Too often books on following Jesus are divorced from the larger biblical framework and given a dysfunctional dose of the contemporary culture. As a result, our picture of following Jesus becomes dangerously familiar and we lose interest. Jon Lunde's *Following Jesus, the Servant King* offers an alternative that is faithfully refreshing. Lunde moves beyond mere description—"10 Easy Steps to Following Jesus"—to explore discipleship in the larger biblical context of covenant. Understanding the covenantal nature of following Jesus provides deeply satisfying answers to the core questions that all disciples ask: *Why follow Jesus since I'm already saved by grace? What does Jesus demand?* and *How do I follow Jesus in a realistic way?* When we see how following Jesus fits into God's larger, covenantal purpose, we will be much more inclined to allow his grace to do its transformative work in our lives. I anticipate that Lunde's thoughtful and insightful contribution will cause many to walk with Jesus at a whole new level of faithfulness.

—J. Scott Duvall, professor of New Testament, Ouachita Baptist University

Discipleship forms the heart of Christian ethics and living, but discipleship too often is reduced to rules or gets sidetracked into personal spirituality. Before one can talk about "following Christ," one must talk about Christ—and only when we get Jesus Christ's image clear can we even begin to talk about discipleship. Jon Lunde, in a book that is excellent for both the classroom and the church, leads us to Christ so we can see what it means to follow as disciples.

—Scot McKnight, Karl A. Olsson Professor in Religious Studies, North Park University

Jonathan Lunde has blessed us with a unique and powerful study of discipleship that avoids simplistic programs. Instead, he takes us deeply into a grace-enabled obedience to Jesus that impels us to live life in this world in the way God intended it to be lived. Jon's learned and impassioned study guides us into the grace of Jesus as our Redemptive Servant, yet also into obedience to Jesus as our Sovereign King. If, as I suspect, God is moving the church into a new and rich phase of discipleship to Jesus, Jon's book will provide the necessary biblical guidance to living in the indispensable balance of grace and demand, of enablement and obedience. Jon gives us a breathtaking glimpse of what God has designed from the beginning of covenantal history—through a truly biblical theology that plumbs the depths of Scripture—to live in an abundant New Covenant discipleship to Jesus as our Servant King.

—Michael J. Wilkins, Distinguished Professor of New Testament Language and Literature, Talbot School of Theology, Biola University

BIBLICAL THEOLOGY FOR LIFE

FOLLOWING **JESUS,** THE **SERVANT KING**

A Biblical Theology of
Covenantal Discipleship

JONATHAN LUNDE

ZONDERVAN.com/
AUTHORTRACKER
follow your favorite authors

ZONDERVAN

Following Jesus, the Servant King
Copyright © 2010 by Jonathan Lunde

This title is also available as a Zondervan ebook. Visit www.zondervan.com/ebooks.

This title is also available in a Zondervan audio edition. Visit www.zondervan.fm.

Requests for information should be addressed to:

Zondervan, *Grand Rapids, Michigan 49530*

Library of Congress Cataloging-in-Publication Data

Lunde, Jonathan.
    Following Jesus, the servant king: a biblical theology of covenantal discipleship / Jonathan Lunde.
       p. cm. (Biblical theology for life)
    Includes bibliographical references and indexes.
    ISBN 978-0-310-28616-5 (softcover)
    1. Christian life. 2. Jesus Christ — Person and offices. I. Title.
  BV4501.3.L8625 2010
  232'.8 — dc22
                                           2010023777

Cover design: Rob Monacelli
Cover photography: Matti Niemi / Getty Images
Interior design: Matthew VanZomeren

Printed in the United States of America

HB 07.27.2018

For my sons, Ryan, Connor, and Trevor

CONTENTS

REFLECTING ON RELEVANCE

DETAILED TABLE OF CONTENTS

QUEUING THE QUESTIONS

ARRIVING AT ANSWERS

REFLECTING ON RELEVANCE

ABBREVIATIONS

Ant.	*Antiquities*
b. Yoma	Babylonian Talmud *Yoma*
CGTC	Cambridge Greek Testament Commentary
CTBT	*Central Themes in Biblical Theology: Mapping Unity in Diversity*, ed. Scott J. Hafemann, and Paul R. House. Grand Rapids: Baker, 2007.
DJG	*Dictionary of Jesus and the Gospels*, ed. Joel B. Green and Scot McKnight. Downers Grove, IL: IVP, 1992.
DOTHB	*Dictionary of the Old Testament: Historical Books*, ed. Bill T. Arnold and H. G. M. Williamson. Downers Grove, IL: IVP, 2005.
DOTP	*Dictionary of the Old Testament: Pentateuch*, ed. David W. Baker and Desmond T. Alexander. Downers Grove, IL: IVP, 2003.
DPHL	*Dictionary of Paul and His Letters*, ed. Ralph. P. Martin, Daniel G. Reid, and Gerald F. Hawthorne. Downers Grove, IL: IVP, 1993.
EBC	*Expositor's Bible Commentary*
EDT	*Evangelical Dictionary of Theology*, ed. Walter A. Elwell. Grand Rapids: Baker, 1984.
ICC	International Critical Commentary
IVP	InterVarsity Press
m. ʾAbot	Mishnah *ʾAbot*
NCBC	New Century Bible Commentary
NDBT	*New Dictionary of Biblical Theology: Exploring the Unity and Diversity of Scripture*, ed. T. Desmond Alexander et al. Downers Grove, IL: IVP, 2000.
NICNT	New International Commentary on the New Testament
NICOT	New International Commentary on the Old Testament
NIDOTTE	*New International Dictionary of Old Testament Theology and Exegesis*, ed. Willem A. VanGemeren. 5 vols. Grand Rapids: Zondervan, 1997.
NIGTC	New International Greek Testament Commentary
NIVAC	NIV Application Commentary
NLT	New Living Translation
NovTSup	Novum Testamentum Supplements
NSBT	New Studies in Biblical Theology
P&R	Presbyterian and Reformed
SNTSMS	Society for New Testament Studies Monograph Series
Str-B	*Kommentar zum Neuen Testament aus Talmud und Midrasch*, ed. H. L. Strack and P. Billerbeck; 6 vols. Munich: Beck, 1922–1961.

TDNT *Theological Dictionary of the New Testament*, ed. G. Kittel and G. Friedrich; trans. Geoffrey W. Bromiley; 10 vols. Grand Rapids: Eerdmans, 1964–1976.

T. Jud. *Testament of Judah*

T. Levi *Testament of Levi*

T. Sim. *Testament of Simeon*

WBC Word Biblical Commentary

SERIES PREFACE

The question "What does the Bible have to say about that?" is, in essence, what the Biblical Theology for Life series is all about. Not unlike other biblical explorations of various topics, the volumes in this series articulate various themes in biblical theology, but they always do so with the "So what?" question rumbling about and demanding to be answered. Too often, books on biblical theology have focused mainly on *description*—simply discerning the teachings of the biblical literature on a particular topic. But contributors to this series seek to straddle both the world of the text and the world in which we live.

This means that their descriptions of biblical theology will always be understood as the important *first* step in their task, which will not be completed until they draw out that theology's practical implications for the contemporary context. Contributors therefore engage both in the *description* of biblical theology and in its contemporary *contextualization*, accosting the reader's perspective and fostering application, transformation, and growth. It is our hope that these informed insights of evangelical biblical scholarship will increasingly become enfleshed in the sermons and discussions that transpire each week in places of worship, in living rooms where Bible studies gather, and in classrooms around the world. We hope that this series will lead to personal transformation and practical application in real life.

Every volume in this series has the same basic structure. In the first section, entitled "Queuing the Questions," authors introduce the main questions they seek to address in their books. Raising these questions enables you to see clearly from the outset what each book will be pursuing, inviting you to participate in the process of discovery along the way. In the second section, "Arriving at Answers," authors develop the biblical theology of the topic they address, focusing their attention on specific biblical texts and constructing answers to the questions introduced in section one. In the concluding "Reflecting on Relevance" section, authors contextualize their biblical theological insights, discussing specific ways in which the theology presented in their books addresses contemporary situations and issues, giving you opportunities to consider how you might live out that theology in the world today.

Long before you make it to the "Reflecting on Relevance" section, however, we encourage you to wrestle with the implications of the biblical theology being described by considering the "Relevant Questions" that conclude each chapter. Frequent sidebars spice up your experience, supplementing the main discussion with significant quotations, illustrative historical or contemporary data, and fuller explanations of the content.

In sum, the goal of the Biblical Theology for Life series is communicated by its title. On the one hand, its books mine the Bible for theology that addresses a wide range of topics, so that you may know "the only true God, and Jesus Christ, whom [he] sent" (John 17:3). On the other hand, contributing authors contextualize this theology in ways that allow the *life*-giving Word (John 1:4; 20:31) to speak into and transform contemporary *life*.

Series Editor

Jonathan Lunde

PREFACE

The vision to write this book emerged gradually during my first few years of teaching classes on Jesus and the New Testament use of the Old Testament at Trinity College in Deerfield, Illinois. As I continued exploring the ways in which the gospel traditions about Jesus connected with Old Testament prophetic expectations, the layers of meaning and significance attached to every aspect of Jesus' ministry were laid open to me. Gradually, the importance of the covenants also came into view, providing the context in which to understand the nature of the relationship that Christians ought to have with God through Jesus, his anointed King.

The result of this, very simply, was a revolution in how I related to Jesus as his follower. Rather than viewing my discipleship through a myopic apprehension of New Testament theology, I realized more deeply than ever that I had been taken up into the grand sweep of God's salvation historical drama. Consequently, I could no longer allow myself to determine the specific contours of my life as a disciple of Jesus. Rather, God's agenda and purposes became the defining context in which I was to live. Since I did not find this perspective well developed in treatments of discipleship, I endeavored one day to write this book. I am thankful to Katya Covrett and the others at Zondervan who have provided me the opportunity to fulfill that intention. Special thanks are owed to Verlyn Verbrugge, whose able editorial work and perceptive critical analysis helped me hone the theses of this book.

It is also with sincere gratitude that I acknowledge the support that I have received from both Biola University and Talbot School of Theology to devote additional time and energy to this project. Apart from Biola's commitment to enabling its professors to pursue scholarship, this book may never have been written. Similarly, several of my colleagues have served as helpful sounding boards along the way. Michael Wilkins has been a particularly important source of exhortation and encouragement. The opportunities he has given me to interact with his DMin students in his summer discipleship classes have proven valuable, furnishing me with feedback that has helped to shape and confirm the usefulness of this approach. Additionally, Matt Williams, Ken Berding, Joanne Jung, Mickey Klink, Darian Lockett, Joe Hellerman, and Tim Muehlhoff have all encouraged me to press forward, sharpening me through our many discussions. I am so blessed to work alongside them. I am also grateful for the insights that my father, Joel Lunde, and father-in-law, Howard Thompson, both gave me as they read portions of the manuscript.

No less significant has been the enduring support from my partner in life and ministry — my lovely wife, Pam. Throughout this long process, when I have frequently had to spend extended hours in the office, Pam has consistently provided sincere encouragement, helpful insights, and prayerful intercession. For more than twenty-five years now, she has served as an ongoing affirmation of the enabling power of grace.

I also want to thank the many students at Trinity College and Biola University whom I have had the privilege of tutoring in the life of Jesus. My interaction with them in the classroom and in countless conversations has helped to sharpen my ability to communicate these concepts clearly and accessibly. In addition, their personal responses have confirmed the effectiveness of this approach to discipleship. Several of them also read portions of the manuscript, offering incisive criticism and suggestions. John Dunne, Brian Asbill, Sam Garcia, and Jesse Ciccotti are especially noteworthy in this regard. Whatever weaknesses and inaccuracies that remain are certainly my responsibility alone.

Finally, I would like to acknowledge the sacrifices that my sons have made while my focus has been distracted by the writing of this book. Rather than responding with distance and resentment to my diminished accessibility and attention, Ryan, Connor, and Trevor have endured these months with patience and support. It is to them that I am dedicating this book. Nothing would be more meaningful for me than that each of them would live their lives, receiving the servant grace of Jesus and responding to his kingly reign with faithfulness.

PART ONE

QUEUING THE QUESTIONS

CHAPTER 1

THE SERVANT KING'S CALL TO DISCIPLESHIP

As he walked along, he saw Levi son of Alphaeus sitting at the tax collector's booth. "Follow me," Jesus told him, and Levi got up and followed him.

Mark 2:14

F ollow me."
With these words, Jesus summarizes his call to discipleship. But what exactly does he mean by this command? What does *following* him involve? How we answer this question is crucially important, because the nature of our lives as disciples— what we actually *do* and how we *live* as Christians—will largely depend on *our* understanding of what Jesus means by these words.

Does following Jesus simply mean confessing him as our Savior, going to church on a regular basis, and giving to Christian causes? Does it entail leaving everything behind and going into full-time missionary work in some far-off land? Or does it mean committing ourselves to obey the Golden Rule throughout our lives, doing our best to love those people who come across our paths? As you know, people who identify themselves as followers of Jesus embrace these and a host of other interpretations, which leads to a wide diversity in Christian expressions, some of which are surely not what Jesus had in mind. And therein lies a significant rub. What people think of Jesus is heavily influenced by what they see in the lives of those who name his name. As recent experience demonstrates, many are turning away from him today *because* of what they see in his followers. One of these disillusioned people recently wrote in a book:

> If the Lord is real, it would make sense for the people of God, on average, to be superior morally and ethically to the rest of society. Statistically, they aren't.... It's hard to believe in God when it's impossible to tell the difference between His people and atheists.[1]

---

1. William Lobdell, *Losing My Religion: How I Lost My Faith Reporting on Religion in America—and* *Found Unexpected Peace* (New York: HarperCollins, 2009), 271.

Since the mission to the world lies close to the center of Jesus' call to discipleship, this represents a major concern for the present state of the church.

JESUS, THE SERVANT KING

Jesus the King

So, what does *Jesus* mean when he beckons, "Follow me"? We don't have to read far into the Gospels before answers begin to emerge. Those alive during Jesus' ministry who hear this call often accompany him physically, following him in his itinerant movements. Peter, Andrew, James, and John all abandon their fathers' fishing nets at Jesus' summons, and Levi's toll booth stands unmanned after Jesus passes by. What's more, as they follow Jesus, their entire life focus is redirected. The fishermen are told that their "catch" will now consist of other *people*. Relational loyalties are also reprioritized, privileging loyalty to Jesus even above those within the immediate family. Finally, Jesus calls on his followers to carry their own crosses — to be willing to face ignoble suffering and death because of their commitment to him. It is clear, therefore, that when Jesus calls people to follow him, he summons them to a life of radical commitment to himself and to his commands.

And what commands they are! Listen to him:

- "I tell you that unless your righteousness surpasses that of the Pharisees and the teachers of the law, you will certainly not enter the kingdom of heaven" (Matt. 5:20).
- "I tell you that anyone who is angry with his brother or sister will be subject to judgment" (Matt. 5:22a).
- "Anyone who looks at a woman lustfully has already committed adultery with her in his heart" (Matt. 5:28).
- "If anyone slaps you on the right cheek, turn to them the other cheek also" (Matt. 5:39b).
- "Love your enemies and pray for those who persecute you" (Matt. 5:44).
- "Be perfect, therefore, as your heavenly Father is perfect" (Matt. 5:48).

As we will see, Jesus is functioning in his role as *King* when he places these demands on his followers, mirroring the relationship that God had with Old Testament Israel. When God entered into covenant with his people, he required that they reflect his character as their Sovereign: "Be holy because I, the LORD your God, am holy" (Lev. 19:2b).[2] Ideally, the Davidic kings would embody this command, ruling in such a way that God's covenantal stipulations were upheld in the nation (Deut. 17:18 – 20). It is this role that Jesus is fulfilling here. As Israel's messianic King, he

---

2. Cf. 1 Sam. 8:7; Pss. 10:16; 24:7 – 9; 68:24; 149:2; Isa. 6:5; 33:22; 43:15; 44:6.

summons his people to follow him, even as he follows God. When Christians follow Jesus *Christ*, therefore, they are following Jesus the *Messiah*—the King whose authority merges with that of his Father, who placed him on David's throne.

But, as any Christian will be quick to point out, this is not the only role that Jesus fills. Although he is the King, he is also the Servant.

Jesus the Servant

We are most familiar with this role in relation to his death on the cross, which the New Testament authors cast in the colors of sacrifice and atonement. But this perspective does not originate with the first disciples. Jesus *himself* takes care to ensure that his followers understand his suffering in these categories. While on the road to Jerusalem and the cross, Jesus takes advantage of the self-seeking dispute between his disciples to interpret his impending death this way: "For even the Son of Man did not come to be served, but to serve, and to give his life as a ransom for many" (Mark 10:45). Then a few days later, on the eve of his death, he confirms this interpretive lens with these graphic words at his last meal with his disciples: "Drink from it, all of you. This is my blood of the covenant, which is poured out for many for the forgiveness of sins" (Matt. 26:27b–28).

In these affirmations, Jesus is clearly signaling to his followers that his death will not simply be a case of his being in the wrong place at the wrong time, unfortunately getting caught up in the political realities of Roman-dominated Jerusalem. Rather, he will be in the *right* place at the *right* time, intentionally entering the capital city for the sole purpose of providing atonement for the very nation that was rejecting him. Therefore, Jesus is more than merely the Davidic Messiah; he is the one who suffers and dies on behalf of others.

In describing himself in this way, Jesus combines his role as King with that of the Servant of the Lord. As Isaiah portrays him, the Servant is the one whose righteous life is ultimately crushed so that mercy might graciously be offered to others.[3] Jesus confirms this identification with an allusion to Isaiah 53 after his Last Supper with his disciples, immediately prior to their departure to the Mount of Olives: "It is written: 'And he was numbered with the transgressors'" (Luke 22:37, quoting from Isa. 53:12). This, then, suggests that Jesus drew on Isaiah 53 in his postresurrection invitations to his disciples to perceive the significance of his death in light of the Scriptures:

> He said to them, "This is what I told you while I was still with you: Everything must be fulfilled that is written about me in the Law of Moses, the Prophets and the Psalms."
>
> Then he opened their minds so they could understand the Scriptures. He told

---

3. Cf. Isa. 53:1–12. The so-called "Servant Songs" are found in Isa. 42:1–7; 49:1–7; 50:4–9; 52:13–53:12.

them, "This is what is written: The Messiah will suffer and rise from the dead on the third day, and repentance and forgiveness of sins will be preached in his name to all nations, beginning at Jerusalem." (Luke 24:44–47; cf. vv. 25–27)

The fact that the apostles frequently use Isaiah 53 in their portrayals of Jesus' work on the cross offers implicit confirmation of Jesus' own use of this text, especially bearing in mind that it was anything but common for the Jews to identify Isaiah's Servant of the Lord with the Messiah.[4] They most likely make this connection because Jesus himself has made it.

Accordingly, Paul testifies later that Jesus provides the righteous, substitutionary life and death for others: "God made him who had no sin to be sin for us, so that in him we might become the righteousness of God" (2 Cor. 5:21; cf. Rom. 8:1–3). The result of this is that people are saved by grace through faith, and not by works of the law:

> But now apart from the law the righteousness of God has been made known, to which the Law and the Prophets testify. This righteousness is given through faith in Jesus Christ to all who believe. There is no difference between Jew and Gentile, for all have sinned and fall short of the glory of God, and all are justified freely by his grace through the redemption that came by Christ Jesus. (Rom. 3:21–24)

Here, then, is the tension that gives rise to some of the diversity expressed by disciples of Jesus today. As the King, Jesus summons his followers to a life of single-hearted commitment and loyalty to himself. As the Servant, Jesus provides the righteous fulfillment of the law's demands and its final sacrifice. The demand of the King is therefore juxtaposed with the grace of the Servant. Rightly resolving the tension created by these two roles of Jesus gets at the heart of discipleship—the heart of what it means to follow him. In order to resolve this tension, we must answer three significant questions. I have identified them as the "Why," the "What," and the "How" questions.

OUR THREE DISCIPLESHIP QUESTIONS
The "Why" Question
The "Why" question wrestles with the place of obedience to the King in the wake of the Servant's provision.

Why should I be concerned to obey all of Jesus' commands if I have been saved by grace?

After all, Paul makes it clear in his letters that righteousness now is "by faith from first to last" (Rom. 1:17) because "Christ is the culmination of the law" as it concerns righteousness (10:4).

---

4. The only explicit example of this comes to us in an Aramaic paraphrase of Isaiah known as the *Targum of Isaiah*. But so problematic is the notion of the Servant's suffering that these elements are diverted to the Gentiles and the wicked in Israel.

In light of these truths, many followers of Jesus respond to his climactic fulfillment of the law on their behalf by *lowering* Jesus' demands to the point where they are *realistic* and then cloaking themselves with his grace for the rest. There is relatively little concern here about what *Jesus* means by his summons to follow him. Rather, those who take this path define discipleship in ways that demand little of them, lest they fall into a legalistic striving for righteousness. They reason, since they are saved by grace and not by works, Jesus' high demand should simply direct them back to him for more grace. If they were to respond by striving to fulfill *all* of Jesus' commands, they would find themselves denying the gracious nature of their salvation. This is the path of *compromise*, and it is rampant in the church today.

To answer the "Why" question, we will need to explore the relationship between grace and demand throughout the Scriptures, preeminently in the biblical theology of "covenant." Our goal will be to discern what it means to live in the New Covenant, graced by the Servant and summoned by the King. How do these two biblical realities hold together? How can I be saved entirely by God's grace in Christ while at the same time be summoned to absolute righteousness? And how can Jesus' teachings be reconciled to Paul's in this regard? Doesn't Paul make it clear that the law's demand has come to its *end* in Christ (Rom. 10:4)? Isn't it the case that Christians are no longer "under" the law's supervision (6:14; Gal. 3:25)? We will discover that the answers to these questions are to be found in what it means to be in covenant with God—a notion far too frequently absent from Christian self-perception. This gives rise to our second question.

The "What" Question

We will learn that the answer to the "Why" question opens the door to a serious consideration of what Jesus commands his disciples to do. This is the "What" question:

What is it that Jesus demands of his disciples?

We could answer this question specifically by working through each of his commands preserved for us in the Gospels. But that would be a book in itself.[5] Our treatment must be more circumscribed, focusing our attention on specific examples that will illumine the whole. We could also approach this question rather generally by evoking Jesus' austere imagery of carrying our own "crosses." But beyond being willing to die for him, how are we to understand what this all-encompassing demand entails? To discern this, we will need to set his commands in relation to the Old Testament law.

Early in his Sermon on the Mount, Jesus responds to a perception that apparently some held regarding his teachings. He declares, "Do not think that I have

---

5. See the recent treatment of each of Jesus' commands in the book by John Piper, *What Jesus Demands from the World* (Wheaton: Crossway, 2006).

come to abolish the Law or the Prophets; I have not come to abolish them but to fulfill them" (Matt. 5:17). Obviously, the important word here is "fulfill." Whatever Jesus means by it, the succeeding verses (5:21–48) make clear that the demands of the law are not *lowered* for Jesus' followers. In fact, they are *preserved* and even *elevated* in some cases. This raises the issue of the relationship of the law to the Christian. How is it that Jesus' commands "fulfill" the law and yet preserve the law's demands for his followers?

To answer the "What" question, we will consider what the prophets declare about the New Covenant and its relationship to the Mosaic Covenant and its law. What do Jeremiah, Ezekiel, and the other prophets teach regarding the law in God's ultimate purposes? What does Jesus mean by his claim to "fulfill" the law? We will discover that the answers to the "Why" and "What" questions will leave Christians with a high covenantal demand of righteousness. This leads us directly into our third question.

The "How" Question

In Matthew 11, Jesus summons his followers to take his "yoke" upon them (v. 29). This agricultural image, pertaining to the pulling of a plow or cart, is stock Jewish symbolism for obedience to the law. Jesus utilizes this same symbol to describe obedience to *his* teachings. And Jesus expects faithfulness. In fact, he places a good deal of weight on his disciples' obedience as the primary evidence of the genuineness of their discipleship: "To the Jews who had believed him, Jesus said, 'If you hold to my teaching, you are really my disciples'" (John 8:31; cf. 13:35). Consequently, his disciples will be known by their "fruitfulness," which must refer to their replication of his life and ministry (Matt. 7:16–20; 21:43; Luke 13:6–9; John 15:8). But *how* is this kind of faithfulness to be accomplished?

Not only is this a major question by itself, but notice also how Jesus characterizes the *experience* of his disciples under his "yoke":

> Come to me, all you who are weary and burdened, and I will give you rest. Take my yoke upon you and learn from me, for I am gentle and humble in heart, and you will find rest for your souls. For my yoke is easy and my burden is light. (Matt. 11:28–30)

How is this possible? Since Jesus' demand preserves the high call to righteousness found in the biblical covenants, this "lightness" seems to be a bit counterintuitive. Thus, our third question:

> *How can the disciple obey Jesus' high demand,*
> *while experiencing his "yoke" as "light" and "easy"?*

That is, how can Jesus' disciples respond faithfully to his righteous commands without falling into binding legalism or into frustration and eventual compromise? In many respects, this is the most important of our three questions. For it often could be said that the problem facing Jesus' followers is not in wondering *what* they are to do, but *how* they are to do it.

To answer this question, we will investigate Jesus' teaching regarding the nature of the kingdom's arrival in his ministry and the implications this has concerning the establishment of the New Covenant. We will also observe how life in the Old Testament covenants was ideally to be lived, perceiving a pattern of life in relation to God that appropriately also applies to Christians—a pattern that will enable Jesus' disciples to experience his yoke as "light."

THE INVITATION OF THIS BOOK

This book, then, addresses disciples of Jesus who struggle with one or more of these three questions. As such, it is for the follower of Jesus who needs to wake up from a lackadaisical discipleship that does not take his demands of righteousness seriously. It is for the one who is bound by a deadening legalism in relation to Jesus' commands. It is for the one who mourns over a frustrating inconsistency in faithfulness to Jesus' summons.

But it certainly is not a "how to" book, replete with ten simple steps to our goal. It is rather a consideration of the biblical theology concerning the consummation of the Old Testament covenants and the interplay between God's righteous demand and his enabling grace. Accordingly, our discussion will be grounded in an awareness of the biblical framework in which each question must be considered. Along the way, we will be keeping watch for covenantal expectations and the dynamic patterns that accompany them. Ultimately, we will perceive how these are confirmed and deepened in the fulfillment that has come in Jesus. Unless we understand him in the broad contours of this context, our discipleship will always suffer from a lack of an appreciation of who he really is.

I have worked with many Christians who apparently have grown bored with Jesus. Once this happens, discipleship is in danger of descending into a state of apathetic inaction, as one's relationship with Jesus recedes into the background like some sort of life insurance policy—easing worry about the future, but not deeply affecting life in the present beyond the bothersome monthly payments.

The thesis of this book is that the answers to our three questions will be found in the realities ushered in by the New Covenant. That is to say, one should not speak about Christian discipleship without also speaking about being "in covenant" with God. If that is true, insight into what it means to follow Jesus necessarily involves understanding more generally the concept of "covenant," and more specifically how the New Covenant brings to culmination the promises, the demands, and the overall relational patterns described in the prior Old Testament covenants. For this reason, we will begin with a survey of these covenants, which will serve as the background for our discussion of discipleship to Jesus.

This book is not a detailed examination of the historical background of the term "disciple" (*mathētēs*) or of the nature of the relationship between Jewish rabbis and their students in first-century Palestine. That sort of thing is readily available in other books on the topic.[6] Rather, this book seeks to develop a more covenantal/theological perspective in which to understand what it means to follow Jesus. Yet since this approach to discipleship is somewhat unexpected, you may need to keep your finger in this introductory chapter to review again the overall structure of the book in light of what I am trying to accomplish.

My underlying assumption is that the only thing that genuinely transforms the heart and enables obedience is *grace*—hardly a new concept. But if this is true, the *persistent* experience of the Servant's grace must be understood as the necessary context in which following Jesus, the King, may be enabled and sustained. What I have therefore written is part biblical theology of covenant, part life of Jesus, and part discussion of discipleship. The reason for this is that these must be kept together, with each one enlightening and enlivening the others. That is the context in which his first disciples were moved to follow him. Unless we too view Jesus in the rich framework of the Old Testament covenantal and prophetic expectations, our perception of him will be too narrow, often leading to imbalanced, impoverished, or even misdirected forms of discipleship.

So, stay with me during the discussions of the Old Testament covenantal background, key texts, or even the ministry of Jesus itself. Such discussions are necessary if our hearts and minds are to be captured by the immensity of Jesus and the fulfillment that comes through him. Only in this way will our continual encounters with him graciously empower us to respond faithfully to his extravagant demands of righteousness.

I invite you, therefore, to a view of Christian discipleship that is grounded in a biblical theology of following Jesus, the Servant King.

---

6. Pride of place here goes to Michael J. Wilkins, *Following the Master: A Biblical Theology of Discipleship* (Grand Rapids: Zondervan, 1992). See also his *In His Image: Reflecting Christ in Everyday Life* (Colorado Springs: NavPress, 1997).

PART TWO

ARRIVING
AT ANSWERS

THE "WHY" QUESTION

Anyone who understands basic Christian teaching knows that Christianity is a religion characterized by grace. The youngest believer is able to express this in simple eloquence: "Jesus died on the cross for me." The "gospel" is "good news" to the Christian because it communicates the gracious truth that Jesus died in place of others so that God could extend forgiving mercy to them. As Paul writes, "it is by grace you have been saved" (Eph. 2:8a).

This grace is grounded in Jesus' righteous life, accomplishing what had previously been impossible for all others before him: "For what the law was powerless to do because it was weakened by the sinful nature, God did by sending his own Son in the likeness of sinful humanity to be a sin offering" (Rom. 8:3a). This means that disciples of Jesus are not dependent on their own demonstration of righteousness through their obedience to the law. Rather, God's righteousness is received solely through faith: "For we maintain that a person is justified by faith apart from observing the law" (3:28).

This is where the "Why" question comes to the fore: "Why should I be concerned to obey all of Jesus' commands if I have been saved by grace?" Doesn't the one who strives to obey all of Jesus' demands risk becoming bound up with a legalism that denies the sufficiency of Jesus' finished work? In fact, aren't the extravagant demands of Jesus better used as prods to goad us back to him for more grace since our salvation is always dependent on his righteous life? Why, then, ought we to be concerned about obedience—especially the extravagant obedience that Jesus demands? The answer to this question turns on the nature of the covenantal relationship we have with God through Jesus. What we discover is that grace has always grounded God's relationships with his people, but that same grace persistently brings the demand of righteousness.

To perceive this pattern, we will need to take into account the covenants into which God and his people have entered throughout history. Then we will consider the prophetic expectations of the New Covenant in this light, as well as Jesus' climactic fulfillment of them. Within this covenantal framework we will find the biblical answer to our question.

COVENANTAL GRACE AND DEMAND

And the LORD God commanded the man, "You are free to eat from any tree in the garden; but you must not eat from the tree of the knowledge of good and evil, for when you eat of it you will certainly die."

Genesis 2:16–17

It is not often that I have heard someone leading a gathering of Christians instruct the people to open their "New Covenants" to a particular passage. Almost universally, we refer to the biblical writings of Jesus' followers as the "New Testament." While there may be good reasons for choosing the title "testament" over "covenant," it has not come without unfortunate consequences. Chief among them is that we do not view ourselves in the theological framework of "covenant." Few today would naturally identify themselves as New Covenant believers. No, we're "Christians," "believers" in Jesus, or "followers" of Christ. In the process, the *covenantal* nature of our relationship with Jesus fades from view.

This is often the case even when the Lord's Supper is celebrated in the church. Too many miss the significance of Jesus' sealing of his relationship with his first disciples in a covenantal rite: "Drink from it, all of you. This is my blood of the covenant, which is poured out for many for the forgiveness of sins" (Matt. 26:27b–28). Rather than using this oft-repeated ritual as an opportunity to help their congregations think covenantally about their relationship to Jesus, pastors generally focus their meditational comments solely on the cross and the good news that it declares. The result of this is that the gospel is set adrift from its covenantal anchorage and discipleship tends to float on the tides of our own definitions. Given this tendency, it is not surprising that "covenant" is almost a foreign concept to many Christians.

But one doesn't have to read far into the Bible to discover the importance of covenant to its overall flow and message. Beginning with Noah and then progressing through Abraham, Moses, and David, God's interaction with humanity, and specifically with Israel, is rooted in and bounded by the various covenants that are established along the way. This also extends into the Christian era, since the heart of its connection to the history and theology of the Old Testament centers on the notion of the New Covenant, which was prophesied explicitly by Jeremiah and implicitly by several of the other prophets.

The fundamental contention of this book is that discipleship to Jesus is best understood in this covenantal context. Indeed, apart from this framework, our tendency is to reduce discipleship to a few of its essential elements, leaving us to define much of the rest of it ourselves. The results are often unfortunate, as is borne out by the wide range of Christian expressions today and the lack of clarity regarding the three main questions addressed in this book. Consequently, if we are to understand Christian discipleship rightly, it is imperative for us to understand the biblical category of covenant, as well as the Old Testament covenantal progression that flows into Jesus' fulfillment of the New Covenant.

If this is the case, what might we learn from the relationships that God initiates with Noah, Abram, Israel, and David? What hints of God's intentions might we gather even from the covenant-like relationship that he has with Adam and Eve in the garden? And how do these covenants prepare for the kind of relationship that ought to characterize the New Covenant prophesied by Jeremiah?

Before we turn to this discussion, however, it will be helpful to understand the category of covenant itself, as well as the two main kinds of covenants that we encounter in the Bible. From this, I will introduce three questions to guide us through our consideration of the biblical covenants, all with the goal of better understanding Jesus and our discipleship to him. In the end, we will discern the covenantal answer to our "Why" question.

Let's begin our look at these relationships by defining what a covenant is.

AN INTRODUCTION TO THE BIBLICAL COVENANTS

The biblical understanding of "covenant" is that of "a solemn commitment guaranteeing promises or obligations undertaken by one or both covenanting parties."[1] To find a similar kind of agreement today, we might think of a "contract." However, we must be careful not to include the notion of "merit" or "payment" that we usually associate with our contracts. Such is not part of the biblical covenants, even though those who enter into a covenant with God are expected to be faithful partners, committing themselves to obedience to God (this is qualified a bit in the Noahic

---

1. P. R. Williamson, "Covenant," *DOTP*, 139. See also the discussion of the meaning of covenant (*berit*) in Ralph L. Smith, *Old Testament Theology: Its History, Method, and Message* (Nashville: Broadman & Holman, 1993), 146–51; John Goldingay, *Old Testament Theology*, vol. 2, *Israel's Faith* (Downers Grove: IVP, 2006), 182. See also D. Hillers, *Covenant: The History of the Biblical Idea* (Baltimore: Johns Hopkins Univ. Press, 1969); M. G. Kline, *Treaty of the Great King* (Grand Rapids: Eerdmans, 1963); Thomas McComiskey, *The Covenants of Promise: A Theology of the Old Testament Covenants* (Grand Rapids: Baker, 1985), 140–44, 223–31.

Covenant). The stipulations governing these behaviors, however, depend on which of the two *types* of covenants is in question.[2]

Covenantal Types

The Grant Covenant

One variety of biblical covenant is known as the "royal grant" or "unconditional" covenant. As it is utilized in the biblical narrative, this type guarantees the promised benefits from God apart from any specific acts of obedience on the part of the people with whom the covenant is made. Its fulfillment is the sole responsibility of God. Those who receive its benefits are those who trust in his trustworthiness. If I were to promise my sons, "I will take you to Disneyland on Saturday," with no mention of any required behavior on their part, I am entering into a sort of "grant" or "unconditional" agreement. The fulfillment of my promise is not tied to anything they must do. Rather, they are to wait in faith, trusting in my fidelity to fulfill my commitment to them.

That is not to say that there are no demands placed on people in a grant covenant. Such are always present. But the reception of the benefits promised in this covenant is not *dependent* on obedience to these demands. In this regard I could follow up my unconditional commitment to take my sons to Disneyland by adding, "So, finish your homework on Friday." This is still a grant "covenant" because obedience to the demand is not stated as the *condition* of the reception of the blessings. Rather, the command to finish their homework is stated as a reasonable *response* of wisdom and even gratitude to the promised blessing.

It must be admitted that this illustration fails to capture the entirety of the relationship depicted in the biblical grant covenants. This is because of the nature of biblical faith, which is the fundamental human response to a grant covenant. The one who has faith in God will respond with obedience to any commands that are given within that covenant. Accordingly, if my sons believe (in a biblical sense) that I will be true to my word to take them to Disneyland, they will respond positively to my instruction to do their homework on Friday. But faith is not the same thing as obedience. Nor is the fulfillment of the blessings of the grant covenant dependent on the obedience of the one who believes. Rather, this is grounded in the faithfulness of the God who makes the covenant. We will see the significance of this, especially as we consider Paul's discussion of justification in the New Covenant.

---

2. For a dissenting view on distinguishing between conditional and grant covenants, see Scott J. Hafemann, "The Covenantal Relationship," in *CTBT*, 20–65. Hafemann helpfully develops the fundamental singularity of the covenant relationship between God and humanity (21–23) and reduces the covenantal framework to a commonly held threefold structure (35). He also convincingly demonstrates the integral role that obedience plays in a biblical understanding of "faith." But his proposal glosses over the distinct formulas pertaining to the various covenants, leading to a diminishment of the important distinction between "faith" and "works" in Paul's New Covenant construal.

The Conditional Covenant

A second type of covenant is known as a "conditional" or "bilateral" covenant. It is patterned after the treaties that conquering kings (known as the "suzerains") established with their subjected rulers (the "vassals") and their people. In this type of covenant, a suzerain pledged to protect a vassal's realm and dynasty. In return, the suzerain demanded from his vassal total loyalty and service. The subjected ruler and his people continued to receive the covenantal blessing of protection as long as he and they remained faithful to the demands of loyalty and service within the covenant.[3] As it is utilized in the Old Testament, however, this treaty form is transformed in relation to God's gracious character, incorporating notions of familial kinship:

> Reflecting its origins, the covenant relationship in the Bible translates the concept of divine kingship in terms of fatherhood, the category of vassal subjects in terms of sonship, the exercise of sovereignty in terms of love, and the call for obedience in terms of faithfulness within a family. With no diminution of God's absolute sovereignty, the biblical covenant thus becomes not only a political arrangement, but also a familial experience of belonging.[4]

Still, the use of this covenantal pattern in the Old Testament highlights God's sovereign identity, to whom his covenant people owe absolute allegiance. Even with its conditional nature, however, obedience in this kind of covenant is never understood to merit or pay for the blessings that are received. Rather, it is once again the appropriate response to the gracious covenantal initiative of God. If I were to restate my promise to my boys — *"If you complete your homework on Friday evening, I'll take you to Disneyland on Saturday"* — my "unconditional" agreement has become a "conditional" one. And yet, while recognizing that they must do their homework if I am to take them to the amusement park, they hopefully also will realize that their academic diligence is not actually *paying* for their day of fun. Rather, the outing is grounded in the relationship that I already have with them as their father.

Recurring Covenantal Patterns

In spite of this diversity of covenantal types, we will discover a consistent pattern that recurs throughout these relationships. On the one hand, the covenants are always grounded and established in the context of God's *prior grace* toward the people entering the covenant, even in the case of the conditional variety. By "grace," I am referring to God's faithful loving-kindness that is repeatedly expressed in his actions of blessing, provision, and restoration throughout the Old Testament narrative. God's grace is always understood to be sovereignly initiated by him, unmerited and grounded in his compassionate disposition. As it pertains to the covenants,

---

3. See esp. George E. Mendenhall, "Covenant Forms in Israelite Tradition," *Biblical Archaeologist* 17 (1954): 50–76.

4. Hafemann, "Covenantal Relationship," 34.

it often appears as deliverance and provisions in the past or present, or as divine promises of future blessings.[5] On the other hand, we will see that God's gracious initiative always brings with it the demand of faithfulness in response, even in the case of the grant covenants. Perceiving the persistence of this demand nuances the overall nature of these covenants and sets up the pattern that will come to full flower in Jesus.

Another pattern that is tied inextricably to the two types of covenants pertains to the role of faith and works of obedience in the reception of the covenantal blessings. The biblical notion of "faith" is much more complex than most Christians might think, nurtured as we are on Paul's covenantal distinction between "faith" and "works." Consequently, we often conceive of "faith" merely as a state of trust in relation to God's promises and provisions

"Brought about by divine initiative, characterized by benevolence and extended to those who are not by nature his own, these divine provisions are acts of unconditional grace. Hence, to speak of a covenant relationship is to speak first and foremost of God's sovereign, self-determined election motivated by his love. Throughout redemptive history, God takes the initiative in establishing, swearing, keeping and remembering his covenant with his people."[6]

apart from active obedience—apart from "works." However, the biblical conception of "faith" is much more robust than this because it is always set in the context of relationship. Because people have faith *in* God, they act in relation *to* him. Accordingly, when genuine faith is present, it will give rise to obedience and fidelity to the commands that God levies.

This means that those who enter into covenant with the faithful God will ideally also live faithfully in relation to him. That is to say, God's true covenant partners always place their faith in him, trusting that he will be true to his Word, *and* they express this faith in lives of faithfulness to him.[7] Even though this is the case, there is a subtle distinction in the role that works of obedience play in relation to the reception of the blessings promised in both grant and conditional covenants.

As we have already seen, the fulfillment of the blessings in a *grant* covenant is grounded in *God's* covenantal commitments. He is the one who will bring them about. Consequently, faith in God's trustworthiness is the fundamental covenantal response by people to a grant covenant. Yet, because of the biblical understanding of faith, the believing recipients of this kind of covenant will also live out this faith in lives of obedience to God. In the grant version of my Disneyland covenant, my boys wait for the fulfillment of my promise, believing that I will be true to my word. Their response of doing their homework on Friday is the natural outworking of that faith.

---

5. The main Hebrew words that convey this notion in the Old Testament are *ḥanan* and *ḥesed*, which are translated by such English words as mercy, compassion, and grace. *Charis* is the main Greek word that carries this notion in the New Testament. See J. B. Green, "Grace," *NDBT*, 524–27; A. B. Luter Jr., "Grace," *DPHL*, 372–74; E. A. Heath, "Grace," *DOTP*, 372.

6. Hafemann, "Covenantal Relationship," 36.

7. See S. S. Taylor, "Faith, Faithfulness," *NDBT*, 487–93; D. C. T. Sheriffs, "Faith," *DOTP*, 281–85.

The ongoing bestowal of the blessings in the *conditional* covenants, however, is dependent not on God's actions—his trustworthiness to act is taken for granted. Rather, the reception of the covenantal blessings is dependent on the people's response of *obedience* that results from their faith in God's trustworthiness. In the conditional version of my Disneyland covenant, my sons will only receive the promised blessing of a day at the amusement park if they fulfill the covenantal condition. Yet it is precisely because my boys *believe* that I will be true to my Disneyland promise that they enthusiastically (or otherwise) complete their homework on Friday. Discerning these distinctions will ultimately prepare us to make sense of the New Testament emphases on faith and obedience and enable us to reconcile Paul's teachings with those of Jesus.

Our Covenantal Questions

In light of this, we will ask three basic questions as we consider each of the main covenants described in the Old Testament:

- First, what is the *gracious context* in which each covenantal relationship is established?
- Second, what are the *demands* that God places on those who enter into covenant with him?
- Third, how do *faith* and *works of obedience* relate to the reception of the blessings of this covenant?

In discovering the answers to these questions, we will discern covenantal patterns and prophetic connections that will help us answer our first major question — the "Why" question. In the next three chapters, then, we will consider the biblical covenants through the lenses of these three questions, concluding with the ways in which Jesus provides the fulfillment of each major covenantal element. But before we move to that discussion, it is worthwhile prefacing our study by considering God's dealings with Adam and Eve—an interaction that is "covenant-like," but should not be considered one of the formal covenants of the Old Testament.

THE COVENANT-LIKE RELATIONSHIP IN THE GARDEN

While scholars debate whether or not it is appropriate to characterize the relationship between God and the first humans as a formal "covenant," it at least can be said that this interaction *anticipates* the covenantal relationships that follow.[8] As such, it

---

8. For a defense of understanding God's interaction with Adam to consist in a covenant, see E. J. Young, *The Study of Old Testament Theology Today* (Westwood, NJ: Revell, 1959), 61–78; see also John Goldingay, *Old Testament Theology*, vol. 1: *Israel's Gospel* (Downers Grove: IVP, 2003), 181; Hafemann, "Covenantal Relationship." For the counterview, see Smith, *Old Testament Theology*, 152–53; Paul R. Williamson, *Sealed with an Oath: Covenant in God's Unfolding Purpose* (NSBT 23; ed. D. A. Carson; Downers Grove: IVP, 2007), 52–58.

is worthwhile to preface our look at the covenants by considering the relationship that prevailed in Eden. Since we are used to thinking of the *commands* that God gives to Adam and Eve in the garden, I am reversing the order of our first two questions in this first relationship.

The "Covenantal" Demands

What demands did God place on Adam and Eve in this relationship? One does not read far in the Genesis narrative before encountering God's first command to Adam and Eve. It is a positive command: "Be fruitful and increase in number; fill the earth and subdue it. Rule over the fish in the sea and the birds in the sky and over every living creature that moves on the ground" (Gen. 1:28b). Although this is written as a word of blessing, it carries with it the command to obey God's assignment to steward the earth as his representatives. This is made clear by noting the previous verse, which specifies humanity's creation in God's "image" (v. 27). Implicit in this, then, is a demand to live righteously in relation to the earth and its creatures. This is a stewardship that reflects God's attributes.

> "Being in God's image, man and woman are to rule the world in God's name. The picture is that of an emperor appointing administrators over his domain and erecting his own statue so that the inhabitants may know whose will it is that rules them. Inherent in this command to rule in God's stead is the God-given capacity to know, worship, and enjoy the Creator."[9]

After this positive command, we find the first prohibition in Genesis 2. God says to Adam: "You are free to eat from any tree in the garden; but you must not eat from the tree of the knowledge of good and evil, for when you eat of it you will certainly die" (Gen. 2:16b–17).

Positively and negatively, then, God asserts from the beginning his reign over his creation, requiring submission from those created in his image. As Adam and Eve are obedient, God allows them to continue to live in the garden and to have constant access to the Tree of Life. That much is clear, but is this the whole picture of this prefall relationship? Our second question reveals that this is not the case.

The Gracious Context

What, then, is the gracious context in which God communicates these demands? It is vitally important to recognize that prior to the giving of either of these commands, Adam and Eve lived *by grace*. That is, God's requirement that they rule over the earth comes in the context of God already having given it to them. As I noted above, while the charge to stewardship is a command, it is also presented as a blessing that God has provided (Gen. 1:28a). God's demand, then, is grounded in the prior giving of the created order to them. It is grounded in grace.

---

9. William Sanford LaSor, David Allan Hubbard, and Frederic Wm. Bush, *Old Testament Survey: The Message, Form, and Back-*ground of the Old Testament (Grand Rapids: Eerdmans, 1982), 24; cf. Williamson, *Sealed with an Oath*, 47.

The same is true of the prohibition regarding the tree. Adam and Eve had already received everything that they needed for living life to the fullest. Eden was lush and safe, providing more than enough food for them to thrive (Gen. 2:8–9). They also were blessed with the relationships they had with each other and with God (2:21–25; implied by 3:8–9). They had merited none of this. It was simply given to them and they received all of it freely—they received it as *grace*. In this, their Creator served them as their Provider, sustaining them out of the goodness of his being. It was in this gracious reality that Adam and Eve were expected to respond in obedience.[10]

This is what makes Adam and Eve's fall reprehensible. Though they are the recipients of remarkably gracious provisions, they reject his commands. But this is not just a rebellion against their Creator's *will*—it is also a spurning of their Creator's *grace*. What God had provided is now not enough! Adam and Eve's rebellion, therefore, involves the abandonment of the posture in which they had lived to this point, harming both sides of their relationship to God. By grasping after God's sovereignty, they simultaneously reject his gracious supply. The result of this is that the gracious enablement to fulfill God's righteous demand is damaged and diminished.

This introduces us to the paradigm on which we will train our focus throughout this book. That is, God's demand of righteousness always comes to humanity in the context of prior grace. This was true even before the fall! While the demand of righteousness is there at the beginning, Eden suggests to us that the *means* by which this demand is to be met is always to be found in the prior reception and experience of grace.

This is not to say that grace is provided only *prior* to the demand. Grace also is granted *after* their failure. Although Adam and Eve are told that the punishment for disobedience will apparently be their abrupt death (Gen. 2:17), God responds to their failure by graciously clothing them in their nakedness and postponing their deaths into the indefinite future (3:21–22). This *subsequent* grace then precedes subsequent obedience. All the way through, the gracious grounding of the divine-human relationship *never* diminishes God's demand of righteousness.

This leads us naturally to our third question.

Faith and Works of Obedience

How, then, do faith and works of obedience relate to the reception of the blessings of this relationship? Although it is merely "covenant-like," if we were to place it into a covenantal category, it clearly belongs to the *conditional* type. This is so because the continued enjoyment of Eden's blessings is tied directly to Adam and Eve's obedience to God's commands. When their rebellion occurs, the "covenant" is broken and the blessings are suspended. They lose the garden.

---

10. So also Thomas R. Schreiner, "The Commands of God," in *CTBT*, 68–69; LaSor, *Old Testament Survey*, 24.

It would be incorrect, however, to deduce from its conditional nature that faith is absent. It is clear that Adam and Eve's obedience to the divine commands implies a profound trust in God that his provisions are not only sufficient, but that they are the best for them. That is to say, Adam and Eve also lived *by faith* in God's ongoing grace to them even before the fall. This is why the tempter cloaks his deception in a question concerning God's truthfulness and good intentions (Gen. 3:4–5). Their obedience is grounded in their trust in God, and their failure is the result of their mistrust — their unbelief.

> "The crucial point for biblical theology is that disobedience to God flows from failure to trust God. All obedience flows from trusting God (Rom. 1:5; 16:26), and conversely "whatever does not proceed from faith is sin" (Rom. 14:23). Adam and Eve transgressed God's command because they believed they would find happiness independently of God's wisdom expressed in his commands; as creatures they therefore displaced the Creator."[11]

THE MAJOR COVENANTS

Before we move from this chapter into discussions pertaining to our three covenantal questions, it will be helpful to summarize the settings in which each of the major biblical covenants appears. Let's take them in chronological and covenantal order.

The Noahic Covenant

The first major covenant we encounter in the Old Testament is the so-called Noahic Covenant (Gen. 8:20–9:17). After the waters of the flood have receded, Noah expresses his gratitude and worship by building an altar and offering sacrifices to God (8:20). God then fulfills his preflood promise (6:18) to establish a covenant with Noah and his descendants (9:9–11).[12] As will become clear in our subsequent discussion, this covenant is a general covenant that goes far beyond the relationship that God has with Noah.

One would think that things would improve after the destruction of Noah's generation and the new beginning offered through the family of this righteous man. Unfortunately, such is not the case, beginning with the individual sin of Ham (Gen. 9:20–25) and culminating in the corporate rebellion at Babel (11:1–9). It is in this context that God singles out one man as his next covenant partner — Abram.

---

11. Schreiner, "The Commands of God," 69.

12. Some have argued that there are two covenants in the Noahic narrative — one that is established with Noah and his family prior to the flood (Gen. 6:18), and one that is universal in scope, established after the flood (8:20–9:17); see Goldingay, *Israel's Gospel*, 173; Bruce K. Waltke, with Charles Yu, *An Old Testament Theology:* *An Exegetical, Canonical, and Thematic Approach* (Grand Rapids: Zondervan, 2007), 289–90. Williamson convincingly contends, however, that the discussion with Noah in chapter 6 is "proleptic," lacking the basic elements of a genuine covenant. As such, the mention of "covenant" in 6:18 only anticipates the covenant that is ratified in chapter 9 (Williamson, "Covenant," 139).

The Abrahamic Covenants

God calls Abram in the aftermath of Babel's rebellion. In the process, God makes three sweeping promises to Abram—promises that set up much of the ensuing biblical narrative and theology (Gen. 12:1–7). These promises orbit around two centers—one that is more narrowly concerned with Abram's natural descendants, and one that is international in scope, including all people groups in its ambit. Then in 15:9–21 and 17:1–21, God incorporates these promises into two distinct, yet related, covenants with Israel's progenitor.

The Mosaic Covenant

While the beginning of Israel's history derives from God's original call of Abram, the actual establishment of the *nation* occurs when God delivers the Hebrews from Egypt. Their deliverance from Pharaoh's clutches effectively sets them apart as a people, culminating in the covenant with God at Sinai in Exodus 19–24. This Mosaic (or Sinaitic) Covenant is comprised of a complex grouping of subcovenants and their stipulations, stretching over the last four books of the Pentateuch. Most significant in this regard is the book of Deuteronomy, which expresses the reestablishment of the covenant on the plains of Moab with the generation of the Israelites that will inherit the land. We will obviously have to be selective in our discussion of this large body of covenantal literature.

The Davidic Covenant

After David successfully secures Jerusalem as his capital and constructs for himself a palace, he tells Nathan the prophet that he intends to build God a house—a temple (2 Sam. 7:1–2). Nathan initially affirms David's plans (7:3). But then the Lord informs the prophet of what he intends to do for David, declaring blessings that intersect strikingly with the Abrahamic promises (7:4–16). It is true that the word "covenant" is not mentioned in this context, nor is there any sacrificial ritual that accompanies the establishment of this covenant. But other biblical texts refer to this interaction as the "covenant" God made with David.[13] Consequently, this passage is usually understood to entail God's covenantal agreement with David and his descendants.[14]

The New Covenant

Each of the previous covenants in its own way anticipates the establishment of the New Covenant, explicitly described in Jeremiah 31:31–34, but implied and referred to by other prophets. Since this is the covenant that Jesus initiates, it is important that we spend a bit more time here to set this covenant in its historical and canonical context.

---

13. See 2 Sam. 23:5; 2 Chron. 7:18; 13:5; 21:7; Pss. 89:3, 28, 34, 39; 132:11; cf. also 1 Kings 8:23–24; Jer. 33:21.

14. See J. J. M. Roberts, "Davidic Covenant," *DOTHB*, 206.

Covenantal Pessimism and Hope

It is interesting that the book of Deuteronomy communicates an increasing pessimism regarding the people's ability to fulfill their obligations in the Mosaic Covenant—even *before* they take possession of the Promised Land. The expected result of their failure will be the enactment of the covenantal curses, culminating in exile. For instance:

> But if your heart turns away and you are not obedient, and if you are drawn away to bow down to other gods and worship them, I declare to you this day that you will certainly be destroyed. You will not live long in the land you are crossing the Jordan to enter and possess. (Deut. 30:17–18)[15]

Faced with the people's repeated failure (1:26–46; 9:1–10:11), Moses knows that their possession of the land they are about to enter will only be a temporary reality.

In spite of this pessimism, however, Moses also anticipates the day in which God will bring his people back to the land and do a new work in their hearts so as to bring about a remnant, faithful to the covenant with Yahweh:[16]

> He will bring you to the land that belonged to your ancestors, and you will take possession of it. He will make you more prosperous and numerous than your ancestors. The Lord your God will circumcise your hearts and the hearts of your descendants, so that you may love him with all your heart and with all your soul, and live. (Deut. 30:5–6)

In other words, God will one day rectify the problem of covenantal disobedience by transforming his people, so that they love him with an undivided heart. This sets up the expectation of the New Covenant and the fulfillment that comes with Jesus.

The Curse of the Covenant

In our discussion of the Davidic Covenant, we will note the responsibility of the kings to rule in such a way as to inspire the people to covenantal faithfulness. Sadly, most of the kings fail miserably in this, impelling the nation toward the kind of unfaithfulness that will eventually incur the covenantal curses. Specifically, because of Solomon's failure (1 Kings 11:1–13) and Rehoboam's arrogance (12:1–17), the Davidic kingdom splits into two realms around 930 BC.

Though the succeeding histories of these two kingdoms are punctuated occasionally by the reigns of godly monarchs, the overall trajectory is that of the kings' and the people's faithlessness in relation to the covenant. Consequently, as Moses had predicted, the two nations experience the ultimate covenantal curse—exile from the land (Deut. 28:36–37, 63–65). The northern kingdom, Israel, is overtaken in 721 BC after a series of invasions by Assyria, and the southern kingdom, Judah, finally

---

15. Cf. also Deut. 4:25–26; 8:18–20; 28:21–24, 63; 29:21–28; 31:16–22; 32:15–25.

16. Williamson, "Covenant," 152–53.

succumbs to the Babylonian armies in 587 BC. In both cases, the prophets make it clear that it is the unfaithfulness of the people that leads to these fates.[17]

The Promise of a New "Exodus"

But the prophets do not leave the Israelites without hope. Remaining true to his covenantal commitments to Abram, God promises the glorious restoration of the people to the Promised Land. Babylon will soon be crushed (Isa. 43:14; 46:1–2; 47:1–15) by God's "anointed one," Cyrus, king of Persia (Isa. 44:28; 45:1–3, 13; 48:14–15; cf. 46:11–13). So Isaiah encourages the exiles with the prospect of their impending return (Isa. 40:1–5).[18] Notice the prophet's use of "wilderness" imagery that likens God's future deliverance from Babylon to the past event of the exodus out of Egypt: "In the wilderness prepare the way for the LORD; make straight in the desert a highway for our God" (Isa. 40:3). This becomes even clearer in chapter 43:

> This is what the LORD says—
>> he who made a way through the sea,
>> a path through the mighty waters,
> who drew out the chariots and horses,
>> the army and reinforcements together,
> and they lay there, never to rise again,
>> extinguished, snuffed out like a wick:
> "Forget the former things;
>> do not dwell on the past.
> See, I am doing a new thing!
>> Now it springs up; do you not perceive it?
> I am making a way in the wilderness
>> and streams in the wasteland.
> The wild animals honor me,
>> the jackals and the owls,
> because I provide water in the wilderness
>> and streams in the wasteland,
> to give drink to my people, my chosen,
>> the people I formed for myself
>> that they may proclaim my praise." (Isa. 43:16–21; cf. also Hos. 11:1–12)

In this way, the prophet evinces the assumption of a recurring *pattern* in God's historical actions. Just as he delivered the people out of Egypt in the original exodus, so also will he do again, this time from the judgment of exile.

---

17. See, e.g., Isa. 1:2–4 in relation to the northern kingdom's exile, and Jer. 2:4–7, 13 in relation to the southern kingdom's exile. Notice that the unfaithfulness of the nations is set in the context of grace spurned and forgotten: "I reared children and brought them up, but they have rebelled against me" (Isa. 1:2b); "They did not ask, 'Where is the LORD, who brought us up out of Egypt…?'" (Jer. 2:6a).

18. Cf. Isa. 48:16–21; 50:2–3; 51:9–11; 52:12; cf. also Ezek. 20:34–42; Hos. 2:14–15; 11:5, 10–11.

This interpretive approach to historical events under God's sovereign direction is known as "historical correspondence" or "pattern in history." Not only will this be visible in the prophets' interpretations of the relationships between God's past and future actions, but we will also frequently discern it in the New Testament writers' interpretive apprehensions of the life and ministry of Jesus.[19]

The Establishment of a New Covenant

The result of God's new act of deliverance will be the arrival of that era when God will pour forth the consummation of his covenantal blessings on Israel. The full-orbed nature of this age entails several dimensions.[20] But preeminent among them is the establishment of a "new covenant." This covenant will address the problems that have plagued the people's relationship with God in the past, bringing the prior covenantal blessings to their culmination. The dimensions of this expectation are found in various passages, but it is only in Jeremiah 31:31–34 that the explicit wording of a "new covenant" appears in the Old Testament: "'The days are coming,' declares the LORD, 'when I will make a new covenant with the house of Israel and with the house of Judah'" (Jer. 31:31).

"The presupposition is that the way God worked in the past is mirrored in the way he works in the present and future. There is a correspondence between what happened to God's people in the past and what happens now or in the future. Climactic events in Israel's history become the paradigms by which new events are explained."[21]

The historical reality experienced by the people after the exile, however, falls short of the preexilic hopes. It is true that the exiles from the south start returning to the land in 538 BC, which leads to the rebuilding of a less glorious temple under Zerubbabel and the walls under Nehemiah. But the consummation of the covenantal hopes once again eludes their grasp. Thus, while Jeremiah and the other preexilic prophets set their expectations of the New Covenant in the context of the return from exile, this event turns out to function as a *foreshadowing* of the future consummation, when the New Covenant is truly established in yet another installment of the return-from-exile pattern. As we will see, this comes with Jesus.

---

19. See Richard Longenecker, *Biblical Exegesis in the Apostolic Period* (Grand Rapids: Eerdmans, 1975), 93–95; Darrell L. Bock, "Use of the Old Testament in the New," in *Foundations for Biblical Interpretation: A Complete Library of Tools and Resources* (ed. David S. Dockery, Kenneth A. Mathews, and Robert B. Sloan; Nashville: Broadman & Holman, 1994), 97–114; Jonathan Lunde, "An Introduction to Central Questions in the New Testament Use of the Old Testament," in *Three Views on the New Testament Use of the Old Testament* (ed. Kenneth Berding and Jonathan Lunde; Grand Rapids: Zondervan, 2008), 19–21, 38–39.

20. These appear to be the main elements of their expectation of God's blessing and vindication, elements that make up the New Testament notion of the kingdom of God: the judgment of Israel's enemies (e.g., Isa. 9:4–7; 11:1–9; 16:5; 32:1–5, 14–20; 42:1–9; 61:1–3; Jer. 30:21–22; 33:15–26; Ezek. 37:21–25; Joel

3:2, 12–13; Amos 9:11–12; Zech. 3:8; 6:12–13; 9:9–10; 1 QM 11:1–18; 4QFlor 1:11–14; 4QPBless 1–7; 4QTestim 9–13; *4 Ezra* 12:31–32; *T. Jud.* 24:1–5); the return of the exiles (e.g., Isa. 11:1, 10–16; Mic. 4:6–8); the renewal of the land (e.g., Amos 9:13–15); the rebuilding of the temple (e.g., Ezek. 43:1–7); the coming of the Messiah (e.g., Ezek. 37:21–25); the establishment of a New Covenant (e.g., Jer. 31:31–34); the outpouring of the Spirit (e.g., Joel 2:28–29); the healing and purification of the people (e.g., Isa. 62:1–3; Jer. 33:6–8); and the inclusion of the nations in the blessings of the kingdom (e.g., Zech. 8:20–23).

21. Klyne Snodgrass, "The Use of the Old Testament in the New," in *New Testament Criticism & Interpretation* (ed. David Alan Black and David S. Dockery; Grand Rapids: Zondervan, 1991), 416.

SUMMARY

We have begun our consideration of the "Why" question by positing the value of the biblical category of "covenant" as a means to define what it is to live in discipleship to Jesus. Indeed, one of the main reasons for our lack of clarity regarding the "Why" question may very well stem from our ignorance of this concept. For it is readily apparent that the central issues of faith, grace, and works are intertwined within the covenantal relationships that God initiates with people. Though always established in grace, each biblical covenant also includes demands of righteousness from those who trust in his faithfulness to fulfill his covenantal promises. This means that covenantal grace *never* diminishes the covenantal demand of righteousness — righteousness that flows out of covenantal faith. As a result, faith and works of obedience will always be found in God's true covenant partners, regardless of the type of covenant in question.

In the case of a grant covenant, the fulfillment of the covenantal blessings is the sole responsibility of God, implying that the fundamental human response to this divine commitment is faith. In the case of a conditional covenant, people continue to receive God's promised covenantal blessings *if* they continue to live faithfully in relation to the demands of righteousness. In both cases, the people's obedience flows out of their faith and in response to God's grace. In no way is this obedience understood to *merit* the covenantal blessings. As we saw, each of these realities is precluded in God's interaction with Adam and Eve in the garden.

What remains for us to do in the next three chapters is to pose our three covenantal questions to each of the main biblical covenants. In the process, we will gain a biblical theological perspective that will enable us to answer the "Why" question. But I hope that the juices are already beginning to run as you think about the implications of these thoughts for discipleship. We have much yet to do before we can answer the "Why" question, but the pathway forward is hopefully already emerging.

RELEVANT QUESTIONS

1. What does the prefall experience of Adam and Eve suggest concerning what it means to live life the way God intended it to be lived?
2. In what ways do people today reenact the twin aspects of the fall, rejecting God's sufficient supply and reaching for what is beyond his limitations?
3. What are some practical ways in which disciples can recover a sensitivity to living in God's grace?

CHAPTER 3

THE GRACIOUS GROUNDING OF THE COVENANTS

"This is the covenant I will make with the house of Israel
    after that time," declares the LORD.
"I will put my law in their minds
    and write it on their hearts.
I will be their God,
    and they will be my people.
No longer will they teach their neighbors,
    or say to one another, 'Know the LORD,'
because they will all know me,
    from the least of them to the greatest,"
                declares the LORD.
"For I will forgive their wickedness
    and will remember their sins no more."

                              Jeremiah 31:33–34

Then he took the cup, and when he had given thanks, he gave it to them, saying, "Drink from it, all of you. This is my blood of the covenant, which is poured out for many for the forgiveness of sins."

                              Matthew 26:27–28

It would be interesting to take a poll among Christians today to see how many of them assume that the Old Testament is mainly about God's demands on his people and his judgment of them when they failed. From what I have seen, my hunch is that the percentage would be high. In step with this is the commonly held impression that the Old Testament describes a religion of legalism that is distinct from the New Testament religion of grace.

I am sure there are many reasons for this state of affairs, but one of the sad corollaries is that the Old Testament has ceased to be useful for much of anything to the contemporary Christian, other than some gripping, moralistic stories about people and their foibles—stories that work especially well in Sunday School lessons for children. In fact, a friend of mine recently told me about an evangelical church he attended for a while that unashamedly proclaimed that they would neither teach nor preach from the Old Testament Scriptures, since they appear to be so irrelevant to Christian experience. How did we end up here?

Certainly, this perspective is distinct from the one we encounter in the New Testament itself. We should remember that writings of the Old Testament were the authoritative Scriptures for the New Testament authors and especially for Jesus himself. And though they do appropriate these texts in ways that sometimes were innovative and different than their non-Christian Jewish contemporaries, Jesus and his apostolic witnesses do not in any way disparage the Old Testament. Indeed, they *ground* their messages in its literature. And this is true even of the gracious foundation of their experience with God. In fact, the closer you look at the Old Testament, the deeper and wider becomes the grace of God in its pages. Grace is certainly not a new reality once we turn the page from Malachi to Matthew, nor does it play a different role in Christianity than in Judaism.

So, what can we learn of the role of grace in the covenantal relationships that God initiates with people in the Old Testament that might shed light on our relationship with Jesus in the New Covenant? To discover this, we will consider each of the main biblical covenants in the light of our first covenantal question: "What is the gracious context in which each covenantal relationship is established?"

COVENANTAL GRACE
The Noahic Covenant

When we think of Noah, most of us focus on the judgment of the flood, the ark, and the blessing of the rainbow in its aftermath, signifying God's pledge not to do this again. But we rarely focus on the covenant itself that God establishes with Noah in Genesis 8–9. When we do so, two gracious aspects step to the fore. The first one, of course, is that God only establishes this covenant once he has graciously delivered Noah from the devastation of the flood.[1] Now, it is true that Noah is described as "a righteous [ṣaddiq] man, blameless [tamim] among the people of his time" (Gen. 6:9).[2] This could be interpreted to mean that Noah was righteous in his own efforts and that the favor given him by God is *merited*. But the text also says that "he walked faithfully with God" (6:9b).[3] It is likely that this intimacy is the

---

1. Williamson observes that this rescue must be seen as God's faithfulness to his declaration to the serpent in Gen. 3:15, that the decisive blow in the ongoing struggle between the seed of the woman and evil would be delivered by her offspring. Preserving one family of descendants from Eve keeps this expectation alive (Williamson, *Sealed with an Oath*, 51).

2. " 'Faithful' (ṣaddiq) designates people who live in right rela-

tionship with God and with their community and in accordance with its standards. 'Whole' (tamim) designates them as complete people, their whole lives lived God's way" (Goldingay, *Israel's Gospel*, 171).

3. Goldingay notes that the phrase "walking with God" "spells out the implications of faithfulness and wholeness, in the kind of relationship of mutuality and friendship that Enoch enjoyed" (ibid., 171).

secret of Noah's "blamelessness." That is, he was the only one of his day who was living life as it was meant to be lived.[4] If Eden is allowed to inform us concerning what this might have entailed, Noah lived in the daily reception of God's gracious provision, leading to the submission of his heart to God. In this close relationship, Noah found divine "favor."

Along with the deliverance from the flood, the second gracious grounding of this covenant is the reestablishment of the conditions that make terrestrial life possible. Although the flood had *undone* the separation in the waters that God had effected in the original creation event (Gen. 1:6–10), Noah and his family are given a world where this separation has once again been accomplished.[6] The waters have returned to their places, with God's promise that they never again will be released with the same destructive force: "I establish my covenant with you: Never again will all life be destroyed by the waters of a flood; never again will there be a flood to destroy the earth" (9:11). Consequently, God guarantees that the seasonal rhythm will continue for the duration of the earth (8:22). With this restoration, the original order before the fall once again appears to be established—with one significant difference.

The word that is translated as "favor" (ḥen) is often also translated as "grace." The nature of "grace" or "favor" in the biblical witness is such that it is never given because of the recipient's merit. Goldingay comments: "If Noah had 'earned' God's grace . . . grace would not be what he had earned."[5] Noah's deliverance therefore should be understood as the culmination of God's gracious work in his life. As he and his family respond to the covenant, they will do so in full awareness of their gracious deliverance from the flood.

This difference is that God commits himself to judicial restraint, *in spite* of human sinfulness. Whereas God previously warned Adam and Eve of the death sentence should they transgress his limitation on the tree—a sentence that is fulfilled eventually both in their own deaths and in the corporate judgment of the flood—God's gracious promises are given in the Noahic Covenant *in full view* of human depravity. Notice that God promises not to curse the ground again in the form of a worldwide flood, "even though every inclination of the human heart is evil from childhood" (Gen. 8:21b). Williamson writes:

> Thus understood, this post-diluvian covenant ... reaffirms God's original creational intent that the flood had placed in abeyance and that humanity's inherent sinfulness would otherwise continue to place in jeopardy.[7]

It is therefore in this gracious context that the covenantal demands are given to Noah. But those will have to wait until the next chapter. Instead, let's move on to the Abrahamic covenants.

---

4. Goldingay opines, "the sentence order suggests that if there is a causal link between finding God's grace and being *ṣaddiq*, it is grace that issues in that moral character rather than the other way round" (ibid., 173).

5. Ibid., 172; cf. Gen. 18:3; 19:19; 30:27.

6. See esp. D. J. A. Clines, *The Theme of the Pentateuch* (2nd ed.; Sheffield: Sheffield Academic Press, 1997), 81. Note also the repopulating of the land by the animals coming out of the ark (Gen. 8:1–3; cf. 1:20–25) and the reestablishment of days and seasons (8:22; cf. 1:14–18).

7. Williamson, *Sealed with an Oath*, 61.

The Abrahamic Covenants

In contrast to the simpler dealings between God and Noah, the interaction between God and Abram stretches out over a series of encounters, involving promises and two covenants of distinct types. But the gracious grounding of both covenants is clear.

The Babel Context

As we noted in the previous chapter, it is important to situate the call of Abram in its larger literary/historical context. In the immediately preceding Babel narrative, the people congregate together to coordinate their self-serving efforts, resisting the command to "fill the earth" (Gen. 1:28; 11:4b). The tower they are building probably refers to an ancient "temple tower" or "ziggurat," on top of which would sit a temple for a deity. The function of these towers appears to have been to provide a means by which their god could descend from the temple on the top to a ground-level temple, thereby coming within the reach of the people.[8] As such, it symbolizes their attempt to reach heaven and assert their importance—to make "a name" for themselves (11:4). Consequently, haunting echoes from Eden reverberate at Babel, as humanity collectively reenacts Eve's fateful reach.

The Babel rebellion perpetuates the pattern that begins with Eve, who takes the fruit so as to be wise "like God" (Gen. 3:5–6). After his expulsion, Cain follows suit, establishing a city known for its power and technology (4:19–24) and "named" after his son (4:17)—a city that has no room for God.[9] The relationship that God desired to have with people is being lost. God intended that people would receive his sustaining provisions and then to respond to this grace by living within the boundaries that he sovereignly establishes. Instead, he is being pushed to the side or brought down to their level.

In a real sense, then, history hangs in the balance here. What will God do? How will he respond *this time* to humanity in rebellion against him? Certainly, the nonrepetition of a summary judgment like the flood should be understood as God's faithfulness to the promise he made to Noah to preserve humanity *in spite* of their sinfulness. This alone is grace. Similarly, his confusing of their languages is likely intended to minimize the potential for evil in a humanity that collectively rebels against God.[10] But God will do more than withhold his hand of judgment and frustrate humanity's sinful designs; he will also reach back to redeem. It is in this context that the Abrahamic call and covenants should be understood.

The Abrahamic Promises

In the wake of Babel's debacle, God calls Abram out of Ur and makes remarkable promises to him—promises that eventually will be given covenantal expression.

---

8. W. Osborne, "Babel," *DOTP*, 74.
9. Ibid., 75.

10. LaSor, *Message*, 30.

Through all of this, the initiative lies solely in God's graciousness. It is for this reason that the silence of the text regarding Abram's character and faith *prior* to God's call is deafening.

In the first promise, God communicates to Abram his intention to raise a great nation through him (Gen. 12:2a). In its covenantal restatement in 15:5, God encourages Abram to envision descendants that mirror the numberless stars of the heavens, in spite of Sarai's barrenness (11:30).[11] The notoriety sought by the throngs at Babel through inappropriate means (11:4) is now graciously given to Abram, whose "name" will indeed be "great" (12:2b).

In the second promise, God declares to Abram that he will become a blessing that will extend to all peoples: "I will bless those who bless you, and whoever curses you I will curse; and all peoples on earth will be blessed through you" (Gen. 12:3). The covenant that especially corresponds to this element is found in Genesis 17. There, the promise that Abram will be the father of a great nation is expanded to include many nations (v. 5), resulting in the changes of Abram's and Sarai's names to Abraham ("father of many"; v. 5) and Sarah (meaning "princess"; v. 15b).[13]

"A promise by definition involves a commitment by one party to another. Through making a promise God not only commits himself to do something, but he creates an expectation or hope for the one who receives the promise. For this reason, divine promises are special because they come from One who has both the power to accomplish what he has said and the faithfulness to ensure that it will happen."[12]

Since only the Hebrews and Edomites are understood to have descended biologically from Abraham and Sarah, this promise must be metaphorical, indicating his role as mediator of the divine blessings to all nations. This helps us see that the primary purpose of Abraham's election and blessing is so that he in turn will be a blessing to all peoples of the earth.[14] Babel's failure is now being addressed positively.

In the third promise, God declares to Abraham that his descendants will inherit the land to which God directs him to go (Gen. 12:1):

> The LORD appeared to Abram and said, "To your offspring I will give this land."
> So he built an altar there to the LORD, who had appeared to him. (12:7; cf. 13:17)

This too finds covenantal confirmation in Genesis 15:7–21 (restated in 17:8). Once again, the gracious nature of this promise is accentuated when viewed in light of the repeated episodes of judgment in the preceding narratives—narratives that describe broken relationships with God.[15] In each instance, this brokenness is symbolized by the loss of land.[16] Adam and Eve were expelled from Eden after

---

11. This stands in stark contrast to the stress in Gen. 1–11 on fertility, genealogies, and the rise of nations. This context signals that God will respond to the need of humanity through the descendants of a couple whose prospects for progeny were nil.

12. T. D. Alexander, "Promises, Divine," *DOTP*, 661.

13. For ease of reference, I will use Abraham and Sarah from this point forward, regardless of the text under discussion.

14. For a defense of the passive Niphil reading of the verb ("will be blessed"), see Williamson, "Covenant," *DOTP*, 144–45.

15. Cf. Gen. 3:14–19; 4:10–16; 7:11–23; cf. 9:24–25.

16. The pattern in the Bible is that possession of the land is contingent on a good relationship between God and the people: "When humans are alienated from God there are significant repercussions, because God uses the land to punish his recalcitrant subjects" (James McKeown, "Land, Fertility, Famine," *DOTP*, 488; cf. Gen. 3:17–19; 4:10–16; 11:5–9; note also the cursing of the land in 3:17–19, 24; 5:29).

their fall, Noah's generation lost the land itself in the flood, and the nations were dispersed from Babel. God began the reversal by giving the cleansed earth back to Noah and his descendants after the flood. The promise to Abraham parallels this pattern, implying almost an Edenic nuance in God's commitment to Abraham in which the Lord said in effect: "I will provide a place for you!"[17] (cf. 15:7; 17:8).

Thus, the relationship that God establishes with Abraham is absolutely grounded in the prior grace of his remarkable promises to him — promises that directly address the need of humanity that has been painted with broad strokes and ominous colors in Genesis 3 – 11. This gracious nature is underscored in the covenantal ceremony of Genesis 15. After restating the promises of progeny (v. 5) and land (v. 7), God confirms his commitment to fulfill them in an ancient covenant ritual that seems rather odd to us moderns. Following God's direction, Abraham splits the corpses of three large animals and arranges the halves opposite each other, along with a couple of birds (vv. 9 – 11). He then falls into a deep sleep, during which God appears in a dream and reaffirms his promises to Abraham. God then passes between the animals in the form of a "smoking firepot" and a "blazing torch" (15:17).

The meaning of the ritual in Genesis 15 is confirmed in Jeremiah 34:18 – 20: "Those who have violated my covenant and have not fulfilled the terms of the covenant they made before me, I will treat like the calf they cut in two and then walked between its pieces. The leaders of Judah and Jerusalem, the court officials, the priests and all the people of the land who walked between the pieces of the calf, I will deliver into the hands of their enemies who seek their lives. Their dead bodies will become food for the birds and the wild animals."

The surprising aspect of this event is that in ancient Near Eastern covenants, *both* parties usually stepped between the riven corpses. Here, however, God *alone* passes between them, so that the responsibility of bringing about the blessings of the covenant is all God's. In effect God is proclaiming, "May what has been done to these animals be done to me, if I fail to fulfill my promises to you." The covenantal relationship that God establishes with Abraham is, therefore, profoundly permeated with his grace — grace that is functionally *prior* to the call to righteousness.

The Mosaic Covenant

At first blush, it seems easy to conclude that the Mosaic Covenant is one relationship that does not have grace as its foundation. Its conditional nature, replete with extensive discussions of cursing and blessing, has led many to the impression that it is grounded preeminently in works of obedience. For instance, Moses declares the *conditional* covenantal blessings to the people before they cross over the Jordan into the land:

> If you fully obey the LORD your God and carefully follow all his commands I give you today, the LORD your God will set you high above all the nations on earth. All

---

17. This is foreshadowed in Noah's reception of the land after the flood. The later occupation of the land is associated with "rest" (Ex. 33:14; Deut. 3:20; 12:9 – 10; 25:19; 28:65). Notice their longing for rest (Gen. 5:29) and the slavery and labor in Egypt.

these blessings will come on you and accompany you if you obey the LORD your God. (Deut. 28:1–2; see 28:3–14; Lev. 26:3–13)

Later in that same chapter, the other foot drops:

However, if you do not obey the LORD your God and do not carefully follow all his commands and decrees I am giving you today, all these curses will come on you and overtake you. (Deut. 28:15; see 28:14–68; Lev. 26:14–39)

Taken at face value without the benefit of the larger historical and literary context, we could understand this covenant as simply a matter of *quid pro quo* ("something in exchange for something"). If the Israelites will obey, God will bless. If they do not, God will visit them in judgment. Understood in this way, the Mosaic Covenant devolves into an economy of merit, where the rewards are *earned* through works of righteousness. Unfortunately, this is a common perception by many people today. But it misses the larger covenantal and historical framework that surrounds this covenant—a framework that underscores the pattern we are tracing.

In the first place, the giving of the law comes in the wake of God's deliverance out of Egypt in the exodus. Chronology is all important here. In Egypt, the Hebrews appear to have been rather ignorant about Yahweh. Apparently, many were idolators, as is implied by their request of Aaron to make the golden calf as soon as Moses turns up missing (Ex. 32:1–6). This suggests that the revelatory purpose of the ten plagues was not simply to confront Pharaoh and the Egyptians with the overwhelming power of the true God. It was also to reveal the same thing to the Hebrews. Had the law been given to the children of Israel while they were still bound to their Egyptian slave masters and living in ignorance of Yahweh's character, the message would have been construed in this way: "If you follow my law, then I will deliver you. Clean up your act and I will save you." The Mosaic Covenant would then truly have been a covenant of works.

But God first of all graciously delivers the Israelites out of Egypt *before* he establishes his law covenant with them. This gracious grounding is asserted repeatedly throughout the final four books of the Pentateuch. For instance, notice how God prefaces the listing of the Ten Commandments at both Sinai and Moab, underscoring their gracious foundation: "I am the LORD your God, who brought you out of Egypt, out of the land of slavery" (Ex. 20:2; cf. Deut. 5:6).[18] Durham writes: "The ten commandments thus present the foundational layer of Yahweh's expectation of those who, in response to his gift of himself, desire to give themselves to him."[19] The gracious foundation of this covenant is clear.

In the second place, it is important to note that God responds to the plight of the Hebrews in Egypt because he remembers his earlier covenant with the patriarchs:

18. This coheres with the ancient suzerain/vassal treaty form, which always grounds the covenantal relationship by means of a historical prologue that details the prior deeds performed by the suzerain on behalf of the vassal. As a result the vassal is obligated to ongoing gratitude to the suzerain: "the vassal is exchanging *future* obedience to specific commands for *past* benefits which he received without any real *right*" (Mendenhall, "Covenant Forms," 58).

19. John I. Durham, *Exodus* (WBC; Waco, TX: Word 1987), 300.

"God heard their groaning and he remembered his covenant with Abraham, with Isaac and with Jacob. So God looked on the Israelites and was concerned about them" (Ex. 2:24–25).

The exodus event must, therefore, be interpreted in the light of the prior grace of the promises and covenant given to Abraham.[20] This also means that the Mosaic Covenant should always be understood as subordinate to the promises made to Abraham in Genesis 12 and the grant covenant of Genesis 15 — the latter unilaterally guaranteeing the promises of people and land. This is the covenantal background that graciously grounds the exodus and the giving of the law at Sinai.[21]

A third aspect of this covenant's gracious grounding comes in the stipulations regarding the removal of guilt through the ministry of the tabernacle. Since God is inflexibly holy, the ministry of the tabernacle provides the means by which God will continue to dwell beneficently with his people without threatening them:

> I will put my dwelling place among you, and I will not abhor you. I will walk among you and be your God, and you will be my people. (Lev. 26:11–12; cf. Ex. 25:8, 22; 29:45; 40:34–38; Num. 9:15–23)

"The law must be interpreted within the context of grace, since God gives commands to people he has redeemed freely and chosen solely because of his great love for them (Deut. 7:7–9). There is no basis, then, for thinking that the Mosaic covenant is a legalistic covenant."[22]

The tabernacle's atoning ministry, therefore, mediates sustaining grace within the covenant, making it possible for the all-holy God to dwell with an unholy people (Lev. 4:31, 35; 16:30; Num. 14:12; etc.).

Thus, the giving of the law is twice grounded in *prior* grace — in the gracious nature of the Abrahamic promises and in the deliverance of the exodus itself — and maintained by *sustaining* grace through the tabernacle. Taken this way, obedience to the law is properly understood not to be a means of *earning* acceptance into the people of God — their inclusion had already been mediated to them through the Abrahamic Covenant and confirmed by the exodus. The command to obedience once again must be seen within this gracious framework.

The Davidic Covenant

There are three gracious elements that are prominent in the establishment of God's covenant with David. The first pertains to God's gracious choice of David. Admittedly, at the time Samuel anoints David, the prophet explains his choice of the youngest son of Jesse because God looks at the heart and not the exterior (1 Sam. 16:7). This indicates God's knowledge of David's character and fitness to become king.

---

20. Note the allusions to the promises made to Abraham, Isaac, and Jacob in Ex. 3:7–8, 16–22; 6:2–6; 13:5–11.

21. That grace is the grounding of the Mosaic Covenant is confirmed by the elements in the narrative that correspond to the expectation of the deliverance that is anticipated in the grant covenant of Gen. 15:13–14. Their growth in numbers (Ex. 1:1–6) begins the fulfillment of Gen. 15:5. They have also become oppressed transients in a foreign land, as predicted in 15:13. Note also how the plagues on Egypt and the exodus itself fulfill 15:14 (Williamson, *Sealed with an Oath*, 94–96).

22. Schreiner, "The Commands of God," 73; see also 100.

However, nothing is said of this in 2 Samuel 7, where God establishes his covenant with David. Rather, the stress there is completely on God's gracious choice of David and the establishment of his rule. God's words to Nathan underscore this emphasis:

> "Now then, tell my servant David, 'This is what the LORD Almighty says: I took you from the pasture, from tending the flock, and appointed you ruler over my people Israel. I have been with you wherever you have gone, and I have cut off all your enemies from before you.'" (2 Sam. 7:8–9)

David had been taken from obscurity to the regal heights of the throne by God's gracious choice and protection.

The second gracious element comes in the form of God's promise to provide peace and security for Israel. Similar to the Abrahamic land promise (Gen. 12:7), God commits himself to provide a place where the oppression of his people will end: "And I will provide a place for my people Israel and will plant them so that they can have a home of their own and no longer be disturbed" (2 Sam. 7:10; cf. Pss. 2:7–9; 89:3–4, 33–37, 39; 132:11). Once again, notions of the reversal of Eden's banishment appear.

The third element consists in the grand promise of an enduring dynasty that will come from David's progeny:

> "The LORD declares to you that the LORD himself will establish a house for you: When your days are over and you rest with your ancestors, I will raise up your offspring to succeed you, who will come from your own body, and I will establish his kingdom.... Your house and your kingdom will endure forever before me; your throne will be established forever." (2 Sam. 7:11b–12, 16)

Since God commits himself to preserve David's line "forever," it is clear that this is a grant covenant. Its divine promise connects retrospectively with the Abrahamic promise of royal descendants (Gen. 17:6, 16) and prospectively to Solomon and the line of kings that would follow. Accordingly, the psalmist prays for a king who idealizes everything that God intends to accomplish through David's royal line:

> Endow the king with your justice, O God,
>   the royal son with your righteousness.
> May he judge your people in righteousness,
>   your afflicted ones with justice....
> May he endure as long as the sun,
>   as long as the moon, through all generations....
> May he rule from sea to sea
>   and from the River to the ends of the earth....
> May his name endure forever;
>   may it continue as long as the sun.
> Then all nations will be blessed through him,
>   and they will call him blessed. (Ps. 72:1–2, 5, 8, 17; cf. 2 Sam. 23:3–4)

This expectation eventually gives rise to the messianic hope concerning a future king who will reign in righteousness, fulfilling in *himself* what originally appears to have been a corporate promise. The pathway to Jesus is already emerging.

The New Covenant

The great articulation of the New Covenant comes to us through the prophet Jeremiah. As he looks past the purifying and atoning judgment of the exile, he describes God's eventual transformative work among his people:

> "The days are coming," declares the LORD,
>   "when *I will* make a new covenant
> with the house of Israel
>   and with the house of Judah.
> It will not be like the covenant
>   I made with their ancestors
> when I took them by the hand
>   to lead them out of Egypt,
> because they broke my covenant,
>   though I was a husband to them,"
>   declares the LORD.
> "This is the covenant *I will* make with the house of Israel
>   after that time," declares the LORD.
> "*I will* put my law in their minds
>   and write it on their hearts.
> *I will* be their God,
>   and they will be my people.
> No longer will they teach their neighbors,
>   or say to one another, 'Know the LORD,'
> because they will all know me,
>   from the least of them to the greatest,"
>   declares the LORD.
> "For *I will* forgive their wickedness
>   and *will* remember their sins no more." (Jer. 31:31–34; emphasis mine)

It is obvious that the blessings spelled out here will come to pass solely because of the divine initiative. Notice the repetition of the "I will" refrain in these verses. God's action clearly grounds the graciousness of this covenant. There are three main dimensions of God's gracious intervention described here.

First, God will write the law on the hearts of his people (v. 33), implying its internalization. This is obviously in contrast to the external commandments engraved on the tablets of stone in the Mosaic Covenant. As such, Jeremiah prophesies an *inner* transformation of the people so that they will no longer harbor hostility or rebellion in relation to the covenant. What Moses looked forward to as the eventual hope of the people (Deut. 30:6) will finally come to pass, as God says through Jeremiah in the next chapter:

> I will surely gather them from all the lands where I banish them ... I will bring them back to this place.... They will be my people, and I will be their God. I will give them singleness of heart and action, so that they will always fear me and that all will then go well for them and for their children after them. I will make an everlasting covenant with them ... I will inspire them to fear me, so that they will never turn away from me. (Jer. 32:37–40)[23]

It is true that the notion of an internalized law and inner transformation is present in the Old Testament (Deut. 10:16; 11:18; 30:6, 14), but apparently only a few among God's people experienced this. What is striking about this expectation in Jeremiah is that *all* of the covenant people will be transformed in this way, leading to a people finally and absolutely faithful to God. By implication, there will no longer be any need to renew this covenant — in stark contrast to the multiple times in which the Mosaic Covenant is renewed.[24]

Second, God will grant profound knowledge of himself to everyone in the covenant community (Jer. 31:34a). Whereas the lack of this knowledge led to the exile (Isa. 2:3; Jer. 2:8; 4:22; Hos. 4:6), in that day there will no longer be any need to exhort another to know the Lord, because all will know him intimately.[25] Undoubtedly, this is the gracious result of the internalization of the law.

Assuredly, both of these two divine initiatives are associated with the new ministry of the Spirit, which will be granted to all and in unprecedented measure. Through Ezekiel God emphasizes the righteous enablement that the Spirit will provide for those who return from exile:

> I will give you a new heart and put a new spirit in you; I will remove from you your heart of stone and give you a heart of flesh. And I will put my Spirit in you and move you to follow my decrees and be careful to keep my laws. (Ezek. 36:26–27; cf. Joel 2:28–29; Isa. 32:15; 44:3; Ezek. 37:14; 39:29)

Notice the purpose of this Spirit-infusion — divine enablement to covenant faithfulness!

Third, God will deal with the sin of his people in a climactic manner. Jeremiah writes, "For I will forgive their wickedness and will remember their sins no more" (Jer. 31:34c). The provocative wording of this promise likely speaks to the notion of a permanently effective atonement. Jeremiah does not define *how* this new atoning

---

23. See also Jer. 24:7; Ezek. 11:19; 37:14.

24. Deut. 27–30; Josh. 24:1–28; 2 Chron. 15; 2 Kings 11:17–18; 23:1–3; Ezra 10:1–5; Neh. 8–10.

25. Contrast this with Jer. 9:26; 16:10–13. The boundaries of this covenant will obviously include Israel, but will also outstrip this national limitation (cf. Isa. 42:6; 44:28; 45:13; 49:6; 55:3–5; 56:4–8; 66:18–24; cf. also Jer. 33:9; Ezek. 36:36; 37:28). This blessing likely does not obviate the need for teachers, but rather the need of a knowledge of the LORD that will lead to obedience (Williamson, *Sealed with an Oath*, 156).

work will be achieved, though he undoubtedly expects it to come about in the context of the impending judgment of the exile that we considered in the previous chapter. Other texts similarly point to God's redemption and cleansing of his people from the exile.[26] But the clearest explication of the means by which this is accomplished is provided by Isaiah in his description of the Servant of the Lord.

Interspersed throughout chapters 42–53 of Isaiah, one finds the Servant Songs.[27] They are so named because of their portrayal of the Servant of the Lord: "Here is my servant, whom I uphold, my chosen one in whom I delight" (Isa. 42:1a). As Isaiah's portrayal develops, it becomes clear that there are actually two "servants." While it is true that each of them is identified as "Israel," their respective behaviors are depicted in stark distinction. The righteous servant is empowered by the Spirit (Isa. 42:1) and persistently follows the Lord:

> The Sovereign Lord has opened my ears;
>> I have not been rebellious,
>> I have not turned away....
> He who vindicates me is near.
>> Who then will bring charges against me? ...
> It is the Sovereign Lord who helps me.
>> Who will condemn me? (Isa. 50:5, 8a, 9a)

The unrighteous servant, by contrast, is described in depressing terms of unfaithfulness:

> Hear, you deaf;
>> look, you blind, and see!
> Who is blind but my servant,
>> and deaf like the messenger I send?
> Who is blind like the one in covenant with me,
>> blind like the servant of the Lord?
> You have seen many things, but have paid no attention;
>> your ears are open, but you hear nothing. (Isa. 42:18–20)

While the identity of the righteous servant has occasioned no little debate,[28] it is enough for us to note that his career culminates in Isaiah 52–53 in a death that serves to atone for the sinful servant's sin:

---

26. E.g., Isa. 41:14; 43:1, 3–4; 44:22–25; 48:17, 20; 49:7, 26; 52:3, 9–10; 54:4–8; 59:16–20; 61:10–11; 63:9; cf. also Isa. 42:16; 43:10–13, 19–21; 44:3; 49:5; 51:9–11; Jer. 33:6–9; 50:20; Ezek. 36:24–27; 37:18–23; Hos. 14:4–7; Zech. 13:1; Mal. 3:1–4.

27. Isa. 42:1–7; 49:1–7; 50:4–9; 52:13–53:12. It is likely that Isa. 61:1–3 ought to be included in this group because of the recurrence of the important servant themes found there. Luke's inclusion of this citation on the lips of Jesus as the summary statement of his ministry (Luke 4:18–19) may indicate that he was interpreting this passage in line with the other servant texts.

28. For concise discussions of the Servant, see Stephen G. Dempster, "The Servant of the Lord," in *CTBT*, 128–78; J. B. Payne, "Servant of the Lord," in *EDT*, 1006–7; Eugene Carpenter, *"ebed,"* in *NIDOTTE*, 3:307; R. T. France, "Servant of Yahweh," in *DJG*, 744–47. See also G. P. Hugenberger, "The Servant of the Lord in the 'Servant Songs' of Isaiah: A Second Moses Figure," in *The Lord's Anointed: Interpretation of Old Testament Messianic Texts* (ed. P. E. Satterthwaite, R. S. Hess, and G. J. Wenham; Grand Rapids: Baker, 1995), 106–38.

But he was pierced for our transgressions,
    he was crushed for our iniquities;
the punishment that brought us peace was on him,
    and by his wounds we are healed....
Yet it was the LORD's will to crush him and cause him to suffer,
    and though the LORD makes his life an offering for sin,
he will see his offspring and prolong his days,
    and the will of the LORD will prosper in his hand....
Therefore I will give him a portion among the great,
    and he will divide the spoils with the strong,
because he poured out his life unto death,
    and was numbered with the transgressors.
For he bore the sin of many,
    and made intercession for the transgressors. (Isa. 53:5, 10, 12)

Although both servants appear to be caught up together in the judgment of exile, the suffering of the righteous servant is discovered to be representative in nature, atoning for the sin of the unrighteous servant and opening the door to a return from exile. Thus, Isaiah's descriptions of the eventual blessing of the returning remnant people must be seen in the light of this gracious substitutionary atonement, by which "her sin has been paid for" (Isa. 40:1–2; cf. 11:10–16; etc.).

It is not surprising, then, that most of the prophetic expectations of redemption are found in this return-from-exile framework. Significantly, Jeremiah's New Covenant passage is set in such a context (Jer. 31:23–30; cf. 30:1–31:22; 16:14–15; 29:10–14), mirroring what is found in other preexilic and exilic prophets.[30] Even in the expectations of the postexilic prophets, we find the repetition of the judgment and redemption pattern.[31] We will see that this pattern culminates in Jesus, the Servant of the Lord, when God once again provides a profoundly gracious context in which to establish his covenant.[32] And this time, the covenant will be eternal (50:4–5).

"Therefore, in its immediate context, Jeremiah's new covenant prophecy serves to explain how God will maintain his relationship with his people in the future and ensure that history does not simply end up repeating itself."[29]

---

29. Williamson, *Sealed with an Oath*, 152.

30. E.g., Jer. 33:6–9; 50:19; Ezek. 36:8–38; 37:18–28; Hos. 1:6–11; 2:14–23; 11:5–11; Joel 3:17–21; Amos 9:11–15.

31. Zech. 8:1–8; 10:8–12; 12:1–13; 13:7–9; 14:1–21; Mal. 3:1–5, 16–17; 4:1–5.

32. The connection between the Servant's work and the establishment of a covenant is strengthened by the characterization of the Servant as a "covenant" for the people (Isa. 42:6; 49:8). Moreover, Isaiah goes on to describe the new conditions resulting from the Servant's removal of the wrath of God, resulting in a permanent "covenant of peace" (Isa. 54:10; cf. Ezek. 34:25; 37:26–27). The implication is that this covenant will culminate all of the prior covenants, each of which is alluded to in verses succeeding Isa. 53: the Abrahamic in Isa. 54:1–3; the Mosaic in vv. 4–8; the Noahic in vv. 9–10; and the Davidic in 55:3–4 (Williamson, *Sealed with an Oath*, 161).

JESUS' FULFILLMENT OF THE GRACE OF THE COVENANTS

"Drink from it, all of you. This is my blood of the covenant, which is poured out for many for the forgiveness of sins" (Matt. 26:27b–28; cf. Mark 14:24). With these words, Jesus interpreted his impending death as the atoning sacrifice that grounds the New Covenant. Luke's version makes this reference even more clear, identifying this covenant as "new" (Luke 22:20).

Now, it is not a new insight to conceive of grace as the ground of the Christian's relationship to God through Jesus. But what may be new for some is the realization that this gracious foundation is shared with *each* of the previous covenants and that the New Covenant brings to culmination this covenantal pattern. What is more, Jesus' life and ministry bring to fulfillment several of the specific prophecies of the earlier covenants, as well as the salvific actions that ground those relationships. We must be selective as we choose from the wealth of themes and texts in the New Testament that expound on these truths, but let's consider a few of the ways in which Jesus fulfills elements pertaining to the Old Testament covenants. We will then be in position to consider important aspects of Jesus' fulfillment of the grace of the New Covenant.

The Edenic Covenant-like Relationship

In our brief discussion of the covenant-like relationship between God and the first humans in the garden, I noted that God had graced them with the physical blessings embodied in the earth as a whole and the garden in particular, prior to the mandate to steward the earth. But I also mentioned the grace of the prefall relationship of intimacy that Adam and Eve enjoyed with God. Sin had not yet gotten in the way, creating distance and estrangement (Gen. 3:8–10). Disobedience had not yet condemned them to death (3:19b).

It is in this context that Paul's majestic comparison in Romans 5 between Adam and Christ must be seen. Whereas Adam's representative disobedience welcomes sin into humanity's experience (vv. 12, 19), leading to death and condemnation for all (vv. 14–15b, 16a, 17a, 18a), Jesus' representative righteous life (v. 18b) mediates life and justification to many (vv. 16b, 17b, 18b, 19b). As the second Adam, Jesus' faithfulness undoes the damage wrought by the first Adam, offering humanity a new beginning that completely outstrips the potential embodied in Noah's family after the flood. Since those who have faith in Jesus' gracious work are also baptized into him, they are joined with him (6:3–4; 2 Cor. 5:14; Gal. 3:3) and are no longer identified in Adam (Rom. 6:6). Now in Christ, they experience what Paul characterizes as the "new creation" (2 Cor. 5:17; Gal. 6:15).

This implies a return to the prefall state of unfettered intimacy with God in the present age (Rom. 8:15; Gal. 4:6) and the prospect of eternal life with him in the age to come (Rom. 5:21; 6:5, 8, 22–23; 1 Tim. 1:16; Titus 3:7). Jesus' faithful life and sacrificial death, therefore, offer humanity the provision of the prefall relationship that Adam and Eve experienced with God. Much of the grace of Eden is restored in Jesus, with the rest still to come (2 Peter 3:13; Rev. 21:1).

The Noahic Covenant

In his discussion of Jesus' atoning death, Peter links Christian baptism with the ark that saved Noah and his family from the devastating flood (1 Peter 3:18–22). Though this is a notoriously difficult text to explicate, what is clear is that Peter is operating on the level of corresponding historical realities. He introduces this theology by appealing to Jesus' death, "the righteous for the unrighteous" (v. 18b). He then speaks of Jesus' preaching to those who disobeyed in the days of Noah, but who perished in the flood (vv. 19–20). If we sidestep the thorny issue of when and where this preaching took place, it appears that Peter is utilizing the flood to illustrate God's just punishment of sin. Given the reference to Jesus' righteous death for the unrighteous, the linkage to the new event of salvation seems to be between the just punishment of sin in the flood and in Jesus' wrath-bearing death on the cross (cf. 1:18–19; 2:24).

If this is the theological correspondence that lies behind Peter's teaching, his correlation of Christian baptism with the "ark" that saved a few people in the flood is understandable. The deliverance of Noah's family was profoundly gracious, as we have seen. Moreover, though they were literally *in* the floodwaters, the ark preserved their lives. Similarly, baptism links believers with the experience of the just punishment of their sin, identifying them with Jesus in his atoning death on their behalf. But since Jesus was raised from the dead and now sits enthroned, baptism is the means by which the believer not only participates with Christ in God's punishment for their sin, but also in God's gracious deliverance through Jesus (1 Peter 3:21b–22). In this way, Jesus fulfills a major aspect of the grace of the Noahic Covenant.

The Abrahamic Covenants

The very first verse of the New Testament celebrates Jesus' identity not only as the "Messiah," the "son of David," but also as the "son of Abraham" (Matt. 1:1). For Matthew, Jesus' genealogy grounds his Jewish pedigree, qualifying him to be the Messiah. But for Paul, Jesus' connection to Abraham is even more tightly drawn.

In the middle of his discussion of the role of faith in the reception of the Abrahamic promises, Paul identifies Jesus as the great "seed" of Abraham through whom the blessings would be mediated (Gal. 3:16–19). In its context in Genesis 12, the word "seed" (Heb. *zerah*; Gr. *sperma*) is clearly a collective singular, referring generally to Abraham's descendants (v. 7). But Paul finds significance in the *singular* nature of this noun, validating his presentation of Jesus as the singular representative of the entire offspring of Abraham. He is *the* Seed!

Since Jesus is the one through whom the curse of the law has been exhausted (Gal. 3:13), the way is now open through him to receive the blessings of the Abrahamic promises by faith (Gal. 3:22–29; cf. Rom. 4:1–25). Thus, though Isaac was the initial descendant through whom the promises were mediated, Jesus now is the preeminent descendant of Abraham who mediates the culmination of those promises. And since those promises include the blessing of all peoples, the door now stands open for the Gentiles to be included among those who are "Abraham's seed" (Gal. 3:29). In Jesus, the gracious promises grounding the Abrahamic covenants have come to their astounding fulfillment![33]

The Mosaic Covenant

In our discussion above, we discerned three major ways in which the Mosaic Covenant is grounded in grace. The first of these is the commitment by God to Abraham to fulfill his promises to him. As we have just now seen, Jesus brings these promises to completion. The other two aspects are the delivering grace of the exodus and the sustaining grace of the tabernacle. Let's briefly consider Jesus' fulfillment of these as well.

The Fulfillment of the Passover Lamb

When Jesus instructs his disciples to drink from the "cup of blessing" during his final meal, he is clearly presenting his impending death as the climactic fulfillment of the deliverance depicted by the Passover meal. You will recall that at the time of the Hebrews' deliverance from their enslavement in Egypt, God was about to afflict Pharaoh's nation with the final plague of the destruction of the firstborn sons (and animals) throughout the land. Since Pharaoh refused to let Israel — God's "firstborn son" — go, God declares that he will kill Pharaoh's firstborn son (Ex. 4:22–23; 11:5).

To avoid this judgment in their own homes, God provided protection for the Hebrews through the spreading of the blood of an unblemished lamb on the door posts and lintels of their dwellings (Ex. 12:7). When the Lord saw the blood on the entryways, he passed over those homes, sparing their firstborn sons (Ex. 12:12–13). The people were to roast and eat the lamb, along with other elements that symbolized their slavery in Egypt and the haste of their departure (12:8–10). Accordingly, they were to eat the meal quickly, aptly attired for their impending flight (12:11). God was to give them deliverance that night. Succeeding generations of Jews continued to celebrate this meal, in effect reliving their miraculous deliverance from Egypt and the grounding of the great Mosaic Covenant.

---

33. See also John 8:56, where Jesus claims to be the one for whom Abraham waited with joy.

But the Passover also becomes the biblical paradigm that depicts the future redemption of the nation—a redemption that would *eclipse* the original exodus in glory. As we saw in the previous chapter, Isaiah parallels the exodus with the return of the Jews from the Babylonian exile (Isa. 43:14), even affirming the superior nature of the latter (Isa. 43:15–21). This helps us perceive the similar use of the exodus imagery in the famous Isaiah 40 passage, again in reference to the return from exile:

> A voice of one calling:
> "In the wilderness prepare
>   the way for the LORD;
> make straight in the desert
>   a highway for our God.
> Every valley shall be raised up,
>   every mountain and hill made low;
> the rough ground shall become level,
>   the rugged places a plain.
> And the glory of the LORD will be revealed,
>   and all people will see it together." (Isa. 40:3–5a)

Strikingly, then, John the Baptist picks this up again and reapplies it to himself as the herald of the deliverance that he expects to come through the "more powerful" one after him: "John replied in the words of Isaiah the prophet, 'I am the voice of one calling in the wilderness, "Make straight the way for the Lord"'" (John 1:23; cf. Matt. 3:11). Thus, in the Passover celebration a backward glance is combined with a forward look to a future deliverance that would amount to a "new exodus," when the Lord would climactically fulfill all of his covenantal promises. Though the return from exile indeed provided one expression of this fulfillment, John's reuse of this imagery demonstrates more was yet to come.

By his evocative presentation of his body and blood at the Passover meal, therefore, Jesus is clearly claiming to be the great fulfillment of the gracious sacrifice that led to the exodus and of the redemptive expectations that came later. As such, he is providing in his death the means by which deliverance for the nation will be accomplished again. As Paul declares, "Christ, our Passover lamb, has been sacrificed" (1 Cor. 5:7). In Jesus, the exodus and its promise find their highest expression!

The Fulfillment of the Atoning Sacrifices

Since the New Testament writers combine Jesus' fulfillment of the Passover lamb with the curse-removing sacrifices that were offered every day by the priests, Jesus also fulfills the sustaining grace of the tabernacle/temple in the Mosaic Covenant. Paul emphasizes this when he interprets Jesus' death in a curse-bearing way: "Christ redeemed us from the curse of the law by becoming a curse for us, for it is written:

'Cursed is everyone who is hung on a pole'" (Gal. 3:13).[34] And yet, since Jesus' sacrifice is presented as the final and climactic sacrifice, it is not to be repeated.

This is the burden of argument in the letter to the Hebrews. There are so many facets to the gemlike portrayal of Jesus in Hebrews, all of which present him as the *better* fulfillment of Old Testament figures, institutions, and events. One of these dimensions has to do with the superior priesthood of Jesus and the sacrifice that he provides. As the high priest who is eternal and perfect (Heb. 6:20; 7:3, 16–17, 21, 24–25, 28), he remains as the everlasting mediator in the heavenly temple (8:1–2; 9:11, 24) and the priest who does not need to offer atonement for his own sin (Heb. 7:26–27). Rather, the atoning sacrifice he provides is the only one that truly brings forgiveness of sin (9:14–15), and therefore it only needs to be offered once (7:27b; 9:25–28; 10:10, 12–14).

Since the sacrifice of Jesus is the sacrifice that provides the permanent forgiveness of sin promised in the New Covenant (Heb. 7:22; 10:15–17), the obsolescence of the sacrificial system in the Mosaic Covenant is obvious: "And where these have been forgiven, sacrifice for sin is no longer necessary" (10:18; cf. 8:13; 10:9, 12). As such, the Mosaic Covenant's foundational (Passover lamb) and sustaining grace (temple sacrifices) is supplied in heightened measure by Jesus.

The Davidic Covenant

In our discussion of the Davidic Covenant, we identified three gracious, foundational aspects. The first had to do with the gracious initiative of God, raising David from obscurity to the kingship (2 Sam. 7:8–9). Without making more of this than we should, it is likely significant that the gospel writers preserve traditions that stress the unlikely nature of Jesus' messiahship, given his obscure and even offensive beginnings.[35]

More relevant for our purposes is the second gracious element of this covenant—God's promise to provide peace and security for Israel through David and his line (2 Sam. 7:10–11a; cf. Ps. 2:8). With this, we are bumping into a topic of immense interpretive difficulty. But it surely does appear that this element is largely postponed until the glorious return of Jesus and the consummation of his kingdom (Matt. 13:43; 25:34; cf. John 18:36; Heb. 11:10, 13–16). Indeed, Jesus reaffirms this promise, declaring that his disciples will one day sit on thrones, occupying positions of leadership over his people. They then will receive recompense for the surrender of family or land as his disciples (Matt. 19:28–29). Yet, in the meantime,

---

34. This theology also comes through in Paul's characterization of Jesus' death as a "sacrifice of atonement" in Rom. 3:25. Note also 2 Cor. 5:21: "God made him who had no sin to be sin for us, so that in him we might become the righteousness of God." For a concise survey of the biblical theology of "atonement," see Frank S. Thielman, "The Atonement," in *CTBT*, 102–27.

35. Nathanael, for example, responds to Philip's invitation to come with him to Jesus by confessing doubt whether anything good could come from Nazareth, Jesus' hometown (John 1:46). This likely is also the intention behind Matthew's obscure reference to Jesus' identity as a "Nazarene" (Matt. 2:23). Jesus is born into poverty (Luke 2:7, 12), confirmed by the lesser sacrifice Joseph and Mary bring to the temple at the time of his consecration (2:22–24; cf. Lev. 12:8).

God is providing a rest for his people through Jesus in the form of the salvation that he has provided (Heb. 4:1–11). One day, the great fulfillment of this Abrahamic/Davidic promise will be consummated in the new creation (Rev. 21:1–22:5; cf. Rom. 4:13; Heb. 2:5–9). Once again, it will come through Jesus.

The third gracious element in the Davidic Covenant flows out of the first and undergirds the second. For Jesus fulfills the great promise that David's son would enjoy a permanent kingship (2 Sam. 7:11b–12, 16; Acts 2:30–31). Even before he was conceived, the angel Gabriel declares to Mary the fulfillment of this promise in Jesus:

> You will conceive and give birth to a son, and you are to call him Jesus. He will be great and will be called the Son of the Most High. The Lord God will give him the throne of his father David, and he will reign over the house of Jacob forever; his kingdom will never end. (Luke 1:31–33)

For this reason, Matthew identifies Jesus in the first line of his gospel as "the Messiah, the son of David" (Matt. 1:1a).[36] Indeed, Jesus is David's greater son, his "Lord" (Matt. 22:41–45; cf. Rom. 1:3–4) and the one who sits at the right hand of God,[37] wielding universal authority.[38] As the final King, Jesus is the fulfillment of the promise of an eternal dynasty, the guarantor of the final consummation of the kingdom.

The New Covenant

Having surveyed some of the ways in which Jesus provides the fulfillment of the gracious foundations of the prior Old Testament covenants, we are finally in position to consider the ways in which Jesus fulfills the grace of the New Covenant.

The Fulfillment of the Servant of the Lord

We've already considered Jesus' fulfillment of the Passover lamb and the entire sacrificial system in our discussion of the Mosaic Covenant. But those elements do not exhaust Old Testament expectations of the atoning grace that Jesus fulfills. Jesus' death is also properly understood to be the consummation of the representative work of Isaiah's Servant of the Lord. As we noted above, Isaiah presents the faithful Servant as the one who lives righteously before the Lord (Isa. 42:1–4; 50:4–9; 53:9), in stark contrast to the unfaithful servant, who apparently represents the remainder of the nation (42:18–20). The righteous Servant's career culminates in his unjust suffering that accomplishes atonement for the unfaithful servant. In this way, the righteous Servant opens the door for the great return from exile (52:1–12; 54:1–8), providing the decisive reenactment of the pattern established by the Passover lamb in relation to the exodus.

---

36. Included in this identification are the hundreds of New Testament uses of "Christ" in reference to Jesus.
37. Matt. 26:64; Luke 22:69; Acts 2:33–35; 7:56; Eph. 2:20–23; Phil. 2:9–11; Col. 3:1.
38. Matt. 28:18; Col. 2:10, 15; Rev. 1:17–18; 5:5; 19:11–16; cf. 1 Cor. 15:24–25.

In the introductory chapter, I mentioned that Jesus himself confirms his identification with this righteous Servant by an allusion to Isaiah 53 after his Last Supper with his disciples: "It is written: 'And he was numbered with the transgressors'" (Luke 22:37; from Isa. 53:12). Jesus, therefore, goes beyond the Passover to present his death as the fulfillment of Isaiah's Servant of the Lord, supplying the grace that enables the nation to be redeemed and brought back to God (Isa. 49:5; 53:4–12). Taken together with the other Servant Songs, this redemption also opens the door for the invitation to be extended also to the Gentiles (49:6; 52:15; cf. also 42:1d, 4c). We will unpack this role of Jesus much more fully during our discussion of the "How" question. For now, it is enough to note Jesus' servant role in shaping the profoundly gracious context in which the New Covenant is established (Mark 10:45; Rom. 3:21–26).

The New Testament authors take for granted that Jesus is the fulfillment of Isaiah's Servant of the Lord figure. In fact, Isaiah 53 stands as the second-most quoted Old Testament chapter by New Testament authors — second only to Psalm 110. However, if New Testament allusions are included, Isaiah 53 far outdistances every other Old Testament passage. What is remarkable is the broad nature of these quotations, including citations by Matthew (Matt. 8:17), Luke (Luke 22:37; Acts 8:32–33), John (John 12:39), Paul (Rom. 10:16), and Peter (1 Peter 2:22). This speaks to the foundational nature of this chapter to New Testament theology about Jesus.

The One Who Supplies His People with the Spirit

One final gracious element that must be seen is the giving of the Spirit through Jesus. God had promised through Ezekiel to transform the heart of his people by means of his indwelling Spirit, enabling them "to follow my decrees and be careful to keep my laws" (Ezek. 36:27; cf. Joel 2:28–29). As the one on whom the Spirit descended (Matt. 3:16; John 1:33), Jesus promises to ask his Father to send this Spirit to his followers after his ascension (Luke 24:49; John 14:15–31; Acts 1:8; cf. 2:33). Paul goes on to emphasize in his letters that the Spirit's indwelling is the mark of the New Covenant (2 Cor. 3:6), enabling believers in Jesus to live lives of righteousness and fidelity (Rom. 8:5–6; Gal. 5:16–18, 22–25; etc.).

This combination of Jesus' fulfillment of the redemptive Servant/Passover lamb role and his provision of the enabling Spirit, by whom God's covenant people will be transformed, confirms the declaration that in Jesus, the grace of the New Covenant comes to its consummation.

SUMMARY

I hope it has now become obvious that God *always* enters into covenantal relationship with his people in the context of his prior, sustaining, and promised future grace. From the general grace of Eden's ample provisions, to the deliverance from the flood, to the promises made to Noah and Abraham, to the exodus out of Egypt, to the sustaining grace of the tabernacle, to the gracious choice of David and the promises granted to him, God consistently grounds his covenants in grace. The New Testament proclamation is that the fulfillment of this covenantal pattern and these covenantal promises has come in Jesus. In addition, Jesus consummates the New Covenant expectations of the permanent forgiveness of sin through his Servant role and the pouring forth of the Spirit upon his glorification. Although this is far from exhaustive, it might be helpful to map out these gracious elements in table format:

Edenic	Noahic	Abrahamic	Mosaic	Davidic	New	Jesus
Creation						New Creation
	Saved from flood					Ident. with Jesus in baptism
Physical provisions	Creation restored and sustained	Promise of land	Exodus	Promise of rest in land	Forgiveness/ end of exile	Fulfillment of Passover/ promise of future rest
			Atonement through tabernacle		Atonement through Servant	Fulfillment of Servant/ sacrifices
Relational provisions		Promise of nation	Abrahamic promises	Gracious choice/ Abrahamic promises		Son of Abraham
		Promise of blessing				Blessing to all nations through Jesus
			Promise of future internaliza- tion of law		Provision of Spirit/ law on hearts/ knowledge of God	Promise of Spirit/law on hearts/ knowledge of God
				Eternal dynasty		Eternal Davidic king

Equipped with this answer to our first covenantal question, we can begin applying this insight to our covenantal understanding of discipleship. If we perceive discipleship within the framework of the New Covenant, an obvious reality is affirmed—discipleship is grounded in prior grace. For Jesus fulfills all of the gracious elements of the prior covenants, bringing to culmination this fundamental covenantal reality. The New Covenant grace, therefore, is to be understood to exist in dynamic continuity with the diverse and manifold grace of the prior covenants. Any conception of discipleship that is not explicitly and intentionally grounded in the grace provided through Jesus is therefore covenantally askew.

For the sake of summarizing this complex background, let's subsume Jesus' grace-providing role under the rubric of the "Servant," recognizing the diversity of the prior events and promises that flow into this role. We then might begin to depict covenantal discipleship in this way:

Servant

Disciple

The direction of the arrow here is absolutely vital, representing the flow of prior grace from Jesus to the disciple. It cannot be reversed. For the nature of the Servant's work makes initial *emulation* impossible. This is because grace is always something that cannot be earned or accomplished in one's own efforts. Otherwise, it would cease to be grace! Covenantal discipleship is, therefore, grounded in the prior grace of Jesus, the Servant.

RELEVANT QUESTIONS

1. What specific things have been reinforced, altered, or transformed concerning how you think about your relationship with God as a result of working through these Old Testament covenants and Jesus' fulfillment of them?
2. How has your view of Jesus been affected by pondering the various ways in which he brings to fulfillment God's gracious provisions?
3. How might reflecting on Jesus' fulfillment of the gracious grounding of these various covenants impact your discipleship?

CHAPTER 4

THE RIGHTEOUS DEMAND OF THE COVENANTS

When Abram was ninety-nine years old, the LORD appeared to him and said, "I am God Almighty; walk before me faithfully and be blameless."

Genesis 17:1

Love the LORD your God with all your heart and with all your soul and with all your strength.

Deuteronomy 6:5

Do not think that I have come to abolish the Law or the Prophets; I have not come to abolish them but to fulfill them.

Matthew 5:17

Whenever I have asked students to give me the first word that comes to their minds when I say the word "disciple," they have consistently offered words like "student," "imitation," "obedience," or "learner." Not one has yet mentioned "grace" or any other word that speaks to the gracious grounding of the relationship. This is not surprising, given the numerous, austere commands that Jesus gives to his followers. We will take a much more detailed look at these commands in our discussion of the "What" question, but these might be epitomized by his command to his disciples to deny themselves and to follow him absolutely, even if that means dying a painful and stigmatized death (e.g., Matt. 16:24). Jesus makes it clear that it will be obedience to him that will make the difference at the final judgment:

> What good will it be for you to gain the whole world, yet forfeit your soul? Or what can you give in exchange for your soul? For the Son of Man is going to come in his Father's glory with his angels, and then he will reward everyone according to what they have done. (Matt. 16:26–27)

Because of sayings such as these, the essence of discipleship is oftentimes reduced to obedience to Jesus' commands. As we will discover, this element is integral to the biblical covenants and must be understood in that context—especially as this pattern is culminated in Jesus' articulation of the New Covenant commands. But, as the previous chapter indicated, they must be perceived as only one side of covenantal discipleship. We will return to the discussion of this covenantal balance later on. It is important at this point, however, to focus on the "demand" side of the covenants, asking our second question: "What are the demands of righteousness that God places on those who enter into each covenant?"

THE COVENANTAL DEMANDS OF RIGHTEOUSNESS

The Noahic Covenant

In the wake of God's gracious deliverance of Noah's family and his giving of the earth back to them, God communicates his covenantal demands to Noah. First, God reaffirms the command that he gave to Adam and Eve: "Be fruitful and increase in number and fill the earth" (Gen. 9:1; cf. also 9:7; 1:28). Implying a new start for creation, God repeats to Noah this blessing/command here, exhorting him to exercise dominion over the earth. Undoubtedly, this entails a continuation of Noah's preflood "faithful" life of "walking with God." Accordingly, there is an implicit command here to live life in consistency with God's character.

Second, God establishes human accountability for respecting animal life in general and human life specifically. God supplements his previous giving of the earth's plant life to Adam by giving to Noah every living creature for food (Gen. 9:3; cf. 1:29). But in so doing, he warns Noah to respect those life forms. This is expressed in the prohibition of eating the meat of animals that still has the lifeblood in it (Gen. 9:5a).[1] God also declares that he will demand an accounting from every person or animal that destroys a human life made in the image of God (9:5b–6).[2] Both of these commands highlight God's character and lordship over all of creation.

The Abrahamic Covenants

Though the gracious grounding of the Abrahamic covenants is emphasized in the biblical texts, this does not mean that God refrains from making demands of Abraham. In fact, his first command comes at the same time he gives to Abraham the promise that he will raise from him a great nation through whom he will bless all peoples: "Go from your country, your people and your father's household to the

---

1. Goldingay notes that this is not to suggest that blood is sacred. Rather, it affirms the sacredness of life since blood is a key symbol of life (*Israel's Gospel*, 180).

2. Even in their postfall condition, humans bear the image of God (Williamson, "Covenant," 140). Goldingay puts it this way — humans are "indirectly sacred, because of the fact that human beings are Godlike. So attacking a human being is like attacking God, and it is because human beings are Godlike that attacks on human beings cannot go unnoticed" (*Israel's Gospel*, 181). It is significant that this affirmation of the value of human life comes in the direct wake of the nearly universal destruction of humanity in the flood. Williamson comments: "Rather than suggesting that 'life is cheap,' the deluge signifies precisely the opposite: the seriousness of the problem that had precipitated the flood" (Williamson, "Covenant," 422).

land I will show you" (Gen. 12:1).[3] This is even before he initiates his first covenant with Abraham.

The Genesis 15 Covenant

When God does initiate that first covenant in Genesis 15, however, he does not issue any commands to Abraham. As I noted in the previous chapter, the entire stress in this covenantal interchange is on God's commitment to fulfill his promise to give Abraham a biological heir. And the inheritance that this heir and his numberless descendants will eventually receive is the land "from the Wadi [river] of Egypt to the great river, the Euphrates" (Gen. 15:18b). The one-sided covenantal ritual makes this gracious emphasis clear (15:9 – 19). Recalling our discussion of the kinds of biblical covenants in chapter 2, we recognize this clearly as a grant covenant.

Since the responsibility of fulfilling the stipulations of this kind of covenant is solely God's, Abraham's response is appropriately identified as faith: "Abram believed the LORD, and he credited it to him as righteousness" (Gen. 15:6). In other words, Abraham receives the blessings God commits himself to provide through taking God at his word and trusting in him.

This, of course, does not mean that Abraham only responds with an intellectual trust. As we have also noted previously, genuine biblical faith inevitably gives rise to actions that demonstrate that faith. This is why Abraham has left Ur in the first place. More important, Abraham's faith is expressed in his obedience to the second covenant that God makes with him.

> "Faith and obedience may be distinguished, but should not be segregated from one another, as if God summons his people to obey him without trusting in him, or as if faith in him could ever be separated from obeying him."[4]

The Genesis 17 Covenant

In contrast to the Genesis 15 covenant, commands are highlighted in the Genesis 17 narrative. This is clear from the outset of the chapter, as God levies an absolute demand on Abraham: "I am God Almighty; walk before me faithfully and be blameless" (17:1). This all-encompassing demand of covenant faithfulness amounts to wholehearted devotion in relation to the sovereign Lord, the only one in position to make such a command.

God's second command appears at first blush to be entirely ritual in nature. The Lord commands Abraham to circumcise all the males in his household (Gen. 17:9 – 14); this will be the sign of inclusion in this covenant. Those who are not circumcised will find themselves cut off from the people, having broken the covenant (v. 14).

---

3. Williamson notes that a second command may be seen at the end of Gen. 12:2, depending on the translation of the verb "to be" here. It could be translated simply as a *consequence* of Abraham's going and God's blessing: "Go so that you will effect a blessing." Alternatively, the verbal form could be taken at face value which amounts to another command: "Be a blessing." If it is understood in this latter sense, then the twofold command of God to Abraham here is "Go ... be a blessing" ("Covenant," 144).

4. Schreiner, "The Commands of God," 101.

Consequently, it functions as the physical sign that preserves the continuation of the covenant from one generation of Abraham's descendants to the next. Located on the male reproductive organ, it serves as a physical *memory aid*, calling to mind God's promise to Abraham that he will have a vast number of descendants.

The ethical dimension of circumcision is confirmed and developed elsewhere in the Old Testament. For instance, Moses writes, "The LORD your God will circumcise your hearts and the hearts of your descendants, so that you may love him with all your heart and with all your soul, and live" (Deut. 30:6; cf. Lev. 26:40–41; Jer. 4:4; 9:24–26; Ezek. 44:7–9).

It is important, however, to set circumcision within the scope of the ethical obligations that God places on Abraham in Gen. 17:1: "Walk before me faithfully and be blameless."[5] Understood in this light, circumcision functions as a sign of the covenant that demands faithfulness to God in all things.[6] It is for this reason that circumcision increasingly takes on notions of internal surrender to God's covenantal demands of righteousness. Moses brings this out clearly as he addresses the people prior to their entry into the land:

> And now, Israel, what does the LORD your God ask of you but to fear the LORD your God, to walk in obedience to him, to love him, to serve the LORD your God with all your heart and with all your soul, and to observe the LORD's commands and decrees that I am giving you today for your own good? . . .
>
> The LORD set his affection on your ancestors and loved them, and he chose you, their descendants, above all the nations—as it is today. Circumcise your hearts, therefore, and do not be stiff-necked any longer. (Deut. 10:12–16)

Notice how the call to a circumcision of the heart concludes Moses' exhortation to an exclusive devotion to God.

It is also significant that individuals from other people groups were to be assimilated into the covenant through circumcision.[7] This implies that the nations will be blessed through Abraham by submitting to the terms of this covenant—terms that include the ethical obligations God places on Abraham in Genesis 17:1. This is affirmed one chapter later, where God states that those who belong to Abraham's family and progeny must also submit to these ethical obligations:[8]

> Abraham will surely become a great and powerful nation, and all nations on earth will be blessed through him. For I have chosen him, so that he will direct his children and his household after him to keep the way of the LORD by doing what is right and just, so that the LORD will bring about for Abraham what he has promised him. (Gen. 18:18–19)

The faithful passing on of the call to righteousness is heard distinctly here in the midst of this covenantal interaction with Abraham.

---

5. P. R. Williamson, "Circumcision," *DOTP*, 123–24; *Sealed with an Oath*, 87–93.

6. In light of foregoing and succeeding episodes implying improper sexual activity (Gen. 6:1–7; 9:20–27; 12:10–20; 18:20–21; 19:1–26; cf. also the consequences of Abraham's mis- guided sexual encounter in 16:1–16), Goldingay suggests that the sign also points to the need for sexuality to be dedicated to God (*Israel's Gospel*, 202).

7. Deut. 17:12–13; cf. Ex. 12:44, 48.

8. See Williamson, "Circumcision," 123.

The Mosaic Covenant

To ask what God demands of his people in the Mosaic Covenant is to broach an immense topic covering commands of wide diversity and purpose. Traditionally, the rabbis teach that there are 613 individual commands in the Torah, mainly given in two historical settings — at Sinai and years later on the plains of Moab just prior to the entry into the land. Detailing these would go far beyond our purpose here.[9] Rather, it is sufficient for us to note two aspects of the covenantal demands that naturally give rise to a third. The first two have to do with the divisions of the Decalogue, and the third with Israel's calling in the world.

Moses declares that the foundational covenantal command is to love God without reserve: "Love the LORD your God with all your heart and with all your soul and with all your strength" (Deut. 6:5). Typical of the kind of devotion owed to a king, this corresponds to the so-called "first table" of the law, whose four commands focus on this vertical relationship between Israel and their electing, redeeming, and reigning God. Far more than merely an emotional expression of love, this command entails complete devotion and obedience to God in all of life (see Deut. 6:6–9; cf. 10:12).

> The specific commands of the Mosaic Covenant are found throughout the final four books of the Pentateuch. Most of them are given at Sinai, including the Ten Commandments and the commands of the covenant (Ex. 20–23), the laws governing the ministry of the tabernacle (Ex. 25–40), and the laws of Leviticus (Lev. 1–27). The last grouping, the laws of Deuteronomy (Deut. 12–26), are given on the plains of Moab just prior to the entry into the land.[10]

To summarize what these commandments require might best be captured by the answer to yet another question — namely, what does the law itself express or reveal? A common answer in this regard is that the law communicates "the will of God" — what God wants his people to do. Obviously, this is not an incorrect answer, but it does not get to the nub of the matter. Rather than simply declaring what God wants his people to do, the law *itself* is an expression of the character and actions of God. The commands, therefore, reflect the truth about God.

> "Yahweh's character was the bedrock of *tora*. It determined the nature of all the laws, commands and instructions as well as the motivation for Israel's response to the laws."[11]

This is easily seen in the Ten Commandments. For instance, the first command, "You shall have no other gods before me" (Ex. 20:2–3), is grounded in the divine reality that Israel's God is the only one.[12] The exclusive nature of this command reflects the truth about the exclusive identity of God. Similarly, the command to revere the name of the Lord (Ex. 20:7) reflects the truth about God; because he is holy, his name is not to be treated casually or with disrespect.[13] God's covenant people are to rest on the seventh day of the week because this reflects God's pattern

9. For a listing and categorization of these commands, see John H. Sailhamer, *The Pentateuch as Narrative: A Biblical-Theological Commentary* (Grand Rapids: Zondervan, 1995), 482–516.

10. See M. J. Selman, "Law," *DOTP*, 500.

11. Ibid., 509.

12. See 1 Sam. 2:2; Isa. 40:12–26; Ps. 18:31.

13. Lev. 20:26; 22:32; 1 Sam. 2:2; Ps. 22:3; Isa. 6:3.

(Ex. 20:8–11), a pattern that declared the creation "good" and abundant in provisions for his people (Gen. 1:29–31). When the law commands truthfulness (Ex. 20:16), this is grounded in God's character as wholly trustworthy; he never lies (Num. 23:19; 1 Sam. 15:29). When the law forbids adultery (Ex. 20:14), this too is grounded in God's character—he always remains faithful to his people.[14] The law forbidding coveting (Ex. 20:17) declares the truth that God will supply what his people need (Deut. 8:6–18). Therefore, those who are in the Mosaic Covenant are summoned to pattern their individual and corporate lives after the very attributes and actions of God: "Be holy because I, the LORD your God, am holy" (Lev. 19:2b).

"Just as ancient law codes generally made a statement about the king who promulgated them, so the covenant obligations revealed at Sinai disclose something of the nature and character of Yahweh. Therefore the law makes a statement not only about Israel . . . but also — and more importantly — about Israel's God."[15]

But then flowing right from this command in Leviticus 19 comes its corollary: "Love your neighbor as yourself" (Lev. 19:18b). This connection is clearly implied in the verses that follow Lev. 19:2, most of which pertain to the horizontal relationship that his people will have with one another (see vv. 3, 9–18). These commands are then summarized by the famous injunction to love others as oneself. But notice that this is followed immediately by a fresh declaration of God's identity: "I am the LORD" (19:18b). That is, one's horizontal relationships are also to be grounded in God's character. Because he is compassionate, his people are to be compassionate (Ex. 22:26–27). Because he is the generous deliverer, his people are to be generous in liberating others (Deut. 15:12–15). Because he is just, his people are to seek justice for others (32:4; 16:18–20; 24:17).

The third aspect of this covenant's demands pertains to Israel's role in relation to the world. God affirms that the nation's obedience within the covenant has a broader, missional purpose to the nations:

> Now if you obey me fully and keep my covenant, then out of all nations you will be my treasured possession. Although the whole earth is mine, you will be for me a kingdom of priests and a holy nation. (Ex. 19:5–6a)

It is true that the people are repeatedly exhorted to remain separate from the surrounding sinful nations (Lev. 20:24, 26; Num. 23:9), but their society also is to serve as a witness to them, declaring who God is. Since the law itself is an expression of God's character and actions, the covenantally faithful nation will reveal God's nature, reflecting his holiness (Lev. 19:2). Thus, when other nations interact with the Israelites, they will come to know Israel's God by observing their society, culture, and religious observances. In this way, they will function as the "priestly nation" in communicating the knowledge of God to the world, fulfilling their role in mediating the Abrahamic covenantal blessings to all nations.[16]

---

14. Deut. 7:9; Ps. 145:13; Isa. 55:3.
15. Williamson, "Covenant," 151.
16. Ibid. 150–51. This conditionality of the Mosaic covenant connects with the conditional covenant that God made with Abraham in Gen. 17. If Abraham's descendants are to continue enjoying the benefits of their special relationship to God,

But the commands of the Mosaic Covenant ought not to be viewed in isolation from the prior Old Testament covenants. In reality, the Mosaic Covenant takes up into itself all of the commands of those other covenants. While the Mosaic Covenant is functionally subordinate to the Abrahamic arrangements, the Mosaic legislation unpacks and clarifies for the nation what it means to walk "faithfully" and "blamelessly" before the Lord (Gen. 17:1; cf. Deut. 11:13; 18:13). This is especially so since the nation's participation in the Abrahamic blessings is contingent on their faithful response to the stipulations of the Mosaic Covenant. Moses also preserves the rite of circumcision, the sign of the Genesis 17 covenant with Abraham (Gen. 17:9–14; cf. Ex. 4:26; Lev. 12:3).

Israel's missional purpose is implied by the observation by other nations of the distinctive laws of Israel and the unique way in which Yahweh interacts with the Israelites: "See, I have taught you decrees and laws as the LORD my God commanded me, so that you may follow them in the land you are entering to take possession of it. Observe them carefully, for this will show your wisdom and understanding to the nations, who will hear about all these decrees and say, 'Surely this great nation is a wise and understanding people.' What other nation is so great as to have their gods near them the way the LORD our God is near us whenever we pray to him? And what other nation is so great as to have such righteous decrees and laws as this body of laws I am setting before you today?" (Deut. 4:5–8).

Similarly, the Noahic command to respect human life (Gen. 9:5–6) finds replication and expansion in Moses' legislation (Ex. 20:13; 21:28–29; Num. 35:33), as does the proscription against drinking the blood of any animal (Gen. 9:5a; Lev. 17:10–14; Deut. 12:23–25). One could even say the Mosaic commands provide specific commentary on what it means to exercise the sort of dominion over the earth that God expected from Adam and Eve (Gen. 1:28) and from Noah (9:1, 7). Notice also the connection that the Sabbath laws (Ex. 20:8–11; 31:14–17) have with the Eden narrative (Gen. 2:2).

"It is clear from the obligations imposed upon Israel that being in special relationship with Yahweh involved more than privilege; it entailed responsibility. Israel, Abraham's promised descendants, could continue to enjoy the divine-human relationship anticipated in Genesis 17:7–8 only by maintaining the socio-ethical distinctiveness enshrined in God's instructions to Abraham ('walk before me, and be blameless' Gen. 17:1). . . . Thus the primary concern of the Sinaitic covenant was on how the promised divine-human relationship between Yahweh and the 'great nation' descended from Abraham . . . should be expressed and maintained."[17]

By means of these connections, then, the covenantal demands communicated through the Mosaic Covenant should be understood to sum up the covenantal demands of each of the prior Old Testament covenants. This sets up the climactic relationship between the demands of the Mosaic and New Covenants. We will return to this issue below, but we first must consider those entailed in the Davidic Covenant.

---

they must also respond to the ethical imperative given to Abraham in Gen. 17:1: "walk before me faithfully and be blameless." While God has guaranteed the promise of people and land to the seed of Abraham, each generation within that covenantal community must also hear the call to do "what is right and just" (Gen. 18:19)—the call to reflect the holy character of their God (Lev. 19:2). God will be faithful to his unconditional commitments in Gen. 15, but it will be with a remnant of his people who respond to his gracious initiative with faithfulness (17:1; 18:19).

17. Williamson, *Sealed with an Oath*, 96.

The Davidic Covenant

It is significant that the choice of David comes in the wake of Saul's failure to obey God's directives through Samuel.[18] God rejects Saul because he is not "a man after his own heart" (1 Sam. 13:14b). It is clear, therefore, that God desires faithfulness from the kings, subservient as they are to God's own sovereign rulership (2 Sam. 7:26; Ps. 2:6). This is why David's heir is to be called Yahweh's "son" (2 Sam. 7:14; Ps. 2:7) and "servant" (2 Sam. 7:5, 19–29). In fact, God's enthronement on Zion precedes the establishment of the covenant (1 Sam. 3–4; 2 Sam. 7:1–17) and is paralleled in Ps. 132:12–14 with the eternal establishment of David's sons in their Jerusalem capital. Consequently, God invites David's heir to sit on the throne at his "right hand" (Ps. 110:1).

Because of this continuity, the sons of David will experience God's fatherly discipline if they do not reign in righteousness: "I will be his father, and he will be my son. When he does wrong, I will punish him with a rod wielded by human beings, with floggings inflicted by human hands" (2 Sam. 7:14). That is to say, when David's heirs rule in ways that are inconsistent with Yahweh's character, reproof will be in the offing. This implies that the same demand of righteousness that permeates all of the previous covenants is also placed on the sons of David.

If we look a bit further afield textually, we can see more of what this demand entails. In Deuteronomy 17, Moses specifies his instructions for the selection of a king once the people are established in the land. To ward off any dependence on alliances, military prowess, and idolatry, Moses prohibits the kings from acquiring large numbers of horses, many wives, or great amounts of silver and gold (Deut. 17:16–17). Rather than counting on these things, the king is to trust in God alone.

More generally, he is to lead the people in fidelity to the Mosaic Covenant. Moses writes:

> When he takes the throne of his kingdom, he is to write for himself on a scroll a copy of this law, taken from that of the Levitical priests. It is to be with him, and he is to read it all the days of his life so that he may learn to revere the LORD his God and follow carefully all the words of this law and these decrees and not consider himself better than his fellow Israelites and turn from the law to the right or to the left. Then he and his descendants will reign a long time over his kingdom in Israel. (Deut. 17:18–20; cf. also Pss. 89:30–32; 132:12)

Since the king reigns as God's representative at the head of the nation, his obedience to the law is vital in leading the people into paths of faithfulness. But, as Israel's and Judah's histories make all too painfully clear, the kings' personal apostasy invariably leads to the corruption of the nation, leading to the eventual enactment of the covenantal curses.

Once again, the demand of righteousness is the same in the Davidic Covenant as was true in the Mosaic Covenant. How, then, do the demands of the Mosaic Covenant relate to those contained in the New Covenant?

18. 1 Sam. 10:8; 13:7–14; 15:3, 7–9, 14–23.

The New Covenant

When Jeremiah characterizes the covenant that God will one day make with his people as "new," he is implying a significant amount of discontinuity between the Mosaic and New Covenants. This is underscored by the affirmation that the New Covenant will *not* be like the covenant that God made with the people who came out of Egypt (Jer. 31:32). Yet we quickly discover that this discontinuity lies not so much in the nature of the covenantal *demands*. Rather, it concerns mainly the nature of the covenantal *people* themselves; rather than breaking the covenant as the Sinai generation did, God implicitly affirms that the people of the New Covenant will prove faithful: "It will not be like the covenant I made with their ancestors … because they broke my covenant, though I was a husband to them" (31:32). The implication here is that the New Covenant people will not break their covenantal relationship with God. Undoubtedly, this anticipated covenantal fidelity will be the direct result of God's transformative work within them. So, the essential demand of conformity to Yahweh's law appears to remain the same between the covenants.

This continuity of demand is asserted by the promise that it will be the *law* that is internalized by the New Covenant people. Whereas in the Mosaic Covenant this law was engraved on tablets of stone, in the New Covenant era it will be written on the people's hearts and in their minds (Jer. 31:33). Consequently, though God's gracious actions in relation to the New Covenant eclipse anything previously experienced, the demand of righteousness that consistently runs through the Old Testament covenants is carefully preserved.[20] Indeed, it appears even to be heightened, since the people of that covenant will prove to be permanently faithful:

> "The glory of the new covenant is not that God's people are freed *from* keeping God's law, but that they are empowered to put it into practice."[19]

"In those days, at that time,"
    declares the LORD,
"the people of Israel and the people of Judah together
    will go in tears to seek the LORD their God.
They will ask the way to Zion
    and turn their faces toward it.
They will come and bind themselves to the LORD
    in an everlasting covenant
    that will not be forgotten." (Jer. 50:4–5)

In contrast to the people in the previous covenants, the permanent faithfulness of the New Covenant people will be evident for all the world to see.[21]

---

19. Schreiner, "The Commands of God," 78.

20. For this reason, Hafemann suggests that the new covenant, though it will be an "everlasting covenant that will never be forgotten" (Jer. 50:5; cf. 32:40), "is a 'renewed' covenantal relationship" ("The Covenant Relationship," 51).

21. Cf. Isa. 4:2–4; 10:20–21; 43:5–7; 51:7–16; 52:1–12; 60:21–22; 61:1–6, 10–11; 62:1–2, 12; 4Q174 4.1–4.

Not surprisingly, this righteous demand is inextricably linked to the reign of the coming Davidic king. Though Jeremiah's promise is situated in full view of the impending exile, the Davidic Covenant's grant nature ensures the eventual coming of a royal heir who will inherit his father's throne (2 Sam. 7:13, 15–16) and rule over his people righteously. Accordingly, Jeremiah declares:

"The days are coming," declares the LORD,
  "when I will raise up for David a righteous Branch,
a King who will reign wisely
  and do what is just and right in the land.
In his days Judah will be saved
  and Israel will live in safety.
This is the name by which he will be called:
  The LORD Our Righteous Savior." (Jer. 23:5–6; cf. Isa. 16:5)

Since the responsibility of the Davidic king was to lead the people into covenantal faithfulness, he was to meditate continually on the law (Deut. 17:18–20). The coming heir of the Davidic Covenant will therefore preserve the Mosaic Covenant's righteous demand as he rules over the New Covenant people. Consistent with this, Ezekiel affirms that the effect of the Davidic king's reign will be enduring faithfulness by the people:

My servant David will be king over them, and they will all have one shepherd. They will follow my laws and be careful to keep my decrees.... I will make a covenant of peace with them; it will be an everlasting covenant. (Ezek. 37:24–26; cf. also Isa. 32:1–5)

The expectation associated with the New Covenant is therefore that of a righteous king reigning over a restored and transformed people whose obedience to the covenant will be absolute. These three great covenants, therefore, converge on this theme.

This combination continues on into the period between the Testaments. A classic example of this comes to us from a first-century BC work known as the *Psalms of Solomon*. Typical messianic themes emerge as the writer describes the career of the coming king, beginning with the judgment and destruction of Israel's enemies:

See, Lord, and raise up for them their king,
the son of David, to rule over your servant Israel
in the time known to you, O God.
Undergird him with the strength to destroy the unrighteous rulers,
to purge Jerusalem from gentiles
who trample her to destruction ...
to smash the arrogance of sinners
like a potter's jar;
to shatter all their substance with an iron rod.[22]

22. *Pss. Sol.* 17:21–24a, in *The Old Testament Pseudepigrapha*, 2 vols., ed. James H. Charlesworth (Garden City, NY: Doubleday, 1985), 2:667.

Then he will reign over a righteous people, demanding righteousness from them:

> He will gather a holy people
> whom he will lead in righteousness;
> and he will judge the tribes of the people
> that have been made holy by the Lord their God.
> He will not tolerate unrighteousness (even) to pause among them,
> and any person who knows wickedness shall not live with them....
> And he will be a righteous king over them, taught by God.
> There will be no unrighteousness among them in his days,
> for all shall be holy,
> and their king shall be the Lord Messiah.[23]

This expectation of righteousness remains strong in various of the Jewish sects on into the time of Jesus.[24]

The demand of righteousness pertaining to the New Covenant is therefore obvious. In fact, since the law is internalized by the people of the New Covenant, and since the Mosaic Covenant subsumes all of the other Old Testament covenants in this respect, it can safely be affirmed that the New Covenant brings the Old Testament covenantal demands to their culminating expression.[25] Thus, while the people of the New Covenant era will be profoundly graced by the representative sacrifice of the Servant of the Lord and the transforming work of the Spirit, they will respond to that grace with lives of righteousness in permanent fidelity to the Messiah, who will then reign in righteousness.

JESUS' FULFILLMENT OF THE COVENANTAL DEMANDS

Jesus' Messianic Authority

As Christian disciples, we generally take Jesus' messianic identity for granted. Unfortunately, however, we sometimes don't discern all of the ramifications of this identity. This is again where a sensitivity to the covenantal expectations of the Old Testament helps us. We have learned that the prophets look forward to the day when God will fulfill his promise to David and send forth the great King who will rule over his people. This one will authoritatively wield the power of the kingdom of

23. *Pss. Sol.* 17:26–32 (in ibid.). These images were expanded to include sweeping eschatological and universal dimensions in some of the apocalyptic literature of the period (e.g., 1 QM 11:1–18; 4QFlor. 1:11–14; *4 Ezra* 12:31–34; *T. Jud.* 24:1–5).

24. Obviously, the Essenes and Pharisees are the classic examples of this. For helpful overviews of each, see T. Beall, "Essenes," *Dictionary of New Testament Background* (ed. Craig A. Evans and Stan-

ley E. Porter; Downers Grove, IL: IVP, 2000), 342–48; S. Mason, "Pharisees," in ibid., 782–87.

25. This is implied more generally by the allusions to the other Old Testament covenants in passages pertaining to the New Covenant, such as Jer. 30–33 and Isa. 54 (see Williamson, *Sealed with an Oath*, 151 n. 16; 160–61).

God, demanding from them the righteousness befitting the New Covenant. Jesus' discipleship summons fits into this picture.

It doesn't take long to discover the New Testament claims in relation to these expectations. As we have seen, the first verse of the New Testament proclaims Jesus' messianic status (Matt. 1:1a). The assumption of his royal identity literally *permeates* the New Testament writings in the oft-recurring title "Christ," which is the Greek translation of the Hebrew word "Messiah." Both words mean "anointed one" and refer to the practice of anointing the king with oil, symbolizing the Spirit's enduing for the purpose of ruling.

When Peter uses this title along with the royal "Son of God" epithet (see Matt. 16:16), the apostle identifies Jesus as the long-awaited fulfillment of the promises made to David and reiterated in several of the prophets.[26] When Jesus accepts these kingly titles (16:17), he clearly agrees with Peter's assessment and claims this identity as his own. His subsequent summons to follow him, even to an ignominious death (16:24 – 27), is therefore consistent with who he is.[27]

Jesus' self-reference as the Son of Man strengthens his authority to demand obedience. In Daniel's great vision of four successive kingdoms, represented by four beasts (Dan. 7:2 – 8), the prophet catches a glimpse of the heavenly throne room where the Ancient of Days is seated in great glory (vv. 9 – 10). "One like a son of man" approaches this throne, riding on the heavenly clouds. Generally corresponding with the destruction of the oppressive fourth beast (vv. 11, 19 – 26), the "son of man" receives from the Ancient of Days "authority, glory and sovereign power," resulting in an "everlasting dominion" that elicits universal worship and submission from all nations and peoples on the

The title "Son of God," when used in a kingly context, is best understood as stemming from the promise God made to David in 2 Samuel 7 regarding the intimate relationship that he will have with his heir: "I will be his father, and he will be my son" (7:14a; cf. Pss. 2:7; 89:26 – 27). It is true that this title takes on notions of deity in the Gospels and the rest of the New Testament, but its Old Testament grounding is that of kingship in the Davidic Covenant.

earth (vv. 14, 27). Whoever this "one like a son of man" turns out to be, he will clearly be a king who will rule the whole world in a kingdom that will know no end.

It is for this reason that the Son of Man title on Jesus' lips causes so much discussion in scholarly circles. For if Jesus applies the title to himself as the fulfillment of the Danielic figure, he is explicitly claiming to be the king who one day will judge the nations and reign supreme on the earth.

Understood in this way, the significance of Jesus' response to Caiaphas at his trial becomes clear: "But I say to all of you: From now on you will see the Son of Man

---

26. As we have already discussed (e.g., Isa. 16:5; 32:1 – 5; Jer. 23:5 – 8; 30:21 – 22; Ezek. 37:21 – 25; Amos 9:11 – 12; Zech. 3:8 – 10; 6:12 – 15; 9:9 – 10).

27. Though not as frequently as we might expect, this acceptance of the messianic identity and role is implied by Jesus in several other contexts; e.g., Matt. 23:8 – 10; 24:5; 26:63 – 64a; Mark 9:41; Luke 24:25 – 27, 44 – 47; John 4:25 – 26; cf. also Mark 11:1 – 11; par. Matt. 21:1 – 9.

sitting at the right hand of the Mighty One and coming on the clouds of heaven" (Matt. 26:64b). Since the context of Jesus' allusion to Daniel 7 includes the judgment of those persecuting God's people (Dan. 7:21–22, 25–27), Jesus' use of this imagery here intimates his own threat to the Sanhedrin; though he is presently under their murderous authority, he will one day be the divinely appointed *king* who will judge them. If Caiaphas perceives this implication, this would explain why he tears his garment as an indication that Jesus has uttered blasphemy.[28] It is clear, therefore, that the Son of Man title further cements Jesus' kingly identity. He is the one who brings in the kingdom of God, possessing absolute authority to place demands on his followers.

The centrality of the kingdom of God to Jesus' preaching is captured in the summary statement of Matt. 4:17: "Repent, for the kingdom of heaven is near" (cf. Mark 1:15).[29] Consistent with this, Jesus declares that in his exorcism of an impairing demon, the kingdom of God has "come upon" his generation (Matt. 12:28). Similarly, in his comments to the crowd after implicitly affirming his messianic identity to John the Baptist's disciples (11:4–6), he explicitly declares that the kingdom is advancing forcefully in and through his ministry (v. 12).[30] Since Jesus identifies the kingdom with his powerful ministry actions, he must not be referring by it to some future "heaven," but to the present exercise of God's kingly power. The inescapable conclusion is that through him the reign of God is breaking in!

It is for this reason that Jesus mirrors John's call for repentance from the people who observed his ministry (Matt. 11:20–24). If the kingdom is present, the time for the righteous remnant of God's people is dawning. This means that the New Covenant demand of absolute righteousness must also be commencing. Jesus' claim to have brought the kingdom, therefore, has great significance for discipleship. As the long-awaited messianic King, who is initiating the New Covenant in the kingdom of God, Jesus levies the absolute demands of righteousness and loyalty appropriate to that era and consistent with his kingly role.

Jesus' Fulfillment of the Law

We have learned in our survey of the Old Testament covenants that God always demands faithfulness and obedience from his covenant partners, even though these covenants are grounded in and sustained by grace. It is appropriate, then, that on the occasion during which Jesus the Servant graciously institutes the New Covenant in his

---

28. Jesus also evokes Ps. 110:1. In that psalm, David declares what God ("the Lord," *yahweh*) says to "my Lord" (*'adoni*). The reference to sitting at the right hand of God clearly identifies David's "Lord" as a king—most likely to be understood as David's heir in fulfillment of God's promise in the Davidic covenant to establish the throne of his son forever (2 Sam. 7:11b–16). Jesus' statement to Caiaphas, then, includes his claim to be the one to fulfill this psalm. In doing so, he will also put down all of those who oppose him; his reign will involve the putting of his enemies "under his feet" as

a "footstool." Judgment is once again implied by Jesus' kingship.

29. Cf. Matt. 4:23; 9:35; 10:7; 11:12; Luke 4:43; 8:1; 9:2, 11; 10:9, 11; 11:20; 22:29. Similarly, Jesus responds to the question of the kingdom's arrival with the bold affirmation that the kingdom was already present "in your midst" (Luke 17:21).

30. This translation takes the verb used here, *biazetai*, as a middle rather than a passive. See D. A. Carson, "Matthew," in *The Expositor's Bible Commentary* (Grand Rapids: Zondervan, 1984), 8:267–68.

own blood and serves his disciples by washing their feet, he also expresses covenantal demands as their King. In the wake of the Last Supper, which is drenched in the grace of the Servant and the lamb, Jesus exhorts his disciples to emulate his actions (John 13:12–17) and to follow his teachings.[31] Covenantal grace and covenantal demand are placed side by side—Servant and King. Since Jesus fulfills the grace of the covenants, he is also the one who expresses the fulfillment of the covenantal demands.

It should not surprise us, therefore, to discover that Jesus intentionally communicates his discipleship demands as the *fulfillment* of the law. In what is perhaps Jesus' most important statement in this regard, he avers in Matthew 5:17: "Do not think that I have come to abolish the Law or the Prophets; I have not come to abolish them but to fulfill them." Christians often interpret these words as referring to Jesus' *living out* of the law perfectly or of providing the final and perfect *sacrifice* that the law requires. Though these statements summarize an appropriate understanding of Jesus' relationship to the law, they are likely *not* what Jesus has in mind in this particular context.

That is because the immediately succeeding verses demonstrate that Jesus identifies his *teaching* as that which brings the law to its ultimate and final form. Notice what he says in Matthew 5:21–22:

> You have heard that *it was said* to the people long ago, "You shall not murder, and anyone who murders will be subject to judgment." But *I tell you* that anyone who is angry with a brother or sister will be subject to judgment. (emphasis mine)

It is likely that when Jesus refers to "the people long ago," he is referring to the Sinai generation who heard Moses declare the Ten Commandments for the first time.[32] If that is the case, when he counters with, "But I tell you," and proceeds to revise this commandment, Jesus is implying that his teachings are authoritatively interpreting the law. He continues making these sorts of claims all the way through this portion of the Sermon on the Mount (Matt. 5:27–44), repeatedly placing his teaching in direct relationship to the law. In this way, he fulfills the law by bringing it to its final *expression* and *demand*.[33]

SUMMARY

We have seen in this chapter the prominent place given to the demand of righteousness within the biblical covenants. Stretching from the covenant-like interaction

31. John 13:34–35; 14:15, 21, 23–24; 15:1–17.
32. E.g., W. D. Davies and Dale C. Allison, *A Critical and Exegetical Commentary on the Gospel according to Saint Matthew* (ICC; 2 vols.; ed. J. A. Emerton, C. E. B. Cranfield, and G. N. Stanton; Edinburgh: T&T Clark, 1988), 1:510–11.
33. Note that this is consistent with Jeremiah's depiction, where the demands of the New Covenant are understood to be in direct relationship to those of the Mosaic Covenant (Jer. 31:31–33). Jesus' role of expressing the culmination of the law is also implied in Matt.

7:21–27, where he declares that only those who do the *will of his Father* will enter into the kingdom (7:21). This is then illustrated by the parable of the wise and foolish builders, which asserts the differing fates of people in the final judgment based on whether or not they heard *his words* and put them into practice (7:24, 26). In this way, Jesus equates his teachings with the will of God (v. 21), accentuating his claim to be communicating the culminating divine commands on his people.

between God and the first humans in the garden and on into each of the covenantal relationships that follow, God calls people to live in consistency with his character and image. It is true that the grant covenant of Genesis 15 does not entail any specific commands, but the appropriate faith response from Abraham brings with it the implied obedience commensurate with that trust, culminating in his response to the demands of the Genesis 17 covenant. As we have seen, all of these covenantal demands flow into those expressed in the Mosaic Covenant, which are then internalized by the people of the New Covenant.

We have also seen the way in which Jesus articulates the goal of these covenantal demands in his kingly role as the Messiah. We will return to the difficult question of the specific ways in which Jesus' commands relate to their counterparts in the Mosaic Covenant in our discussion of the "What" question. For now, we simply need to perceive Jesus' intention to couch his commands in the context of *covenant* in claiming to bring the fulfillment of the law. And since the law in the Mosaic Covenant summarizes the demands of all of the Old Testament covenants, we can see how Jesus' discipleship summons brings to culmination all of the Old Testament covenantal demands. Once again, I will summarize these observations in table format:

Edenic	Noahic	Abrahamic	Mosaic	Davidic	New	Jesus
Steward the earth	Steward the earth	Go to land				
Obey God by avoiding the fruit	Obey God by respecting life	Obey God by walking blamelessly	Love God completely/ obey all commands so as to be the priestly nation	Obey the law	Obey internalized law	Obey the law as he teaches it
		Circumcise males				
		Be a blessing				

In light of this, the nexus between the demands of the Old Testament covenants and those of the New Covenant is precisely the relationship between the Old Testament law and the fulfillment that comes through Jesus and his teachings. While scholars will continue to debate the precise nature of this relationship, it is enough for us to see Jesus' call to discipleship as the demand of the New Covenant.

With Jesus' role as King, then, the second movement in the discipleship diagram that we are drawing comes into focus. Having been graced by the Servant, Jesus summons his followers to follow him as their King. In this way, the grace/demand dynamic in the covenants is preserved in relating to Jesus in these two roles:

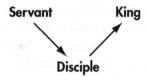

But since following the King involves living out the commands that he himself embodied perfectly, and since surrendering to his reign will result in the internalization of the attributes that emanated from his heart, following Jesus involves *emulation*. And since Jesus lived out the life of the Servant, his disciples will emulate his Servant life as they follow him. This is why the Christian's life is one that ultimately is characterized by the cross and the washing of the feet of others. The triangle is thereby completed:

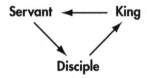

Having been graced by the Servant, the disciple follows the King, inevitably emulating the Servant.

By casting Jesus' discipleship commands in the covenantal framework, which always includes demands of righteousness and obedience as part of its matrix, we are close to answering the "Why" question. But the nagging issue of how to reconcile this perspective with Paul's statements about the absolutely gracious nature of the New Covenant remains to be addressed. To this we turn in the next chapter.

RELEVANT QUESTIONS

1. When you think of the demands of discipleship, do you often think of the command, "walk before me faithfully and be blameless" (Gen. 17:1), or, "Be holy because I, the LORD your God, am holy" (Lev. 19:2)? Does this often connect in your mind with Jesus' command, "Be perfect, therefore, as your heavenly Father is perfect" (Matt. 5:48)? How does this consistency of covenantal demand impact your understanding of discipleship?

2. When you think about these covenantal demands, do you find yourself becoming concerned that they may lead you into a legalistic fixation on obe-

dience? How might the covenantal framework that we have been discerning help in this regard?

3. In your opinion, which aspect of the "love" command does the contemporary church emphasize—the command to love God or to love one's neighbor? Why do you think that is the case?

4. In what ways is thinking about discipleship in the context of the New Covenant changing your prior perceptions of the Christian life?

5. How does the missional goal of the Mosaic Covenant impact the importance of covenant faithfulness?

CHAPTER 5

THE COVENANTAL RELATIONSHIP BETWEEN FAITH AND WORKS OF OBEDIENCE

For I tell you that unless your righteousness surpasses that of the Pharisees and the teachers of the law, you will certainly not enter the kingdom of heaven.

Matthew 5:20

For in the gospel the righteousness of God is revealed—a righteousness that is by faith from first to last, just as it is written: "The righteous will live by faith."

Romans 1:17

And if by grace, then it cannot be based on works; if it were, grace would no longer be grace.

Romans 11:6

I hope it is becoming clear that we are getting close to answering the "Why" question: "Why should I be concerned to follow all of Jesus' commands if I have been saved by grace?" In the two previous chapters, we have seen how Jesus fulfills the corresponding sides of the covenantal relationship between God and humanity. As the great Servant of the Lord, Jesus brings to culmination the gracious provisions and promises that ground and sustain the covenants. As the messianic King, Jesus brings to final expression the demands of righteousness that permeate the covenants. When we move from these observations to answer the "Why" question, it is tempting to respond with a straightforward covenantal answer.

Since it is true that all biblical covenants are grounded in grace, the New Covenant in Jesus is not unique. Moreover, since the expressions of covenantal grace do not nullify or diminish the covenantal call to righteousness, disciples of Jesus should indeed be concerned to respond to all of Jesus' New Covenant commands with obedience. This is the plain covenantal pattern—a pattern that Jesus validates. His righteous commands make it clear that entrance into the kingdom is dependent on actual, lived-out righteousness (e.g., Matt. 5:20; 7:19–27). The prophetic expectations of righteousness coming from a faithful people in the New Covenant, living in submission to the righteous messianic King, further corroborate this answer.

But then Paul chimes into this biblical conversation with statements that seem to qualify this perspective. That is to say, Paul makes it clear that Jesus has accomplished on our behalf all of the works of the law, so that righteousness is now completely provided by him through faith: "Christ is the culmination of the law so that there may be righteousness for everyone who believes" (Rom. 10:4). Indeed, it is those who come to him by faith rather than by works of righteousness who actually obtain a right standing before God: "What then shall we say? That the Gentiles, who did not pursue righteousness, have obtained it, a righteousness that is by faith" (9:30). This is because of Jesus' completion of the law's requirements in our stead:

> For what the law was powerless to do because it was weakened by the sinful nature, God did by sending his own Son in the likeness of sinful humanity to be a sin offering. (Rom. 8:3)

From statements such as these, many Christians pass over commands that are especially troubling and demanding. Since Jesus the Servant accomplished everything on our behalf that he as the King requires of us, we must respond with faith alone—as Paul says, resting in Jesus' sufficiency. Anything beyond this threatens to reduce us to legalists who deny God's grace in Christ.

For this reason, we need to ask one additional question of the covenants to find insight into how Jesus' absolute covenantal demands of righteousness might be reconciled with Paul's statements about grace and faith. Our third question, therefore, is this: "How do faith and works of obedience relate to the reception of the blessings of this covenant?" We will discover that the answer to this question always turns on the nature of the covenant in question. Let's return, then, to the covenants to see if we can find more light to shed on this issue.

FAITH AND WORKS IN THE COVENANTS
The Noahic Covenant

It is obvious that the Noahic Covenant is a grant covenant. Having established in the flood his posture in relation to sin, God declares his commitment to sustain the earth for *sinful* humanity. As I noted in chapter 3, God's gracious promises in this covenant are given in full view of human *depravity*. Accordingly, God promises not to curse the ground again in the form of a worldwide flood, "even though every inclination of the human heart is evil from childhood" (Gen. 8:21b). In fact, not even faith is required to receive its benefits. Goldingay writes:

Noah and the other recipients of God's pledge contribute absolutely nothing to the covenant relationship. They do not even have to believe in it. It will still be a reality. Out of God's own being comes the one-sided pledge that there will be no more world-denying catastrophes.[1]

As such, this covenant is a pure example of the grant type: its benefits are unconditional, grounded solely in God's commitment to provide them. Every ensuing divine command must, therefore, be understood to be given in this general, gracious context.[2] For unless God holds to his covenant with Noah, a recurrence of the flood is inevitable.

In spite of the unconditional character of this covenant, we have seen that God still places demands on people in it—to steward the earth and to respect both human and animal life. And though the ongoing seasonal blessings are not tied to human obedience to these commands, this does not mean that the divine directives are inconsequential. The threat of divine recrimination apart from a summary flood for those who disobey makes that clear.

"Creation's existence is profoundly endangered by all the things that constantly happen in it, which are anything but good. The fact that it still goes on existing in spite of this is due to God's self-imposed obligation, his covenant with Noah. And that is the reason why human beings can have confidence in creation."[3]

Nor is faith completely absent among this covenant's partners. Though all of earth's inhabitants receive the covenantal benefits because of God's unconditional commitment, the *proper* stance on the part of people in this covenant is to trust in God's faithfulness to perpetuate the seasonal rhythm. This is surely communicated through the sign of the rainbow. While it functions as a reminder to God concerning his pledge not to destroy the earth through another flood (Gen. 9:12–17), those who have faith in God's truthfulness are implicitly invited to be comforted by its appearance. In this way, the seasonal rhythm can be *perceived* and *experienced* as grace by the one who trusts in God's ongoing commitment to sustain life on the earth. So also is faith implied in the obedience of the one who respects human and animal life. Such obedience flows out of an awareness of God's sovereignty and his just relationship to all of life within his creation.

Thus, though all will receive this covenant's blessings, the appropriate posture for those in it is that of trusting in God's faithfulness both to sustain the seasonal order and to hold people accountable to his commands. Those who live this way are exhorted to express this faith by responding to God's covenantal commands with obedience.

1. Goldingay, *Israel's Gospel*, 182. Goldingay emphasizes this lack of conditionality even more strongly, contending that the Hebrew particle (*ki*) that is translated in the TNIV as "even though" in Gen. 8:21 should receive its usual translation of "because": "Never again will I curse the ground ... because every inclination of the human heart is evil from childhood." This introduces a jarring tension into the covenantal wording—the promise of never cursing again is made *because* every inclination of humanity's heart is evil.

God's response to evil from this point forward will be quantitatively different than his actions in the flood.

2. Williamson writes: "Since the Noahic covenant has never been abrogated ..., subsequent divine-human covenants must be viewed within the context of its all-encompassing framework" ("Covenant," 143).

3. R. Rendtorff, *Canon and Theology: Overtures to an Old Testament Theology* (Edinburgh: T&T Clark, 1993), 109.

The Abrahamic Covenants

As I suggested in the previous chapter, it seems best to conclude that God establishes two distinct covenants with Abraham, each being a different type. The traditional interpretation is that there is only one Abrahamic Covenant expressed in two stages. This surely fits nicely with Paul's reference to God's interactions with Abraham as a singular entity.[4] But Williamson convincingly argues on the basis of several textual features that it is far more appropriate to treat them as separate covenants of distinct types.[5] Consequently, faith and works interact with each of them in slightly different ways.

The Genesis 15 Covenant

The first Abrahamic covenant is clearly of the grant variety. As we learned in chapter 2, this becomes clear in the covenant ritual of Genesis 15, when God *alone* passes between the animal corpses. In so doing, God declares that the fulfillment of the covenant promises is dependent solely on his own faithfulness. Abraham responds by demonstrating an obedience that springs forth from his faith that God would be true to his word: "Abram believed the LORD, and he credited it to him as righteousness" (Gen. 15:6). But, as I noted in the previous chapter, this is not the first time Abraham believed God. He would never have left Ur in the first place unless he had taken God at his word from the beginning.

Once again, faith is the appropriate response to the grant covenant. Distinct from the Noahic Covenant, however, the implication here is that the blessings of this covenant will be experienced by those who trust in the God who has promised. Faith, therefore, is the *means* through which the blessings of this covenant are received. But it is also important to note that the demand of obedience is not absent, even though this covenant is unconditional in nature. Though God's initial command appears in the context of his gracious promises, prior to the establishment of the Genesis 15 covenant, Abraham is commanded in that original call to leave his homeland and settle in the land that God would indicate. The confirmation of his belief is his obedience to this demand.[7] What is most important for us to note is that Abraham's obedience is summoned in the context of God's remarkable promises of blessing — it is grounded in the grace of a grant covenant.

"Abraham's obedience, then, flowed from his faith, so we can say of Abraham that he was justified by faith alone, as long as we recognize that such faith always issues in obedience (Jas 2:14–26)."[6]

---

4. E.g., Rom. 4; Gal. 3; cf. also 1 Chron. 16:15–18.

5. Williamson, "Covenant," 146–48; *Sealed with an Oath*, 84–91; cf. also McComiskey, *Covenants of Promise*, 59–66.

6. Schreiner, "The Commands of God," 101.

7. Hafemann is right to highlight the inextricable connection between faith and obedience, unifying both of the Abrahamic covenants ("The Covenant Relationship," 44). Certainly, all of the covenants are "conditional" in the sense that the necessary response to God's covenantal initiative is *always* the obedience that comes

from faith (34–40). But his attempt to suppress any distinction in kind between these covenants results in the loss of the supremacy of the Genesis 15 covenant and its grand fulfillment in the New Covenant. As one moves from a grant covenant to a conditional one, the subtle shift regarding the responsibilities of the covenant partners in relation to the fulfillment of the covenantal commitments is an important distinction to maintain. As we will see, Paul seems to base his whole argument on this distinction.

The Genesis 17 Covenant

Somewhat surprisingly, the second Abrahamic covenant appears to be of the conditional variety. This is suggested first of all by God's promise in Genesis 17:2 to establish his covenant with Abraham at some point in the *future*, significantly *after* the first covenantal ceremony. As it turns out, thirteen years elapse between the covenants. Moreover, God indicates that he will do this once Abraham demonstrates his faithfulness to him. God says to Abraham:

> I am God Almighty; walk before me faithfully and be blameless. Then I will make my covenant between me and you and will greatly increase your numbers. (Gen. 17:1b–2; repeated in 17:7)

This futurity, coupled with the typical reciprocal wording of the conditional covenants — "As for me, this is my covenant with you ..." (Gen. 17:4a); "As for you, you must keep my covenant ..." (17:9b) — strongly suggests that this second Abrahamic Covenant is conditional. That is to say, Abraham's reception of the covenant blessings in this covenant is dependent on his faithfulness to walk before God blamelessly.[8]

When one looks for an occasion when this condition might have been met, Abraham's successful passing of the stringent test in relation to Isaac comes quickly to mind (Gen. 22:1–18).[9] This hunch finds confirmation when God responds to Abraham's mountaintop obedience by reiterating the international blessing element of the Genesis 17 covenant.[10]

> I swear by myself, declares the LORD, that *because* you have done this and have not withheld your son, your only son, I will surely bless you and make your descendants as numerous as the stars in the sky and as the sand on the seashore ... and through your offspring all nations on earth will be blessed, *because* you have obeyed me. (Gen. 22:16–18; emphasis mine)

In other words, the condition of wholehearted obedience is met in Abraham's near-offering of Isaac on the altar. Whereas the grant covenant of Genesis 15 focuses on God's oath to multiply Abraham's descendants into a great nation, God's promise to bless the entire world through Abraham is covenantally confirmed in Genesis 17 to all who would enter into the same life of obedience.

The conditionality of the second Abrahamic covenant is also affirmed by the command to circumcise his offspring and all foreigners who come into his household (Gen. 17:9–10; cf. vv. 11–13). The necessity of circumcision for the ongoing reception of the blessings in this covenant becomes clear when God concludes with

---

8. Williamson, *Sealed with an Oath*, 87–89.

9. Though the word "covenant" does not appear in Gen. 22, the covenantal nature of the Isaac event is suggested by the necessity of the sacrifice, even after Isaac is spared (22:13). The extraordinary nature of this test and the stress on Abraham's obedience (22:16b;

18b; cf. 26:5) serve to confirm Abraham's sincerity to walk before God blamelessly (Williamson, "Covenant," 147–48).

10. Gen. 22:17–18; cf. 17:4, 16b. The realization of this universal potential is also contingent on the positive response of the world's peoples to Abraham (12:3a).

this warning: "Any uncircumcised male, who has not been circumcised in the flesh, will be cut off from his people; he has broken my covenant" (17:14).

Commensurate with the conditionality of this covenant, Abraham responds immediately with obedience. That very day Abraham himself is circumcised, along with Ishmael and all the males in his household (Gen. 17:23–27). The prerequisite to the reception of the blessings of this covenant is, therefore, the fulfillment of the command to live faithfully before God, symbolized by circumcision.

The conditionality of the Genesis 17 covenant helps to shed light on what appears to be a random episode in Moses' life. While Moses is on his way back to Egypt to carry out the Lord's commands, God meets him at a lodging place and threatens to kill him (Ex. 4:24–26). The narrative does not indicate the reason for this confrontation, but it becomes obvious that it is because of Moses' neglect to circumcise his son. When his wife, Zipporah, intervenes and circumcises Moses' son, the divine threat is removed. Surely this confirms the conditionality of Abraham's second covenant.

Yet again, we must not overlook the presence of faith. For Abraham would certainly not have obeyed the command concerning circumcision had he not believed that God would be faithful to him in return. Abraham's faith may also be seen on the path up Mount Moriah when he replies to Isaac's query about the absence of a sacrificial lamb: "God himself will provide the lamb for the burnt offering, my son" (Gen. 22:8).[11]

Nor should we let the conditional nature of the Genesis 17 covenant nullify the gracious context in which its demands are expressed. As we learned in chapter 2, God has already promised the benefits of this covenant to Abraham (12:1–7), and he has already bound himself to the fulfillment of the people and land promises in the grant covenant of Genesis 15. Having received these divine commitments, Abraham's obedience in this covenant is predicated upon his faith in God's gracious faithfulness to him.

The Mosaic Covenant

We have learned that the Mosaic Covenant as a whole is a prime example of a conditional covenant. As such, the ongoing experience of its blessings is dependent on the continued faithful obedience of the covenant people. Therefore, living as a faithful member of this covenant *necessarily* involves works of obedience. When such is not forthcoming, the covenantal relationship between God and the nation is thrown into jeopardy.

This is poignantly illustrated by the crisis caused by the golden calf incident (Ex. 32–34), precipitating judgment (32:27–28, 35) and the threat of God's destruction of them (32:9–10), or at least his nonaccompaniment (33:3–5). Significantly, God restores his covenantal relationship with his people after Moses appeals to the

---

11. Gordon J. Wenham, *Genesis 16–50* (WBC; ed. David A. Hubbard, Glenn W. Barker, and John D. W. Watts; Waco, TX: Word, 1994), 2:108–9.

promises guaranteed in the grant covenant of Genesis 15 (Ex. 32:13–14). Accordingly, it is restored by grace.

It is important at this point, however, to remember that the exodus from Egypt and the subsequent giving of the law at Sinai are presented as the result of God's election of Abraham and the promises he made to him. Consequently, the Mosaic Covenant is best understood as an "administrative covenant" in relation to the Abrahamic Covenants,[12] providing the grand explication of what it means to walk before God blamelessly (Gen. 17:1).

In other words, the Mosaic Covenant administers or mediates the Abrahamic blessings to the nation. As the nation responds to God's prior grace on their behalf with obedience to the law's provisions, they will continue to experience the Abrahamic blessings, restated in their Mosaic expressions (Deut. 28:1–14). Set within this context, it is obvious that the people's obedience does not by any means *merit* or *earn* the blessings, for these have already been granted to Abraham's seed by means of gracious promises (Gen. 12:2–3, 7) and a grant covenant (15:9–21). Works of obedience to the law, therefore, are simply the means by which the reception of these gracious covenant blessings is maintained. When the people fail in this regard, the atoning ministry of the tabernacle is available to restore their covenantal relationship.

Once again, however, faith in God is fundamental to the obedience of the people in this covenant, even though faith by itself is not stressed throughout the Pentateuch. As we learned in chapter 2, the biblical understanding of faith in God implies the response of faithfulness. Where there is obedience, therefore, faith is assumed. But apart from faith, no obedience would be forthcoming and consequently no reception of the covenantal blessings.

This is confirmed in the failure of the people at Kadesh Barnea to trust the Lord's promise that he was giving them the land. When they turn away from God's command to take possession of the land, they immediately experience the suspension of the Abrahamic land promise (Deut. 1:19–36, esp. v. 32; cf. Num. 13:1–14:45). Moses indicts their disobedience because of their lack of trust in God: "But you rebelled against the command of the LORD your God. You did not trust him or obey him" (Deut. 9:23b; cf. 1:32).

By contrast, Caleb receives his inheritance because he "followed the LORD wholeheartedly" (Deut. 1:36b). Set in contrast to the failure of the people to trust God (v. 32), this implies that Caleb follows God because he trusts in him. This confirms the nature of biblical faith—it is expressed in obedience. Where there is faith, there will inevitably be obedience. But this can also be stated in the obverse: where there is obedience, there is faith.[13]

---

12. See esp. McComiskey, *Covenants of Promise*, 66–76, 150–53.

13. Schreiner concurs, commenting on this concomitance in the discussion in Heb. 3 and 4: "The oscillation between disobedience and unbelief in Hebrews demonstrates that the two are intimately related, and we have good reasons to conclude that they failed to obey because they failed to believe.... On the other hand, we see that Abraham (and Moses, Joshua, Caleb, and the generation who inherited the land under Joshua) obeyed God and were blessed because they believed" ("The Commands of God," 74).

The apparent underemphasis in the Pentateuch on the explicit discussion of faith in God is more than compensated by the prevalence of this theme throughout the psalms and prophets. Such notions as trusting, fearing, and waiting on the Lord reverberate throughout the literature, describing the life of faith that results in covenantal faithfulness.

The Davidic Covenant

Since the Davidic Covenant is a grant covenant, its fulfillment is ultimately not ensured by the righteous obedience of God's covenant partners. Failure will occur in the reigns of David's descendants (2 Sam. 7:14b), but this will not invalidate the covenant:

> But my love will never be taken away from him, as I took it away from Saul, whom I removed from before you. Your house and your kingdom will endure forever before me; your throne will be established forever. (2 Sam. 7:15–16)

Given this unconditional nature, faith in the God of the promise is the appropriate covenant response. And this is what we find here. In the wake of Nathan's announcement of the covenant terms, David prays before the Lord, expressing gratitude for God's gracious promises and affirming his faith that God will prove true to his word:

> Sovereign LORD, you are God! Your covenant is trustworthy, and you have promised these good things to your servant. Now be pleased to bless the house of your servant, that it may continue forever in your sight; for you, Sovereign LORD, have spoken, and with your blessing the house of your servant will be blessed forever. (2 Sam. 7:28–29)

This posture of trust in God likewise fills David's psalmic expressions. Indeed, his faith in God's trustworthiness grounds his oft-repeated expectation of deliverance from his enemies[14] and leads to deeds of righteousness.[15] It is for this reason that the king must take refuge in God alone; he must not place his trust in the strength of his military might (Deut. 17:16; Ps. 20:7), in wealth (Deut. 17:17b), or in treaties with other rulers (Deut. 17:17a; Isa. 30:1–2; 7:7–9).

As we have seen, however, the demand of righteousness is also communicated through this covenant, for the king's responsibility is to lead the nation in fidelity to the Mosaic Covenant. This responsibility explains the notes of *conditionality* that do appear from time to time in relation to the covenant. For instance, in his final charge to Solomon before he dies, David implies that the continuation of the Davidic blessings is tied to obedience to the law:

> So be strong, act like a man, and observe what the LORD your God requires: Walk in obedience to him, and keep his decrees and commands, his laws and regulations,

---

14. Pss. 3:2–6; 4:1; 6:4, 8–10; etc.

15. Ps. 4:3–5; etc. Yet because the king also participates in the Mosaic Covenant, expectations of blessings in response to righteousness can also be found (e.g., Ps. 7:8).

as written in the Law of Moses. Do this so that you may prosper in all you do and wherever you go and that the LORD may keep his promise to me: "If your descendants watch how they live, and if they walk faithfully before me with all their heart and soul, you will never fail to have a successor on the throne of Israel." (1 Kings 2:2b–4)

Notice that last line: "If your descendants watch how they live ... you will never fail to have a successor on the throne of Israel" (v. 4b). It sounds as though conditionality has crept into the Davidic Covenant! This conditionality is also implied in Psalm 132:11–12:

> The LORD swore an oath to David,
>   a sure oath that he will not revoke:
> "One of your own descendants
>   I will place on your throne.
> If your sons keep my covenant
>   and the statutes I teach them,
> then their sons will sit
>   on your throne for ever and ever."

The failure of the covenant is even agonizingly asserted in Psalm 89:39: "You have renounced the covenant with your servant and have defiled his crown in the dust."

But these conditional expressions should not be interpreted as indicating the overall conditional nature of the covenant. For even in these contexts where conditionality seems to be implied, the inviolability of God's oath to David is asserted.[16] The reason for this unevenness is best explained by the close relationship that the kings have with the conditional Mosaic Covenant. Since the nature of their reign would greatly influence the nation to fidelity to the covenant or apostasy from it, individual kings participated in its conditionality. As is obvious, the burden of 1 and 2 Kings is to demonstrate that the nation went into exile largely as a result of the failure of their kings.

It is likely, therefore, that this conditionality pertains to the *unbroken* nature of the reign of the Davidic kings: "you will never fail to have a successor on the throne of Israel" (1 Kings 2:4b). Thus, if the sons of

"Yhwh is unconditionally committed to David's line. David's successor must be uncompromisingly committed to Yhwh if the promise is to be fulfilled. Yhwh's commitment must not be allowed to take away from the reality of human obligation, and the necessity of human obligation must not be allowed to take away from the reality of divine sovereignty. The absoluteness of the promise is relativized by the requirement of obedience, and the requirement of obedience is relativized by the absoluteness of the promise."[17]

David reign faithfully in relation to the law, the nation likewise will remain faithful and the curses of the Mosaic Covenant will not be enacted. If, however, the Davidic kings stray, the nation eventually will suffer the ultimate covenantal curse—the exile—and the Davidic line will experience a *suspension* of the fulfillment of God's covenant promise to David.[18] Yet because of the grant nature of this covenant, the hope for the future fulfillment of the divine promise to David after the exile remains intact.[19]

The New Covenant

The prophets appear to depict the New Covenant as being of the grant variety. Two closely related reasons give rise to this conclusion—the prophetic emphasis on God's action and the absence of the language of conditionality.

First, the prophets unanimously emphasize *God's* actions in bringing about the New Covenant realities—realities that revolve around redemption and enablement. As we have seen, Jeremiah declares that the redemption provided by God in the New Covenant will be permanently effective, strikingly different from the repetitious nature of the temple sacrifices: God will "forgive their wickedness and will remember their sins no more" (Jer. 31:34c). We noted above that this atonement will be accomplished in the context of God's redemption from exile.[20] This is true of Jeremiah's presentation (30:1–31:29) and is commonplace in other prophetic expectations of God's end-time blessing of his people.[21] We have also seen that Isaiah's description of the Servant of the Lord's representative work brings into specific focus the means by which this atoning redemption will be accomplished (Isa. 53:4–12).

But since God will no longer remember the sins of the people who experience this redemption, the complementary implication is that the people of that covenant will be climactically transformed by God. The prophets use different language, but agree on this glorious result. Since God will put his law in their hearts and minds (Jer. 31:33ab) and provide them with intimate knowledge of himself (31:33c, 34ab), they will remain steadfast as a faithful covenant partner. When God makes an "eternal covenant" with his people, he will continually bless them and "inspire them to fear [him], so that they will never turn away from [him]" (32:40). In place of their "heart of stone," God will give them a "heart of flesh" that will be

---

18. The conditionality in this covenant, therefore, pertains to the individual kings. In Ps. 132:11–12, the psalmist seems to suggest that the continuance of the sons of David on the throne is dependent on their faithfulness to the law. But this likely indicates the conditionality that pertains to *individuals* within the Davidic line. Those who forsake the covenant will experience God's judgment. As successive members of the line fail, there also is the threat of the suspension of the throne altogether. This, obviously, is what transpired in the Babylonian exile and its aftermath. But the unilateral nature of the covenant assures us that God's commitment to David will eventually come to pass—an assumption that grounds the messianic hope (cf. Roberts, "Davidic Covenant," 210).

19. E.g., Isa. 9:1–7; 11:1; Ezek. 37:24–25; etc.

20. Hafemann concludes from the consistency in the exile/return

framework of the covenants "that there is no difference in the covenant formula or its constituent structure when it is related to the patriarchs, exodus, Sinai or new covenant" ("The Covenant Relationship," 52). But this commonality of imagery does not necessarily imply an identity in covenantal form. The dramatic movement from the conditional Mosaic Covenant to the grant New Covenant declares the culmination in God's gracious intervention to bring about the *final* return from exile. Hafemann is certainly right in affirming the condition of faith in response to the New Covenant (64). But this basic commonality should not obscure the significance of the distinct wording associated with this covenant in comparison to that which accompanies the Mosaic Covenant.

21. E.g., Jer. 24:4–7; 32:36–44; Ezek. 11:14–17.

"undivided" (Ezek. 11:18–19; 36:26–27). In this transformed reality, the Spirit's presence within his people will serve to move them to "follow [his] decrees and be careful to keep [his] laws" (Ezek. 36:27).

Second, the language of conditionality is strikingly absent from the discussions of that covenant. One does not find in the prophetic depictions of the New Covenant era the conditional formulas, "As for me ... as for you," or the "If you do this ... I will do this." Rather, the emphasis is on God's action that will *inevitably* result in transformation, fidelity, and righteousness in his people. Since God will give them "singleness of heart and action," they will "always fear" him; "they will never turn away" from him (Jer. 32:36–41; 24:7; Ezek. 14:11; 37:23). Conditionality is, therefore, not in view. God's transforming and enabling action will be so complete that the people will not fail in their response.

> "Thus the new covenant is the climactic fulfillment of the covenants that God established with the patriarchs, the nation of Israel, and the dynasty of David. The promises of these earlier covenants find their ultimate fulfillment in this new covenant, and in it such promises become 'eternal' in the truest sense."[22]

If the New Covenant belongs in the grant category, the reception of its blessings must be solely dependent on faith. Though this is not spelled out explicitly in the Old Testament covenantal passages, it is likely implied in the repeated phrase, "I will be their God, and they will be my people."[23] While this affirmation obviously includes actions of covenantal faithfulness, it especially depicts the nature of the people's wholehearted trust in God alone. Elsewhere, God proclaims through Jeremiah:

> I will give them a heart to know me, that I am the LORD. They will be my people, and I will be their God, for they will return to me with all their heart. (Jer. 24:7)

Indeed, their worship and trust will be in God alone; no longer will they turn to other gods:

> They will no longer defile themselves with their idols and vile images or with any of their offenses, for I will save them from all their sinful backsliding, and I will cleanse them. They will be my people, and I will be their God. (Ezek. 37:23)

This, in turn, will lead to consistent covenant faithfulness:

> They will be my people, and I will be their God. I will give them singleness of heart and action, so that they will always fear me and that all will then go well for them and for their children after them. (Jer. 32:38–39)

Significantly, this hearkens back to Genesis 17:7–8, where God promises in connection to his "everlasting covenant" with Abraham that he will be the God of his descendants. The New Covenant people, therefore, will experience the fulfillment of this covenantal promise: no longer will they turn to another deity or trust in any other god. Rather, their faith and security will be in Yahweh alone.

---

22. Williamson, *Sealed with an Oath*, 181.   23. Jer. 31:33c; cf. Ezek. 11:20b; 14:11; 37:27.

Since God will indeed be their God in whom they trust, they will live out this faith in lives of faithfulness.[24] As we have seen throughout the covenantal conversations, this expectation is consistent with the biblical notion of "faith," preserving the covenantal demand of righteousness. Indeed, because of the nature of the divine provisions in this covenant, the expectation of righteousness is *absolute*—they will no longer turn away! Rather, they will remain faithful to God, submitting to the reign of David's righteous heir.

FAITH AND WORKS IN JESUS' NEW COVENANT FULFILLMENT

How, then, should we answer this question when we turn to the New Testament portrayal of Jesus and the disciple's relationship to him? This is not an easy task, requiring us to reconcile Jesus' rigorous commands of righteousness with Paul's theological affirmations of grace.

As I noted at the outset of this chapter, it is tempting to assume that Jesus depicts the New Covenant as conditional in nature because of his stringent call for obedience. For instance, he declares that those who do not pick up their crosses cannot be his disciples (Matt. 10:38; par. Luke 14:27). Similarly, survival at the judgment is dependent on his disciples doing the will of the Father as it is expressed by Jesus (Matt. 7:24–27; par. Luke 6:46–49). Indeed, he echoes the Old Testament in demanding that his disciples be "perfect" as God is perfect (Matt. 5:48; cf. Lev. 19:1). These commands reveal that the New Covenant blessings will be received only by those who live lives of robust faithful discipleship to Jesus. Seen through this lens, the New Covenant appears to be a continuation of the conditional Mosaic Covenant, albeit mediated through Jesus' authoritative teachings.

Paul identifies himself as a minister of a "new covenant" (2 Cor. 3:6; cf. 1 Cor. 11:25), emphasizing the internal ministry of the Spirit as its defining characteristic (2 Cor. 3:3, 6–18). In this way, Paul clearly is appealing to the covenant faithfulness that would characterize the transformed and Spirit-filled New Covenant people (Ezek. 36:26–27). Yet, Paul makes it clear in his letters that righteousness in this new covenantal era is "by faith from first to last" (Rom. 1:17). Salvation is not received "by works" (Eph. 2:9a), but "through faith" (2:8b). Indeed, Christ is the "culmination of the law so that there may be righteousness for everyone who believes" (Rom. 10:4).

Thus, Jesus seems to be all about the demand of righteous obedience, while Paul revels in the gracious reception of righteousness by faith. Many resolve this tension by interpreting the teaching that Paul is countering as a form of legalism. In support of this, there is ample evidence in contemporary Jewish literature that many Jews

---

24. The connection with Gen. 17 underscores this expectation. For those whose God is the Lord will walk before him blamelessly (17:1).

of that time conceived of law obedience as the basis of their eventual vindication by God.[25] Paul, then, is responding to an aberrant form of Judaism, rectifying first of all the assumption that justification would be based on law observance rather than faith in God's grace. To do so, he appeals to Abraham's justification, which came about by faith, several centuries prior to the giving of the law (cf. Rom. 4:9–12; Gal. 3:6, 17). Paul then goes on to affirm that Jesus is the fulfillment of the grace of the Old Testament curse-removing sacrifices (Gal. 3:13; cf. 2 Cor. 5:21), so saving faith must now be in Christ (Rom. 3:21–26; Eph. 2:8–9).

Since this sort of "legalistic" thinking has been convincingly demonstrated to have been entertained by some in that era, this "traditional" approach to Paul's teaching has a great deal to say for itself. Indeed, it is quite possible that some kind of legalism is within Paul's purview in some texts. Paul's nullification of Jewish "boasting" in their knowledge of God through the law seems to run in this direction (Rom. 3:27; cf. 2:17, 23). Similarly in this regard is his denial of any merit attained by Abraham, which rules out any "boast" by him before God (Rom. 4:1–12)

Reconciling Paul with Jesus, then, turns on this important observation that justification before God is solely based on faith in Jesus' atoning sacrifice (Rom. 3:21–28). Jesus' call to righteousness is therefore understood to reflect the conditionality that exists in all covenants, since faith necessarily gives rise to obedience (1:5).

This perspective may accurately capture Paul's teaching on this issue. But is there any insight that our study in the covenants might contribute to this debate?

The New Covenant as a Grant Covenant

Anyone who reads New Testament scholarship or simply has studied the Scriptures is aware that we are bumping into a massive question that puzzles the best of minds.[26] A book of this sort certainly cannot aspire to make any significant contribution to this discussion. But I do believe that the covenantal perspective that we have gained may suggest a way forward.

25. See, e.g., Simon Gathercole, *Where Is Boasting: Early Jewish Soteriology and Paul's Response in Romans 1-5* (Grand Rapids: Eerdmans, 2002), 37–194; idem, "Justified by Faith, Justified by his Blood: The Evidence of Romans 3:21–4:5," in *Justification and Variegated Nomism*, vol. 2, *The Paradoxes of Paul*, ed. D. A. Carson, Peter T. O'Brien, and Mark A. Seifrid (Grand Rapids: Baker, 2004), esp. 150–61.

26. For further discussions of the issues involved, see Frank Thielman, "Law," *DPHL*, 529–42; D. J. Moo, "Law," *DJG*, 450–61; Willem A. VanGemeren, Greg L. Bahnsen, Walter C. Kaiser Jr., Wayne G. Strickland, and Douglas J. Moo, *The Law, the Gospel, and the Modern Christian: Five Views* (Grand Rapids: Zondervan, 1993); John Piper, *The Future of Justification: A Response to N. T. Wright* (Wheaton: Crossway, 2007); N. T. Wright, *Justification: God's Plan and Paul's Vision* (Downers Grove: IVP, 2009).

For more scholarly discussions, see Stephen Westerholm, *Perspectives Old and New on Paul: The "Lutheran" Paul and His Critics* (Grand Rapids: Eerdmans, 2004); James D. G. Dunn, *The New Perspective on Paul* (rev. ed.; Grand Rapids: Eerdmans, 2005); idem, *The Theology of Paul the Apostle* (Grand Rapids: Eerdmans, 1998), 334–89; D. A. Carson, Peter T. O'Brien, and Mark A. Seifrid, eds., *Justification and Variegated Nomism*, vol. 1, *The Complexities of Second Temple Judaism* (Grand Rapids: Baker, 2001); and idem, vol. 2, *The Paradoxes of Paul*; Frank Thielman, *Paul & the Law: A Contextual Approach* (Downers Grove, IL: IVP, 1994); A. Andrew Das, *Paul, the Law, and the Covenant* (Peabody, MA: Hendrickson, 2001); Seyoon Kim, *Paul and the New Perspective: Second Thoughts on the Origin of Paul's Gospel* (Grand Rapids: Eerdmans, 2002); Guy Prentiss Waters, *Justification and the New Perspectives on Paul: A Review and Response* (Phillipsburg: P&R, 2004).

We concluded in our discussion of the New Covenant that the prophets appear to present it as a grant covenant. Paul confirms this thesis by repeatedly and adamantly asserting that *faith* is the sole means of receiving the blessings of what has come through Jesus. This helps to explain why Paul is careful to separate the gospel from any notion of receiving the New Covenant blessings through works of obedience to the law. There has been a change in the covenants that is not merely *sequential*; it is also a change in *kind*. Whereas the Mosaic Covenant was a conditional one that demanded faithful works of obedience for the ongoing reception of its blessings, the New Covenant in Jesus is a grant covenant, whose blessings are only dependent on God's faithfulness to fulfill them.[27]

The nub of Paul's argument, then, is that those who seek to receive the blessings of the gospel as if they were mediated through a *conditional* covenant—conceiving of obedience to the law as the continuing means by which the blessings are received—miss the point entirely. At one level, then, Paul is not rebuking a legalistic merit theology so much as a fatal misrepresentation of the New Covenant that leads *unintentionally* to legalism.[28] In other words, because of the *nature* of Jesus' fulfillment of the Mosaic Covenant, those who treat the law as if it were still in effect place themselves back under the demand of the law and therefore under its conditional curse. This seems to be the way in which Paul is arguing in Galatians 3.

In the seminal discussion of Galatians 3, Paul implies that he is thinking covenantally in several ways. First, note that he refers to his readers' reception of the Spirit (which Paul understands to be the hallmark of the New Covenant; cf. 2 Cor. 3:2–6), which is contrasted with life in the law (Gal. 3:2). He then cites Genesis 15:6, summarizing the essence of Abraham's grant covenant (Gal. 3:6). But most tellingly, he explicitly differentiates between the covenant established in promises to Abraham (vv. 15–16) and the law, which was given 430 years later (v. 7). Given this context, Paul's reference to "this faith" that has "come" (v. 23; cf. v. 19) must refer to the grant covenant that has come in Christ—a covenant whose benefits must be received "by faith."

This helps to explain, then, why Paul emphasizes that the law's requirements of obedience also carry a curse for those who fail in this regard (Gal. 3:10).[29] This is the nature of the conditional covenant, as we have seen. Then Paul states categorically that "no one is justified before God by the law, because 'the righteous will live by faith'" (3:11b). Paul is therefore nodding to two realities: the inability of anyone to fulfill the righteous demands of the law entirely (Rom. 2:17–23; 3:9–20; 7:7–25; 8:3a) and the consequent necessity of faith in the person who is justified by God.

---

27. In this regard, see esp. the salvation-historical argument by Silva (Moisés Silva, "Faith versus Works of Law in Galatians," in *Paradoxes of Paul*, 236–44), who writes, "The Galatians' most fundamental error was precisely their blurring the distinction between the time of law, of curse, of flesh, or guardianship, of slavery, and the time of faith, of blessing, of the Spirit, of sonship, of freedom" (241).

28. Cf. also Das, *Paul, the Law, and the Covenant*, 161–63. It is important to recognize along with Silva that the view that Paul is countering in Gal. 3:17, 23–24 is his own view and not some misunderstanding of the law (Silva, "Faith versus Works," 243).

29. Obviously, I am assuming that Paul is referring to the entirety of the law's commands by means of his phrase (lit.) "works of the law" (e.g., Gal. 2:16; 3:2, 5, 10; cf. Rom. 3:20, 28) or the more abbreviated "works" (e.g., Rom. 4:2, 6; 9:12, 32; 11:6; Eph. 2:9).

Paul defends this theology in Romans 4 by appealing to Abraham's experience of justification by faith before he was circumcised (Rom. 4:3, 9–11). As a result, Abraham functions as the paradigm of being justified apart from the law, anticipating the state of affairs pertaining to believers in the New Covenant era (Gal. 3:6–9, 16–18).[30] But Paul goes beyond Abraham to David (Rom. 4:6–8), who exemplifies the true Israelite *under* the law—those of the "circumcision" who *also* follow "in the footsteps of the faith that our father Abraham had before he was circumcised" (4:12b). Justification before God has *always* been dependent on faith, even during the era of the law. This is because faith has always been the necessary response to God's gracious initiative, as well as the means by which restoring grace through the sacrificial system was received.[31] So even when the conditional Mosaic Covenant was in place, faith was the means by which atoning grace was received by the penitent sinner, who could never have kept the law in its entirety.

Paul therefore assumes that it is possible to be a Jew under the law without the faith of Abraham (Rom. 4:16). And since his faith lays hold of the promises of God that find their fulfillment in Jesus (Gal. 3:16, 19, 22–25; 2 Cor. 1:20; implied in Rom. 4:19–25), those Jews who deny Jesus' role to be that of bringing the era of the law to an end are found *not* to be children of Abraham (Gal. 3:26–29).[32] This, then, sets the table for Jesus.

Jesus, the Faithful Covenant Partner and the Curse Remover

Paul summarizes the gracious provision of Jesus under two major headings: his role as the faithful covenant partner and his role as the righteous curse remover. These roles can be perceived in Paul's pithy statement in Romans 5:9–10:

> Since we have now been justified by his blood, how much more shall we be saved from God's wrath through him! For if, while we were God's enemies, we were reconciled to him through the death of his Son, how much more, having been reconciled, shall we be saved through his life!

Paul refers in the first place to Jesus' role as the curse-bearer so that we who trust in Jesus will be protected from God's wrath. Paul then notes how we are saved through Jesus' righteous life, which the apostle describes in 5:12–21 as the grand replacement of Adam's unrighteous failure. We will take them both of these affirmations in turn.

Jesus was born under the law (Gal. 4:4) and therefore lived under its condition-

---

30. Gathercole ("Justified by Faith," 164–65) helpfully observes that Abraham's faith does not merely function as an analogy of faith in Christ, but it also communicates the *content* of saving faith, which is grounded in God's power to bring to life that which is dead (Rom. 4:19–25).

31. Das, *Paul, the Law, and the Covenant*, 213.

32. See Silva ("Faith versus Works," 227–36) for a defense of the view that Paul understands faith to be in Jesus (and not Jesus' faithfulness).

ality. Unlike all of Abraham's previous descendants, however, Jesus proved to be the sole faithful covenant partner without sin (2 Cor. 5:21a). As the representative of both Israel (the "Seed"; Gal. 3:16, 19) and humanity as a whole (our second "Adam"; Rom. 5:15–19), Jesus meets the conditionality of the covenant perfectly, without the need of personal atonement. He thereby fulfills the law's demand of a faithful covenant partner (5:18–19)—something that Israel and all the descendants of Adam had failed to be (5:12, 14–19a).

Jesus' righteous life also qualified him to die in the place of humanity, taking onto himself the curse of the Mosaic Covenant and thereby removing it:

> Christ redeemed us from the curse of the law by becoming a curse for us, for it is written: "Cursed is everyone who is hung on a pole." (Gal. 3:13; cf. 1 Cor. 10:16; 2 Cor. 5:21; Gal. 2:20)

By virtue of this fulfillment, however, Paul affirms that Jesus also renders *ineffective* the curse-removing function of the temple sacrificial system; those sacrifices have now been fulfilled by Jesus.[33] This means that those who seek to perpetuate the Mosaic Covenant effectively reject the covenantal grace that has come through Christ (Gal. 5:2–4). The unfortunate consequence of this, however, is that they end up returning to the conditional nature of that covenant with its ongoing demand of obedience, seeking in the process to establish their own righteousness through the works of the law (Rom. 10:2–3). But since Jesus has made obsolete the curse-removing sacrifices of the temple, there is no longer any possibility of atonement in that covenant.

As a result, such individuals are now exposed to the demand of perfect obedience according to the requirement of the conditional Mosaic Covenant. The law has always required absolute fidelity (Gal. 3:10b, citing Deut. 27:26).[34] But since the Levitical sacrifices are no longer effective to remove the law's curse, there is no longer any restoring grace available. Consequently, the law has become a messenger of death (Rom. 7:21–24; 2 Cor. 3:7a, 9a),[35] for there is no way any longer to avoid its curse. In this way, we can speak of "legalism" entering in through the back door of an obsolete covenant.

Whereas the Mosaic Covenant came with restoring grace to compensate for the inevitable failure of the people, the New Covenant provides both permanent atonement (1 Cor. 11:25) *and* a representative covenant partner (Rom. 5:18–19), who fulfilled the law's demands perfectly. The result is that the blessings of the Abrahamic Covenant are no longer mediated through the conditional Mosaic Covenant

---

33. Ibid., 144; Schreiner, "The Commands of God," 87.

34. See esp. Das, *Paul, the Law, and the Covenant*, 145–70. He writes, "The summaries in Deut 27:26; 28:1, 15, 58, 61; 30:10 consistently emphasize obedience of all that God commands in the law. The language is comprehensive; the law is an organic whole, and all of it must be obeyed" (157).

35. Ibid., 144: "Paul is saying that the Jew who disobeys the law has no effective path to resolve the situation caused by sin, since its resolution can be found only in Christ. The Mosaic law has been severed from its context and forced to function as an empty series of demands requiring obedience with no solution for failure—hence, Paul's negative view of the law."

but through Jesus, who is the representative covenant partner for everyone. God has therefore provided what he demanded, fulfilling the grant nature of the Genesis 15 covenant and allowing the Abrahamic blessings now to be received solely by *faith*.

Paul can thus stridently affirm that the righteousness that God demands is now received by faith "from first to last" (Rom. 1:17). This must mean that Paul understands the New Covenant (1 Cor. 11:25) to be a grant covenant—one that does not depend on our continuing works of righteousness to receive its blessings.

"His point is that reverting to the Sinai covenant now that Christ has come denies the fulfillment of the covenant in Christ and places one in the impossible position of having to do everything the law says to be saved, apart from its provisions for forgiveness. Since all sin, all need atonement. Those who do not accept Jesus as their atonement have no atonement. Their position is hopeless."[37]

Prior to Jesus' fulfillment, the Jews were "held in custody under the law" (Gal. 3:23), most likely referring to its conditional nature and its concomitant curse. But now that "this faith" has come—this grant covenant whose benefits are provided through Christ's finished work by faith—the "supervision of the law" has come to an end (Gal. 3:25).[36]

God, in Christ, has reconciled the world to himself (2 Cor. 5:19; Col. 1:19–20). This means that the guarantee of the fulfillment of the covenant requirements lies in him alone; all of the covenantal promises of God find their "yes" in Jesus (2 Cor. 1:20). Seeking to receive its blessings through obedience to the law is now covenantally *anachronistic* and salvifically *bankrupt*! Disciples of Jesus enter and remain in this New Covenant solely by *faith*.

Reconciling Jesus' Demand with Paul's Gospel

If the foregoing argument for the grant nature of the New Covenant is correct, how are we to reconcile Jesus' all-encompassing demand of righteousness with Paul's grace-filled message of the gospel?

Let's begin with Jesus. At least two things should be said in this regard. First, if my presentation of Paul's argument is on target, Jesus functions as the true covenant partner on behalf of those who trust in him. As a result, Jesus does fulfill his own commands. These commands, therefore, come to his disciples already as *fulfilled* commands. This is surely the implication of Jesus' presentation of himself as the lamb and the Servant at the Passover meal. Those who trust in him receive his gracious provision of righteousness through faith.[38]

But we have also seen that the grace of the covenants never nullifies nor diminishes the demand of righteousness. One of the most important findings that our

36. Similarly also Silva ("Faith versus Works," 240), who stresses the implicit connection with Jesus' coming.

37. Schreiner, "The Commands of God," 87.

38. It is significant that Jesus repeatedly recognizes and validates people's faith in him (e.g., Matt. 8:10; 15:28; Mark 2:5; 5:34, 36; 10:52; 11:23–24; Luke 17:19; John 6:29; 14:12; cf. John 4:42; 8:24; 9:35; 10:38; 11:42; 17:20–21; 20:27), and censures others' lack of faith (e.g., Matt. 8:26; 14:31; 17:20; Mark 6:6; Luke 12:28; John

5:38–47; 6:64; 8:45–46). Although many of these instances come in the context of faith for healing, the prevalence of this theme demonstrates Jesus' stress on the importance of faith in him. When we understand that all of Jesus' ministry actions are interwoven into a seamless whole, faith in Jesus for one thing has the potential of becoming expanded with added insight into the kind of faith that Paul discusses, though it also may be abandoned (e.g., Luke 8:13; John 6:66).

covenantal study has demonstrated is that the grace/demand structure is fundamental to the way in which God interacts with humanity. And this is true even
in the case of the *grant* covenants, whose benefits are received *by faith*. As we have
discussed previously, this is because the biblical notion of faith always carries with
it the implicit expectation of an obedience that demonstrates its reality.

When God established his grant covenant with Noah, the appropriate (though
admittedly, not necessary) posture of those in that covenant was implicitly one of
faith in God's trustworthiness to sustain life on the earth. Yet even within this grant
covenant, notions of conditionality appear in the threats of divine recrimination for
those who do not respect human and animal life. Those who obey these commands
implicitly do so because of their belief that God will be true to his warnings of justice.

When God established his grant covenant with Abraham, the patriarch's
response was again that of faith (Gen. 15:6). But this faith resulted in obedience that
eventually was expressed in the demand of all-encompassing faithfulness in the conditional covenant of Genesis 17 and the test surrounding Isaac on Mount Moriah.

When God established his grant covenant with David, the king's response was
also that of faith. But his faith too resulted in obedience to the conditional Mosaic
Covenant under which the entire nation lived, such that he was identified as a man
after God's "own heart" (1 Sam. 13:14; Acts 13:22). Seeking to avoid Jesus' demands
of righteousness by an appeal to the grant nature of the New Covenant is to overlook this consistent covenantal pattern.

It is true that in the case of the New Covenant, there is no correlating conditional
covenant—those covenants have now been superseded in Jesus' fulfillment. This must
be why Paul stresses that our relationship to God is from faith "from first to last." That
is to say, in place of the conditional reception of the New Covenant blessings through
the ongoing demand of obedience, we have Jesus, our representative covenant partner.
That conditional demand has been met in his righteous life. As we have argued, this
is the reason why the transition from the Mosaic Covenant to the New Covenant has
occasioned a change in covenant types. But what stands in the place of a conditional
covenant are the expectations of righteousness from the people of the New Covenant.
Jesus' requirement of absolute righteousness makes perfect sense in this context.

This is because those disciples who have entered the New Covenant established
by Jesus are also those who have received that covenant's grace. And what grace it
is! Those graced in the New Covenant have experienced the transforming power of
God's redemptive work, including:

- the permanent atonement for their sin (Jer. 31:34b; Matt. 26:28; Heb.
  10:12–14, 18)
- the internalization of the law (Jer. 31:33b; 2 Cor. 3:3–18; Col. 2:11–12)
- the provision of a new heart that is receptive to his call (Ezek. 36:26; Matt.
  5:8; 7:16–20; 13:8–9; 22:37; John 3:3–7; 1 Peter 1:23)

- the granting of an intimate knowledge of God (Jer. 31:34a; Matt. 13:11, 16–17; 1 Cor. 2:9–16)
- the empowerment of the indwelling Spirit (Ezek. 36:27; Joel 2:28–29; Rom. 8:4–6, 9, 13b–17; Gal. 5:22–23)
- the reign of the righteous King (Isa. 32:1–5; Ezek. 37:24–28; Matt. 16:15–17, 24–27; Mark 12:28–34)

Put into this context, Jesus' demand of righteousness is exactly what would be expected of the people in the New Covenant. Though these demands are not part of a conditional covenant—that covenant form is now obsolete!—anything less than this level of righteousness would fail to cohere with the expectations of the New Covenant people, who will never forget their covenantal commitments (Jer. 50:4–5).

And Paul does not disagree with this! While he consistently defends the doctrine of salvation by grace through faith, he also strongly affirms the necessity—indeed, the *inevitability*—of a life of righteousness. For instance, right after he affirms God's fulfillment of the law's demands in Christ (Rom. 8:3), he identifies its purpose: "in order that the righteous requirement of the law might be fully met in us, who do not live according to the sinful nature but according to the Spirit" (Rom. 8:4; cf. Gal. 5:13–25). That is to say, the result of receiving Jesus' gracious fulfillment of the law's demands through faith will be the fulfillment of the law's demands by his people, now empowered by the promised Spirit. Those who live according to the Spirit—and therefore keep in step with the Spirit (Gal. 5:25)—*inevitably* will please God (implied by the contrast between Rom. 8:8 and 8:9–13) and will live in the intimacy and freedom of adoption into his family (Rom. 8:14–17; Gal. 4:4–7). This is what being led by the Spirit is all about.

In response to the all-encompassing grace in Christ, therefore, Paul exhorts his readers to present themselves to God as "living sacrifices" (Rom. 12:1), resulting in lives of righteousness that fulfill the law (13:8–10) and the kinds of commands that come through Jesus (13:9–21; Eph. 4:17–5:20; Phil. 4:8–9; Col. 3:5–17). There is, therefore, no disagreement between Jesus and Paul concerning the nature of the demand of righteousness for those who are disciples of Jesus—for those who are in Christ!

SUMMARY

What I hope has become clear through this chapter is the importance of understanding the grant nature of the New Covenant and the relationship of faith and works of obedience within that kind of covenant. Seen in the context of the covenantal pattern that we traced through the Old Testament, the answer to the "Why" question is becoming more obvious. Let me summarize these relationships once again in table format.

Grant covenant	Demand of righteousness
Noahic	Respect for life forms
Abrahamic (Gen. 15)	Conditional covenant of Gen. 17
Davidic	Conditional Mosaic Covenant
New	Jesus' commands

In each case, the faith associated with the grant covenants gives rise to obedience. But the attachment of conditional covenants to the Genesis 15 Abrahamic and the Davidic covenants has not been continued into the New Covenant era. This has been replaced by Jesus' discipleship commands, which are commensurate with the transformation of the New Covenant people.

In the end, I hope that this chapter's argument has helped to correct misunderstandings of both Jesus and Paul and, in the process, facilitated the reconciliation of their messages. On the one hand, Jesus should not be understood to be perpetuating the conditional nature of the Mosaic Covenant. Rather, he should be seen as articulating what disciples graced by the New Covenant blessings ought to live like. On the other hand, Paul should not be understood as diminishing Jesus' high call to lived-out righteousness by means of his stress on salvation by grace through faith. Rather, his concern should be interpreted as safeguarding the grant nature of the New Covenant, grounded in Jesus' twofold fulfillment of the Mosaic Covenant as the representative covenant partner and the righteous curse remover.

Both Jesus and Paul should, therefore, be understood to be in agreement that those who follow Jesus and trust in the good news of the gospel must respond with a New Covenant, Spirit-empowered righteousness that outstrips that which was possible under the Old Testament covenants. The question that naturally arises at this point has to do with the dissonance between this expectation and the reality of the contemporary disciple's life. For the answer to that question, however, we will have to wait until we address the "How" question. It is sufficient at the present time to draw the strings of these chapters together to answer the "Why" question.

RELEVANT QUESTIONS

1. In what ways has this discussion of faith and works of obedience in relation to the types of biblical covenants influenced your understanding of discipleship in the New Covenant?
2. Have you encountered in others or perceived in yourself a diminishing of the

concern to obey Jesus' commands because of Paul's theology of grace? How has this chapter's discussion affected that understanding?

3. In light of this chapter's argument, what are some of the typical misunderstandings of Christian discipleship? How might these be addressed?

4. In what ways should Christian evangelistic presentations of the gospel change in light of the answer to the "Why" question?

THE ANSWERS TO
THE "WHY" QUESTION

We are finally ready to draw the strings of our biblical theology together to answer the "Why" question: Why should I be concerned to obey all of Jesus' commands when I have been saved by grace? Why should I be concerned about what Jesus says concerning how I handle my money, or how I interact with issues pertaining to justice, or what I do in the private world of my thought life, or …? You finish that sentence. Our answer comes to us in the covenantal matrix of faith, grace, and demand that we have been considering. In answering this question, we will move from the more general covenantal perspective to the more specific insights we have gained from Jesus and Paul.

IMPLICATIONS FROM
THE COVENANTAL PATTERNS

We should begin answering this question from the insight that we have gained concerning the covenantal patterns that consistently appear in Scripture. Though there is great diversity in the specific covenantal stipulations pertaining to the various biblical covenants, in each case God initiates those covenants in actions of creating, providing, redeeming, and promising. Therefore, the covenants are alike in the gracious foundations that they all exhibit. In fact, we also discovered that the New Covenant is intimately tied to these gracious covenantal actions, since Jesus provides their climactic fulfillments.

This realization, then, helps us to avoid one common mistake right away — that of appealing to the gracious nature of the New Covenant to set it off from the prior covenants and seeking by this to excuse a negligence regarding righteousness. While the grace that has come through Jesus is deeper and wider and higher and better than any of the gracious provisions in the prior covenants, it is at the same time *continuous* with those prior expressions, even as their *fulfillment*. Since the grace of the Old Testament covenants did not diminish the call to righteousness, neither can we assume that the grace of Jesus would lead to any different result.

A second pattern that has manifested itself has been the consistent presence of demands of loyalty and righteousness throughout the biblical covenants. This is because God's great desire is to have a people for "his own possession" who will reflect his character in the earth. From Eden's mandate to steward creation in God's image and under his sovereignty, to the Abrahamic command for an all-encompassing faithfulness symbolized by circumcision, to the Mosaic call for a holiness that mirrors God's character, to the Davidic responsibility to rule in God's stead in faithfulness to the law—all of these covenants communicate God's consistent demand of righteousness. Though each of these covenants is grounded in and sustained by grace, the requisite covenantal response is that of righteous obedience.

The New Covenant continues this pattern. Though it is rooted in the grace that fulfills all of God's prior provisions and promises, the expectation of righteousness from its covenant partners remains that of the all-encompassing demand of faithfulness and obedience. There is no negative correlation between the amount of grace and the demand of righteousness in this covenant. Though the gracious provision of the New Covenant provides a transformation and enablement that exceeds anything before it, the resulting demand is absolute covenantal faithfulness.

As we saw in chapter 3, New Covenant people will not forget the covenant, nor will they break it—obviously in sharp contrast to the people of the Mosaic Covenant (and all other covenant partners). When Jesus initiates the New Covenant at the Last Supper, this new state of affairs is being established. Given this context, Jesus' commands should be understood as "covenantal" demands. And this is what we find consistently in Jesus' teachings as he repeatedly situates his commands in the neighborhood of the law, intentionally communicating its culmination. Disciples of Jesus are, therefore, summoned to follow him in a faithfulness befitting those in the New Covenant.

IMPLICATIONS FROM JESUS' MESSIANIC AUTHORITY

This understanding finds resounding confirmation in Jesus' messianic identity and kingdom ministry. As the long-awaited fulfillment of the heir to David's covenantal promise, Jesus is the righteous King who reigns over God's restored people, leading them in righteousness and covenantal fidelity. Accordingly, his bracing call for righteousness and faithfulness to himself above all other loyalties resonates with prophetic significance. The kingdom of God has arrived! The time of the righteous king's reign over a righteous people has dawned!

IMPLICATIONS FROM THE SPIRIT'S OUTPOURING

Similarly, Jesus' disciples are those who have experienced the fulfillment of the prophetic expectations of the Spirit's outpouring on God's covenant people. As the prophetic portrayals make clear, the effect of this divine endowment will be a deeper enablement for righteousness. Paul echoes this in his discussion of the Spirit's effect on God's people. Those who are led by the Spirit will inevitably produce the fruit of the Spirit and fulfill the law of Christ. As Spirit-enabled New Covenant partners, those who follow him ought to be continually concerned regarding obedience to all of Jesus' covenantal demands.

THE AGREEMENT BETWEEN JESUS AND PAUL

This is not to be understood, however, to contradict Paul's assertions that God's salvation in Christ is available only by grace through faith. Given the nature of Jesus' perfect fulfillment of the Mosaic Covenant as the Passover lamb and the Servant of the Lord, the Abrahamic blessings are now available to his disciples solely by faith in him. Jesus' righteous demands, therefore, are to be obeyed within the context of the grant nature of the New Covenant, for Jesus' commands are *fulfilled* commands. Legalism is simply not in the picture! Rather, in response to its profound culmination of the covenantal grace of God in Christ—the complete satisfaction of the conditional demand of the Mosaic Covenant, the culminating atonement through Jesus' crucifixion, and the pouring out of his transforming and enabling Spirit—those of us who follow Jesus must realize the vital nature of our covenant faithfulness to *all* of our King's commands.

Having answered the "Why" question, the logical flow of this book is easy to see. If it is the case that we as disciples ought to be concerned to obey all of Jesus' commands, it is important for us to understand *what* those commands are, especially as they intersect with the law of the Mosaic Covenant. For this reason, we will turn next to a consideration of the "What" question. But it should also be clear by now that there is a sharp *dissonance* between what Jeremiah and the other prophets depict in their discussions of the New Covenant people and what is presently visible among the followers of Jesus. Why is this dissonance the case? This will eventually lead us to ask the "How" question, focusing on the reasons for this discrepancy, but more importantly on *how* covenant faithfulness might be increasingly true of Jesus' disciples today.

THE "WHAT" QUESTION

So, what does Jesus command us to do?

We learned in our discussion of the "Why" question that the fundamental reason we should be concerned to obey all of Jesus' commands is because the New Covenant is the fulfillment of the previous Old Testament covenants. Thus, the grace/demand dynamic appropriately persists for God's New Covenant partners. Although this covenant is a grant covenant, such that the absolute righteousness demanded by God is received by faith in Jesus' representative obedience, we have learned that God's righteous demand never diminishes in the wake of his grace.

In addition, New Covenant people are those in whose minds the law has been inscribed, in whose hearts the Spirit has been given, and over whom the Messiah reigns. God has done all of this for the expressed purpose of bringing about a righteous people who will make him known throughout the earth. Biblically speaking, those who experience these covenantal fulfillments will, by virtue of their transformed nature, *inevitably* be concerned to respond with passionate obedience to the New Covenant expectations of righteousness. Since Jesus is the messianic King who articulates this demand, his genuine disciples will hear his summons and follow.

It is easy to see that the "What" question follows naturally from this discussion: "What is it that Jesus commands me to do as his disciple?" To answer this question, we will need to perceive ways in which the covenantal demands are mediated to us through Jesus. He doesn't speak to us out of a covenantal vacuum! Rather, since he is the long-awaited Messiah, we will begin by reviewing the expectations embodied in the Davidic Covenant. What does it look like to live in his "kingdom"? What does it mean to follow this King who lived his life as the Servant in faithfulness to the Mosaic law? This will lead us into a consideration of the ways in which Jesus mediates the law to those who belong to the New Covenant era.

We have also learned that central to the promises God made with Abraham is his overarching desire to bless all nations by filling the earth with the knowledge of himself. Not surprisingly, then, to speak of discipleship necessarily includes the language of "mission." How does God's promise to bless all nations flow into Jesus' discipleship commands? How does our following him actually contribute to the big picture of God's missional purposes in the world?

As we turn to the "What" question, we are opening a topic that easily exceeds our ability to ferret out every aspect of its answer. But my goal is not to provide an exhaustive discussion of all of the issues and all of the texts. Such are readily available in commentary discussions, specialized monographs, and learned journal articles. My purpose is a much more modest one: to trace the broad strokes of the massive portrait that God has drawn for us in the Scriptures. Consequently, we will concentrate our focus on those ways in which Jesus' demands intersect with the covenantal expectations that we considered in our discussion of the "Why" question. Given these limitations, let's engage the "What" question in pursuit of more answers.

CHAPTER 6

THE PROPHET WHO IS THE KING

The LORD your God will raise up for you a prophet like me from among you, from your own people. You must listen to him.

Deuteronomy 18:15

You still lack one thing. Sell everything you have and give to the poor, and you will have treasure in heaven. Then come, follow me.

Luke 18:22b

Throughout his ministry, Jesus calls people to follow him. This certainly indicates his intention as a teacher and mentor to mold and to shape them; as a result, we often consign the significance of this summons to that role. But if we look at this action in relation to the covenantal expectations that we considered in the first section of this book, another dimension emerges that demands our consideration. We have learned that the Old Testament prophets look forward to the New Covenant era when the Messiah will reign over God's transformed people, demanding from them the profound righteousness befitting his kingdom. In this chapter, we will consider Jesus' absolute summons to follow him in the context of these expectations. We will see that the fulfillment of the ideal expressed in the Davidic Covenant has come through the King who is also the Prophet.

JESUS' COMPLEMENTARY ROLES

When we ask the "What" question, two of Jesus' roles come together—those of king and prophet. The latter is obvious, because his authoritative teaching on the will of God (along with his miracles) moves people to the inescapable conclusion that a great prophet has arisen among them.[1] Jesus himself agrees with this assessment (Luke 13:33) and acts it out with great authority (e.g., Matt. 5:21–48). This appropriately leads some to conclude that he is the fulfillment of Moses' promise regarding *the* Prophet who would come:

---

1. E.g., Matt. 14:5; 21:46; Mark 6:15; Luke 7:16; 24:19; John 4:19; 9:17.

The LORD your God will raise up for you a prophet like me from among you, from your own people. You must listen to him.... I will raise up for them a prophet like you from among their people, and I will put my words in his mouth. He will tell them everything I command him. (Deut. 18:15, 18; cf. John 6:14)

In its original context, Moses' reference appears to be the ongoing line of prophets who would follow him and serve the people in many of the ways he had. This is implied by his cautions against being deceived by false prophets and the criteria by which they might know a prophet truly speaks from God (Deut. 18:19–22). But God's purposes usually lead to the climactic fulfillments of their approximate and iterative expressions. This is as true of his actions of judgment and redemption as it is of the fulfillment of the promises regarding the roles of king and prophet. Understood within this salvation-historical context, Jesus is indeed the climactic fulfillment of the line of prophets that leads from Moses on down through the likes of Nathan, Elijah, Elisha, Isaiah, and Jeremiah. He is *the* Prophet like Moses.[2]

Yet, it is also clear that he is the climactic fulfillment of the promises made to David concerning the line of kings that would come from his progeny (2 Sam. 7:11b–16). Although kings like Solomon, Rehoboam, Josiah, and Hezekiah represent punctuated fulfillments of God's promise, Jesus brings the ideal fulfillment of the Davidic line, exhausting the extravagant language of "sonship" pertaining to David's heirs: "I will be his father, and he will be my son" (2 Sam. 7:14). Consequently, he is the one who ultimately fulfills the Davidic Covenant.

Both of these roles of Jesus are in play when we ask the "What" question. But what is clear is that both God and Jesus *subsume* his prophetic role to his kingly role.

The Great Prophet Who Is the Great King (Matt. 17:1 – 8)

When Jesus is transfigured on the mountain, Moses and Elijah appear with him, obviously representing the prophets. Whereas Moses' face radiated in the aftermath of standing in the presence of God (Ex. 34:29–30), Jesus' face is *transformed*, apparently from within, and even his clothing emanates glory (Matt. 17:2).[3] Then, from the engulfing cloud that likely hearkens back to the cloud that shrouded Sinai when Moses ascended its slopes to meet God (Ex. 19:9, 16–18; 24:15–18) and the subsequent Shekinah glory that descended on the tabernacle signaling God's presence (e.g., Ex. 40:34–38; Lev. 16:2; Num. 9:15–22), the divine voice addresses Peter, James, and John: "This is my Son, whom I love; with him I am well pleased. Listen to him!" (Matt. 17:5).

---

2. See esp. Dale C. Allison Jr., *The New Moses: A Matthean Typology* (Minneapolis: Fortress, 1993). Allison's thesis takes this role of Jesus far beyond that of merely fulfilling the Deut. 18 promise to typologically fulfilling the role of Moses in relation to God's people.

3. For a discussion of the Old Testament allusions reflected in this text, see esp. Davies and Allison, *A Critical and Exegetical Commentary on the Gospel according to Saint Matthew*, 2:693–705.

This pithy statement echoes the divine affirmation at Jesus' baptism in evoking two important Old Testament passages. "This is my Son" alludes to Ps. 2:7, which comes in the middle of a psalm that likely was read on the day a king acceded to the throne: "I will proclaim the LORD's decree: He said to me, 'You are my son; today I have become your father'" (Ps. 2:7). Strengthening these kingly connections, the psalmist himself alludes back to the promises God made to David in 2 Samuel 7:14: "I will be his father, and he will be my son." The words "with him I am well pleased," however, refer to his role as the Servant of the Lord, described in Isaiah 42:1a: "Here is my servant, whom I uphold, my chosen one in whom I delight."

What is *new* here, however, is God's directive: "Listen to him!" This alludes to Deuteronomy 18:15: "The LORD your God will raise up for you a prophet like me from among you, from your own people. You must listen to him." Accordingly, God is identifying Jesus as *the* prophet who ultimately fulfills Moses' prophecy. Accentuated by the departure of the two Old Testament prophets, Jesus' authority to declare God's will is here hailed as greater than that of Moses, Elijah, and the remainder of their ilk. And yet, his prophetic role is placed *within* the scope of Jesus' royal sonship: "This is my Son." Jesus is the great Prophet, but he performs this role as the great Son of David — the King!

> "The present-day church needs once again to discover the absolute authority of the teaching of Jesus. Jesus, as our passage shows, stands in continuity with the revelation of the OT, symbolized by Moses and Elijah, but because of who he is and what he brings (i.e., the kingdom of God, the climax of salvation history), his utterances have a final and incomparable authority. The transfiguration dramatically underlines that fact."[4]

The Son Who Is the Heir (Matt. 21:33 – 41)

Equally telling is Jesus' parable of the tenants. There he likens the prophets to "servants" of the vineyard owner, sent to collect the rent from his antagonistic tenants. Given the prominence of the use of the "vineyard" to represent Israel in the Old Testament (e.g., Isa. 5:1 – 10; cf. Ezek. 17:5 – 10; Hos. 9:10), this reference is likely in view here. The focus, however, is on Israel's religious leaders, to whom has been entrusted the care of the nation. One by one, the vineyard owner (= God) sends his servants (= the prophets) to Israel's leaders throughout the generations. Consistently, however, the tenants refuse to comply with the owners' wishes and abuse the servants, indicating the persistent rejection of the prophetic message. Finally, the owner sends his "son" in the hope of a different result (Matt. 21:37). Tragically, he too is rejected and killed (v. 39).

Placed within the larger context of Jesus' ministry, it is not difficult to perceive Jesus' intentions. Surely he is alluding to himself as the "son," whose purpose in being sent is the same as when the owner sent the servants. As such, Jesus is align-

---

4. Donald A. Hagner, *Matthew 14–28* (WBC 33B; ed. David A. Hubbard, Glenn W. Barker, and Ralph P. Martin; Dallas: Word, 1995), 495.

ing himself with the prophets. But he also sets his prophetic role within his identity as the owner's *son*. Almost certainly, Jesus' use of the "sonship" motif here implies kingship.[5] Jesus confirms this reference by warning the religious leaders through the words of Psalm 118:22 — "The stone the builders rejected has become the cornerstone" (Matt. 21:42) — words best understood in their original context to refer to the Israelite *king*, acting as the representative for the nation.[6] Once again, Jesus' prophetic role is subsumed under his royal identity.

Jesus' Absolute Summons (Luke 18:18 – 23)

These observations set us up for perceiving the significance in Jesus' absolute summons to discipleship. When God established his covenant with the Sinai generation, he made it clear that there was to be no rival to his lordship over their lives — no other gods, no idols, no sinful patterns. It was to be an *exclusive* relationship. Moses reminded the people of this fact again and again, summoning them to obey God and faithfully to follow his decrees: "It is the LORD your God you must follow, and him you must revere. Keep his commands and obey him; serve him and hold fast to him" (Deut. 13:4).[7] And though the people asked Moses to mediate between them and God (Ex. 20:19), Moses persistently exhorts the people to follow *the Lord*. This is the role of the prophet.

It is in this light that Jesus' summons to follow *him* exclusively is striking. Parents (Matt. 8:21 – 22), family members (Luke 14:26 – 27), occupational responsibilities (Matt. 4:18 – 22; Mark 2:14; Luke 5:1 – 11), wealth (Luke 18:18 – 30), and even life itself (Mark 8:34) must play second fiddle compared to one's loyalty to him. This priority goes well beyond that of the prophet. For in the process, Jesus demands the sort of devotion that only a king has the right to demand.

This coheres nicely with Jesus' consistent identification of himself as the Son of Man (e.g., Matt. 26:64), which we have already seen hearkens back to Daniel's vision of a regal figure who is given kingly authority from Yahweh (Dan. 7:13 – 14). When Jesus adds to this his claim before Caiaphas that he is the one who will sit at God's right hand (Matt. 26:64), he is alluding to Psalm 110:1 and its glorious vision for the greater son of David, making his kingly self-identification unmistakable. As such, his demand that people follow him merges with the same demand from Yahweh, Israel's true King.

This identity of demand finds strong confirmation in Jesus' interaction with a wealthy ruler, who comes to inquire regarding the deeds necessary to inherit eternal life (Luke 18:18 – 30). As he does so, the man addresses Jesus as "good teacher." Within the status consciousness of the ancient Near Eastern social system, it is possible that the ruler was lauding Jesus for the purpose of receiving a similarly

5. Cf. 2 Sam. 7:14; Ps. 2:7; see esp. Matt. 22:41 – 45.
6. Cf. Craig Blomberg, "Matthew," in *Commentary on the New Testament Use of the Old Testament* (ed. G. K. Beale and D. A.

Carson; Grand Rapids: Baker, 2007), 73 – 74.
7. Cf. also Deut. 4:1 – 13; 5:1 – 33; 8:1; 15:5; 27:10; 28:1, 15, 58; 30:8; 31:12; Lev. 18:4; 19:37; 20:8, 22; 22:31; 25:18; etc.

impressive response.[8] But Jesus will have nothing of this, responding immediately by reminding him that God alone is good: "'Why do you call me good?' Jesus answered. 'No one is good—except God alone'" (Luke 18:19).

Jesus then answers the man's question, listing various commands from the Decalogue—commands that the man claims to have kept from his youth (Luke 18:21). Rather than disputing this claim, Jesus proceeds to identify the one thing he lacks. He commands him to sell all of his possessions and to give the proceeds to the poor (v. 22b). Last of all, he summons the man to follow him (v. 22c).

A few items are of special significance here. In the first place, it is telling that Jesus only lists for the man commands that pertain to loving *others*. He completely passes over the first four commandments dealing with love for *God*. It is possible that he does this because obedience to these commands is more measurable than in the case of the commands to love God. He then expands the man's understanding of his love for others in demanding the wholesale surrender of his wealth for the benefit of others. Since the law demands that people love others as they do themselves (Lev. 19:18b), Jesus may be seeking to send the message that the man's significant wealth indicates that he has not, in fact, kept all of the commands. This certainly must be in play.

But it may go deeper than that. Jesus' directive to sell everything in the context of his passing over of the first table of the law may also have the goal of identifying the man's love for

Bailey unpacks the social context in which to understand the ruler's interaction with Jesus: "Thus Jesus is best understood as responding to a tendency on the part of the ruler to 'overdo it.' The ruler is trying too hard. He tries to impress with a compliment and perhaps hopes to be greeted with some lofty title in return. In the Oriental world, one compliment requires a second. The ruler starts with 'Good Teacher' and may expect 'Noble Ruler' in response from Jesus."[9]

wealth as the idol that also keeps him from loving *God* with his whole heart. On both accounts, then, Jesus is demonstrating to the man the impossibility of meeting the all-encompassing demand of the law so as to inherit eternal life. To this point in the narrative, Jesus is filling the role of the prophet.

If this is on target, it is significant that Jesus pairs the command to the ruler to sell his belongings with the summons to follow him. In this context, Jesus' invitation suggestively implies that the man will fulfill what it means to love God with all of his heart in the context of discipleship to *him*. Jesus, in other words, does more than fulfill the prophet's role in *declaring* the will of God to this man. Rather, his summons expresses his implicit claim to embody God's will so intimately that following him will be the equivalent of loving God.[10]

Consequently, Jesus' mild rebuke at the outset of the conversation invites a double take. On the first read, it appears that Jesus is distancing himself from God as he

---

8. Kenneth E. Bailey, *Through Peasant Eyes*, in *Poet & Peasant and Through Peasant Eyes: A Literary-Cultural Approach to the Parables in Luke* (comb. ed.; Grand Rapids: Eerdmans, 1976), 162.

9. Ibid., 162.
10. See also ibid., 163.

scolds the man for using the adjective "good" for anyone but God alone. But when he calls the man to follow him in the context of loving God above all else, Jesus' reprimand likely implies that the man's show of respect toward Jesus was actually too *low*. Addressing Jesus as "good" will only be appropriate if it is used with the same weight as when it applies to God. That is because following Jesus absolutely amounts to loving God above all other things.

JESUS' SUMMONS TO KINGDOM DISCIPLESHIP
The King after God's Own Heart

How does all of this fit into the covenantal flow that we have been tracing? You will recall the ideal reality pertaining to the king's relationship with God was that of a son to a father (2 Sam. 7:14a; Ps. 2:7). Implied by this metaphor are notions of intimacy, devotion, and obedience, sustained by daily meditation on the law (Deut. 17:18–20; Pss. 1:1–3; 19:7–14; 119). Such a king would reign faithfully in the place of Yahweh, making God's will known through his embodiment of God's just and merciful nature. Sadly, the historical reality of the kings' history was anything but this. Israel's and Judah's rulers all too frequently abandoned the covenant, leading to the exile of the nation and the temporary fall of David's house.

But God promised David an *eternal* dynasty (2 Sam. 7:11–14). If this was to become a reality, a king would have to arise one day who would consistently reign in harmony with God, so that the curses of the covenant would no longer threaten the nation (Deut. 17:20b) or the royal line. Such a king would walk faithfully with God and lead his people into faithfulness. Jeremiah's description of this king bears repeating here:

> "The days are coming," declares the LORD,
>   "when I will raise up for David a righteous Branch,
> a King who will reign wisely
>   and do what is just and right in the land.
> In his days Judah will be saved
>   and Israel will live in safety.
> This is the name by which he will be called:
>   The LORD Our Righteous Savior." (Jer. 23:5–6; cf. Isa. 9:6–7; 16:5;
>   32:1–2; Ezek. 37:21–26)

When that king comes, God will finally have the great fulfillment of the ideal that David only foreshadows. God will have a man "after his own heart" on the throne (1 Sam. 13:14), who will lead the people in righteousness and faithfulness to the law:

My servant David will be king over them, and they will all have one shepherd. They will follow my laws and be careful to keep my decrees. (Ezek. 37:24)

It is not too big of a jump to see the appropriateness of such a king summoning his people to follow him as one would follow God.

Jesus' demand of righteousness and all-encompassing discipleship must be encountered in this framework. Since he is the one who knows the Father uniquely and has received the singular authority to make him known to others (Matt. 11:27–28), he is the only one who faithfully reveals God's character.[11] He is indeed the great Prophet who fulfills the prophetic ideal (Deut. 18:15–18). But while he authoritatively declares the will of God, he also commands his hearers to follow him as the embodiment of God's kingly reign over them. He is indeed the Prophet, but his prophetic cloak is worn under his royal mantel, as was David's before him (Acts 2:30).

Obeying the King's Demands

As David's great heir who reigns faithfully as Yahweh's Anointed King, then, Jesus appropriately summons us to an *absolute* discipleship. And we dare not blunt the sharp edges of this demand. Recalling the vision of the New Covenant people who will bind themselves to the Lord in a covenant that will not be forgotten (Jer. 50:5), Jesus musters us to a discipleship that holds to him as we would hold to God. Such a discipleship brooks no rivals (Luke 14:26), permits no turning back (14:27–35), and takes precedence even over life itself (Matt. 10:38; 16:24).

But what exactly does this look like? Even a cursory read of the Gospels will reveal Jesus' preference for the notion of the "kingdom."[12] Fundamentally, Jesus means by this term the exercise of God's kingly rule—the exertion of his royal dominion. Wherever a king exercises this kind of power, the result is that his character is made manifest in that territory. That is to say, his *realm* displays the contours of his nature. As we have seen, this explains the covenantal demand that God places on the people whom he delivered and set apart for his very own. As their King, he demands that they submit to his reign by reflecting his attributes, making known his nature to the surrounding nations. Unfortunately, this ideal was never fully realized in the history of Israel—indeed, in the history of the human race.

But when Jesus announces that the kingdom of God has arrived in his ministry, he is claiming that God is exercising his kingly power, transforming the world to reflect his character. Zechariah had prophesied that one day, "the LORD will be king over the whole earth. On that day there will be one LORD, and his name the only name" (Zech. 14:9). Jesus is declaring that that day has arrived in his ministry. Those who follow him come under his kingly reign and enter the kingdom,[13] even though

---

11. Cf. Matt. 11:27; John 1:14, 18; 12:45; 14:9–10; 2 Cor. 4:4; Col. 1:15; Heb. 1:3.
12. E.g., Matt. 4:17, 23; 6:10; 9:35; 10:7; 11:12; 12:28; 13:1–52; 24:14; and parallels.
13. Matt. 5:3, 10; 18:3; 19:23; 21:31; cf. Matt. 19:14; Mark 12:34.

a reference to the future consummation of his reign is preserved.[14] Jesus therefore summarizes his discipleship command in this way: "seek first his kingdom and his righteousness" (Matt. 6:33). In the larger context of his teachings and claims, this is an invitation to submit to his ruling authority and to emulate his righteous character.

Obeying Jesus' Fulfillment of the Law

Lest this remain fuzzy and undefined, Jesus fulfills his prophetic role by articulating the specific nature of this discipleship by authoritatively teaching the fulfillment of the law. In chapter 4, we learned that Jesus takes care to explain that he is not abolishing the law or the prophets (Matt. 5:17). Such is impossible, Jesus affirms, since the law's permanence — down to the smallest letter (Gr. *iōta*, which may refer to the smallest Hebrew letter) or even portions of letters (Gr. *keraia*, which likely refers to projections of Hebrew letters) — mirrors the duration of the heavens and the earth (v. 18). Rather than abolishing the law or its prophetic advocates, Jesus claims he has come to "fulfill" them (v. 17).

"In Jesus, God has become present among men and redemptively active. In its dynamic meaning, the Kingdom of God is God himself, not merely ruling in the universe but actively establishing his rule among men."[15]

In the light of how he interacts with individual commands in the succeeding verses (Matt. 5:21 – 48), we will see that Jesus is best understood here to be bringing to final expression the law and the prophetic articulations of its message. Instead of *diminishing* the law's requirement of righteousness for his disciples, Jesus exhorts wholehearted commitment to *all* of its demands (v. 19). Indeed, he warns that those who enter the kingdom of heaven will be characterized by a righteousness that exceeds that which was exemplified by the scribes and Pharisees (v. 20). As his teaching in vv. 21 – 48 reveals, Jesus considers the interpretations and practices of those religious leaders to be superficial and inadequate.

Jesus' summons, therefore, is to a robust obedience to the law as he authoritatively mediates it to his New Covenant disciples. But since he is also the great King who embodies this demand in God's stead, he calls us to follow *him* absolutely. We might update our diagram in light of these observations in this way:

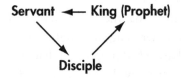

As I noted previously, to answer the "What" question fully would require us to discuss *each* of Jesus' commands, as well as the remainder of the New Testament teaching

---

14. Matt. 5:20; 7:21; 8:11; 13:43; 25:34; 26:29.

15. George Eldon Ladd, *The Presence of the Future: The Eschatol-* *ogy of Biblical Realism* (Grand Rapids: Eerdmans, 1974), 145.

on the topic. This goes well beyond the space we have available here. More complete treatments are available.[16] What I am concerned to accomplish in this section is to consider a sampling of Jesus' interactions with the law so as to get a glimpse of the ways in which he mediates the covenantal demands to his disciples. We will discover that the more things change with the covenants, the more things remain the same.

SUMMARY

When we begin to ask the "What" question, we are thrown into the context of Jesus' roles of Prophet and King. We have seen that Jesus surely is the culmination of the line of prophets announced by Moses (Deut. 18:18–19). But both Jesus and the gospel writers *subsume* this role to his identity as the King, as he fulfills the prophetic expectations of an ideal ruler expressed in the Davidic Covenant, reigning as God's true Son over his people.

As the fulfillment of these expectations, Jesus authoritatively articulates the will of Yahweh as the Prophet who carries the authority to mediate the final expression of the law to his people. But he also summons people to follow him absolutely as the King, who faithfully represents Yahweh's righteous reign. Jesus' disciples follow him as their King, even as he articulates God's demand as the great Prophet. Let's turn to a closer consideration of these demands as we continue asking the "What" question.

RELEVANT QUESTIONS

1. Bearing in mind that centuries of time elapsed as people awaited the arrival of the Prophet like Moses and the King like David, do you feel the enormity of your privilege to live on this side of Jesus' ministry and to know him as the Gospels present him? How might you allow that privilege to impact you on a more regular basis?

2. How does your perception of Jesus change as you begin to view him as the Prophet whose authority to articulate the demands of God outstrips that of Moses?

3. Do you think that Christians today find it uncomfortable to interact with Jesus as their high King? Is it awkward to envision Jesus standing before you as your King, demanding absolute obedience to his commands? If so, why do you think that is the case?

4. Are you beginning to understand what it means to live in God's kingdom today? How is this different from what most people today envision by the term *Christian*?

---

16. See Piper, *What Jesus Demands from the World.*

CHAPTER 7

JESUS,
THE "FILTER"

"Their sins and lawless acts I will remember no more." And where these have been forgiven, sacrifice for sin is no longer necessary.

Hebrews 10:17–18

So I say, walk by the Spirit, and you will not gratify the desires of the sinful nature. For the sinful nature desires what is contrary to the Spirit, and the Spirit what is contrary to the sinful nature.... But if you are led by the Spirit, you are not under the law.

Galatians 5:16–18

There is a sense in which my parents and my wife's parents are parenting my sons. This is the case even though the only times our sons have been in their grandparents' homes have been during occasional visits on family vacations. But the influence that our parents have had on the shaping of our sons is immense. That is because there are countless ways in which our own approach to parenting is reminiscent of the ways in which our parents reared us. Since Pam and I eventually came to embrace the Christian worldview and the ethical standards that our parents sought to instill in us, we interact with our own children in countless ways that are similar to how our parents trained us.

That is not to say that our parenting is *identical* in every instance. There are times when our guidance on particular moral issues is more pointed and developed than what we received. Many things have changed since we were children, so the specifics of the behaviors that we yearn to see in our children are sometimes more carefully defined than what our parents required of us. In other matters, our parenting may appear to have let go of some things that were really important in the past. The culture has changed, and along with it have certain contextualized expressions of Christian behavior.

Does that mean we are no longer concerned with the same fundamental issues as our parents were? No. It means rather that we are addressing them in different cultural expressions than did our parents. Even with these modifications, however, it remains essentially true that our parents are participating in the parenting of our children. But their instruction and discipline are being *mediated* through us in a new era.

In certain ways, my sons' relationship to their grandparents' instruction is similar to the Christian's relationship to the law. While the law impacts our morality and worldview in massive ways, this influence is not *immediate*. Rather, it is mediated to us *through* Jesus' teachings. We have learned that one of the great blessings of the New Covenant era is the writing of the law on the hearts and minds of God's covenant people. Should we interpret that to mean that we are still under the law and obligated to fulfill each command as if there were no shift in covenant? No, not at all. As we have seen, this is because Jesus claims that he is *fulfilling* the law (Matt. 5:17). The implication of this is that however the law may affect us, it does so *through* Jesus.

As I discussed in chapter 3, the New Testament's portrayal of Jesus' fulfillment of the law includes the provision of the climactic atoning sacrifice for sin (e.g., Rom. 3:24–25). It is also true that Jesus himself lives out the demands of the law on our behalf (e.g., 8:3). These aspects are vital to this discussion. But Jesus' claim in Matthew 5:17 goes beyond these notions to refer to his prophetic role of *articulating* the law's end-time expression (5:21–48). Therefore, when we ask the "What" question, each of these three notions of fulfillment comes into play, for we are necessarily entering into the discussion of how the law is mediated to us through Jesus.

But this process is not as easy to answer as we might initially assume. Since Jesus fulfills the law in diverse ways, we must not paint using a broad brush and only one color in asserting that his fulfillment does merely *one* thing to the law. As is the case with our mediation of our parents' instructions, certain things are preserved, others are sharpened, and still others are sloughed off, yet endure in different ways. Accordingly, we need to take a careful look at examples of the various ways in which Jesus fulfills the law to discern this diversity.

Doing this exhaustively would require a large tome focused on this issue alone. We only have a few chapters here to introduce the topic. Thus, we need to be selective, focusing on specific passages so as to provide hints regarding how other aspects might also be interpreted. To accomplish this, I will use three metaphors (each of which relates to "light") to characterize the distinct ways in which Jesus has brought the law to its fulfillment. Some requirements become obsolete and are transformed, others are recovered and explained, and still others are elevated.

The complexity of Jesus' interaction with the law certainly implies that additional metaphors could be employed. These are not exhaustive. In addition, there are times when Jesus' teaching straddles the boundaries of more than one category. Still, we will find these three metaphors helpful as an organizing rubric by which we might begin to grasp how the law comes to us as his disciples, and therefore what Jesus is demanding of us.

JESUS' FULFILLMENT AS "FILTER"

Recently when I was using a pair of sunglasses to illustrate for my students how a filter affects light, a bright science major raised her hand to explain how sunglasses work. She talked of such things as "polarization," "ultraviolet wave frequencies," and the like. Essentially, she explained that good sunglasses have grids and coatings that block certain damaging frequencies of light, while permitting nondamaging frequencies to pass through the lenses to our eyes. It was an "enlightening" explanation!

When we speak of Jesus functioning as a "filter" in relation to the law, a similar reality is being suggested. That is, the nature of Jesus' fulfillment of the law at times brings certain things to their *culmination*, rendering the continuation of their practice inappropriate. Our metaphor breaks down at this point, of course, since those things that are discontinued in Jesus' fulfillment should never be considered harmful or wrong! But the reality remains that the fulfillment brought by Jesus has *blocked* certain aspects of the law from passing through to his disciples. Their practice has now become obsolete, even though their significance is permitted to pass through to the New Covenant era.

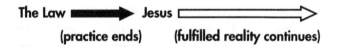

The Law ➤ Jesus ⇒
(practice ends)   (fulfilled reality continues)

Accordingly, for each aspect of the law under consideration, we will look first of all to Jesus' fulfillment of that aspect, and then consider its ongoing significance—its covenantal demand for the disciple of Jesus.

As will become evident, the New Testament explicitly applies this role of Jesus to only a few aspects of the law, even though many Christians interpret some of Paul's comments—such as, "you are not under the law, but under grace" (Rom. 6:14b)—to imply that the *entirety* of the law and its significance has been blocked by Jesus. Our discussion in the succeeding chapters will demonstrate that this is far from the truth.

The Law's Atoning Sacrifices (Matt. 26:17–29; Heb. 7–10)

The Gracious Fulfillment

We learned in chapter 3 that during his last meal with his disciples, Jesus implicitly presents himself as the fulfillment of the Passover lamb. Picking up elements of the meal, Jesus declares that the bread is to be identified with *his* body and the cup with *his* blood. But Jesus goes even beyond the Passover in endowing his death with atoning potency for the forgiveness of sins (Matt. 26:26–28). In this act, brimming with far-reaching implications for the temple, Jesus asserts his claim to be providing what the Passover lamb had come to signify and foreshadow—God's climactic deliverance of his people. What is important here is that Jesus presents himself as the atoning sacrifice *apart* from the provision mediated through the temple.[1]

Though the theological significance of this event took a while to settle out, by the time the writer to the Hebrews pens his letter, things have become clear. By virtue of offering himself as the sinless sacrifice (Heb. 7:26–27), Jesus establishes the New Covenant prophesied by Jeremiah (8:7–12), fulfilling both the Passover lamb and the atoning sacrifices of the Mosaic Covenant so as to render them obsolete (8:13; 10:8–18). Since Jesus has now provided the culminating atoning sacrifice by which God will no longer remember sins, "sacrifice for sin is no longer necessary" (10:18b).[2]

Jesus himself anticipates this conclusion by his allusive words after his clearing of the temple courts. When challenged regarding his authority to do such a thing, he replies, "Destroy this temple, and I will raise it again in three days" (John 2:19). John explains Jesus' reference to be that of his own body (v. 21), but the replacement implications are suggestive. By making this statement in the temple courts, Jesus ties his body to the nearby physical temple, whose continuation is now gravely in doubt.

Three of the gospel writers preserve Jesus' allusion to Jeremiah 7:11 as he explains his motivation for his temple tirade: "but you are making it 'a den of robbers'" (Matt. 21:13b; Mark 11:17; Luke 19:46). In its original context, Jeremiah rails against his contemporaries for the ways in which their day-to-day lives betray their misuse of the temple—as if they could go on living immorally, but then repeatedly run back to the temple for protection the way thieves retreat to their hideout (see Jer. 7:1–11). Such mockery of the covenant will not be countenanced, declares Jeremiah. No, the destruction that consumed Shiloh (v. 12), the place where the tabernacle once stood, will soon happen to Solomon's temple (vv. 14–15). Six centuries later, Jesus' use of Jeremiah's indictment implicitly indicates that history will again repeat itself, as God reenacts the covenantal curses.

By establishing this connection, Jesus ties his own death to the impending destruction of the temple. But the relationship here is one of ironic fulfillment. That is, by rejecting and killing Jesus, the Jews would reject the institution that had stood for centuries as a pointer to Jesus. The destruction of the temple would then be assured,[3] giving way to the temple's fulfillment in Jesus' resurrection body! Similarly, by crucifying Jesus, the Jews would bring about the very sacrifice that would make those offered in the temple *obsolete*—Jesus' sacrifice was once for all!

This is Jesus' role as the "filter," rendering the ongoing observance of the Levitical laws pertaining to sacrifices completely inappropriate—even heretical! The result, of course, is the absence of any additional atoning sacrifices in Christian practice. To insist on the continuation of the sacrifices of the Mosaic Covenant

---

1. A similar implication comes through Jesus' fulfillment of Isaiah's Servant of the Lord, as we have seen.

2. For a helpful word-study-based examination of the concept of "atonement" in the Scriptures, see Leon Morris, *The Apostolic*

Preaching of the Cross (3rd ed.; Grand Rapids: Eerdmans, 1965).

3. See Jesus' escalating threats of judgment, both against Jerusalem as a whole and against the temple in particular, in Matt. 21:38–44; 22:1–7; 23:37–38; 24:1–2, 15–21; Luke 19:41–44.

would imply a return to that covenant, along with its conditionality. But, as I suggested in chapter 5, the sacrifices of that covenant are now of no benefit, since Jesus' curse-bearing fulfillment has rendered their function obsolete.

"Therefore it is the human body of Jesus that uniquely manifests the Father, and becomes the focal point of the manifestation of God to man, the living abode of God on earth, the fulfillment of all the temple meant, and the centre of all true worship.... In this 'temple' the ultimate sacrifice would take place; within three days of death and burial, Jesus Christ, the true temple, would rise from the dead."[4]

This does not mean that Leviticus ceases to be relevant for the Christian, however. Something is still allowed through. One aspect of this is the role of Leviticus as an ongoing pointer to the significance of Jesus' death, even in the New Covenant era! That is to say, "until everything is accomplished" (Matt. 5:18), Leviticus will stand as an explanatory witness to its fulfillment in Jesus' crucifixion, communicating the unyielding holiness of God, the dire gravity of sin, and the inescapable need of atonement. Since neither "the smallest letter" nor "the least stroke of a pen" will "disappear from the Law" (Matt. 5:18), even Leviticus continues to declare authoritative truth about Jesus.[5]

The Covenantal Demand

Since Jesus fulfills this element of the Mosaic Covenant, is there any demand that passes into the New Covenant era? We could answer that question in the affirmative by simply noting Jesus' expectation that his followers would remember his self-sacrifice through their repetition of the Lord's Supper: "do this in remembrance of me" (Luke 22:19c). It is obvious that the early church responded faithfully to this command, regularly repeating this meal (Acts 3:42; 20:7; 1 Cor. 10:14–22; 11:17–34). But since Jesus is consciously fulfilling Old Testament sacrificial institutions, he is certainly also expecting from his disciples the behaviors appropriate for the beneficiaries of those sacrifices.

Surely, then, Jesus is implicitly calling for repentance and confession of sin by those who come to the meal that proclaims his atoning death. Those who received forgiveness through the sacrifices offered at the temple did so with repentant hearts. Lacking this, no atonement was granted. Hosea, for instance, declares, "For I desire mercy, not sacrifice, and acknowledgment of God rather than burnt offerings" (Hos. 6:6). The Lord decries his people's lack of repentance through Amos, even as they continue practicing the formal rituals of the sacrificial cult:

Go to Bethel and sin;
　go to Gilgal and sin yet more....
I gave you empty stomachs in every city
　and lack of bread in every town,
　yet you have not returned to me. (Amos 4:4a, 6)[6]

4. D. A. Carson, *The Gospel according to John* (Grand Rapids: Eerdmans, 1991), 182; so also C. K. Barrett, *The Gospel according to St. John* (2nd ed.; Philadelphia: Westminster, 1978), 201.

5. I was first exposed to this approach to the ongoing relevance of Leviticus and similarly fulfilled portions of the Old Testament through the able instruction of D. A. Carson.

6. Cf. also Amos 5:21–24; Mic. 6:6–8; cf. 1 Sam. 15:22–23; Isa. 1:11–17; Jer. 7:21–23.

Given this background and Jesus' frequent calls for repentance on the part of people who observed the graciousness of his kingdom ministry (Matt. 11:20–24; cf. 4:17; Mark 6:12; Luke 13:3–5), it is unthinkable to suggest that repentance would not accompany the highest expression of that grace. Anyone who understands the origins of the American holiday known as Thanksgiving does not need to be told what posture of the heart *ought* to be true of those who enter into that celebration. Some things do not need to be said since they are assumed by the cultural context. Consequently, although Jesus does not explicitly demand that his followers enter into their reenactments of his Last Supper with repentance, this must have been his expectation. Indeed, the Passover celebration was itself followed immediately by the week-long Feast of Unleavened Bread (Ex. 12:17–20), which involved the careful removal of all leaven from their homes—a practice that eventually took on moral overtones.

For many Christians, communion has become something of a perfunctory, occasional addition to the Sunday service. For many others who celebrate it weekly, it has become a routine ritual without impact. But coming to grips with its significance as the celebration of the sacrifice by which God's ultimate deliverance is provided should move us to deep expressions of repentance. Paul's exhortation to the Corinthians to engage in self-reflection so as not to eat the meal "in an unworthy manner" (1 Cor. 11:27–29) confirms this perspective. To participate in the Lord's Supper without this is to repeat the error of Israel in the past, when they partook of the temple sacrifices with unrepentant hearts.

For this reason, those who come to the Lord's table are implicitly summoned to a life of repentant righteousness. Paul also confirms this when he uses Passover imagery to exhort the church to rebuke and remove a grossly sinning brother from their fellowship: "Get rid of the old yeast, so that you may be a new unleavened batch— as you really are. For Christ, our Passover lamb, has been sacrificed" (1 Cor. 5:7).[7] Drawing on the Jewish practice of removing sin-referring leaven from their homes, Paul exhorts a similar elimination from the Corinthian assembly.[8] This removal of the old yeast, then, ought to be the response of all Christians to Jesus' death as the fulfillment of the temple sacrifices (cf. also Rom. 6:11–13).

---

7. Thistleton (citing C. L. Mitton, *The Gospel according to St. Mark* [London: Epworth, 1957], 61) notes the ancient practice of holding over a piece of dough from the previous week's baking so as to instigate the leavening process in a fresh batch. Though useful, this practice also invited the carryover of disease and dirt from one week to the next. Once a year, therefore, Jews would start all over with fresh yeast in a new lump of dough. "Hence the influence of a small amount of material carried over from the past was eradicated, and a new beginning took place" (*The First Epistle to the Corinthians: A Commentary on the Greek Text* (NIGTC; ed. I. Howard Marshall and Donald A. Hagner; Grand Rapids: Eerdmans, 2000], 401). It is easy to see how this analogously points to the break with past patterns of sin.

8. Several commentators interpret Paul's use of "yeast" to refer to the sinful man who must be removed (cf. 1 Cor. 5:13; so Thistle-ton, *The First Epistle to the Corinthians*, 388; Gordon D. Fee, *The First Epistle to the Corinthians*, NICNT [Grand Rapids: Eerdmans, 1987], 216). This is strengthened by the explicit command to remain separate from those who would claim faith in Christ but whose lives are inconsistent with that profession (vv. 9–11). An alternative view understands Paul to be referring rather to the Corinthians' pride in tolerating this man in their midst (cf. 1 Cor. 5:2, "And you are proud!"). This view is strengthened by Paul's preceding comment, "your boasting is not good." It is this that must be expelled. By removing the sinful man from their fellowship, the Corinthians will be ridding themselves of the cause of their boasting. Viewed in this way, the church's repentance becomes even more forceful (see Verlyn Verbrugge, "First Corinthians," in *Romans–Galatians* [EBC, rev. ed.; ed. Tremper Longman III and David E. Garland; Grand Rapids: Zondervan, 2008], 11:302–3).

In Jeremiah's New Covenant text, the grounding for the people's pervasive knowledge of God and their covenantal faithfulness appears to be the new act of atonement on their behalf. Notice the logical connection between the internalized blessings of God's New Covenant work and his forgiveness:

> "No longer will they teach their neighbors,
>   or say to one another, 'Know the LORD,'
> because they will all know me,
>   from the least of them to the greatest,"
>   declares the LORD.
> "*For* I will forgive their wickedness
>   and will remember their sins no more." (Jer. 31:34; emphasis mine)

Thus, God's climactic work of atonement is the basis for this New Covenant intimacy. In the wake of Jesus' consummating fulfillment of this promise, how can disciples of Jesus respond in any other way than repent, leading to the offering of themselves to God as "living sacrifices" (Rom. 12:1)?

The Food Laws (Mark 7:1 – 23)
The Gracious Fulfillment

As early as the second century BC, some Jewish groups were voluntarily applying to themselves the ritual cleansing requirements governing the priests who ministered before the Lord in the tabernacle or temple (Ex. 30:17–21; cf. 40:13). The Pharisees of Jesus' day (along with the Qumran community) were the preservers of this perspective, fastidiously washing their hands before morning prayers and meals.[9] In their concern to deepen the people's fidelity to the law, the Pharisees' agenda included extending the priestly purity laws to the entire nation. Accordingly, they were likely seeking to foster the sort of purity expected of the remnant returned from the exile (cf. Ezek. 36:25). It is for this reason, that the Pharisees confront Jesus when they observe his disciples' neglect of ritual purity:

> So the Pharisees and teachers of the law asked Jesus, "Why don't your disciples live according to the tradition of the elders instead of eating their food with defiled hands?" (Mark 7:5)

Jesus responds to this complaint in two ways. He first of all indicts their traditions as actually working against the fulfillment of the demand of righteousness:

> "You have let go of the commands of God and are holding on to human traditions."
> And he continued, "You have a fine way of setting aside the commands of God in order to observe your own traditions!" (Mark 7:8–9)

---

9. William Lane, *The Gospel according to Mark: The English Text with Introduction, Exposition, and Notes* (NICNT; Grand Rapids: Eerdmans, 1974), 245–46.

It is important to remember that the Pharisees' standards regarding the washing of hands were grounded not in the law but in their traditions, as they voluntarily extended the priestly obligations to themselves. Jesus' point is that the Pharisees' fixation on their traditions was diverting attention away from the important things. Rather than being concerned with merely external cleansing, they ought to be consumed with internal purity toward God. Unfortunately, as they focused on the external, they lost the internal.

"In the outward appearance of their piety the Pharisees were impeccable since they scrupulously observed numerous prescriptions and commandments. It was, nevertheless, a lie because they had not surrendered themselves to God."[10]

To dramatize this, Jesus appeals to Isaiah's condemnation of his own generation, who majored on external religious expression while neglecting the heart submission to God:

He replied, "Isaiah was right when he prophesied about you hypocrites; as it is written:

" 'These people honor me with their lips,
    but their hearts are far from me.
They worship me in vain;
    their teachings are but merely human rules.' " (Mark 7:6–7; citing Isa. 29:13)

Since the people were neglecting to love God with all of their hearts, Isaiah declares that their religious activities were odious to God. Similarly, Jesus rebukes the Pharisees for ironically neglecting God's command by holding to their traditions that were intended to assure the fulfillment of the law. Unfortunately, the heart of the law was being lost.

To this point in the narrative, Jesus has merely stripped away traditional interpretations, functioning in the role of "lens"—a role I will develop more fully in the next chapter. But then Jesus goes beyond this, rejecting the possibility of becoming defiled by *anything* that enters into a person (Mark 7:15, 18–19). What truly defiles, Jesus says, is what comes *out* of the person:

Corban was a technical priestly term denoting an offering made to God. If a man wanted to eliminate the possibility of his parents gaining benefit from his financial means, this tradition allowed the man to place a ban on his money, removing it from any use by his parents and reserving it for sacred use. If the son had a change of mind and wanted to remove this ban, the priests held him to his vow and would not allow him to do anything for them. In this way, obedience to the Pharisees' traditions actually enabled disobedience to the law's commandment to honor one's parents.[11]

For from within, out of your hearts, come evil thoughts, sexual immorality, theft, murder, adultery, greed, malice, deceit, lewdness, envy, slander, arrogance and folly. All these evils come from inside and defile you. (Mark 7:21–23)

10. Ibid., 248.
11. *Corban* placed a character of an "offering" on something, exemplified by this inscription found on an ancient ossuary (bone box): "All that a man may find-to-his-profit in this ossuary (is) an offering to God from him who is within it" (cited in Lane, *Mark*, 250–51).

Jesus thereby implies that observing the external purity requirements of the law *itself* will not necessarily result in true purity. Avoiding defilement requires something more than merely the external observance of clean and unclean foods. Seeking to ensure understanding on the part of his readers, Mark inserts at this point his parenthetical comment regarding the significance of Jesus' statement: "In saying this, Jesus declared all foods clean" (Mark 7:19b).[12] Thus interpreted, Jesus here impugns the ongoing legitimacy of the food laws themselves. With but one swipe, Jesus nullifies a large and influential swath of the Mosaic legislation (Lev. 11:1–23; Deut. 14:3–21). How is Jesus' interpretive method to be understood?[13]

As we have seen, Jesus' fundamental relationship with the law is one of fulfillment (Matt. 5:17). Therefore it will not do to interpret his statements here as simply Jesus' arbitrary disparagement of this portion of the law. Unfortunately, however, nothing in this immediate context offers us any illuminating light into his rationale. Consequently, to discern what Jesus is doing, we must pull together strands of his teaching and ministry from elsewhere.

Jesus surely seems to be suggesting that preeminent among the purposes of the food laws is their role of reminding the people to be set apart to God from the heart. Every day, with every bite of food, Jews under the Mosaic Covenant were reminded to think covenantally to remember who they were in relation to the God who had created, called, and redeemed them. The recurring question, "Is this food clean or unclean?" at least potentially would summon people to faithfulness to God—a faithfulness that would be expressed in their reflection of his character in their lives. Thus, Jesus' identification of the things that defile a person from within does not amount to a *disparagement* of the food laws, but the identification of their *goal*!

So why does Jesus abrogate them? Whatever else might be said in this regard, the answer must surely be found within the context of Jesus' awareness that he is bringing the kingdom and the end-time expression of the law.[14] In his teaching, the fulfillment of the law has come. With this also is coming the New Covenant reality, including the inner transformation of the people through the Spirit (e.g., John 3:3–8; cf. Ezek. 36:26–27). Accordingly, though the Spirit would not be poured out until after Jesus' resurrection and departure (John 14:15–31; Acts 2:1–21), Jesus seems to be referring to the Spirit's ministry here, which would replace the external food laws in calling the people to inner purity. Jesus' teaching, therefore, turns on his awareness of his New Covenant ministry, by which he is indicating

12. Note that this is lacking in Matthew's version—see Matt. 15:16–20. This is obviously the perspective of later clarity, for Jesus' allusive statement surely was not sufficient for the early Christians to settle the matter of the food laws without some discussion, as Acts informs us (cf. Acts 15:28–29).

13. The discernment of the rationale and organizing principles governing the area of "clean and unclean" foods and practices in ancient Hebrew religion is an area of great complexity and easily eclipses our purpose here. For a helpful overview, see W. J. Houston, "Foods, Clean and Unclean," *DOTP*, 326–36.

14. So C. E. B. Cranfield, *The Gospel according to St. Mark* (CGTC; ed. C. F. D. Moule; Cambridge: Cambridge Univ. Press, 1959), 244–45.

the true purpose of the purity laws and the replacement of their function by the soon-coming Spirit.[15]

The Covenantal Demand

What, then, does Jesus expect of his followers here? Given these implications of the New Covenant era, Jesus is demanding the righteousness foretold by the prophets, when the law will be written on the hearts of the people and the Spirit will enable them to purity from within. Whereas under the previous covenant, the possibility existed that the external could become separated from its corresponding internal reality, in the New Covenant ministry of the Spirit, this apparently will not take place. Consequently, the precursors to the Spirit's work in calling forth this inner righteousness have been fulfilled and set aside. Jesus would certainly have agreed with Paul's exhortation, "let us keep in step with the Spirit" (Gal. 5:25).

As a result, the continuing observance of the food laws has been "filtered" out by virtue of their fulfillment by the internalization of the law and the Spirit's ministry. Retaining the food laws as a demand within the New Covenant would therefore deny the reality of the covenantal shift that has come through Jesus and would obscure the enabling and transforming work of the Spirit. And yet, the food laws remain valid as authoritative pointers to the fulfillment that has come through Jesus. As in the ideal of the Mosaic Covenant, gauging purity must extend past external observances to the very thoughts and intentions of the heart.

Could it be said of contemporary Christians that we are less concerned with inner purity than were our Old Testament forebears? Such certainly would be shocking, given the nature of the enabling fulfillment that has come through Jesus. In light of this, might it not be appropriate for us to spend time mulling over the food laws, remembering their purpose and reflecting on the nature of their fulfillment? Should we not respond to our culinary freedom by reflecting on what we ought now to have as our focus — the fulfillment of the food laws through the Spirit's work of convicting sin and enabling righteousness? It is significant that Paul's lists of works of the flesh are similar to Jesus' list of defiling actions in Mark 7:

> The acts of the sinful nature are obvious: sexual immorality, impurity and debauchery; idolatry and witchcraft; hatred, discord, jealousy, fits of rage, selfish ambition, dissensions, factions and envy; drunkenness, orgies, and the like. (Gal. 5:19–21; also Eph. 5:3–7; cf. Mark 7:21–22)

As Paul reminds us, "anyone [who] does not have the Spirit of Christ" — and therefore bears the fruit of the Spirit — does "not belong to Christ" (Rom. 8:9).

15. The ending of the food laws is similarly implied by the heavenly voice in Acts 10:11–16, instructing Peter to kill and eat animals previously forbidden to Jews under the Mosaic food laws. As the narrative unfolds, Peter realizes that the ultimate point of the vision has to do with the inclusion of Gentiles into the people of God without their conversion to Judaism (10:28, 34–48). But this also indicates a change in the covenantal framework governing the people of God — a shift that includes the cessation of the purity laws. This is later confirmed by the gathered church in Acts 15:4–21, even though James' letter exhorts converting Gentiles to conduct themselves according to a bare minimum of cultic purity to minimize offense among the Jewish Christians.

Jesus' implicit command is then made explicit by Paul's exhortation to a life in the Spirit that produces different fruit:

> But the fruit of the Spirit is love, joy, peace, patience, kindness, goodness, faithfulness, gentleness and self-control. Against such things there is no law. Those who belong to Christ Jesus have crucified the sinful nature with its passions and desires. (Gal. 5:22–24)

Circumcision (Rom. 2:25–28; Col. 2:11–12; etc.)
The Gracious Fulfillment

The Gospels preserve no explicit word from Jesus on the topic of circumcision. Considering the enormity of the controversy that eventually arose in the churches surrounding this issue, this silence surely indicates the reticence of the first generation Christian community to supplement Jesus' teachings with later ecclesial doctrine. Even though no word from Jesus regarding circumcision is preserved, however, it is clear from his focus on the "heart" as the source of good and evil in the person that the trajectory of his teaching points directly at the fulfillment of circumcision. It is, therefore, important that we address this topic here since this is one of the most important aspects of the law that are "filtered out."

We learned in chapter 4 that circumcision was instituted by God in his second covenant with Abraham. There God commanded the patriarch and his descendants to circumcise each of their sons and any foreigner who came into their households (Gen. 17:9–14; cf. Lev. 12:3). Integral to this covenant, which is directly connected to God's promise to bless all nations (Gen. 17:3–6, 16; 22:18; cf. 12:3), God clarified that this blessing would be passed on to those who followed in Abraham's instruction to "keep the way of the LORD by doing what is right and just" (18:19). From the beginning, then, external circumcision was intended to remind those in the covenant to follow in Abraham's footsteps of faith (22:8) and obedience (22:16–18).

This external/internal circumcision relationship shows up again in various Old Testament contexts, anticipating the time when the divine intention symbolized by circumcision would be realized in a pervasive manner. As we saw in chapter 2, Moses prophesied of the day in which God would restore his people to the land and complete the work of circumcision in their hearts:

> He will bring you to the land that belonged to your ancestors, and you will take possession of it. He will make you more prosperous and numerous than your ancestors. The LORD your God will circumcise your hearts and the hearts of your descendants, so that you may love him with all your heart and with all your soul, and live. (Deut. 30:5–6; cf. 10:16; Jer. 4:4)

Although some in that era likely experienced this internalization, the prophets anticipate the climactic fulfillment of circumcision's goal in the New Covenant era, when the internalization of the law (Jer. 31:33–34) and the internal work of the Spirit (Ezek. 36:27; Joel 2:28–29) will occur in *all* of God's people. As we have already noted, the effect of this divine intervention will be a people characterized by righteousness and covenant fidelity:

> "In those days, at that time,"
>   declares the LORD,
> "the people of Israel and the people of Judah together
>   will go in tears to seek the LORD their God.
> They will ask the way to Zion
>   and turn their faces toward it.
> They will come and bind themselves to the LORD
>   in an everlasting covenant
>   that will not be forgotten." (Jer. 50:4–5; cf. Isa. 60:21; 62:12)

Paul picks up this thread in numerous places in his letters, demonstrating that the covenantal and prophetic ideal expressed by circumcision has now come about through the work of the Spirit in the New Covenant. The apostle agrees with the Old Testament in identifying obedience to the law as the underlying goal of circumcision: "Circumcision is nothing and uncircumcision is nothing. Keeping God's commands is what counts" (1 Cor. 7:19). In other words, physical circumcision without covenantal obedience amounts to an *uncircumcised* life (Rom. 2:25–27).

Thankfully, the goal of circumcision has now been accomplished by the Spirit who has been poured out in this new covenantal era: "No, a person is a Jew who is one inwardly; and circumcision is circumcision of the heart, by the Spirit, not by the written code" (Rom. 2:29; cf. Col. 2:11).

Since this prophesied fulfillment has now come, the external pointer (similar to the food laws) has been rendered obsolete: "For in Christ Jesus neither circumcision nor uncircumcision has any value. The only thing that counts is faith expressing itself through love" (Gal. 5:6). For this reason, returning to circumcision as a covenantal requirement is not only incorrect, it is even disastrous (Gal. 5:1–4), since this would involve a return to a conditional covenant whose atoning grace has been made obsolete.

Commenting on Romans 2:29, Moo writes, "Paul's 'letter'/'Spirit' contrast is a salvation-historical one, 'letter' describing the past era in which God's law through Moses played a central role and 'Spirit' summing up the new era in which God's Spirit is poured out in eschatological fullness and power. It is only the circumcision 'in the Spirit' that ultimately counts."[16]

The Covenantal Demand
Once again, although circumcision has been "filtered" out by the fulfillment that has come in and through Jesus, this does not in any way diminish the expectation of righteousness. In fact, the opposite is the case. Now that the Spirit has been

16. Douglas J. Moo, *The Epistle to the Romans* (NICNT; ed. Gordon D. Fee; Grand Rapids: Eerdmans, 1996), 175.

poured out in God's people, the long-expected righteousness of the New Covenant people ought to be forthcoming. So dramatic is this transformative work that Paul characterizes it as a "new creation" through our union with Christ in his resurrection: "Neither circumcision nor uncircumcision means anything; what counts is the new creation" (Gal. 6:15; cf. 2 Cor. 5:17). To accomplish this, more than merely a portion of the flesh is removed. Rather, the removal of the entire body of sin, representing our identity with Adam, is accomplished and replaced by our identity with the second Adam, Jesus (Rom. 6:6; cf. 5:12–21).

We should, therefore, not respond to the discontinuance of the circumcision command by simply being grateful that the Mosaic Covenant has been superseded. The fulfillment of circumcision carries with it the demand of Spirit-enabled righteousness. As always, prior covenantal grace gives rise to a corresponding response of faithfulness. Now, as those who have been joined with Christ in his death and resurrection (Rom. 6:3–10; Gal. 2:20; Col. 3:1) and who have been vivified by the enabling Spirit (Rom. 8:5–16, 26–27), we are called to live out the righteous fulfillment of this aspect of the law by keeping in step with our new reality (Rom. 6:11–14; Gal. 5:16, 22–25; Col. 3:1–17).

THE DIVORCE LAW (MARK 10:2 – 12)
The Gracious Fulfillment

Mark and Matthew record Jesus' interaction with Pharisees who inquire about his position on divorce. It is possible that these religious leaders had already picked up Jesus' strict interpretation of the divorce law and were now seeking to trap him by appealing to Moses' somewhat permissive legislation on the topic (Mark 10:4; cf. Deut. 24:1–4). Jesus responds by nodding to Moses' permission, but goes on to explain that their hardness of heart had precipitated it (Mark 10:5). He then appeals to Genesis 1:27; 2:20b–24, effectively pitting Moses against Moses and defusing the strategy of their attack.

> But at the beginning of creation God "made them male and female." "For this reason a man will leave his father and mother and be united to his wife, and the two will become one flesh." So they are no longer two, but one. Therefore what God has joined together, let no one separate. (Mark 10:6–9)

Consequently, Jesus recovers the "one flesh" intention that has always been God's design for marriage. What naturally follows is a much more stringent stance on divorce than what Moses eventually permitted (Mark 10:11–12; cf. v. 8b). The upshot is that Jesus greatly restricts the Mosaic legislation permitting divorce. Moses' broad concession has ended! This again is Jesus' role as "filter," ending something that pertained to the previous covenantal reality.[17]

---

17. One could easily argue that the other two metaphors that we will discuss are also active in this fulfillment of the law. As the "lens," Jesus recovers the original intention concerning marriage. As "prism," Jesus raises the bar of righteousness above that which prevailed under the Mosaic Covenant.

Why does Jesus do this? We must again recall that his kingdom ministry brings the New Covenant reality, in which the covenant people are transformed by the Spirit and enabled to live out a righteousness that outstrips what was true of the Mosaic Covenant era. Because this is the case, the temporary concessions to the hardness of the people's hearts have come to an end. Ezekiel prophesied that a day would come when God would replace the people's "heart of stone" with a "heart of flesh" (Ezek. 36:26). Jesus' teaching on divorce here intimates his assertion that this great day has arrived. If so, then he also is implying his intention to rectify the people's problem, bringing about soft hearts that are supple in the hands of the Spirit of the Lord (36:27).

"With the advent of the eschaton toleration and 'realism' and the mass of makeshift legal arrangements giving them effect are rendered obsolete. The provisional — and now even the Torah is seen in its provisional aspects — is finished. Such is the thrust of Jesus' word on divorce."[18]

The Covenantal Demand

Consistent with the other elements of the law that are filtered out, what endures from this fulfillment is a deep summons to righteousness of life. The complexities of the theological and biblical issues raised by the contemporary problem of divorce far eclipse our ability to address them adequately here. It is enough for us to recognize that Jesus' mediation of the law in this instance involves a termination of an allowance of divorce, calling his disciples to an even higher standard of righteousness than prevailed in the era of the Mosaic Covenant.

Do we hear this demand from Jesus today? Surely, the current high rate of divorce within the church suggests otherwise. Divorce ought not to be known among us who name the name of Jesus. Instead, marital faithfulness in enduring marriages should be our hallmark. It is at this point that the "How" question again rears its hoary head. We will wrestle with that question eventually, but before that we must do more on the "What" question.

"The implication is that the new era of the present kingdom of God involves a return to the idealism of the pre-fall Genesis narrative. The call of the kingdom is a call to the ethics of the perfect will of God ... one that makes no provision for, or concession to, the weakness of the flesh."[19]

SUMMARY

We began this chapter by introducing the way in which the Christian relates to the law of the Mosaic Covenant. As I noted, this relationship is more complex than most think, involving significant aspects of discontinuity and continuity. The key, of course, is discerning how the law is mediated to us through the fulfillment that comes in Christ. In his role as "filter," Jesus brings certain elements of the

18. Ben F. Meyer, *The Aims of Jesus* (London: SCM, 1979), 140.
19. Donald Hagner, *Matthew 1–13* (WBC 33a; Dallas: Word, 1993), 549.

law to their culmination, thereby rendering their ongoing observance covenantally improper. Accordingly, Jesus' fulfillment brings to an end the Old Testament sacrifices, food laws, circumcision, and largely even Moses' provision for divorce.

It is significant that when Jesus abrogates these aspects of the law, the result is not a *lowering* of the law's demand of righteousness. In fact, the opposite is true. What continues on in each case is a summons to a life of righteousness befitting the New Covenant era, to which each superseded element was pointing all along. For this reason, it is appropriate that disciples of Jesus continue to reflect on these Old Testament realities, allowing their obsolescence to remind them of the righteousness that God expects from his Spirit-filled, New Covenant people.

RELEVANT QUESTIONS

1. Has it ever occurred to you how convenient it is not to have to bring animal sacrifices to church with you? How might meditating on Leviticus influence your appraisal of Jesus' work on the cross, as well as your attitude toward sin in your life? How might reflecting on the Feast of Unleavened Bread move you to renewed repentance in response to the Lord's Supper?

2. How might an awareness of your freedom to eat any food translate into a deeper consciousness of the New Covenant era in which we live? What are some ways in which Jesus' rescinding of the food laws might remind you of the work of the Spirit and the demand to keep in step with him?

3. Have you sensed a tendency to focus on the external demands in Christian discipleship, rather than living in the reality and enablement of the internalizing work of the Spirit? How might meditating on the eclipse of circumcision help you in addressing this?

4. Do you believe that living faithfully in an enduring marriage is a central aspect of what it means to be a disciple of Jesus? How might you tap into the gracious provisions that have come through Jesus as you seek to be faithful as a spouse?

CHAPTER 8

JESUS, THE "LENS"

One of them, an expert in the law, tested him with this question: "Teacher, which is the greatest commandment in the Law?"

Jesus replied: "'Love the Lord your God with all your heart and with all your soul and with all your mind.' This is the first and greatest commandment. And the second is like it: 'Love your neighbor as yourself.' All the Law and the Prophets hang on these two commandments."

Matthew 22:35–40

Anyone who has spent time in the church has wrestled with the problem of discerning which aspects of one's traditions are reflective of New Testament teaching and which are simply culture-bound attempts to apply that teaching to life. It's not an easy task, evinced by the diversity of opinions that oftentimes characterizes these discussions. Distinguishing between what is normative and what is either temporary or even misguided requires a clear grasp on biblical theology as well as a humility that permits correction. It calls for the ability to bring into focus matters that are not so clearly perceived so that others too might see things as they really are.

A lens *focuses* light. It brings things into clarity.

In several of his interactions with the law, Jesus' teachings function in this way. In these cases, Jesus doesn't really do anything to the law itself. Rather, he brings back into focus an aspect of the law that the teachers of his generation had obscured through the encumbrance of their traditional interpretations. When Jesus functions as a lens, he strips away these traditions as he reestablishes and recovers the law's teaching so that its original intent and demand might be perceived.

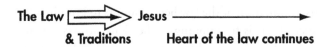

We will consider a few examples of this as we continue to seek the answer to the "What" question.

JESUS' FULFILLMENT AS "LENS"
Clarifying the Greatest Commands
(Matt. 22:34 – 40)

During the final week of Jesus' life, he evidently spent long hours of each day in the courts of the temple, dialoguing with various groups on a variety of issues. On one of those occasions, a Pharisee scholar addresses Jesus to get his take on the question of the law's greatest commandment. Since the rabbis regularly debated which commandments were "weighty" and which were "light," this was not an unusual question. Jesus responds by identifying "love for God" (the vertical relationship) and love for "one's neighbor" (the horizontal relationship) to be the two greatest. He then goes on to say that on these two commands, all the law and prophets *hang* (Matt. 22:40; cf. 7:12; 9:13; 12:7; Mark 2:27). What does Jesus mean by this?

One way this has been interpreted is that these two commands so outweigh all of the other commands that occasionally they justify the disobedience of a command if these are in conflict; that is, if doing the loving thing necessarily means disobeying another of the law's commands, then so be it. But this misses the more nuanced integration of love and the law in Jesus' ministry. Rather than an either/or approach, Jesus teaches that the *heart* of the law's intention is the expression of love to God and to one's neighbor. In other words, the law's commandments or the teachings of the prophets will not be fulfilled *unless* love for God and love for others vivify the actions of obedience. For this reason, Jesus attacks hypocrisy in religious activities with withering intensity (e.g., Matt. 6:1 – 6; 15:3 – 9; 23:1 – 36; Luke 13:15).

But love ought not to be reduced simply to an emotional response. Love for God involves more than a feeling of warm devotion during the singing of a praise chorus. Rather, it entails reverence, commitment, and obedience to God that reflects the acknowledgment of God's roles as Creator and Redeemer in life.[1] This obviously involves knowing God and his will in Scripture and living in alignment with his character. If people love God in this way, their hearts will be conformed to God's compassion and concern in relation to other people. But here, too, it must not be reduced simply to being a friendly person who waves at the neighbors down the street. Loving one's neighbor "means acting toward others with their good, their well-being, their fulfillment, as the primary motivation and goal" of interacting with them.[2]

Clearly, Jesus' summation of the law here amounts to bringing its core teachings into focus. As such, Jesus is functioning as the "lens" to recover the law's original intention. He is not changing anything in the law, though he may be interacting with competing views that people at that time were defending concerning the question of the law's weightiest commands.

---

1. Hagner, *Matthew 14 – 28*, 648.   2. Ibid.

What does Jesus require of us as his disciples here? By reiterating these seminal commands, Jesus affirms that his fundamental demand remains the same as it had been throughout the history of the law's reign over God's people. As the expanded articulation of the Abrahamic injunction to walk faithfully before God (Gen. 17:1), the law demands an all-encompassing love for God and for one's neighbor. Anything short of this fails to match the extent of God's disarming command to Abraham to sacrifice his own son, Isaac. These are the core demands of the law, and Jesus mediates them to us. In so doing, he serves notice that all of the rest of his teachings on the law assume these two commands as their foundation.[4] Thus, it is this high demand of righteousness that is at the core of the answer to the "What" question.[5]

> "These are the greatest commandments because they go to the essence of the way God has created humans to live: giving oneself to God and to others to fulfill his purposes for us as the crown of his creation in displaying in our lives the glory of God's kingdom on earth."[3]

Recovering the Demand of Mercy (Matt. 9:9 – 13)

One of the more offensive actions of Jesus was his penchant for associating with a variety of people in the context of a meal (e.g., Matt. 11:16 – 19; Mark 2:13 – 17; 7:1 – 5; Luke 15:1 – 2). This was offensive because impurity was believed by some to be *contagious* in that culture. McKnight explains this for us:

> To eat with people of a different rank or class, to eat with murderers, or to eat with the unclean was to defile oneself and accept their status as either acceptable or equal to one's own. Thus, eating with such people was taboo and unacceptable.[6]

Consequently, groups such as the Pharisees believed that sitting down with sinners resulted in the spread of their defilement. The Pharisees, therefore, extended the law's purity requirements by their traditions, seeking to maintain in their homes and social gatherings the sort of purity that was expected of the priests and longing for the day when all Israel would live in such holiness. By their example, they exhorted the nation toward greater purity, seeking to hasten the arrival of the day when God would fulfill his covenantal promises to Israel. To

> The residents of the Dead Sea community called Qumran especially emphasized separation from sin and sinners: "One of the main reasons for the Qumranians' withdrawal into the wilderness was to form the truly righteous remnant of God's people and spur his apocalyptic intervention to redress the horrible injustices of the present age, an intervention for which no other segment of Judaism was, in their opinion, properly preparing."[7]

---

3. Michael Wilkins, *Matthew* (NIVAC; Grand Rapids: Zondervan, 2004), 726.

4. Several of the passages that fit into this category deal with the second table of the law, governing behavior in relation to other people. As we reflect back on the interaction between Jesus and the expert in the law (Luke 18:18 – 30; see ch. 6), Jesus' summons to follow him as the fulfillment of what it means to love God with all of one's heart could also be listed in this chapter as an example of Jesus' "lens" work.

5. In this regard, see esp. Scot McKnight, *The Jesus Creed: Loving God, Loving Others* (Brewster, MA: Paraclete, 2004).

6. Scot McKnight, "Who Is Jesus? An Introduction to Jesus Studies," in *Jesus under Fire* (ed. Michael J. Wilkins and J. P. Moreland; Grand Rapids: Zondervan, 1995), 64.

7. Craig L. Blomberg, *Contagious Holiness: Jesus' Meals with Sinners* (NSBT; ed. D. A. Carson; Downers Grove, IL: IVP, 2005), 84.

relax these boundaries was to allow the defilement of sinners to spread throughout the community and send the message that repentance was unimportant, further delaying the coming of the kingdom.

The Romans recruited people from among the Jewish population to collect at ports and near city gates the customs taxes levied on transported goods. These tax collectors, who bid to acquire their positions, earned their living from their commission on the taxes they collected. Although these commissions were regulated, the tax collector's authority to determine the value of the goods taxed opened the door for abuse. It is understandable, therefore, why the tax collectors were assumed to be unscrupulous and held in high contempt. Not only did they collect taxes for the godless Roman oppressors, they were also getting rich by their unjust additions to the already burdensome tax liabilities of the people.[8]

Jesus obviously does not share this perspective as he enters Matthew's house to mingle with the tax collector's friends. When he is subsequently confronted by the Pharisees, he responds by instructing them to learn the message of Hosea: "I desire mercy, not sacrifice" (Hos. 6:6a; Matt. 9:13). God had castigated Hosea's contemporaries for their lack of love toward both himself and their fellow Israelites:

> There is no faithfulness, no love,
> no acknowledgment of God in the land.
> There is only cursing, lying and murder,
> stealing and adultery;
> they break all bounds,
> and bloodshed follows bloodshed. (Hos. 4:1b–2)

Lacking devotion to the two central commands of the law, the Israelites' attempts to seek the Lord through the fulfillment of the ritualistic commands were unsuccessful:

> When they go with their flocks and herds
> to seek the LORD,
> they will not find him;
> he has withdrawn himself from them....
> When they celebrate their New Moon feasts,
> he will devour their fields. (Hos. 5:6, 7b)

In appealing to Hosea, Jesus affirms that his religious detractors had repeated the error of their apostate forebears. And yet there are subtle distinctions. Whereas in Hosea's day the people were doggedly obeying the *law* that required sacrifices, in Jesus' day the leaders were tightly clutching their *traditions* about the law. Furthermore, the ritualistic observances of Hosea's generation were not themselves the reason for their failure to fulfill the law. It appears rather that they assumed they would be safe from God's wrath if they followed the ritualistic requirements, while at the same time pursuing other gods and neglecting justice and mercy in their society. In Jesus' day, the Pharisees' traditions *themselves* were hindering the genuine

---

8. See T. E. Schmidt, "Taxes," *DJG*, 804–7.

obedience of the command to show mercy to others. While outwardly pious in their external observances, those very practices impeded any attempt to act in redemptive ways toward those around them.

Jesus' teaching here calls his hearers back to the heart of the law, cutting through their traditions that were inhibiting their merciful pursuit of others. By preserving an impenetrable boundary between themselves and the so-called "sinners," they obviated the possibility of drawing people to repentance through their experience of pursuing grace. The implication of Jesus' rebuke is therefore crystal clear: any *traditional* application of the law that gets in the way of showing love and mercy to others is to be rejected as wrong.

Jesus' interaction with the Pharisees unfortunately has as much relevance today as it ever has. Too many of us who follow Jesus have developed pious traditions that have muzzled God's command to show mercy and compassion to those around us. Jesus' actions and teaching here ought to serve as a much-needed rebuke to those of us who claim to be following him, but who do not compassionately pursue those who are "unclean." Is our church culture structured in such a way that sinners are welcomed in gracious ways? Are our activities solely focused on fellowship and the building up of the body? In what ways are we reaching into groups that are "defiled" from a Christian standpoint?

Surely, ministries to the poor and homeless, to AIDS victims, and to the prison population come quickly to mind as the sorts of activities Jesus would have endorsed. Why are these under-represented in many churches today? What traditional notions regarding purity are inhibiting our fulfillment of the heart of the law, both corporately and individually? If we are the New Covenant people, why are we oftentimes caricatured in the public eye as the *least* loving and the *least* concerned about mercy? Since our love for our neighbor flows out of our love for God, might not our anemic compassion also expose our shallow love for the Lord?

> "[Jesus'] point is not that the moral Law ... takes precedence over the ceremonial Law ... nor that being merciful to people is more important than obeying the Law, but that one has failed to understand God's intention in the Law if rigid adherence to oral tradition ... is retained at the expense of showing God's compassion on sinners."[9]

Recovering the Demand to Love Our Neighbors (Luke 10:25 – 37)

Jesus' concern over traditions that limit the scope of the law's command resounds in boundary-breaking clarity in his parable of the good Samaritan. The introductory context is important. In his discussion with an expert on the law, Jesus confirms the man's conclusion that obedience to the twofold love command entails the requisite obedience for obtaining eternal life (Luke 10:26 – 28). Jesus' affirmative response certainly does not indicate a works righteousness approach to salvation. Rather, he is

---

9. Moo, "Law," 452.

evincing a covenantal understanding. Within the confines of the Mosaic Covenant (which was then still active), responding to God's prior grace with faithfulness to the law is the condition on which the gracious covenant blessings are given. Where there is no action, there certainly is no faith in God's provision or promises!

But then the man, wanting "to justify himself," presses Jesus for more explanatory commentary: "And who is my neighbor?" (Luke 10:29). Jesus then tells the shocking story of a despised Samaritan caring for an unfortunate Jew at great personal expense and effort (vv. 30–35). Significantly, Jesus concludes his teaching by compelling the expert in the law himself to confess the correct interpretation of the story (v. 37a):

> "Which of these three do you think was a neighbor to the man who fell into the hands of robbers?"
>
> The expert in the law replied, "The one who had mercy on him."
> (Luke 10:36–37a)

Jesus then delivers his forceful command: "Go and do likewise" (v. 37b).

In this highly subversive yet compelling way, Jesus clarifies what is meant by the law's demand to love our neighbors as ourselves (Lev. 19:18b). Since Jesus' discussion partner is an expert in the law who is seeking "to justify himself," Jesus is inducing him to find his own reflection in the failed examples of the religious leaders in the story—people whose interpretation of this demand was too narrow. For whatever reason, those leaders' interpretation of the love command did not include assisting the unfortunate traveler. Jesus' interpretation, however, *obliterates* any religious limitation of the love command, stripping the man of any possibility of self-justification. Jesus then encourages the expert on the law to move beyond this failed paradigm to find himself in the two remaining figures.

One of the theories as to why the two religious leaders did not assist the man is that they were concerned to avoid defilement through contact with a corpse (Lev. 21:1–4; 22:4–7; Ezek. 44:25–26). But two Jewish beliefs ought to have mitigated this concern: "First, Jews were required on religious grounds to bury a neglected corpse.... Second, at least for most Jews, nothing — not even purity laws — legitimately stood in the way of saving a life. Laws were suspended when life was endangered."[10] Regardless of whether the two Jewish passersby thought the man was dead or in dire need, they would have been obligated to get involved.

In the first place, Jesus invites the man to identify with the unfortunate traveler lying wounded by the road. Since the law demands that we love others in the manner that we love ourselves, Jesus must be encouraging the man to think about how he would treat *himself* if he were to fall into such misfortune. If such injustice were to happen to him, anything less than being brought to a place of safety and care would be considered inadequate. The depth of this command is thereby implied

---

10. Klyne Snodgrass, *Stories with Intent: A Comprehensive Guide to the Parables of Jesus* (Grand Rapids: Eerdmans, 2008), 355.

by the interruption in the Samaritan's own journey and the cost required of him to love his neighbor to this extent.

But Jesus also explains the breadth of the command by implying that the man should also find himself in the Samaritan — of all people! As is well-known, the Samaritans were despised by the Jews of that day, who viewed them (inaccurately, in most cases) as the descendants of marriages between Jews of the northern kingdom and displaced, non-Jewish residents of the old Assyrian empire. By presenting a Samaritan as the one who fulfills the commandment, Jesus extends the horizontal boundaries of the meaning of "neighbor," removing the possibility of using racial identity to limit the horizons of this command. Any limitation that turns on the identity of the person is thereby nullified. In this way, Jesus' answer quashes the question's premise that the boundaries of "neighbor" can be defined. Snodgrass's comments are apt:

> The question "Who is my neighbor?" ought not be asked. No thought is allowed that a human can be a non-neighbor. Franz Leenhardt's often used statement is compelling: One cannot define one's neighbor; one can only be a neighbor.[11]

Once again, Jesus clarifies the nature of the law's demands and exhorts his followers to similar obedience.

The sheer immensity of today's societal problems threatens to overwhelm us and cow us into inactivity and noninvolvement. "What can I do in the midst of such need?" we ask. But Jesus' command here is uncomplicated, permitting no diluting interpretation. Surely acknowledging the impossibility of *individually* tackling the entirety of the needs of the oppressed is appropriate. This only encourages the involvement of the corporate body of Christ. But Jesus does not leave us any room to excuse our lack of costly and sacrificial involvement in the extension of our love to those who lie in need around us.

Richard Hays applies Jesus' teaching here to the issue of the unborn: "The point is not that the unborn child is by definition a 'neighbor.' Rather, the point is that we are called upon to *become* neighbors to those who are helpless, going beyond conventional conceptions of duty to provide life-sustaining aid to those whom we might not have regarded as worthy of our compassion. Such a standard would apply both to the mother in a 'crisis pregnancy' and to her unborn child. When we ask, 'Is the fetus a person?' we are asking the same sort of limiting, self-justifying question that the lawyer asked Jesus: 'Who is my neighbor?' Jesus, by answering the lawyer's question with this parable, rejects casuistic attempts to circumscribe our moral concern by defining the other as belonging to a category outside the scope of our obligation."[12]

Do we conduct ourselves with this perspective? Are we keeping an eye always open to those coming across our paths who need mercy and love? Do we recognize that extending ourselves toward others in these ways is not merely the "right thing

11. Ibid., 357; citing F. J. Leenhardt, "La parabole du Samaritain," *Aux sources de la tradition chrétienne* (Neuchâtel: Delachaux & Niestlé, 1950), 136.

12. Richard Hays, *The Moral Vision of the New Testament: Community, Cross, New Creation: A Contemporary Introduction to New Testament Ethics* (San Francisco: HarperOne, 1996), 451 (emphasis his).

to do," but rather it is what Jesus *commands* us to do? Does even putting it this way sound like legalism to us? If so, our need to recover what it means to be in covenant with God is hereby exposed.

Recovering the Demand of Sabbath Provision (Luke 13:10 – 17)

Consistent with his preference for stories of Jesus' compassionate ministry, Luke recounts the intriguing interaction between Jesus and a deformed woman in a synagogue on a Sabbath. Luke tells us that the woman's back had been perpetually bent over for eighteen years. Seeing her enter the synagogue, Jesus summons her forward and heals her, setting her free from Satan's imprisonment (Luke 13:16). Jesus' action is then censured by the ruler of the synagogue:

> Indignant because Jesus had healed on the Sabbath, the synagogue leader said to the people, "There are six days for work. So come and be healed on those days, not on the Sabbath." (Luke 13:14)

Jesus angrily responds by pointing out the hypocrisy in this response, evidenced by a Jew's care for animals on the Sabbath (Luke 13:15). One could deduce from Jesus' defense that he is affirming his healing was a case of a "gracious violation" of the law in the interest of showing mercy.[13] But this misses Jesus' subtle point here about the nature of the Sabbath.

The original intention of the Sabbath was to declare the truth about the created order and the Creator himself.[14] God's cessation of work was obviously never to imply his *fatigue*. Rather, it was God's declaration that his creation was ready to go. That is, everything that his creatures would need in the world was prepared for them. Nothing further was required.

Human cessation of work assents to the truth of God's assessment of the world, at the same time also expressing faith in God's continuing provisions. It was this trust that was seriously damaged in Satan's original deception. Understood in this context, Sabbath offers to humanity a realignment to the posture of reception and dependence that was rejected in Eden. This means that actions on the Sabbath that are theologically aligned with the truth of God's provision are not to be rejected as *violations* of the Sabbath. Rather, they are to be celebrated, for they proclaim the truth of God's sustaining care. Resting on the Sabbath becomes the primary way in which this is demonstrated.

But it can also be declared in the occasional provision of needs for those who

---

13. It is true that this sort of reasoning stands behind some of the exceptions pertaining to work allowed on the Sabbath. For instance, it was apparently taken for granted that the work of the priests in the temple superseded the Sabbath prohibitions (Num. 28:9 – 10; 1 Chron. 23:31). Yet even in these cases, the ministry of the priests could be viewed as the necessary conduit of God's merciful provision for the people on the Sabbath.

14. For helpful discussions of Sabbath, see P. A. Barker, "Sabbath, Sabbatical Year, Jubilee," *DOTP*, esp. 695 – 99; S. Westerholm, "Sabbath," *DJG*, 716 – 19; Moo, "Law," 452 – 55.

come into our care. This is why Jesus uses the example of feeding one's animals on the Sabbath. Rather than a Sabbath violation, caring for them gets at the *core* of the Sabbath, because the animal owners are the necessary conduits through whom God's sustaining provision for the animals is provided.

We can now see why Jesus' healing of the woman is not a gracious violation of the law in favor of love. Rather, since Jesus knows he is to be the conduit of God's provision for that woman, he perceives not only the *allowance* for his healing action on the Sabbath, but the *appropriateness* of it. Jesus declares: "... *should not* this woman, a daughter of Abraham, whom Satan has kept bound for eighteen long years, be set free on the Sabbath day from what bound her?" (Luke 13:16; emphasis mine).

The Greek brings this "appropriateness" out even more forcefully. Jesus literally says, "Was it not necessary [*edei*] for her to be set free from this bondage on the day of the Sabbath?" In Jesus' merciful act, God's Sabbath provision for the woman entailed both her healing and her release from Satan's grip. Jesus' gracious actions are therefore seen to press into the very *heart* of the Sabbath. In this way, Jesus again functions as a "lens," clarifying the original intention of the law.

In light of Jesus' teaching, those who observe a Sabbath rest today ought to think through the theology that undergirds and informs it.[15] Much more than simply a day off from work, it amounts to a celebration and acknowledgment of God's sustaining provision, both for that day of rest and throughout the remaining work week. Since loving God must inform all acts of covenant obedience, pausing from work without this God-honoring posture does not fulfill the commandment. Mindless observance is not obedience. Similarly, Jesus' example reminds us to be quick to spring to the aid of those who come across our paths on our Sabbaths, taking seriously our privilege to be the conduit of God's supply to them as he provides opportunity. Loving God with one's whole heart in no way nullifies the command to love others.

Recovering the Demand of Truth (Matt. 5:33 – 37)

In Matthew 5:21 – 48, we encounter the section of Jesus' teachings known as "The Antitheses." They get their name from the structure of Jesus' didactic approach. Repeatedly, Jesus introduces his discussion of individual commandments with a version of this phrase: "You have heard that it was said to the people long ago...." He then follows this with, "but I tell you ..." (Matt. 5:21a; cf. vv. 26 – 27, 33 – 34, 38 – 39, 43 – 44). There is much disagreement about what it is that "was said." Some think that this merely refers to the traditions of the elders and not the law itself. But Jesus is more likely referring to the Mosaic law that was declared to the ancient

---

15. There are obviously differing opinions on whether or not an ongoing Sabbath observance is expected of New Covenant believers. See, e.g., D. A. Carson, ed., *From Sabbath to Lord's Day: A Biblical, Historical and Theological Investigation* (Grand Rapids: Zondervan, 1982).

people at Mount Sinai.[16] Understood in this way, Jesus is explicitly demonstrating his "fulfilling" authority (5:17), identifying the true direction in which the law points.

Unfortunately, identifying these as "antitheses" sends the message that Jesus is undoing or combating the law's requirements. In reality, he is either *recovering* those demands or even *raising* them: "The contrast involves not contradiction but transcendence."[17] Thus, calling them "antitheses" is a misnomer. But it does highlight Jesus' astounding claim to authority in relation to the law of Moses. We will return again to this section in the next chapter. But the "antithesis" concerning oaths merits our attention here.

Jesus' claim to authority is discerned clearly in the Greek translation of Jesus' Aramaic diction. In each instance, Jesus responds to what "was said" by Moses with the refrain, "but I say to you." In Greek, the pronoun "I" is unnecessary, unless the speaker wants to emphasize himself as the actor. For this reason, it is significant that in each of these "antitheses," the first person pronoun is used to introduce the verb: "I say" (*egō legō*). Our translation of Jesus' words here ought to preserve this stress: "Moses said this, but *I* say to you. . . ."

A vow is a solemn promise, pledge, or commitment to another party. One takes an oath to buttress the truthfulness of the vow by means of an association with something that is greatly valued by the oath maker or with something that is of greater power and significance. The one who would swear by God presumably recruits God's testimony to vouch for the truthfulness of the promise. Should the person fail in following through on the promise, God himself would somehow be implicated in that falsehood. Moses underscores the serious nature of vows and the necessity of fulfilling them:

> When a man makes a vow to the LORD or takes an oath to obligate himself by a pledge, he must not break his word but must do everything he said. (Num. 30:2; cf. Ex. 22:10–13; Lev. 19:12; Deut. 5:11; 6:3; 22:21–23)

Unexpectedly, however, Jesus seems to do away with oaths altogether:

> But I tell you, do not swear an oath at all: either by heaven, for it is God's throne; or by the earth, for it is his footstool; or by Jerusalem, for it is the city of the Great King. And do not swear by your head, for you cannot make even one hair white or black. (Matt. 5:34–36)

The seemingly categorical nature of Jesus' prohibition might suggest that this is yet another law that is "filtered out." Several groups throughout church history have interpreted these statements of Jesus in just this way, disallowing their members from taking any oaths whatsoever (e.g., Anabaptists, Quakers, Mennonites, and Jehovah's Witnesses). This remains a possible interpretation.

But the issue that concerns Jesus here is *truthfulness*, which was being subverted

16. E.g., John Nolland, *The Gospel of Matthew* (NIGNT; Grand Rapids: Eerdmans, 2005), 229; Hagner, *Matthew 1–13*, 115; Davies and Allison, *Matthew*, 1:510–11; and most commentators.
17. Davies and Allison, *Matthew*, 1:507.

through traditional formulas surrounding oaths. Contrary to the law's demand, traditions existed in Jesus' day that governed how compulsory certain oaths were. Sometimes the degree to which oaths were binding turned on which grounding was chosen or even the preposition introducing the grounding. Carson comments, "Swearing by heaven and earth was not binding, nor was swearing by Jerusalem, though swearing toward Jerusalem was."[18] This casuistic approach to oaths eventually required an entire tract in the Mishnah.[19]

Given this religio-cultural situation, it is likely that Jesus is not actually abrogating oaths altogether. Rather, the direction of his teaching seems to return to the original intent of the law—namely, that truthfulness among God's people is necessary and ought not to depend on anything outside of their own control. As Nolland writes:

> The challenge is to stand, as far as one's word is concerned, nakedly on one's own integrity: neither by the introduction of an oath implicitly to downgrade the commitedness [sic] of one's word without an oath nor by the use of the oath to seek to take hostage the honour of anything else to our own claim to truthfulness. Nothing by which I might swear can be made to carry responsibility for my truthfulness; the responsibility is my own.[20]

This explains the logic of Jesus' progression. Since God has full claim on heaven and on earth, neither is within the power of the oath taker to control and must not be employed to strengthen the truthfulness of one's own word. The same applies to Jerusalem since it is God's city. Finally, since it is only God's place to extend one's life so as to increase one's honor (implied by the graying of one's hair), even that is not within the control of the oath taker.[21]

In the situation where people were unnecessarily appealing to things outside of their control somehow to enhance their truthfulness or, worse yet, utilizing various formulas to do end runs around the truth, Jesus would rather do away with oaths altogether. Only trustworthy statements should come from the mouths of his disciples: "All you need to say is simply 'Yes' or 'No'; anything beyond this comes from the evil one" (Matt. 5:37).[22] Taken in this way, Jesus does not so much set aside oaths as he does the traditions that had grown up around them. He therefore recovers the original intent of the law and functions once again as the authoritative "lens" by which to interpret the law's demand rightly.

As I am writing this chapter, the daily U.S. news broadcasts are nauseatingly repetitive in their detailing of tales of deception committed by people in the financial and investment world. Those who ought to be trustworthy by virtue of their professional roles are repeatedly being found to be liars and cheats, bilking their

18. Carson, "Matthew," 153.
19. Šebuʿot; cf. m. Sanhedrin 3.2.
20. Nolland, Matthew, 251.
21. Ibid., 251–52.
22. See Moo, "Law," 456.

trusting investors out of billions of dollars. While one can only speculate on the damage that this is inflicting on the general public's concern for truthfulness, it certainly is breeding a culture of cynicism and pessimism over the truthfulness of people. It has never been more important than in the present day for those who confess Jesus' name to be counterculturally *honest*. Since the God we serve is faithful to the covenantal oaths he has taken, so also must his people be faithful in *all* of their dealings with others. Whether this be in our daily speech, our interaction with our spouses and children, our handling of our responsibilities at our places of employment, or the reporting of our income on our tax forms, our "yes" must mean yes, and our "no," no.

SUMMARY

As if he were turning the focus wheel, Jesus brings several of the law's commands back into clarity, dispensing with various traditions that had obscured the view. Most fundamentally, Jesus identifies as the heart of the law an all-consuming love for God and a love for our neighbors that is commensurate with our own self-love (Matt. 22:34–40). Lacking these, no efforts to obey the law will be successful. Accordingly, Jesus confronts traditional conceptions of purity that inhibit the merciful pursuit of others (9:9–13). He explodes culturally and racially defined limitations on what it means to be compassionate toward another (Luke 10:25–37). He recovers the heart of the Sabbath and illustrates how its provision leads to mercy toward others (Luke 13:10–17). And he restores the law's straightforward demand of truthfulness from God's people (Matt. 5:33–37).

In each case, it is important to see that Jesus' interpretations consistently recover the *greater* scope of the law's commands—a scope that traditional interpretations and applications of the law had truncated. The answers that we are discovering to the "What" question certainly do not permit any *diminishment* of the law's demand. On the contrary, Jesus *recovers* and *preserves* this demand, mediating it on to his New Covenant disciples.

RELEVANT QUESTIONS

1. Does the twofold command of Jesus—to love God with everything we have and to love those around us as ourselves—often govern your life in conscious ways? What actions come to mind that alternately express your obedience and your neglect of these commands?
2. What are some traditional expressions of Christian behavior that inappropriately obstruct Jesus' command to show love and mercy to others? How might these be addressed and changed in light of Jesus' teaching and example here?

3. In what specific ways does Jesus' parable of the good Samaritan confront the church today? How might your church respond? How might you respond?

4. In light of Jesus' clarification of the purpose of Sabbath-keeping, do you feel it is common for Christians to spend time searching the Scriptures to understand the rationale for God's commands? What might be different in your own obedience to God's demands if this happened?

5. In what ways are you untruthful in how you live your life? What steps might you take to bring your behavior into line with Jesus' command to reflect God's truthful nature?

CHAPTER 9

JESUS,
THE "PRISM"

You have heard that it was said to the people long ago, "You shall not murder, and anyone who murders will be subject to judgment." But I tell you that anyone who is angry with a brother or sister will be subject to judgment.

Matthew 5:21–22

You have heard that it was said, "You shall not commit adultery." But I tell you that anyone who looks at a woman lustfully has already committed adultery with her in his heart.

Matthew 5:27–28

Be perfect, therefore, as your heavenly Father is perfect.

Matthew 5:48

The rainbow is a beautiful phenomenon of nature. When someone says, "Look, there's a rainbow," most people swivel their heads with interest and enthusiasm. This is because of the stunning beauty that results from the *prismatic* effect of the raindrops on the light that is passing through them.

A prism refracts, or bends, light. Consequently, light coming out the other side of a prism will be moving in a slightly *different* direction than when it entered. In the process, white light is refracted into its different frequencies, allowing the colors of the spectrum normally hidden from view to be seen in their distinctive beauty. When I speak of Jesus' role as "prism," I am referring to his "refraction" of the law into the New Covenant era, occasionally raising its demand and displaying its inherent beauty.

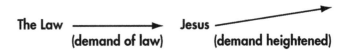

The Law ⟶ Jesus ⟶
(demand of law)   (demand heightened)

As the King who reigns over the people of the New Covenant, Jesus demands the *heightened* righteousness befitting the era in which the covenants have come to their fulfillment. In the process, Jesus brings out the colorful panoply of the law's ultimate intentions, now in its New Covenant expression.

JESUS' FULFILLMENT AS "PRISM"

In the previous chapter, we considered one of "The Antitheses" in Jesus' Sermon on the Mount. There we observed how Jesus recovers the law's intention regarding truthfulness in speech. Let's return again to this portion of Matthew for four more of Jesus' interactions with the law, this time looking for his "prismatic" mediation.

Elevating the Murder Prohibition (Matt. 5:21 – 26)

In Matthew 5:21 – 26, Jesus deals with the command that proscribes murderous acts:

> You have heard that it was said to the people long ago, "You shall not murder, and anyone who murders will be subject to judgment." (v. 21; citing Ex. 20:13)

Jesus affirms here that anyone who commits murder will be hauled before the court and condemned. But then he gives his authoritative revision:

> But I tell you that anyone who is angry with a brother or sister will be subject to judgment. Again, anyone who says to a brother or sister, "Raca," is answerable to the Sanhedrin. And anyone who says, "You fool!" will be in danger of the fire of hell. (v. 22)

Whichever way Jesus' intended meaning is construed, it is unavoidable to conclude that obedience to this command now consists in more than simply avoiding murder. This is because Jesus extends the demand to include resisting even the anger that expresses itself in lesser ways to bring division. Shockingly, those who allow anger to well up within them will be held to the same condemnation as was the murderer in the law. Lest there be any misunderstanding, Jesus states his warning three times, identifying demeaning denunciations of others as anger's telltale mark.[2]

Bietenhard notes that demeaning someone verbally in the ancient world was considered to be much more serious than in most modern societies because of the importance given to the meaning of names: "Throughout the OT there is a sense of the significance of the proper name. The name denotes the person, establishes its identity, and is a part of it. It can often be said: 'As a man is named, so is he.' "[1]

This is an obvious example of the misleading nature of the "antithesis" label. For Jesus is in no way *rejecting* the Old Testament command. Instead, he preserves

---

1. Hans Bietenhard, "ὄνομα," *TDNT*, 5:254.

2. There is no progression implied in the final two statements of judgment, as if calling someone "fool" (*mōros*) merits eternal punishment but the demeaning "empty head" (*rhaka*) only brings judgment on earth. Rather, the judgment of the human court (the Sanhedrin) is identified as the place where the judgments of the law are enacted, corresponding to v. 21b. The transition to the heavenly assize only shows the divine authority that the law's judgment carries. Understood in this light, the final two statements are equivalents, implying no progression in the condemnation of those who call others "Raca" to those who use the word *mōros* ("You fool") to express their anger. See Ulrich Luz, *Matthew 1 – 7: A Commentary* (Hermeneia; trans. Wilhelm C. Linss; Minneapolis: Augsburg, 1989), 282 – 84.

its requirement by *elevating* the standard of behavior that is required in it. Most likely, Jesus is interpreting the command proscribing murder in light of the love command: "The murder commandment becomes to some degree a negative formulation of the love commandment."[3] Accordingly, Jesus' role as "prism" emerges here as he brings the law's commands together, refracting the requirement attached to the individual command to a higher standard. The difficult question pertains to how far he raises it.[4]

A common interpretation takes Jesus' words at face value, concluding that he views anger *itself* to be sinful.[5] Understood in this way, Jesus is viewed by some as teaching an unreachable ethic. Since anger is an apparently unavoidable emotion, this amounts to an impossible command. But this might be a slight misreading of Jesus' summary statement here, because Jesus *himself* seems to have gotten angry:

> He looked around at them *in anger* and, deeply distressed at their stubborn hearts, said to the man, "Stretch out your hand." He stretched it out, and his hand was completely restored. (Mark 3:5; emphasis mine)

Likewise, his anger is apparent when he clears the temple courts of the sale of the animals in Matthew 21:12–13 and when he confronts the hypocrisy of the religious leaders in Matthew 23. In fact, Jesus calls his opponents "fools" in 23:17, using the same word (*mōros*) that Jesus disallows here in 5:22. Consequently, unless we are prepared to conclude that Jesus breaks his own command, he is certainly not equating anger in itself with sin.[6]

Rather, he must be speaking about a specific kind of anger. Whatever might be said about the specific focus of Jesus' ire in his temple action (Matt. 21:12–13), his anger is certainly justified and faithfully communicates God's perspective on the current state of affairs. The same is true of Jesus' anger at the hypocrisy of the religious leaders in Matthew 23 and the hardness of the synagogue crowd in response to the need of the man with the deformed hand in Mark 3. His anger on these occasions is in response to unrighteousness. The reality is that we Christians ought to experience this kind of anger more often than we typically do. Any follower of Jesus who learns some of the details regarding modern slavery, human sex trafficking, and child abuse (to name but a few) should feel bile rising in the throat. It is to our shame that we remain unmoved at the deepest level of our beings in response to such depravity.

So how should we interpret Jesus' command here? It is better to understand Jesus' raising of the bar here not to consist in proscribing anger wholesale, but

3. Nolland, *Matthew*, 232.

4. Sentiments similar to Jesus' ethic can be found in extrabiblical Jewish literature. For instance, the rabbi Eliezer ben Hyrcanus teaches, "The one who hates his neighbor, behold, belongs to those who shed blood" (see Str-B, 1:282; cited in Luz, *Matthew 1–7*, 284). A comparable outlook is expressed in *2 Enoch* 44:3, though the date of this work is the subject of much debate: "He who expresses anger to any person without provocation will reap anger in the great judgment. He who spits on any person's face, insultingly, will reap the same at the Lord's great judgment."

5. Apparently, Luz, *Matthew 1–7*, 287; Davies and Allison, *Matthew*, 1.521.

6. Cf. Hagner, *Matthew 1–13*, 118; Carson, "Matthew," 149.

rather in disallowing the anger that conflicts with the command to love others. For this reason, he summons his hearers to the careful avoidance of relational anger in general, and he especially targets anger that is permitted to linger.

Jesus' illustrations take things in this direction. Instead of allowing the cauldron to simmer or relational ruptures to persist, Jesus exhorts his followers to hasten toward reconciliation, bearing in mind the condemnation awaiting those who remain angry (Matt. 5:23–26). Rather than remaining unreconciled in their anger, Jesus commands his followers to take the initiative in peacemaking efforts: "Go and be reconciled to that person.... Settle matters quickly with your adversary." This is the way of reversing the cycle of anger and avoiding sin in it. Note how Paul also writes: "'In your anger do not sin': Do not let the sun go down while you are still angry" (Eph. 4:26). Those who do not curb such anger, Jesus warns, will be condemned in the final judgment.[7]

One of the most difficult things to do is to initiate reconciliation after a falling out has occurred. I have lived long enough to have observed many relationships suffer and, in some cases, die as a result of one or both parties not being willing to come together for restoration. Whether it has been neighbors, friends, colleagues, spouses, or in-laws, once-close relationships around me have degenerated into cold indifference or even outright hostility following even the smallest of slights.

New Covenant disciples are not to be this way. Rather, Jesus commands us to be those who are known for our willingness to seek reconciliation, even at the cost of personal pride and position. If we put this into the larger context of our role as salt and light in the world, our seeking reconciliation almost certainly will be noticed by others around us, if nothing else because of its countercultural nature.

This in itself can serve as a pointer toward the deeper reality in our lives that produces this softness — namely, the grace of God. We are the people whose sin has been forgiven in the most dramatic and permanent of ways. It is unthinkable that those who have truly experienced this kind of grace would not be softened in their hearts toward those with whom tensions have arisen. Having been pursued by the reconciling grace of the Servant, how can we not respond similarly toward others so as to humbly initiate reconciliation and declare the truth about God in the process? Jesus demands that we do.

Elevating the Adultery Prohibition (Matt. 5:27–30)

Adultery occurred under the Mosaic law when a man had sexual intercourse with an engaged or married woman. The death penalty applied to both of them (Lev. 20:10;

---

7. The TNIV's "fire of hell" translates a Greek reference to the Valley of Hinnom, which is situated to the south of the temple mount. It is the site where sacrifices and rituals associated with the pagan god Molech were once practiced (cf. 2 Chron. 28:3; 33:6; Jer. 7:31; Ezek. 16:20). Eventually, it became the place where animal corpses and garbage were thrown and burned (2 Kings 23:10). Given its association with abominable practices and the perpetual smoke plumes rising from its refuse fires, it became a symbol for end-time condemnation and punishment.

Deut. 22:23–24) because it effectively destroyed the "one flesh" union that God created between spouses. It also marred the metaphor of the divine-human relationship that marriage depicts (e.g., Isa. 54:4; 62:5; Jer. 3:1–20; 31:32; Hos. 2:1–23; 3:1). As God was faithful to his covenant people, so his people were to mirror this faithfulness in their marriage covenants (Mal. 2:11–16).

Jesus underscores the serious nature of sexual unfaithfulness by taking this command to the depth of prior thought and intent:

> You have heard that it was said, "You shall not commit adultery." But I tell you that anyone who looks at a woman lustfully has already committed adultery with her in his heart. (Matt. 5:27–28)

Clearly, Jesus is indicting any contemplation of a woman for the purpose of sexual arousal in one's imagination. How are we to understand his radical treatment of this commandment?

It is clear that Jesus' demand eclipses the horizon of the seventh commandment that prohibits the actual sex act (Ex. 20:14). Jesus most likely does this by bringing its focus together with that of other commands. Similar to Jesus' interpretation of the murder command in relation to the love command, Jesus deepens the adultery prohibition in light of the command that prohibits a man from coveting his neighbor's wife (Ex. 20:17; Deut. 5:21).[8] And yet, Jesus' command is more focused on the sexual imagination than a more "general" covetous desire.[9]

"The righteousness to which Jesus' followers are called intensifies and exceeds the most rigorous standards of Israel's most scrupulous interpreters of the Law. Thus, the six antitheses ... raise the ante by radicalizing the demands of the Law.... Even though this portrayal of the community of disciples is new and revelatory, it is at the same time a fulfillment of the deepest truth of the Law and the prophets."[10]

In so doing, Jesus' prismatic effect on the law is seen, refracting upward the standard of the adultery command, while sharpening the focus of the coveting command. As a result, one might say that Jesus' roles as prism and lens coalesce. In the process, Jesus' refraction of the demand results in revealing the rainbow of the fuller dimensions of the law's requirements.

A person living in most modern cultures simply cannot escape the permeating themes of sexuality that accost the senses every day. Whether driving in one's car, walking through a mall, listening to the radio, watching television, surfing the internet, or attending a movie, sexual themes are incessantly present. Given this saturation, it is inevitable that the relaxed ethical standards of those all around us will threaten to erode our own boundaries.

The result of this has been the wounding of countless minds and marriages among those who claim to follow Jesus. Consequently, Jesus' austere command and warning concerning sexuality must be clearly heard today, illustrated by the shocking images of the gouging out of a lustful eye or the cutting off of a rebel-

8. Wilkins, *Matthew*, 244.

9. Nolland, *Matthew*, 237.

10. Hays, *Moral Vision*, 321.

lious hand. The force of these pictures should be understood as communicating the drastic measures that his disciples must take to preserve their sexual purity. Nolland writes: "By taking up dramatic and extreme instances, the text urges such a level of seriousness about avoiding sin that there will be unrestrained commitment to the use of all possible means to avoid it."[11]

Obedience to this command, therefore, must be taken seriously by the disciple of Jesus. Doing so will likely best be done by drawing on a combination of defensive and offensive strategies. For instance, establishing an accountability relationship with a trusted confidant, where honesty and transparency prevail, is a vitally important *defensive* measure. Linking computers by means of internet monitoring software can be an essential aspect to this kind of relationship. But reflecting positively on the beautiful potential within the biblical design for sexuality offers an important *offensive* approach to this struggle. Similarly, working hard to strengthen and deepen one's marital relationship helps immensely in preserving fidelity between two people whose love for each other is growing.

"The radical treatment of parts of the body that cause one to sin ... has led some (notoriously Origen) to castrate themselves. But that is not radical enough, since lust is not thereby removed.... Cutting or gouging out the offending part is a way of saying that Jesus' disciples must deal radically with sin. Imagination is a God-given gift; but if it is fed dirt by the eye, it will be dirty. All sin, not least sexual sin, begins with the imagination. Therefore what feeds the imagination is of maximum importance in the pursuit of kingdom righteousness."[12]

Since sexuality is one of the covenantal blessings of the one-flesh marriage, participating in those blessings *outside* of that context serves to make a mockery of the covenant itself. Jesus reminds us who are in covenant with God that we must understand and embrace the immense theological significance of covenantal faithfulness in the area of sexuality. In so doing we will also declare to a watching world that God is always faithful to his people. This is the righteousness of the New Covenant people, set apart unto their God.

Revising the Justice Provision (Matt. 5:38–42)

In Matthew 5:38, Jesus cites the law's provision that governed legal retribution: "You have heard that it was said, 'Eye for eye, and tooth for tooth'" (citing Ex. 21:24). This injunction likely served to limit justice to measures commensurate with the harm that had been inflicted. When applied in this way, it avoided an ugly escalation in retributive actions, yet it allowed for a violent—albeit, just—cycle to ensue. Nolland points out, however, that in the Old Testament contexts in which this principle is employed, the emphasis falls on the side of ensuring that the perpetrator bears the full weight of the crime.[13] In other words, the commandment was apparently used mainly to ensure people did not get off easy.

11. Nolland, *Matthew*, 239.
12. Carson, "Matthew," 151.

13. Nolland, *Matthew*, 256 (cf. Lev. 24:20; Deut. 19:21).

Jesus instructs his disciples to respond in a very different way, but he applies this text to a variety of situations:

> But I tell you, do not resist an evil person. If anyone slaps you on the right cheek, turn to them the other cheek also. And if anyone wants to sue you and take your shirt, hand over your coat as well. If anyone forces you to go one mile, go with them two miles. Give to the one who asks you, and do not turn away from the one who wants to borrow from you. (Matt. 5:39–42)

Given his citation of Exodus 21, we would expect Jesus' applications to concern instances of physical injury and abuse. But of the illustrations he offers, only the first one functions in that way. The others turn out to depict different situations altogether. Consequently, Nolland concludes that Jesus is using the Old Testament text "to stand for a principle of aggressive protection of one's own interests."[14] Seen within this framework, the illustrations follow more naturally.

Jesus' first scenario (Matt. 5:39) envisages a right-handed slap on the right cheek of another. In that culture, this kind of back-handed blow was considered to be a high insult. But rather than responding in a legally acceptable way to protect one's honor, Jesus demands that his followers respond with forbearance and a willingness to suffer further insult.

Nolland notes that "a slap with the back of the hand calls for twice the payment in recompense as for other blows; in terms of dishonor it is on the same level as tearing an ear, plucking out hair, spitting on someone, pulling a cloak off, and loosing a woman's hair in public."[15]

In the second scenario (Matt. 5:40), Jesus implies that the reason for the lawsuit is a genuine debt. On the surface, then, Jesus is not describing a criminal or oppressive act. Yet, when it becomes clear that the protagonist is suing a poor man for the only thing he has left — the clothing he is wearing — the unmerciful nature of this action becomes visible. Jesus' illustration specifically envisions someone suing for a man's inner garment. This comes close to violating the law's provision that safeguards a person's outer cloak, which was essential for protection against the elements:

> If you take your neighbor's cloak as a pledge, return it by sunset, because that cloak is the only covering your neighbor has. What else can your neighbor sleep in? When he cries out to me, I will hear, for I am compassionate. (Ex. 22:26–27)

Jesus' followers who find themselves oppressed in this sort of way are to respond not with a close-fisted protection of their basic needs. Instead, Jesus surprisingly exhorts his followers to exceed the extent of their aggressor's demand, surrendering even what the law specifically protected. In the process, however, the immoral and excessive nature of the protagonist's action will also be exposed.

Most likely the third scenario (Matt. 5:41) involves unpaid service or labor demanded by Roman officials or soldiers. Jesus' exhortation to render this service

---

14. Ibid., 257–58.

15. Ibid., 258, n. 235.

willingly and even generously has the potential of transforming the situation into a much more positive encounter. Rather than resisting and resenting their occupation, Jesus fosters a spirit of cooperation and accommodation even with those who were their oppressors. Once again, Jesus' teaching moves in the direction of the surrender of the need to defend one's personal rights.

Jesus' final scenario functions as the obverse of the earlier court example. Whereas in that case, disciples found themselves cast in the role of a poor debtor being taken to court, in this last case they are approached by a needy person seeking financial help. Rather than protectively preserving one's wealth in view of the riskiness of such a loan, the disciple of Jesus is to respond with mercy and openhandedness.

Various interpreters have concluded from Jesus' treatment of the law here that his disciples are to be total pacifists, should never take another to court, and must avoid service in the military or police force.[16] But these deductions may go beyond the undefined boundaries of Jesus' instruction here and may conflict with other New Testament teaching concerning the God-ordained place of the government (e.g., Rom. 13:1 – 4).[17] Rather than getting stuck in the quagmire of the specific application of Jesus' commands, however, it is best that we focus on the fundamental issue of how Jesus' disciples ought to respond to similar threats and demands.

It is important in this regard to note that Jesus resisted evil during his ministry. He refused to bow to Satan's wiles in the wilderness (Matt. 4:1 – 10), confronted bigoted hypocrisy head-on (23:1 – 39), and rebuked Peter for his naïve censure (16:22). He also cryptically advised his disciples to purchase a sword in the new situation of persecution that was coming on him and his followers (Luke 22:36). Jesus is therefore not disallowing the action of resisting evil. Rather, he is disallowing responses that demand the protection of personal rights.

Note Paul's similar teaching: "Do not repay anyone evil for evil. Be careful to do what is right in the eyes of everyone. If it is possible, as far as it depends on you, live at peace with everyone. Do not take revenge, my dear friends, but leave room for God's wrath, for it is written: 'It is mine to avenge; I will repay,' says the Lord. On the contrary:

'If your enemy is hungry, feed him;
    if he is thirsty, give him something to drink.
In doing this, you will heap burning coals on his head.'

Do not be overcome by evil, but overcome evil with good" (Rom. 12:17–21).[18]

Since Jesus himself exemplifies this all the way to the cross, it is not inappropriate once again to suggest that he is using the image of the Servant of the Lord as a paradigm for his followers' lives of discipleship. Strikingly, in his four initiatives here,

---

16. Hays (*Moral Vision*, 320) provides a summary of interpretive approaches that have sought to avoid the absolute nature of Jesus' injunctions.

17. See attempts to apply these illustrations in Glen H. Stassen and David P. Gushee, *Kingdom Ethics: Following Jesus in Contemporary Context* (Downers Grove, IL: IVP, 2003), 138.

18. Cf. also Luke 6:27–36; 1 Thess. 5:15; *Didache* 1:4–5; cf. also 1 Peter 2:21–23.

Jesus uses seven of the Greek words used in the Greek Bible's translation of Isaiah 50:4–9: "*resist, slap, cheek, sue, coat, give* and *turn away.*"[19] Davies and Allison write:

> Is not the imitation of Christ implicit in [Matt.] 5.39–40? Jesus himself was struck and slapped (26.67 ...), and his garments (27.35 ...) were taken from him. If his followers then turn the other cheek and let the enemy have their clothes, will they not be remembering their Lord, especially in his passion?[20]

As Jesus' disciples mirror his servant life, they will also manifest his character, offering opportunities for others to perceive the grace and mercy of God. Jesus does not explicitly *rescind* the Old Testament command of commensurate justice. But he does demand that his followers go *beyond* that law, setting aside its provisions for personal retaliation. Once again, Jesus functions as the prism, refracting the demand of righteousness to a higher standard.

For most of us, following this command of Jesus pushes us into a posture that is radically foreign. For westerners, at least, the preservation and protection of one's personal rights lies close to the heart of what it means to be a human being. Surrendering this dignity is shockingly countercultural. But that may be exactly why it has the potential not only to short-circuit the spirals of violence and aggression, but even to bring about the transformation of those involved.

What might happen in the workplace if a Christian employee exceeds an unrealistic supervisor's demands? What will go through the minds of those watching if a disciple intentionally refrains from responding to a verbal assault, but rather whose restraint invites the person to try another? What truth about God might be communicated through the willing lending of money to someone whose credit is anything but watertight? Throughout the history of the church, disciples of Jesus who have faithfully imitated Jesus in this servant life have made visible to the watching world the sort of grace that befuddles the wise and melts the hearts of the hardened. In so doing, they have invited others to receive from the true Servant the same grace that has already transformed them.

This does not mean, of course, that disciples of Jesus should not be on the front lines of those working toward and calling for justice and the protection of the powerless. Although Jesus surrendered his own rights, he championed those of the poor and the weak. Being faithful to this command of Jesus, therefore, involves articulating a balance between social activism and the entrusting of personal rights to God.

Extending the Love Command (Matt. 5:43–47)

In Matthew 5:43, Jesus extends the command to love others. He begins by citing the love command in relation to one's neighbors (Lev. 19:18), but then appends to it a sentiment that does not explicitly appear in the Old Testament: "and hate your

---

19. Stassen and Gushee, *Kingdom Ethics*, 139 [emphasis theirs]; see also Wilkins, *Matthew*, 251.   20. Davies and Allison, *Matthew*, 1:546.

enemy." Jesus does not give us any delimitations regarding who fits into the "enemy" category, so it is best to consider that he is referring to anyone who acts in a hostile manner toward us. This also means that his use of "neighbor" must be the equivalent to a "friend," since it is set in opposition to one's "enemy." As such, Jesus' summation of "what has been said" captures the reciprocity sentiment that governed social life in the Greco-Roman world.[21] It finds expression, for example, in the Dead Sea writings:

> He is to teach them to love everything He chose and to hate everything He rejected, to distance themselves from all evil and to hold fast to all good deeds.... He is to teach them both to love all the Children of Light ... and to hate all the Children of Darkness, each commensurate with his guilt and the vengeance due him from God. (1QS 1:3b–4, 9b–11; but contrast 1QS 10b:17–21)

This was possibly an extension of God's hatred of evil along the lines of the imprecatory psalms (cf. Pss. 26:4–5; 139:21–22) and the commands to exact divine justice on surrounding nations who had mercilessly attacked Israel in the past (e.g., Deut. 25:17–19).

Jesus' disciples are not to live this way. Rather, they are to show kindness and mercy to *everyone*, without distinction. It is true that the Old Testament law required the Israelites to love the foreigners who lived among them:

> He defends the cause of the fatherless and the widow, and loves the foreigners residing among you, giving them food and clothing. And you are to love those who are foreigners, for you yourselves were foreigners in Egypt. (Deut. 10:18–19; cf. Ex. 22:21)

But this obviously refers to foreigners who had chosen to live *peacefully* among them.

Other Old Testament texts push the boundaries further. In Exodus 23:4–5, Moses enjoins the people to assist their enemies in their retention and care for their livestock. So also in Proverbs 24:21–22, readers are to respond to the needs of their enemies with gracious provision. Similar injunctions can be found in the literature of other cultures of that era as well.[22]

Jesus, too, goes well beyond the command to love one's neighbor: "But I tell you, love your enemies and pray for those who persecute you, that you may be children of your Father in heaven" (Matt. 5:44). Rather than retaliating or looking for an opportunity to take one's "pound of flesh," Jesus' disciples are to love their enemies and even to pray for their persecutors (cf. 5:10). In this, they will transcend the reciprocal love that is common even among notorious sinners (vv. 46–47) and will demonstrate their true identity as children of the Father.

The logic of Jesus' deduction is explained by God's own actions. Just as God provides generally for all without regard for the specific morality of his benefactors, so also must Jesus' disciples mirror God's all-inclusive love, expressed in his

---

21. See Nolland, *Matthew*, 264, for references.   22. See ibid., 265–67.

common grace: "He causes his sun to rise on the evil and the good, and sends rain on the righteous and the unrighteous" (Matt. 5:45). Echoes from the Noahic Covenant are unmistakable here, as Jesus refers to God's promise to sustain nature's seasonal processes for people whose hearts are ever prone toward evil and unrighteousness (Gen. 8:21 – 22).

In this way, Jesus affirms the necessity of imitating God. Yet, in contrast to the Dead Sea text cited above, this does not include all of his attributes. Throughout the Old Testament, God is presented as the one who wrathfully judges sin. In this the New Covenant people are not to follow him.[23] Rather, their calling is to entrust their vindication to him, trusting that he will in fact make things right in the end. Since Jesus here raises the law's demand to the highest of its expressions found here and there in the Old Testament, he is once again acting as the prism, requiring of his disciples a level of obedience that is fit for the kingdom (Matt. 5:20).

Yet again, Jesus pushes us well beyond the limits that are comfortable for us. Inviting friends and colleagues over for meals or looking for ways to serve them seems both logical and righteous (cf. Matt. 5:46 – 47). But when we do so, there is a sense that we are serving ourselves, since we will most likely experience benevolent reciprocation. But praying for one's persecutors and seeking ways to provide for them seems to go over the top. Jesus' teachings here remind us that he is not interested in a halfhearted discipleship that can be mirrored by those in the world who are not transformed by his grace. Rather, his command to extend love to one's enemies is situated in the neighborhood of God's radical command to Abraham concerning Isaac. Once more, Jesus' commands embody the kind of righteousness expected from those who live in the New Covenant era.

Jesus therefore fittingly summarizes both this command and this whole section by means of his restatement of Leviticus 19:2. Rather than, "Be holy because I, the LORD your God, am holy," however, Jesus substitutes a word that is translated into Greek as *teleios*: "Be *teleioi*, therefore, as your heavenly Father is *teleios*" (Matt. 5:48). Though this word can bear different nuances in various contexts, here it certainly has to do with faithfulness to God's character.[24] It is used in the Greek Old Testament to refer to the nature of Noah's life as he walked faithfully with God (Gen. 6:9) and to God's demand to resist imitating the pagan practices of the nations surrounding Israel in the land (Deut. 18:13). As such, it refers to *wholehearted* commitment to God's will. Jesus' role as prism truly does refract the law in higher directions, bringing out at the same time the beauty of God's nature as it is seen in Jesus' ultimate expression of the law's demands. Nolland's comments sum this up nicely:

> The call is to go all the way with the will of God, now seen with fresh clarity. The completeness here answers to the fulfilling promised in Mt. 5:17 and to the sense

---

23. Obviously, this does not conflict with the need to practice church discipline when needed (Matt. 18:17).

24. Wilkins, *Matthew*, 261.

in vv. 18–19 that nothing should be missing from obedience to the whole claim of the Law. One must go all the way in obeying the will of God; one cannot be content with some circumscribed version of obeying God's will, as witnessed to in the Law and the Prophets.[25]

SUMMARY

As the "prism" in relation to the Old Testament law, Jesus refracts its commands to new levels of demand, displaying in the process the glory of God's ultimate desire for his people. Accordingly, his disciples are not to allow relational anger to run interference with the command to love others. Rather, they are to pursue reconciliation passionately and intentionally. Similarly, they are to remain sexually pure, resisting even the temptation of entertaining another in one's thoughts for the purpose of sexual arousal.

Jesus also summons his followers to the uncomfortable position of responding positively to people who put impinging pressure on their personal rights, whether that be responding passively to personal insults, exceeding the unmerciful demands of others, generously offering service to people who would otherwise resort to forceful compulsion, or even making risky loans to those in need. Such openhandedness and forbearance is reminiscent of the Servant of the Lord, demonstrating the kind of grace that carries with it the potential of the genuine transformation of others. Finally, Jesus extends the love command to include even those who are hostile. In so doing, Jesus' followers demonstrate their true identity as children of God, imitating his indiscriminate inclusion of all within his common grace.

In the end, it is obvious that Jesus' call to this transcending obedience amounts to the end-time expression of God's demand of obedience encapsulated in Abraham's mountaintop test and the law's overall summons. Jesus' teachings here make it clear that God is still seeking people who will reflect his character in the costliest of ways, so that others might indeed perceive who he is. In the process, we have discerned more of the answer to the "What" question, encountering the high demand of righteousness that Jesus requires from those who claim to be his followers. Jesus, therefore, stands before any would-be disciple and conveys commands that cannot be avoided.

RELEVANT QUESTIONS

1. What are some of the ways in which Christians fail to follow Jesus' command about the avoidance of divisive anger and the need for active efforts toward reconciliation? Do many seem to take seriously Jesus' warnings about the

---

25. Nolland, *Matthew*, 271.

effect that failure in relation to these commands will have on their relationship with God?

2. How are Christians falling short of Jesus' demand regarding sexual purity, even at the level of the imagination? What might be some practical steps toward addressing this lack?

3. Does Jesus' command to relinquish the need to protect one's own rights or to extend love to those who are hostile to us even sound realistic in our world? What would have to happen to our hearts in order for this to begin to happen more often?

4. In light of the answers to the "What" question that we have perceived so far, does the biblical presentation of New Covenant Christianity sound like the Christianity practiced by most people today? What are your thoughts in relation to this?

CHAPTER 10

JESUS' KINGLY SUMMONS TO THE MISSION

Therefore go and make disciples of all nations, baptizing them in the name of the Father and of the Son and of the Holy Spirit, and teaching them to obey everything I have commanded you. And surely I am with you always, to the very end of the age.

Matthew 28:19 – 20

And this gospel of the kingdom will be preached in the whole world as a testimony to all nations, and then the end will come.

Matthew 24:14

At the outset of his public ministry, Jesus recruits people to join him in his work. "Come, follow me," he says to Peter and Andrew, "and I will send you out to fish for people" (Matt. 4:19). Clearly, their discipleship has as its ultimate goal to prepare them to carry Jesus' ministry far beyond the scope of what he himself could accomplish in his short time. Consequently, having designated his disciples as "apostles" (meaning, "sent ones"; Matt. 10:2; Mark 6:30; Luke 6:13), Jesus dispatches them as workers into the Galilean "harvest" of burdened and vulnerable people (Matt. 9:36 – 37; 10:5 – 42; Mark 6:6b – 13; Luke 9:1 – 6). He does the same thing on a larger scale as he approaches Judea, to prepare for his ministry there (Luke 10:1 – 16).

Finally, following his resurrection, Jesus confers on his disciples the responsibility of continuing his ministry into the entire world. Known as "the Great Commission" (Matt. 28:18 – 20), Jesus commands them to represent him, making disciples of all nations through baptism and instruction. The mission is there at the beginning, in the middle, and at the end of Jesus' interaction with his disciples.

Any discussion of Christian discipleship must, therefore, wrestle with Jesus' missional command. How are we to understand this mission responsibility? What exactly are we commanded to do? Is it primarily to engage people in apologetic conversations that will lead to evangelism? After all, Jesus said, "And this gospel of the kingdom will be *preached* in the whole world as a testimony to all nations, and then the end will come" (Matt. 24:14; emphasis mine). Is it, rather, to engage in social activism that transforms the lot of the disadvantaged and reveals the character of the reigning King? As we bring our all-too-brief discussion of the "What" question to an end, it is appropriate that we consider this culminating command once again in the context of God's overarching covenantal purposes.

THE COVENANTAL EXPECTATIONS
The Abrahamic Covenantal Expectations

When God declared his commitments to Abraham, included among them was his intention to bless all nations through him and his descendants (Gen. 12:3). In chapter 3, we observed that this promise came hard on the heels of the rebellion at Babel. Since this corporate apostasy culminated humanity's godless, postflood pursuits and mirrors their preflood rebellion, the Abrahamic promise of universal blessing should be seen as God's gracious response to the depressing legacy of Genesis 3–11.

"We cannot speak biblically of the doctrine of election without insisting that it was never an end in itself but a means to the greater end of the ingathering of the nations. Election must be seen as missiological, not merely soteriological."[1]

What was this blessing to entail? Obviously, it takes the remainder of the covenantal flow and the historical narrative of the Scriptures to flesh this out. But pondering the beginning of this sequence will help us avoid the tendency of truncating Jesus' missional command, reducing it to something that does not retain God's original intention. It is significant in this regard to recall that God's blessing would flow to all nations only as Abraham's descendants experienced God's holistic provision on their own behalf. That is, as God shaped them into a people and provided for them in the land, they would serve as a testimony of God's nature to the rest of the world.

Therefore, one might expect that Israel's experience in covenant with God would become a paradigm for God's intentions for the rest of humanity. As the historical narrative of the Old Testament unfolds, this expectation is found to be correct, with the epic events of the exodus from Egypt, the provision of the land, and the return from the Babylonian exile serving as the patterns of salvation and blessing that image God's expansive agenda of blessing. Although the spiritual dimension is at the heart of this blessing, God's holistic deliverance extends into the physical, social, and political spheres. In many ways, this ought not to be surprising, given God's comprehensive provision for Adam and Eve in the garden prior to any redemptive need. When we ask what Jesus is commanding his followers to do when he confers on them his mission, *each* of these dimensions must be kept in view.

But *how* is this mediation of the blessing to be accomplished? We learned in chapter 4 that the covenant most closely tied to the promise of universal blessing

---

1. Christopher J. Wright, *The Mission of God: Unlocking the Bible's Grand Narrative* (Downers Grove, IL: IVP, 2006), 369.

is the conditional covenant of Genesis 17, where circumcision sealed Abraham's covenantal commitment to walk before God faithfully and blamelessly (17:1). The implication here is that the extension of this blessing to all nations will be accomplished through people who follow Abraham's example of faithful obedience to God. The Lord's confirmation in Genesis 18 bears repeating here:

> Abraham will surely become a great and powerful nation, and *all nations* on earth will be *blessed* through him. For I have *chosen* him, so that he will *direct* his children and his household after him *to keep the way of the LORD* by doing what is right and just, so that the LORD will bring about for Abraham what he has promised him. (Gen. 18:18–19; emphasis mine)

In other words, the mission will not be accomplished by mere *proclamation*. Rather, the mediating element between Abraham's election and the blessing to all nations is *ethics*. As Wright insightfully observes,

> *the ethical quality of life of the people of God is the vital link between their calling and their mission.* God's intention to bless the nations is inseparable from God's ethical demand on the people he has created to be the agent of that blessing.
> There is no biblical mission without biblical ethics.[2]

Thus, through the community of those who have embraced God's demand to live life in alignment with his character, symbolized by circumcision, the blessing will spread to the nations. As we have seen, this is where the Mosaic Covenant enters.

The Mosaic and New Covenantal Expectations

We learned in chapter 4 that the people's obedience to the Mosaic Covenant's demand of righteousness was the means by which Israel would serve as the priestly nation to all other nations, mediating the knowledge of Yahweh to the world. God's statement in this regard also bears quoting again here:

> Now if you obey me fully and keep my covenant, then out of all nations you will be my treasured possession. Although the whole earth is mine, you will be for me a kingdom of priests and a holy nation. (Ex. 19:5–6a)

Through Israel's obedience, Abraham's blessings would extend to all nations (Deut. 4:5–8; Isa. 49:6).

When the nations look at Israel, they ought to discern the singular nature of Yahweh's claim — he is the only true God (Deut. 10:12–17; Josh. 24:14–15)! Similarly, they should perceive Yahweh's righteous attributes as they are displayed through the nation's obedience to the Ten Commandments and related legislation (Deut. 4:5–8). They should understand Yahweh's just demand and the need for the

---

2. Ibid., 369; emphasis his.

reception of his atoning grace through the ministries of the temple (Lev. 1:1–17; 4:1–6:13, 24–30; 7:1–6; 8:14–21; 16:3–24). They ought to realize God's compassion and mercy, as his people reach out to care for the poor, the powerless, and even the foreigner among them (Lev. 19:33–34; Deut. 10:18–19; 24:17–22). This would foreshadow the day when no one would be marginalized or disadvantaged (Isa. 55:1–2; 61:1–3; 65:13–16; Ezek. 47:22–23).

Though the people of the Mosaic Covenant largely failed in this, we have also seen the prophetic expectation that this ideal will finally be fulfilled in the people of the New Covenant, in whose minds God's law will be written and in whose hearts his Spirit will dwell. Through this transformed and enabled remnant of his people the character of Israel's true King will be seen. Such transformation will point ahead to the day when his reign is absolute in the earth. At that time, God's people will finally follow him into covenantal faithfulness.

The Davidic Covenantal Expectations

This is obviously where God's promises to David come in. When the great and righteous Son of David reigns over the transformed nation, his covenantal inheritance will be realized (Ps. 2:8–12). This will lead to the submission of all nations to him and their consequent participation in Abraham's blessings through him. The psalmist writes:

> Endow the king with your justice, O God,
>> the royal son with your righteousness....
> May he rule from sea to sea
>> and from the River to the ends of the earth....
> May his name endure forever;
>> may it continue as long as the sun.
> Then all nations will be blessed through him,
>> and they will call him blessed. (Ps. 72:1, 8, 17; cf. 2 Sam. 23:3–4;
>>> Amos 9:11–12)

This expectation is paralleled in Daniel's vision of the royal Son of Man, who must be linked with the Davidic line. When the "one like a son of man" comes to the Ancient of Days, all nations will submit to him:

> In my vision at night I looked, and there before me was one like a son of man, coming with the clouds of heaven. He approached the Ancient of Days and was led into his presence. He was given authority, glory and sovereign power; all nations and peoples of every language worshiped him. His dominion is an everlasting dominion that will not pass away, and his kingdom is one that will never be destroyed. (Dan. 7:13–14; cf. v. 27)

At the time when God fulfills this promise of the coming king (Zech. 9:9–10), Zechariah tells us that all nations will be drawn to Israel's God:

This is what the LORD Almighty says: "In those days ten people from all languages and nations will take firm hold of one Jew by the hem of his robe and say, 'Let us go with you, because we have heard that God is with you.'" (Zech. 8:23; cf. Isa. 49:6; 62:1–2, 10c)

Even more stunningly, Isaiah affirms that the Gentiles will be included *within* God's people:

In that day Israel will be the third, along with Egypt and Assyria, a blessing on the earth. The LORD Almighty will bless them, saying, "Blessed be Egypt my people, Assyria my handiwork, and Israel my inheritance." (Isa 19:24–25; cf. Ps. 87:4–6; Zech. 9:7)

God will then be the King over all:

The LORD will be king over the whole earth. On that day there will be one LORD, and his name the only name. (Zech. 14:9; cf. v. 16)

The kingdom of God will be consummated on the earth!

In this way, the Abrahamic, Mosaic, and Davidic covenants all coalesce on this notion of "mission." That is to say, God's holistic blessing will be mediated to all nations through the community that faithfully submits to the righteous King and responds to the covenantal demand of reflecting Yahweh's character in the earth. Then the knowledge of Yahweh will permeate the earth as Abraham's blessing is poured out to all nations. All of this converges in Jesus' missional command.

JESUS' MISSIONAL COMMAND

When placed against this covenantal backdrop, we can see the significance of Jesus' sending of his disciples into the mission. For the fulfillment of these covenantal hopes has now arrived. There are several dimensions of this.[3]

The Covenantal Pattern

As we have seen, God's missional strategy is to mediate his blessing to all nations through Abraham's descendants. Paul follows this tack in his affirmation that God's salvific grace came "first to the Jews, then to the Gentile" (Rom. 1:16; cf. 2:9–10; Acts 26:23) and in his missionary strategy of going first to the synagogues in each of the cities in his journeys,[4] even though he was explicitly sent to the Gentiles (Acts 9:15; 13:47; 22:21; 26:17–18). His expectation obviously was that God would use those Jews who came to faith in each city to be the means by which those in the surrounding region would hear the good news.

---

3. For a robust treatment of this subject, see Wright, *Mission of God*; see also his *The Mission of God's People* (Biblical Theology for Life; Grand Rapids: Zondervan, 2010).

4. Acts 13:5, 14; 14:1; 17:1, 10, 17; 18:4, 19; 19:8; cf. 13:46; 18:6.

Jesus too follows this pattern. Though he eventually grants the request of a Canaanite woman to help her demonized daughter, Jesus initially fends her off by asserting that he was sent "only to the lost sheep of Israel" (Matt. 15:24). Similarly, when he sends his disciples on their missionary journey, he carefully delineates their focus: "Do not go among the Gentiles or enter any town of the Samaritans. Go rather to the lost sheep of Israel" (10:5–6; cf. 23:34). It comes as a bit of a shock, then, when he sends them to the *world* at the end of his earthly ministry: "Therefore go and make disciples of all nations . . ." (28:19a; cf. 24:14; Acts 1:8). When his actions are set in the context of the Abrahamic promises, however, it is clear that he is following the covenantal pattern, whereby God's blessing of the Gentiles is mediated through Abraham's descendants. Covenantally speaking, Jesus *had* to begin with Israel. But since the ultimate covenantal horizon has always been the entire world, Jesus' final commissioning widens out accordingly.

The Light of the World (Matt. 5:13 – 16)

Second, Jesus confirms the covenantal means by which the world will be included in the blessing. As we learned in the covenantal interactions between God and Abraham as well as with the people of Moses' day, the means by which the world would come to participate in the covenantal blessings would be through the witness of those in covenant with him.

This is where Jesus' call to obedience that we have been considering in these chapters comes to the service of the mission. It is significant that immediately prior to his declaration of the fulfilled law, Jesus specifies their role as "salt" and "light" to the world:

> You are the salt of the earth. But if the salt loses its saltiness, how can it be made salty again? It is no longer good for anything, except to be thrown out and trampled underfoot.
>
> You are the light of the world. A city on a hill cannot be hidden. Neither do people light a lamp and put it under a bowl. Instead they put it on its stand, and it gives light to everyone in the house. In the same way, let your light shine before others, that they may see your good deeds and glorify your Father in heaven. (Matt. 5:13–16)

Whatever Jesus intends by the images of "salt" and "light," it is clear that his followers are to be *different* from those surrounding them in the world. Salt was used in the ancient world for flavoring, for fertilizer, and especially as a preservative. Jesus does not identify which of these functions he has in mind, but the attribute common to each of them is that salt is *distinct* from what is around it, bringing with it some kind of benefit.

The function of "light" here is clearer. Those who light a lamp put it on the stand so that it gives light to all who are in the house. Once again, the image of "light" communicates a dramatic *difference* between it and the state of affairs in that house prior to its lighting. It was dark! As Jesus goes on in the Sermon on the Mount to discuss how his followers are to live, it becomes clear that this difference is a *moral* difference—they are salt and light as they live their lives in morally distinct ways from those around them. Whereas the world is lan-guishing in sin, in squalor, in meaninglessness, and in the relentless pursuit of things that ultimately do not satisfy, Jesus' followers are to be identified by their purity, their devotion to God, and their commitment to love others.

> "The world will see no reason to pay any attention to our claims about our invisible God, however much we boast of his al-leged nearness to us in prayer, if it sees no difference between the lives of those who make such claims and those who don't."[5]

The prophets had looked forward to the day when God's redeemed covenant people would serve as a beacon for the nations. Isaiah affirms that when God redeems his people, their "salvation" will shine forth "like a blazing torch," which the nations will see (Isa. 62:1–2). As they respond with the sort of covenant faithfulness that pursues justice for the powerless and extends compassion for the poor (Isa. 58:6–7, 10), they will stand as light bearers in the world, drawing them to Yahweh (Isa. 58:8, 10b). Isaiah writes:

> It is too small a thing for you to be my servant
>> to restore the tribes of Jacob
>> and bring back those of Israel I have kept.
> I will also make you a light for the Gentiles,
>> that my salvation may reach to the ends of the earth. (Isa. 49:6)

Consequently, Isaiah exults, "Raise a banner for the nations" (Isa. 62:10e), for at that time the blessing will go forth through this purified remnant of the nation to all the nations of the world: "Nations will come to your light, and kings to the brightness of your dawn" (60:3).

Therefore, when Jesus declares to his disciples that they are the "light of the world," he is claiming that the time of the fulfillment of these prophetic hopes has finally arrived! *It is time!* Those who respond to Jesus' call to the sorts of things we have been considering in this section will be the ones through whom he will shine the light of his truth and mercy to all nations.

The People of the King (Matt. 28:18)

Jesus also evokes the Davidic Covenant in his missional command. This is espe-cially evident in his prefatory comment to the Great Commission. Jesus asserts, "All authority in heaven and on earth has been given to me" (Matt. 28:18). This surely echoes the wording found in Psalm 2 and Daniel 7:

> Ask me, and I will make the nations your inheritance,
>> the ends of the earth your possession. (Ps. 2:8)

5. Wright, *Mission of God*, 380.

•   •   •

He was given authority, glory and sovereign power; all nations and peoples of every language worshiped him. (Dan. 7:14a)

By virtue of his resurrection, Jesus has entered into his inheritance. As the great Davidic King, his reign over all nations has begun (Acts 2:32 – 36). In light of this, his disciples are to go forth in the confidence that Jesus is truly the Sovereign of the world, even though the consummation of this reign lies yet in the future.[6]

But notice also the remarkable way in which this sovereignty is to be established. If we glance back at the contexts of the Old Testament passages I listed above, we see that the establishment of the king's dominion is expected to be achieved through forceful means. When he comes, the opposing kingdoms will be undone (Dan. 7:11 – 12, 17 – 26), and any rebellion will be met with swift justice (Ps. 2:9 – 12). Yet, surprisingly, such is not to be the case in the present age of Jesus' reign. Rather, the nations will bow before his throne through their reception of the gracious message of the gospel: "Therefore go and make disciples of all nations ... teaching them to obey everything I have commanded you" (Matt. 28:19 – 20a; cf. 24:14). There will come a day when the nations will be forcefully subjugated to him,[7] but in the interval between Jesus' resurrection and his glorious return, the nations will be graciously won through the call to *discipleship*!

The Command to Preach, to Serve, and to Suffer

How is this call to be communicated to others? What is it explicitly that his disciples are to do as they go forth in the mission?

A Holistic Mission (Matt. 10:1, 5 – 42)

Since God's salvation fulfills the exodus/return-from-exile pattern, it is not surprising that Jesus' missional summons entails a holistic ministry. As Israel was enslaved, poor, oppressed, and helpless before God's past actions of deliverance, so also will Jesus' salvific mission focus on the same conditions experienced by the poor, disease-stricken, and ostracized. This is borne out by Jesus' instructions to his disciples as they go out on their missionary journey.

Jesus called his twelve disciples to him and gave them authority to drive out evil spirits and to heal every disease and sickness.... "As you go, proclaim this message: 'The kingdom of heaven has come near.' Heal the sick, raise the dead, cleanse those who have leprosy, drive out demons. Freely you have received, freely give." (Matt. 10:1, 7 – 8)

---

6. Whether you interpret the referent of James' words as the resurgence of David's line or the building of the end-time temple, the prophetic appropriateness of the inflowing of the Gentiles into the covenant is similarly tied to the end-time fulfillment of promises made to the Davidic line (Acts 15:15 – 19; cf. Amos 9:11 – 12).

7. E.g., Matt. 24:36 – 25:46; 1 Thess. 5:1 – 3; Rev. 19:11 – 21.

If these instructions are understood to provide a sort of shorthand agenda for disciples in every age, several things are evident. First, Jesus' mission summons involves proclamation and teaching. His missionaries are to make disciples by *teaching* others all that Jesus had taught them (Matt. 28:20), including especially the announcement that the kingdom had drawn near (10:7; 4:7; Luke 10:11) and was even present (Matt. 12:28). Central to this is the surprising proclamation that Jesus is the long-awaited Messiah (16:16–17). The unexpected nature of the kingdom brought by Jesus and his eventual crucifixion would be major reasons why some in their Jewish audience would respond with skepticism (Matt. 12:38; 16:1; Mark 8:11; John 2:18; 6:30) and rejection (Matt. 27:42). His missionaries are those in every context who embrace the offense of Jesus' cross as they confess his kingship (1 Cor. 1:18–31).

Second, also important is the announcement that through Jesus' representative death, the grand redemptive moments in Israel's history had come to their consummative fulfillment (Luke 4:16–21). Accordingly, the great exodus for his people and their long-awaited return from exile had somehow taken place in this surprising manner. We will explore several dimensions of this in the next section. It is enough for us here to note that the upshot of Jesus' fulfillment is that forgiveness of sins would no longer come through the sacrifices offered up each day in the temple, but through the crucified heir to David's throne![8] In the pluralistic age in which we live, affirming that forgiveness is available solely through Jesus is nothing if it is not insultingly offensive. But such is what Jesus commands his followers to proclaim.

Jesus summarizes his own ministry by claiming to fulfill Isaiah's return from exile description: "The Spirit of the Lord is on me, because he has anointed me to proclaim good news to the poor. He has sent me to proclaim freedom for the prisoners and recovery of sight for the blind, to set the oppressed free, to proclaim the year of the Lord's favor" (Luke 4:18–19; citing Isa. 61:1–2a). In claiming to fulfill this return-from-exile prophecy (Luke 4:21), Jesus affirms that his ministry culminates the pattern of deliverance that began in the exodus and recurred in the return from Babylon.

Third, since Jesus' death also institutes the New Covenant (Luke 22:20), the ways in which Jesus mediates the law to his followers certainly also formed a central pillar of this proclamation. Communicating some of the material we have gone over in chapters 6 through 9 undoubtedly became important as the church began to settle into the new covenantal era. Unfortunately, few in the church today are able to do this sensitively. So if New Covenant Christianity is to be clearly articulated to the world, a renewed commitment to equipping Christians with this sort of knowledge is imperative.

Fourth, Jesus also instructs his disciples to go beyond mere *proclamation*. Since God's kingdom was arriving in fulfillment of his historical actions of deliverance,

---

8. Matt. 26:28; Mark 10:45; John 3:16–17; 6:42–59; Acts 2:23–39.

Jesus' disciples were to *demonstrate* its presence in tangible ways that image its presence. *Proclamation* and *demonstration*—these dimensions belong inextricably together. Without either of them present, God's mission is only partially realized.

So Jesus graciously confers on his disciples the authority to perform exorcisms and healings (Matt. 10:7–8). When God's kingdom comes in its fullness, Satan will no longer be free to work his mayhem. Consequently, the casting out of Satan's minions in the present age presages the kingdom's culmination in the future. Similarly, when God's full blessing is poured out, sickness and death will cease. The healings effected through his disciples by the power graciously given to them (10:8b) foreshadow that great day.

Finally, though he does not specify it here, Jesus also must have exhorted his disciples to utilize their wealth in ways that would ameliorate the plight of the poor (Matt. 11:5e; Luke 4:18b). Since God's deliverance in the exodus and his provision of the land graced the Hebrews in their poverty, the law included provisions for the poor at harvest time (Lev. 19:10; 23:22; Deut. 24:19–22; cf. Amos 5:11) and for the payment of tithes, some of which would be given to the poor.[9] Accordingly, however one interprets the difficult parable of the shrewd manager (Luke 16:1–13), central to its meaning is the command to use money in gracious ways that incline others toward the master.

This is confirmed by the rich man's condemnation in the next parable for not actively reaching out to Lazarus in his misery, even though he lay at his gate (Luke 16:19–31).[10] It is for this reason that any declaration of the kingdom's presence necessarily includes acts of mercy, compassion, and justice, even as Jesus' own mission targeted the poor. Whatever monetary resources that are granted to us must, therefore, be stewarded in such a way that inclines others toward God as they see and experience grace through us.

A Vulnerable Servant Mission (Matt. 25:31–46)

Finally, Jesus' summons to the mission involves the willingness to undergo persecution and suffering. Earlier I described the discipleship dynamic: having been graced by Jesus the Servant, disciples are summoned to follow Jesus the King. But since Jesus lived out the life of the Servant, following him amounts to emulating his servant life. This helps to account for Jesus' repeated command that his disciples pick up their own crosses in following him. That is to say, they are to be prepared to endure the same treatment that he experienced as he fulfilled his kingdom-centered calling of mercy and love.

This is the reason for the *vulnerability* that Jesus sets up for his missionary disciples, sending them forth without resources and dependent on those who will

---

9. Lev. 27:30; Num. 18:26; Deut. 14:22, 28; Neh. 10:37; Mal. 3:8–10.

10. Closely related to this, the law required that justice on behalf of the poor and powerless was to be protected; cf. Ex. 22:22; Deut.

1:16; 10:18–19; 24:14–15, 17; 27:19; cf. Amos 2:7; 5:12; 8:4–6; Mal. 3:5. See M. D. Carroll R., "Wealth and Poverty," *DOTP*, 881–87.

provide for them along the way (Matt. 10:9–11, 16, 40–42). As Jesus was vulnerable to rejection and attack during his Servant ministry, so also will his disciples be (vv. 17–25, 28, 38). This, in turn, also offers to those who hear their message the opportunity to demonstrate their acceptance of it in tangible expressions of mercy toward the very ones who have brought the gospel. This helps us understand Jesus' meaning in one of his best-known, but often misinterpreted stories.

Given its resonance with Jesus' concern for the poor elsewhere, it is tempting to interpret Jesus' parable of the sheep and the goats in Matthew 25:31–46 as promising salvation for those who show mercy to the homeless and impoverished in the world. Those who see it this way note Jesus' close identification with the need of the poor, so that acts of mercy done to any impoverished, imprisoned, or otherwise vulnerable person are also done to Jesus.[11]

But this reading struggles to convince for several reasons. First, Jesus makes it clear that those who will enter into the kingdom of heaven will be those who confess him before others and who keep his teachings (Matt. 7:21–27; Mark 8:37–38). He also explains that those who are his disciples will receive forgiveness of sin by receiving his sacrificial provision on the cross (Matt. 26:28), not by washing his feet or feeding him. Construing mercy to the disadvantaged as the sole criterion for entrance into the kingdom sits uncomfortably with the full range of Jesus' teachings, especially when people opposed to Jesus are oftentimes heavily engaged in these kinds of merciful acts. Indeed, those who interpret Jesus' parable as exhorting mercy to the poor in general usually have to supplement Jesus' simple words here with other dimensions of discipleship, such as faith and the reception of grace.[12]

Second, when Jesus metaphorically employs the term "my brothers" in Matthew, he does not use it to refer to the impoverished in general, but to his disciples who do the will of God (Matt. 12:48–50; 28:10; cf. 18:15, 35; 23:8). Most of the remaining instances of "brother" refer to actual familial ties and not to people in general.

Third, Jesus does not use the adjective "the least" in any other text to describe people, but he does employ its conceptual cousin, "little ones," to characterize his disciples (Matt. 10:42; 18:2–14; Mark 10:15; cf. Matt. 11:25; Luke 12:32).

These considerations set us up to see the significance of the most convincing evidence of all, namely, the parallel descriptions between Jesus' instructions to his disciples in Matthew 10:40–42 and his portrayal in Matthew 25. Notice first of all the identity that Jesus establishes between himself and his disciples in Matthew 10:40: "Anyone who welcomes you welcomes me, and anyone who welcomes me welcomes the one who sent me." Jesus' depiction in Matthew 25:40 echoes this

---

11. For a recent defense of the general interpretation of the "least," see Klyne Snodgrass, *Stories with Intent*, 551–61.

12. This is also implied by Jesus' words to the sheep, "Come, you who are blessed by my Father; take your inheritance, the kingdom prepared for you since the creation of the world" (Matt. 25:34b).

The very nature of an inheritance is that it is not something that is earned — as may be implied by the popular interpretation regarding the homeless and the poor. Rather, an inheritance is solely at the discretion of the giver to *give*.

identification: "The King will reply, 'Truly I tell you, whatever you did for one of the least of these brothers and sisters of mine, you did for me.'"

In addition, those who showed mercy to the disciples on their missionary journey and welcomed them into their homes were those who had heard their message and embraced it. This is what is implied by the examples of the reception by people in Matthew 10:41. They receive a reward for their reception of these individuals because they embraced *what they stood for*:

> Whoever welcomes someone *known to be a prophet* will receive a prophet's reward, and whoever welcomes someone *known to be righteous* will receive a righteous person's reward. (Matt. 10:41; emphasis mine)

All of this prepares us for the nearly verbal parallel between the two passages:

> And if anyone *gives even a cup of cold water* to one of these *little ones* who is known to be my disciple, truly I tell you, that person will certainly be rewarded. (Matt. 10:42; emphasis mine)

•   •   •

> Come, you who are blessed by my Father; take your inheritance, the kingdom prepared for you since the creation of the world. For I was hungry and you gave me something to eat, I was thirsty and *you gave me something to drink*.... Truly I tell you, whatever you did for one of the *least of these* brothers and sisters of mine, you did for me" (Matt. 25:34b–35a, 40; emphasis mine).

Significantly, the acts of mercy toward the missionaries of Matthew 10 are done in full knowledge of their identity as Jesus' disciples. Set in the context of the mission, this strongly suggests that those homes that turn out to be "deserving" (Matt. 10:13) are those whose inhabitants demonstrate their acceptance of the disciples' *message* by their *actions* of hospitality. Notice Jesus' confirmation of this in the description of those who, by implication, are undeserving: "If anyone will not welcome you or listen to your words ..." (10:14a). Their demonstrations of mercy and hospitality or the withholding of them are therefore set in the context of hearing or not hearing their *message*.

The same must then be true of the "least" in Matthew 25:34–40. Seen through this lens, "the least" must be those of his disciples who make themselves vulnerable in going forth into the mission to the nations, confidently proclaiming the gospel (24:14), compassionately serving the poor, and authoritatively exorcising demons and healing the sick in Jesus' name (cf. 10:1, 7–8).

SUMMARY

Jesus' discipleship summons, therefore, comes to each one of us: "Are we willing to be the least?" That is, are we willing to become vulnerable so as to present the good news of Jesus' kingdom ministry to others? As we have seen, this is the very place where the Abrahamic, Mosaic, Davidic, and New Covenants all converge. As God's remnant people respond to the covenantal demand of reflecting his character in the earth, submitting in the process to the reign of David's righteous heir, God's holistic blessing will be mediated to all nations. Then the knowledge of Yahweh will permeate the earth as Abraham's blessing is extended to all nations.

As such, this is not a call that comes only to the "really committed" minority of Jesus' followers. Its summons comes right along with the grace of atonement. It is heard with the call to discipleship. There is no avoiding it. Jesus fully intended to reach the world through the bright light and penetrating salt of his faithful disciples. This is because God's purpose in gathering a people to himself is so that he can gather some more!

As a result, we must ask ourselves:

- Are we willing to be the least?
- Are we willing to declare the presence of the kingdom in this era of such suffering and evil?
- Are we bold enough to affirm the unique kingship of Jesus in the midst of modern attacks on the veracity of the gospel witness and the pluralistic relativization of Jesus' singular claim to truth?
- Do we dare to assert the redeeming nature of Jesus' self-sacrifice in an age increasingly opposed to the notion of the atonement of sins done against an all-holy God?
- Are we willing to live lives shaped by the true Servant, so that others might see him through us?
- Will we step into the role of being the conduit of Abraham's blessing, whether that be responding to the call to demonstrate the kingdom's presence in a crosscultural setting, participating in an urban ministry to the homeless, sharing our beliefs with a coworker, or extending love to our indifferent neighbors?
- Are we serving God rather than money, generously using our resources to further the mission next door and throughout the world?
- Are we bold enough to confront the powers of darkness in the authority of Jesus' name?
- What's more, are we filling the role of the "sheep," participating in the mission of the "least" around the world, supporting them with acts of mercy and hospitality—either in our own homes or through our investment in their care from afar?

If we aren't, there is little hope for those still languishing in the exile of the nations to see the gracious and compassionate nature of the Servant King who died for them and now sits on the throne. Those of us who have received Jesus' holistic gospel are commanded to respond by participating in this mission to the world. In these ways, we have the astounding privilege of contributing to the fulfillment of God's promise to bless all nations through Abraham.

RELEVANT QUESTIONS

1. How has viewing the Great Commission within the framework of the covenants changed your perspective?
2. Has the call to righteousness taken on a new urgency when it is viewed as the means by which the nations will see the truth of the kingdom and hear its good news?
3. Is the contemporary church succeeding in displaying the fullness of the kingdom message? What might be needed to strengthen its witness?
4. What might it mean for you to begin living as one of the "least" of Jesus' brothers and sisters? Are you presently living as one of his "sheep"?

THE ANSWERS TO
THE "WHAT" QUESTION

I t's time now to survey the ground we've covered in pursuit of the answer to the "What" question. As we have seen, its answer emerges from the general and specific ways in which Jesus mediates the fulfillment of the demand of the Old Testaments covenants. Since he is their fulfillment, the answer flows through him and from him.

THE DISCIPLESHIP IMPLICATIONS
OF JESUS' PROPHETIC KINGSHIP

We began by considering his fulfillment of the Davidic Covenant. Since God promised David an eternal dynasty, there had to arise one day a faithful king who would match the ideal described in the Father/Son relationship that God promises to have with David's son. When that one comes, he will reign in righteousness and justice, leading his people into covenant faithfulness. As the one who fulfills this ideal, Jesus perfectly embodies Yahweh's character and reigns as "a man after his own heart" (1 Sam. 13:14). For this reason, he commands people to follow him in a discipleship that expresses the righteousness of God.

Jesus is also the Prophet, the one in whose mouth God put his words so as to communicate to his people "everything I command him" (Deut. 18:18b). Consequently, Jesus is authorized to articulate the final expression of God's will that had already been revealed in the previous covenants, especially the Mosaic. Jeremiah prophesied that God would write his law on the hearts and in the minds of his New Covenant people. As the great Prophet, Jesus articulates this law and summons his followers to live out absolutely Yahweh's character (Matt. 5:48).

THE MORAL IMPLICATIONS OF
JESUS' FULFILLMENT OF THE LAW

We therefore discovered three of the significant ways in which Jesus mediates the fulfilled law to us. As the "filter," he fulfills elements of the law in such a way as to render their ongoing observance obsolete. But in each instance, what is mediated through Jesus into the lives of his people is the demand of righteousness to which the fulfilled Old Testament provisions pointed. Accordingly, his disciples are to respond to Jesus' climactic fulfillment of God's atoning grace by living lives characterized by repentance and wholehearted devotion to him. Their Spirit-circumcised hearts are to be characterized by purity rather than defilement, and faithfulness in their relationships rather than the failure expressed by divorce. In light of these themes, it is remarkable that any Christian would ever entertain the notion that Jesus' fulfillment of the law would result in a *diminishment* of the demand of righteousness for New Covenant believers. For even when elements of the law are fulfilled in such a way as to render them obsolete, their rescision has given way to the greater righteousness expected to come in the New Covenant.

As the "lens," Jesus recovers and preserves the law's commands by bringing their original intent back into focus and interpreting them in the greater scope of their entirety. In the process, he sweeps away traditional interpretations that had obscured their force and hindered their fulfillment. Preeminent among these observations is Jesus' identification of the heart of the law to be an all-consuming love for God and a love for one's neighbors that matches one's own self-love (Matt. 22:34–40). In many respects, these two commands capture the essence of the law—everything else is commentary. As a result, if they are lacking in any individual, no efforts to obey the law will be successful. Moreover, any tradition that stands in the way of fulfilling the command to love others is simply wrong. Any interpretation of the law's commands that does not result in preserving love both for God and for one's neighbor is similarly imbalanced. Mercy, compassion, and truthfulness are to be the hallmarks of Jesus' disciples. Once again, Jesus' fulfillment of the law restores the covenantal demand of righteousness.

As the "prism," Jesus "refracts" the law to new levels of demand. This is consistent with both the ideal expectations within the law itself, as well as the anticipations of the greater righteousness that would characterize the New Covenant community. Consequently, Jesus commands his followers not only to reject murder, but even anger that disrupts relationships and festers long afterward. Likewise, they are not only to avoid adulterous relationships, but even the entertainment of thoughts for the purpose of sexual arousal. Although the law permitted people to exact just payment for injuries and the infringement of personal rights, Jesus exhorts his disciples to go beyond the law in their willingness to bear additional insults, exceed the unreasonable demands of others, generously offer service to those who would compel it, and lend to those who likely may not be able to repay. Finally, Jesus commands his disciples to imitate God in extending love and care even to those who are hostile to them. The sheer intensity of these demands matches the depth of Abraham's test on the mountain and the all-encompassing demand of the law. The command to reflect God's character is alive and well in Jesus' teachings.

Each of these aspects of Jesus' teaching illustrates his surpassing authority to communicate the covenantal demands. As the great fulfillment of the line of prophets, he articulates the end-time expression of God's will. But since he also embodies this fulfillment in his role as the great Son of David, his prophetic role is subsumed under his kingly role. So, while he echoes and strengthens the call to righteousness found in the Law and the Prophets, he also summons people to follow *him* as the King whose reign is extending across the earth.

THE MISSIONAL IMPLICATIONS OF JESUS' FULFILLMENT OF THE ABRAHAMIC BLESSINGS

Those who have submitted to Jesus' reign are therefore commanded to participate in the fulfillment of the Abrahamic promise to bless all nations by proclaiming and demonstrating the presence of his kingdom. Not only does this include the affirmation of Jesus' messianic identity, through whom atoning grace is now available, but it also involves the compassionate ministries of healing, exorcism, and mercy to the poor. Since Jesus lived out the life of the Servant, his imitating disciples are to be willing likewise to make themselves vulnerable in this mission, giving others the opportunity to respond to the good news of the gospel in tangible expressions of mercy and hospitality.

The answer to the "What" question is, therefore, found to fit into God's strategy of bringing to consummation his desire to have people respond to his prior grace in making his righteous glory known throughout the earth. In light of the biblical answer to the "Why" question, there is no avoiding this answer to the "What" question.

But this then leaves us with the "How" question: How is faithfulness to this summons to be realized in our lives?

THE "HOW" QUESTION

We have finally reached the "How" question: How can the disciple obey Jesus' high demand? If you are like me, Jesus' teachings do not often allow you to feel good about the consistency of your discipleship. What's more, as I noted in the first chapter, Jesus seems to suggest that following him will not be burdensome. In fact, those who come to him will find "rest," as well as a yoke that is "easy" and "light." Having seen Jesus' bracing call to righteousness, it is hard to imagine how following him would be "light" in any sense of the word!

This is why this third question brings us to the crux of our dilemma. How is the disciple of Jesus to follow him with single-hearted devotion, without becoming bound up with crippling legalism? How is the lethargic heart of the contemporary Christian to be moved to a righteousness that is not compromised? As we have seen, both of these discipleship mutations mock the great desire of the heart of God! Thankfully, clarity once again comes from the covenants.

When we considered the covenantal patterns, we discovered that grace was always provided *prior* to the giving of God's commands of obedience. Divine grace also *sustained* those in covenant with God. This provides the obvious hint concerning the answer to our question: prior and sustaining grace must always be understood as the enabling context in which God's demands are given, received, and responded to. That is to say, covenantal faithfulness will only be possible as people within the covenant live *in* and respond *to* grace.

But as we have also seen, one of the devastating results of Eden's tragedy is the human propensity to reject grace altogether or at least to take it for granted, which thereby nullifies its transforming power and muzzles its consequent demand of righteousness. By taking of the fruit, Eve declared her independent sufficiency. From that moment on, the natural posture for us humans has been a close-fisted, straight-backed resistance to grace and an adolescent insistence on defining our own boundaries. And even though a significant softening of this posture has come with our conversion to Christ, it is clear that more is yet to be accomplished within us. Given the present state of our transformation, in spite of the arrival of the New Covenant, Eden's heritage still stalks our paths and haunts our minds. How then are we to live faithfully in this age when this dissonance lurks deep within our hearts?

THE "HOW" QUESTION

CHAPTER 11

DISCIPLESHIP DISSONANCE IN THE INAUGURATED KINGDOM

But if it is by the Spirit of God that I drive out demons, then the kingdom of God has come upon you.

Matthew 12:28

The kingdom of heaven is like a mustard seed, which a man took and planted in his field. Though it is the smallest of all seeds, yet when it grows, it is the largest of garden plants and becomes a tree, so that the birds come and perch in its branches.

Matthew 13:31–32

In our consideration of the "Why" and "What" questions, we have learned that Jesus claims to have brought the kingdom in his ministry. Accordingly, Jesus presents himself as the righteous heir of David, demanding absolute righteousness from his followers who have been graced by the New Covenant blessings. Thankfully, Jesus also functions as our representative covenant partner so that the blessings of this covenant are received by faith. Yet even with that gracious provision, our answers to the "What" question have informed us that Jesus' demand of righteousness is not diluted. Along with the absolute grace of the New Covenant has come the absolute demand of the kingdom.

This is obviously where the tension within us threatens to drag us either into legalism or compromise. For who is able to respond faithfully to Jesus' demands so as to meet these New Covenant expectations? *No one!* How then can Jesus' claims about bringing the kingdom, about establishing the New Covenant, and about giving his disciples the Spirit be reconciled with the stark contradiction of our frail and inconsistent devotion to God and love for our neighbors?

Any honest follower of Jesus knows only too well the dissonance of which I am speaking—the recurring tug-of-war between our passion for righteousness and our drooling after the lusts of the flesh. After reading the prophetic descriptions of the New Covenant people, one would not expect this to be the case. But it *is* the case! Consequently, the "How" question confronts us, caught between the unyielding constancy of Jesus' summons and the inconsistency of our devotion to him. To begin to answer it, we must first of all understand the age in which we live—an age that was apparently *not* foreseen by the prophets.

THE INAUGURATED KINGDOM

As we learned in our discussion of the first two questions in this book, the prophets anticipate a time when God will consummate his covenants with a climactic exercise of his sovereign power, transforming the world and his people in it. To use Jesus' favorite word for it, the "kingdom" will arrive. Then will come the long-awaited righteousness of God's people, and the earth will be filled with the knowledge of the Lord. Since the kingdom is the centerpiece of Jesus' teachings, it is there that we must look for clues regarding the answer to the "How" question. We have already seen that his answer to the "What" question reinforces the higher demand of righteousness that should be characteristic of the kingdom. But is there anything else here that might shed additional light on our struggle? Let's start with a review of the typical Jewish expectations that were aloft in the first-century Palestinian air, and then consider Jesus' teachings in this context.

The Jewish Expectations of the Kingdom

Even a casual reading of the prophets will reveal their general "two-age" perspective on history. While this age is a time of sin, suffering, and oppression, the next age will be a time when these conditions will cease, and peace, comfort, and joy will reign:

> "The days are coming," declares the LORD,
>> "when the reaper will be overtaken by the one who plows
>> and the planter by the one treading grapes.
> New wine will drip from the mountains
>> and flow from all the hills,
>> and I will bring my people Israel back from exile.
> They will rebuild the ruined cities and live in them.
>> They will plant vineyards and drink their wine;
>> they will make gardens and eat their fruit
> I will plant Israel in their own land,
>> never again to be uprooted
>> from the land I have given them,"
>>> says the LORD your God. (Amos 9:13–15)

Accordingly, the Lord reigns now (Ps. 99:1–4), but a far greater expression of his dominion is yet to come: "The LORD will be king over the whole earth. On that day there will be one LORD, and his name the only name" (Zech. 14:9). When this consummated kingdom comes, the righteous will be vindicated and blessed in the renovated creation (sometimes depicted as a new creation; e.g., Isa. 65:17–19), resulting in overwhelming fecundity and abundance (Amos 9:13–15). It will be the time when the great covenantal promises of God will be fulfilled — when Israel is reconstituted as a nation in the land (Ezek. 37:16–23) and given God's eternal protection and blessing (Zech. 9:8), and its sin will be atoned for permanently (Jer. 31:34). Then the

"The curse which lies upon nature because of man's sin means that it cannot be the scene of the final realization of God's Kingdom apart from a radical transformation; and the new age of the Kingdom will therefore be so different as to constitute a new order of things. The Kingdom cannot be produced by the normal flow of events but ... only by a cataclysmic irruption of God into history; and the resultant order will be something which is concrete and earthly and yet at the same time supramundane."[1]

nations will throng to Jerusalem to participate in the worship of Yahweh (Zech. 8:20–23) and in the blessings he promised to them through Abraham (Gen. 12:3).

Since all of this is apparently to occur after the cataclysmic day of the Lord, the coming of the kingdom is expected to be sudden and overwhelmingly transformational. Obadiah's perspective is typical: when the final day of the Lord comes, the oppressors of Israel will be judged and the remnant of God's people will be vindicated in God's kingdom:

"The day of the LORD is near
   for all nations.
As you have done, it will be done to you;
   your deeds will return upon your own head....
But on Mount Zion will be deliverance;
   it will be holy,
and the house of Jacob
   will possess its inheritance...."
This company of Israelite exiles who are in Canaan
   will possess the land as far as Zarephath;
the exiles from Jerusalem who are in Sepharad
   will possess the towns of the Negev.
Deliverers will go up on Mount Zion
   to govern the mountains of Esau.
   And the kingdom will be the LORD's. (Obad. 15–21)[2]

Consequently, many Jews of Jesus' day envisaged a *dramatic* in-breaking of God's absolute rule that would usher in the age of his kingdom in a torrent of sovereignty:

---

1. Ladd, *The Presence of the Future*, 64.
2. Cf. also Isa. 13:9; 14:1–2; Ezek. 30:1–19; Joel 2:1–11,
18–32; 3:14–21; Mal. 4:1–5.

In the fire of his jealousy
the whole earth will be consumed,
for he will make a sudden end
of all who live on the earth. (Zeph. 1:18b)

We could diagram this traditional perspective in this way:

This Age	The Age to Come (the Kingdom)

What is important about this vision for our purposes is that the divine transformation of the people of that age is similarly depicted as happening *wholesale*. We've already seen these expectations. Having been purged in the fires of God's covenantal judgment, Israel will climactically return to the Lord and bind themselves to him permanently (Jer. 50:4–5). The blessings of the New Covenant will transpire, resulting in their internalization of the law and their enablement by the Spirit (Jer. 31:33; Ezek. 36:26–27). They all will have an intimate knowledge of the Lord and finally be faithful to the covenant (Jer. 31:32–34). Accordingly, those who return from the exile will be called by God's name (Isa. 43:5–7) and will have turned from evil (Isa. 59:19–20). They will be called "righteous" (Isa. 60:21; 61:2–3; 62:1–5, 12) and "priests" (Isa. 61:6).[3]

So the problem is obvious. With the fulfillment that came with Jesus, the New Covenant was established and the Spirit was poured out on his people. Nevertheless, even though we are the beneficiaries of these blessings, we don't match the prophetic descriptions. How do we account for this? Fortunately, Jesus' claims regarding the nature of the kingdom's presence shed explanatory light on the dissonance of our hearts.

The Inauguration of the Kingdom in Jesus' Ministry

It has become commonplace these days to speak of the "now" and the "not yet" in New Testament kingdom theology. What is meant by this is that the powerful exercise of God's kingly reign has indeed broken into the present, although not in its final form. As we have already noted, Jesus affirms that the kingdom has been "forcefully advancing" since the days of John (Matt. 11:12).[4] By this, Jesus is no doubt referring to his ministry actions: "The blind receive sight, the lame walk, those who have leprosy are cleansed, the deaf hear, the dead are raised, and the good news is proclaimed to the poor" (v. 5). God's reign is afoot in Jesus' ministry, bringing the people's well-being and the social order into alignment with his character. And yet, the nature of the kingdom's arrival with Jesus is sufficiently distinct from the stock

3. Ladd, *The Presence of the Future*, 70–75.
4. As in the NLT translation. This rendering takes the verb *biaze-*   *tai* as a middle with active force, rather than a passive (cf. Carson, "Matthew," 267).

Jewish expectations that Jesus invites John (through his disciples) not to "stumble" over him (v. 6). The kingdom *is* here, but not in a way that would convince everyone.

Jesus even more clearly affirms the kingdom's presence in Matthew 12, responding to his detractors' assertion that his exorcisms were accomplished through his allegiance with Beelzebul. Such is ludicrous, Jesus says, because that would mean Satan is attacking his own house (12:25 – 26). The reality is just the opposite: Jesus is "tying up the strong man" (= Satan) in order to set people free (v. 29). So he concludes, "But if it is by the Spirit of God that I drive out demons, then the kingdom of God has come upon you" (12:28).

Jesus usually characterizes the kingdom as "having drawn near" (captured by the Greek verb *ēngiken*; e.g., Matt. 3:2; 4:17; 10:7), indicating the kingdom's impact on the present by the sheer imminence of its arrival. But on the occasion in Matthew 12:28, his choice of verb is distinct (the Greek verb *ephthasen*—"has come upon"). The kingdom is *here*, demonstrated by his powerful dismissal of a servant of Satan! Yet room remains for the willful rejection of this reality (12:31 – 32). This must mean that the *consummation* of the kingdom, which will be overwhelmingly obvious to everyone when it comes, awaits its grand fulfillment at some time in the apparently imminent future. Further confirmation of this perspective comes especially in a few of Jesus' kingdom parables. One will suffice for us here.

In Matthew 13:24 – 30, 37 – 43, Jesus likens the kingdom to a field in which weeds have been sown surreptitiously among the wheat. When the weeds emerge along with the wheat, the field owner rejects the option of pulling up the weeds. Rather, to preserve the wheat, he instructs his workers to let both grow until the harvest. Only then should they pull up the weeds along with the wheat, gathering the wheat into his barn and burning up the separated weeds (vv. 29 – 30, 40 – 42). Jesus then explains that the wheat represents the people of the kingdom, while the weeds depict the people of the evil one. When the harvest comes, the angels sent out by the Son of Man will harvest both from the "field," which Jesus identifies as "his kingdom" (v. 41). Then the righteous will experience the blessings of the "kingdom of their Father" (v. 43). What, then, is the important aspect of this parable for us? The answer becomes obvious through a comparison with the common Jewish expectations regarding the kingdom.

On the one hand, the rewarding of the righteous and the condemnation of the unrighteous at the judgment is exactly what the kingdom-pining Jews of that era anticipated. There is nothing new here, and Jesus affirms its correctness! On the other hand, the notion of a *present* expression of the kingdom that does not immediately bring about the expected division between the people of the kingdom and the people of the evil one is surprising, to say the least! In fact, it requires a massive alteration in the usual Jewish expectation. Jesus even characterizes this as the "mystery" of the kingdom (cf. Matt. 13:11). It's a mystery because the prophets did not anticipate its arrival without bringing the harvest at the end of the age. This is the "*inaugurated*" kingdom—an era where the two ages *overlap*. We might depict this modification in this manner:

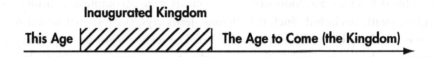

While preserving the Jewish expectation of the climactic judgment, Jesus introduces this new stage. It is the era of the kingdom in which you and I live.[5]

THE INAUGURATED NEW COVENANT

What, then, are the implications of this inaugurated kingdom for discipleship? Simply this: since the kingdom has only been inaugurated by Jesus' coming, we should not be surprised if some aspects of the New Covenant initiated by Jesus are similarly only inaugurated. We need to speak carefully here, of course. It is the unanimous conviction of the New Testament writers that the atonement that Jesus provides is complete and unrepeatable. There remains no need for any further sacrifice for sin. But that does not necessarily mean that all of the other New Covenant blessings have similarly been consummated. In fact, it is obvious that they are not.

It is true that disciples of Jesus have received forgiveness of sins (Eph. 1:7), they have been regenerated by the power of the Spirit (Gal. 5:25), and the will of God has been written on their hearts (2 Cor. 3:3). Moreover, the blessings of the Abrahamic Covenant are breaking through to many nations of the earth (Rom. 15:19–20). But have all of these blessings been consummated and fulfilled in absolute terms? *Hardly!*

Although the atonement has been consummated, the absolute nature of the people's transformation remains unfulfilled. The Spirit has indeed been poured out into the hearts of God's people in the New Covenant, but the flesh continues to war against his influence, giving rise to the struggle that plagues the disciple in this era:

> For the sinful nature desires what is contrary to the Spirit, and the Spirit what is contrary to the sinful nature. They are in conflict with each other, so that you are not to do whatever you want. (Gal. 5:17)

---

5. The inaugurated stage of the kingdom is also expressed in the parables of the mustard seed (Matt. 13:31–32) and the leaven (Matt. 13:33). In the first case, Jesus utilizes traditional images that emphasize opposite degrees of size. The mustard seed in the Middle East is proverbially the smallest of the seeds. Conversely, the mature mustard plant is not actually a "tree," but rather a large bush. In the second parable, Jesus sets up a rather unlikely scene, with the woman making the equivalent of twenty-two liters of dough—about fifty pounds. This then is contrasted with a "lump" of leaven that is hidden in the dough. In both instances, the end result matches with the usual Jewish conception of the kingdom—it will be *big*! A tree in which birds can roost or fifty pounds of leavened dough! But it is the unexpected *smallness* of the initial form of the kingdom that grabs the attention. To think that the kingdom could ever be characterized as a mustard seed or a small lump of leaven is revolutionary, yet this is what Jesus is affirming. Although the kingdom is here, it is only here in an inaugurated, partially-fulfilled form. One day, it will be consummated at the return of the Son of Man.

Indeed, all creation awaits the consummation:

> We know that the whole creation has been groaning as in the pains of childbirth right up to the present time. Not only so, but we ourselves, who have the firstfruits of the Spirit, groan inwardly as we wait eagerly for our adoption, the redemption of our bodies. (Rom. 8:22–23)

This means, then, that disciples of Jesus are literally caught in the tension between two salvation-historical realities—between the ongoing frailty characteristic of the old era and the Spirit-enabled, absolute demand of righteousness pertaining to the new era. Though the transformation of the people has begun, it is only partially realized in the inaugurated kingdom.

Consequently, it seems appropriate to understand that the inaugurated nature of the *kingdom* implies a similar inauguration of the *covenant* that is associated with it. The New Covenant has been established in Christ, and we have already now begun to experience its benefits. But we have not yet experienced its full consummation.[6] The prophetic vision regarding the transformation of the people has begun, but it has not been fully realized. In this age, Jesus alone is completely faithful. Only when the consummated kingdom comes will the rest of us experience the complete transformation of our hearts, such that we will no longer disrupt our relationship with God through sin. What we must do, therefore, is to learn how to live ever-increasingly faithful lives within the inaugurated New Covenant blessings of the inaugurated age of the kingdom.

SUMMARY

This is the challenge facing Jesus' disciples in this era. In contrast to the Jewish expectation that the kingdom would arrive in a cataclysmic and sudden manner, resulting in the wholesale transformation of the New Covenant people, the reality in which we live falls somewhat short of this. This is because Jesus clarifies that he has merely inaugurated the kingdom, leaving its consummation to an undefined time in the future. The significance of this observation is that the covenant blessings associated with the kingdom are likewise also merely inaugurated. That is to say, while we as disciples of Jesus have received his atoning grace and experienced the provision of the Spirit, our hearts are not completely surrendered to his enablement.

How then can we live faithfully without falling into a legalism that will shackle our fickle hearts in the chains of our failure? The answer once again is to be sought in the framework of covenant—specifically, in learning how life is to be lived in covenant with God. Therefore, let's return once again to the Old Testament for insight into what life was like in the covenants, looking for more answers and for hope.

---

6. Williamson, *Sealed with an Oath*, 208–10.

RELEVANT QUESTIONS

1. When you compare your life to the glorious prophetic expectations of the people who will live in the New Covenant era, what thoughts come to mind?

2. How does the notion of the inaugurated kingdom and New Covenant in Jesus' ministry affect how you assess the present state of the church? In what ways does it help to explain things?

3. How might the theology of the inaugurated kingdom be used inappropriately to excuse and minimize the gravity of sin? In what ways do the answers to the "Why" and "What" questions help us avoid this pitfall?

4. As you think about the nature of the covenants, what is your expectation regarding the answer to the "How" question?

CHAPTER 12

LIFE IN COVENANT WITH GOD

Remember that you were slaves in Egypt and the LORD your God redeemed you from there. That is why I command you to do this.

Deuteronomy 24:18

[The Spirit] will glorify me because it is from me that he will receive what he will make known to you. All that belongs to the Father is mine. That is why I said the Spirit will receive from me what he will make known to you.

John 16:14–15

When we reflect on the high demands that Jesus places on his followers, anything but the adjectives "easy" and "light" come to mind! So how is it possible that Jesus' followers would experience his "yoke" that way? When we considered the covenantal conversations under the "Why" question, we discovered that grace was always prior to the demands. This provides the obvious hint concerning the answer to the "How" question: prior and sustaining grace, in all of its forms, is *always* to be understood as the enabling context in which God's demands are to be responded to. That is, covenant faithfulness will only be possible as disciples experience the enabling power of grace.

But remember that one of the devastating results of the fall is the posture of autonomy and independence that Eve and Adam assumed in relation to God when they grasped the fruit, rejecting the sufficiency of God's provision on their behalf. The damaging result has been that the ongoing, enabling power of grace has been minimized or lost altogether, leading to compromise, unfaithfulness, and outright rebellion.

So how was this state of affairs addressed in the Old Testament, specifically in the context of the Mosaic Covenant? We will discover that life in the Mosaic Covenant was lived in yet another covenantal pattern:

- the frequent *remembrance* of God's provisions
- the present celebration of the *reception* of those provisions
- (leading to) the enabled *response* of obedience and faithfulness

This, in turn, will provide us with insight into the answer to the "How" question. Once again, let's return to the Old Testament.

REMEMBERING, RECEIVING, AND RESPONDING

We learned in chapter 4 that God's overarching covenantal demand is to love him with all of one's being: "Love the LORD your God with all your heart and with all your soul and with all your strength" (Deut. 6:5). This entails *complete* devotion and obedience in all of life, as Moses goes on to explain:

> These commandments that I give you today are to be upon your hearts. Impress them on your children. Talk about them when you sit at home and when you walk along the road, when you lie down and when you get up. Tie them as symbols on your hands and bind them on your foreheads. Write them on the doorframes of your houses and on your gates. (Deut. 6:6–9; cf. 10:12)

Wherever his people went, they were to remain faithful to their God. But the important question is *how* this was to come about. As we will see, the enablement for this kind of single-hearted devotion was to be received through the frequent *remembrance* and *reception* of God's prior and sustaining grace toward them as a people — grace that softened their hearts, renewed their fear of the Lord, reinforced their dependence on him, and moved them to follow him as their King. To discern this, let's once again consider the Old Testament covenantal reality, looking for various ways in which this dynamic is woven into the fabric of covenantal life.

The Exodus and the Provision of the Land

A major focus of the Israelites' remembrance is their gracious deliverance from Egypt and the eventual provision of the Promised Land. But the practice of this remembrance is not simply for the sake of remembering their beginnings as a nation. Rather, their remembrance is to reinforce and catalyze their covenant faithfulness in the wake of God's gracious deliverance and provision:

> Be careful to *follow every command* I am giving you today, so that you may live and increase and may enter and possess the land that the LORD promised on oath to your ancestors. *Remember* how the LORD your God led you all the way in the wilderness these forty years, to humble and test you in order to know what was in your heart, whether or not you would keep his commands. He humbled you, causing you to hunger and then feeding you with manna, which neither you nor your ancestors had known, to teach you that people do not live on bread alone but on every word that comes from the mouth of the LORD. (Deut. 8:1–3; emphasis mine)

This theme continues on into their experience of life in the land:

When the LORD your God brings you into the land he swore to your fathers, to Abraham, Isaac and Jacob, to give you—a land with large, flourishing cities you did not build, houses filled with all kinds of good things you did not provide, wells you did not dig, and vineyards and olive groves you did not plant—then when you eat and are satisfied, *be careful that you do not forget the LORD, who brought you out of Egypt, out of the land of slavery.* (Deut. 6:10–12; emphasis mine)

In other words, Moses exhorts the people to covenant faithfulness as they settle into their mundane, daily life in the land; though they themselves work the land and derive food and wealth from it, they are not to allow the illusion of their independence from God to result in covenantal infidelity:

For the LORD your God is bringing you into a good land—a land with streams and pools of water, with springs flowing in the valleys and hills....

When you have eaten and are satisfied, praise the LORD your God for the good land he has given you. Be careful that you *do not forget* the LORD your God, failing to observe his commands, his laws and his decrees that I am giving you this day. Otherwise, when you eat and are satisfied, when you build fine houses and settle down, and when your herds and flocks grow large and your silver and gold increase and all you have is multiplied, then your heart will become proud and you will *forget* the LORD your God, *who brought you out of Egypt*, out of the land of slavery.... You may say to yourself, "My power and the strength of my hands have produced this wealth for me." But *remember* the LORD your God, for it is he who gives you the ability to produce wealth, and so confirms his *covenant*, which he swore to your ancestors, as it is today. (Deut. 8:7–18; emphasis mine; cf. also Josh. 1:12–15; 23:3–6)

Thus, Israel's obedience to all of the law's commands is to be grounded in the memory of what God has done on their behalf in the exodus and wilderness wanderings. Whether this concerned orderliness in relation to marriage and divorce (Deut. 24:1–4) or compassionate and just treatment of poor laborers, widows, and foreigners (24:10–15, 17, 19–21), the memory of God's deliverance and gracious provisions on their ancestors' behalf is the catalyst for righteousness:

Remember that you were slaves in Egypt and the LORD your God redeemed you from there. That is why I command you to do this. (Deut. 24:18; cf. v. 22)

Even the tassels, worn on the corners of men's garments to remind them of the Lord's commands, are themselves to be perceived in the prior grace of the exodus:

You will have these tassels to look at and so you will remember all the commands of the LORD, that you may obey them and not prostitute yourselves by chasing after the lusts of your own hearts and eyes. Then you will remember to obey all my commands and will be consecrated to your God. I am the LORD your God, *who brought you out of Egypt* to be your God. I am the LORD your God. (Num. 15:39–41; cf. Deut. 5:15; 15:7–15; 16:3; emphasis mine)

Obviously, the memory of their slavery will encourage them to reflect on their present experience of freedom as an expression of God's ongoing grace to them as a people.[1]

Sadly, when the people forget this gracious nature of their existence, they will prove unfaithful to the Lord, even turning to other gods:

> No sooner had Gideon died than the Israelites again prostituted themselves to the Baals. They set up Baal-Berith as their god and *did not remember* the LORD their God, *who had rescued them* from the hands of all their enemies on every side. (Judg. 8:33 – 34; cf. Deut. 32:12 – 19; Isa. 1:2 – 5; Jer. 2:11 – 14; Hos. 11:1 – 4)

This confirms our general perspective. Only as people live in the remembrance and conscious reception of the prior and sustaining grace of God do they remain faithful to God's call to righteousness. We will see the recurrence of the exodus and the provision of the land in several aspects of Israelite life in covenant with the Lord.

Sabbath

A major focus of Israelite remembrance is embodied in the Sabbath, whose weekly observance set them apart from the surrounding nations. In Exodus 31, we learn that the Sabbath is understood to be the sign of the Mosaic Covenant, even as the rainbow was the sign of the Noahic Covenant and circumcision the sign of the Abrahamic Covenant: "The Israelites are to observe the Sabbath, celebrating it for the generations to come as a lasting covenant. It will be a sign between me and the Israelites forever" (Ex. 31:16 – 17a). Two theological reasons are given for the Sabbath, both of which appropriately would be in the minds of those observing its pattern.

God's Provision in Creation

The first motivation appeals to the obvious connections the Sabbath had with the ending of God's creative activity:

> Remember the Sabbath day by keeping it holy. Six days you shall labor and do all your work, but the seventh day is a sabbath to the LORD your God. On it you shall not do any work.... For in six days the LORD made the heavens and the earth, the sea, and all that is in them, but he rested on the seventh day. Therefore the LORD blessed the Sabbath day and made it holy. (Ex. 20:8 – 11; cf. also Ex. 31:12 – 17)

---

1. This awareness is clearly demonstrated by the postexilic community as they gather in Jerusalem and recall their past failures and God's compassionate faithfulness (Neh. 9:6 – 31). They then appeal to their covenant God to respond once again to their hardship as a people (Neh. 9:32 – 37). Finally, in light of God's past faithfulness and the expectation of future deliverance, they recommit themselves to faithfulness: "all these now join their fellow Israelites the nobles, and bind themselves with a curse and an oath to follow the Law of God given through Moses the servant of God and to obey carefully all the commands, regulations and decrees of the LORD our Lord" (Neh. 10:29). This was to include respecting the Sabbath, bringing in the full tithe, and remaining set apart to God (Neh. 10:30 – 39). Cf. similar portrayals in Psalms 77; 105; 106.

The reason for God's rest is here identified as a divine declaration that everything needed for life to thrive on the earth had been provided.[2] As Hafemann puts it:

> [God's] Sabbath was like the rest a metalsmith takes after the final polishing has been applied and the pendant is complete. God rested because the world was now perfectly suited to meet the needs of mankind and, in doing so, to display the glories of its Creator.[3]

Regular Sabbath observance, therefore, enabled the people to live out the reality of their dependence on God's sovereign provision in ruling over his creation. During the six work days, they fulfilled their God-given role of subduing and stewarding the creation as God's image-bearing representatives. But on the seventh day, they were to receive again the promise of God's provision for the task. Resting on the Sabbath reminded the people of their utter dependence on God for all of life, including the ability to obey his demands in relation to the created world.

"Thus, by keeping the Sabbath, God's people were to proclaim about creation what God himself said about it when he 'rested': God's provision is all they need to fulfill his calling in their lives. Like God, his people were not to rest on the Sabbath because they were exhausted or needed a break, but because they were content in God and his will. God's own pleasure in his provisions, signified by his 'rest,' was to be marked by and embodied in his people's pleasure in what he had provided — likewise signified by their rest. In this way, keeping the Sabbath expresses what it means to be created in the 'image of God' (Gen. 1:27)."[4]

God's Provision in the Exodus

The second reason for the Sabbath lies once again in its appeal to Yahweh's redemption of Israel from slavery:

> Observe the Sabbath day by keeping it holy, as the LORD your God has commanded you. Six days you shall labor and do all your work, but the seventh day is a sabbath to the LORD your God.... *Remember* that you were *slaves in Egypt* and that the LORD your God *brought you out of there* with a mighty hand and an outstretched arm. Therefore the LORD your God has commanded you to observe the Sabbath day. (Deut. 5:12–15; emphasis mine)

In a sense, God's creative work at the beginning of the universe was *reenacted* in the exodus. By delivering the Israelites out of their bondage in Egypt, God created for himself a people of his own possession — a people to whom he committed himself

---

2. It is interesting that in Gen. 2:1–3, no "evening and morning" formula is attached to the seventh day. This suggests its nature as "an endless day, anticipating the ideal for God's creation. It is to this that Exodus 20 appeals, inviting Israel to participate in a weekly Sabbath modeled on the original, very good creation" (Barker, "Sabbath, Sabbatical Year, Jubilee," 697).

3. Scott J. Hafemann, *The God of Promise and the Life of Faith: Understanding the Heart of the Bible* (Wheaton: Crossway, 2001), 45.

4. Ibid., 46.

in the Mosaic Covenant and then sustained in their travels to the land of promise so they could become the nation of priests to the world (Ex. 19:6).[5]

This complements the first grounding of the Sabbath, adding God's gracious deliverance to his sustaining grace. By observing the Sabbath each week, therefore, Israel's memory was jogged to recall her complete dependence on Yahweh for everything, ensuring the conscious *reception* of his blessings. In this way, it corrected the posture of independence left over from Eden's fall. The response of obedience and faithfulness to God appropriately was to flow forth from their ongoing experience of God's prior and sustaining grace.

Festival Celebrations of Redemption and Material Provision

Other dimensions of remembrance come through the Jewish festivals. While the Sabbath occurs every week, these festivals are grouped at three intervals in the year—in the early spring, the summer, and the fall.[6]

Early Spring: The Passover, the Feast of Unleavened Bread, and the Firstfruits

To preserve the significance of the Passover event in the national consciousness, succeeding generations were to reenact God's remarkable deliverance in the Passover meal, repeating the story to themselves and their children. Accordingly, each generation reentered their nation's seminal history by reenacting it:

> Obey these instructions as a lasting ordinance for you and your descendants. When you enter the land that the LORD will give you as he promised, observe this ceremony. And when your children ask you, "What does this ceremony mean to you?" then tell them, "It is the Passover sacrifice to the LORD, who passed over the houses of the Israelites in Egypt and spared our homes when he struck down the Egyptians." (Ex. 12:24–27)

It is significant that the original meal was celebrated *prior* to the actual deliverance provided by Yahweh. Thus, it was eaten in faith that God would soon set them free. By reenacting the meal, each generation actively reentered their beginning, rendering them once again "the exodus people."[7] Accordingly, they *remembered* God's provision and *received* afresh its implications.

Preeminent among these was the urgent call to *respond*, imaged by the week-long Feast of Unleavened Bread (Ex. 12:15–20). As we have noted previously, the removal of yeast from their homes symbolized the haste with which they departed

---

5. Ibid., 47–48.

6. See C. E. Amerding, "Festivals and Feasts," in *Dictionary of the Old Testament: Pentateuch* (Downers Grove: IVP, 2003); J. E. Hartley, "Atonement, Day of," in *Dictionary of the Old Testament:*

Pentateuch (Downers Grove: IVP, 2003).

7. John Goldingay, *Old Testament Theology: Vol. 3: Israel's Life* (Downers Grove, IL: IVP, 2009), 162.

Egypt. By the time of the first century AD, the permeating qualities of yeast had led to its association with sin, explaining Paul's use of the imagery in 1 Corinthians 5:6–8. There may be traces of this development in the prohibitions against mixing the sacrifices with yeast (Ex. 34:25; Lev. 2:11; 6:17), although some offerings included leavened bread (Lev. 7:13; 23:17). At the least, the Feast of Unleavened Bread allowed succeeding generations to reenact their history and to join with their forebears in urgently responding to God's deliverance (cf. 1 Cor. 5:6–8).

"The remembering involved in the event is a conscious application of the mind that takes one into another reality. It accompanies this by activity of the body that ensures that the whole person is engaged.... As the event recurs it embraces the participants once again and takes them in their own experience from bondage to freedom. If they are actually living in some Egypt, its doing so is the more important, so that the real world in which service of the king gave way to service of Yhwh becomes again the world that shapes the lives of people who are tempted to live as if the world in which this does not take place is the truly real world."[8]

Along with the celebration of God's past deliverance, on the Sunday morning after the Passover Sabbath they also presented to the Lord a sheaf of barley to represent the firstfruits of that harvest. In this way, the deliverance of the past was also connected to the present provision of sustenance in the land that God had given to them:[9]

> So the Lord brought us out of Egypt with a mighty hand and an outstretched arm, with great terror and with signs and wonders. He brought us to this place and gave us this land, a land flowing with milk and honey; and now I bring the firstfruits of the soil that you, Lord, have given me. (Deut. 26:8–10a)

It is evident from these texts that God's past, present, and future grace functions in these festivals to engender a corresponding faithfulness from the covenant people.

Early Summer: The Feast of Weeks/Pentecost

Seven weeks after the Feast of the Firstfruits, the Israelites observed the Feast of Weeks. It came to be called "Pentecost" (from the Greek number fifty), according to the days between it and the Feast of Firstfruits:

> Count off seven weeks from the time you begin to put the sickle to the standing grain. Then celebrate the Feast of Weeks to the Lord your God by giving a freewill offering in proportion to the blessings the Lord your God has given you. And rejoice before the Lord your God at the place he will choose as a dwelling for his Name—you, your sons and daughters, your male and female servants, the Levites

---

8. Ibid., 162. Das, too, notes the present reference to this celebration: "In the Mishnah the Passover memorial was more than a remembrance of God's deliverance of the firstborn of Israel from the destroying angel; it came to signify the entirety of God's saving deliverance of Israel from the bondage and oppression of Egypt. As Exod 13:8 and the Mishnah (*m. Pesaḥ* 10:4–5) show, the Passover is a celebration of God's saving activity *in the present* and of God's *continued* redemption of Israel" (Das, *Paul, the Law, and the Covenant*, 112; emphasis his).

9. Allen P. Ross, *Recalling the Hope of Glory: Biblical Worship from the Garden to the New Creation* (Grand Rapids: Kregel, 2006), 230–33.

in your towns, and the foreigners, the fatherless and the widows living among you. (Deut. 16:9–11; cf. Ex. 34:22; 2 Chron. 8:13)

In this festival, the people celebrated the wheat harvest, though it was also connected to the more general provision of the land (Deut. 26:1–11). Along with various sacrifices, they presented two loaves that symbolized the blessing of the harvest with which God had blessed them in the land. As such, this festival continued the pattern of reiterated celebrations of God's gracious provisions toward them as a people.

Fall: The Feast of Trumpets, the Day of Atonement, and the Feast of Tabernacles

Three festivals marked the fall season. The first was called the Feast of Trumpets, taking place in the seventh month called Tishri (September/October). This festival celebrated the ending of the agricultural year and the beginning of the next. Trumpet blasts figured prominently in this festival, summoning the people to join in the festival:

Say to the Israelites: "On the first day of the seventh month you are to have a day of sabbath rest, a sacred assembly commemorated with trumpet blasts. Do no regular work, but present a food offering to the LORD." (Lev. 23:24–25; cf. Num. 29:1–6)

Those who gathered together reflected not only on the ending of one year's harvests and the promise of the next, but also on the ultimate ending of the age and the consummation of God's overarching purposes and blessings. In light of this, repentance, forgiveness, and restoration were prominent themes associated with this feast.[10]

The second fall festival transpired ten days after the Feast of Trumpets. This was the Day of Atonement (*yom kippur*), and it was viewed as the holiest day of the Jewish year:

The LORD said to Moses, "The tenth day of this seventh month is the Day of Atonement. Hold a sacred assembly and deny yourselves, and present a food offering to the LORD. Do no work on that day, because it is the Day of Atonement, when atonement is made for you before the LORD your God." (Lev. 23:26–28)

In addition to making provision for his own purification (Lev. 16:1–6, 11–14), the high priest selected two goats as the means by which God's gracious provision for the people was enacted (16:5, 7). One of these goats was slaughtered, and the priest carried its blood into the Most Holy Place to be sprinkled on the cover of the Ark of the Covenant. In this way, atonement was made for the uncleanness and rebellion of the people (Lev. 16:15–16). The priest placed his hands on the head of the other goat and confessed the sins of the nation. Then the "scapegoat" was led into the wilderness, symbolically carrying away into exile its defiling burden (16:20–22). Finally, the high priest offered burnt offerings for himself and for the people (16:23–27).[11]

---

10. Ibid., 234–35.   11. Ibid., 235–36.

The significance of the Day of Atonement was obvious in the life of the nation. When observed correctly, it was a day of solemnity and fasting, as the people reflected on their deep need before God. Positively, it effected the forgiveness of the nation's sins committed since the previous Day of Atonement, enabling God to continue to live among them and to bless them.

Only five days after the Day of Atonement, the Israelites celebrated their last harvest festival—the Feast of Booths (Lev. 23:34) or Ingathering (Ex. 34:22). In addition to the sacrifice of a large number of animals (Num. 29:12–40), they reentered their past history once again, living the week in simple booths made of branches to recall the experience of the wilderness generation. On the final day of the weeklong feast, the people moved back to the comfort of their own homes with great celebration, recalling the provision of the land of Canaan after the hardship of the wandering:

> Live in temporary shelters for seven days: All native-born Israelites are to live in such shelters so your descendants will know that I had the Israelites live in temporary shelters when I brought them out of Egypt. I am the LORD your God. (Lev. 23:42–43)

As it developed, this festival symbolized the future consummation when people from all over the world would come to Jerusalem to celebrate it (Zech. 14:16).

Much more could be said about the feasts, but what we have seen confirms our basic thesis—that the twin themes of redemption and material provision are interwoven throughout these celebrations of life with Yahweh. Those who lived within the Mosaic Covenant were continuously *drenched* with celebrations of the past, present, and future grace of Israel's covenant God.

The Tabernacle/Temple

Since the temple was the place where God objectively dwelt, climbing the temple mount or approaching the tabernacle was to come into the very presence of Yahweh (Ps. 42:4). As the center of the religious life of the people, the tabernacle/temple served as a constant reminder to the nation of God's nature and what he demanded of them. On the one hand, God's holiness and corresponding righteous demand were proclaimed. On the other hand, his profound grace toward his sinful people was dramatized.

Righteous Demand

The priesthood itself communicated the Lord's righteous demand. Since no one could approach God in a sinful state, the people needed a blameless mediator to stand between him and them. Thus, even the priests needed purification through the temple rituals, cleansing them of impurity and moral guilt. Only then could they approach God to make intercession and sacrifice for the people. Even so, God's unapproachable holiness was symbolized by the increasingly restricted access, moving from the outer courts all the way into the Most Holy Place, which could only be penetrated by the high priest once a year on the Day of Atonement.

Gracious Provision

But God's profound graciousness to his people was also celebrated in the temple. Though his holiness far outstripped the people's reach, the various atoning sacrifices met the people in their penitent defilement and opened the way to reconciliation and peace with their God. The temple made it clear that these twin themes were to be held together:

> When worshippers were reminded of the high standard of holiness, they did not despair; rather, they acknowledged their deficiency with contrition and humility and prepared to make the appropriate sacrifices. They would have rejoiced that they could yet celebrate communion with the living God in the sanctuary, *because what God's holiness demanded his grace provided.*[12]

Demand and Enablement in the Mosaic Covenant

Each of these institutions and festivals helps to confirm the nature of life lived in covenant with Yahweh. Although the law communicated his righteous demand, the people's faithful response was repeatedly set in the context of the remembrance and celebration of God's prior, present, and future provisions on their behalf. Properly understood, then, obedience in the Mosaic Covenant was empowered by the ongoing remembrance and reception of God's grace. Taken together, this provides us with vital insight for discipleship in the inaugurated kingdom.

ENABLEMENT IN THE NEW COVENANT

In our discussion of the New Covenant in chapters 3 and 4, I suggested that discipleship to Jesus can be depicted in a triangular fashion:

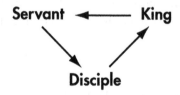

Having been graced by the Servant, the disciple is summoned to follow

---

12. Ibid., 197–98, emphasis mine.

the King. But since the King lived out the life of the Servant, the disciple ends up emulating the Servant. The only problem with this is that we disciples have experienced merely the *inauguration* of the New Covenant, such that we still often live inclined away from receiving and living in God's gracious provisions. How are we to respond faithfully to the absolute, kingdom demand of righteousness when our hearts are only intermittently attuned to the reception of God's sustaining grace?

Fighting for the Threshold

When I was in my doctoral program, I was privileged along with other doctoral students to spend an evening with Dr. John Stott. While on a speaking tour in the Chicago area, he graciously agreed to share some of his wisdom with us aspiring scholars. I confess that I remember little of what Stott said to us that evening — other than one memorable illustration.

Stott recounted the story of an Anglican bishop whose spiritual life had come under fire for one reason or another. Because of this, a group of hecklers had gathered outside of a building where the bishop was attending a meeting. As he emerged from the structure, one of these sang out, "Hey Bishop! How much time have you spent in prayer today?" Without hesitation, the clergyman turned to the man and calmly responded, "Three minutes." But then, before his challenger could say anything further, the bishop added, "But I spent thirty minutes fighting for the threshold." Dr. Stott used this interchange to exhort us to "fight for the threshold" in our prayer lives so that we would not allow form to replace substance in the ministry of the Word entrusted to us. Routine repetition of sanctified words, no matter how frequently uttered or how long in duration, can never accomplish what an intimate interchange with the Lord of the universe can — even if it is momentary.

What Stott's story says about prayer might also be applied to our reception of grace. It is one thing to *think* about grace, remembering its multifaceted expressions in Scripture or in our own lives. It is another thing to pause in those reflections long enough to *receive* that grace afresh, allowing God's faithfulness in the past and present, as well as his promises regarding the future, to wash through our souls, renewing our faith, softening our hearts, and aligning our wills once again with our Lord. It is the kind of encounter with Jesus that the woman with the ongoing hemorrhage had (Mark 5:24 – 34). Though many others were jostling Jesus in the excitement and curiosity generated by his agreement to go to Jairus's ailing daughter, it was only that needy woman who *received* anything from him (5:29 – 34). When we "fight for the threshold" with Jesus, we sit with him, believing that what he said, accomplished, and promised are true — this is the vital role of faith — until we receive from him his renewing, transforming, and enabling grace. And when his grace is received, transformation happens.

The Gospels are sprinkled with these kinds of encounters with Jesus. Think about the "sinful woman" in Luke 7, who ignores the horror in the room caused by her weeping over Jesus' feet. Undoubtedly, a prior encounter with Jesus had melted her wayward heart, moving her to express her repentance and gratitude in this shocking manner. Peter, Zacchaeus, Thomas, Mary Magdalene, and a host of others are all transformed by their encounters with Jesus because of their reception of his grace. Many people talk about the *motivation* that grace gives for righteous living. This is appropriate, of course. But in many ways it fails to do justice to the effect that grace has on those who truly receive it, underestimating its power. Stated as the *motivation* for obedience, the final emphasis lands on what *we* do in response to it.

But grace does more than merely motivate. When it is actually received, grace *empowers*. That is to say, the heart that receives it will not be left in the same hardened and rebellious condition. As such, rather than *motivation*, we should speak rather of the *enablement* that grace provides. I believe this is why God promises through Ezekiel that he will "move" his people to covenant faithfulness through the gift of his Spirit (Ezek. 36:27).

Thus, the answer to the dilemma facing us as New Covenant members in the inaugurated kingdom is obviously to return *repeatedly* to the Servant for renewing and transforming grace. This is one of the main benefits of having "gospels" in the New Testament. Similar to the festivals of Old Testament Israel, which reenacted the salvific and sustaining events of its history with God, the Gospels permit us to insert ourselves into the narrative, watching Jesus as he engages people, pursues them, invites them, touches them, cleanses them, and transforms them. And then they invite us to allow him to do the same with us!

The lessons we have learned from life lived in covenant with God suggest that only in this way will we be progressively wooed away from our inherited-from-Eden posture of independence and restored to the posture of reception. As this happens, we will be *enabled* to follow Jesus as King in ever nearer approximations of what we will be like in the next age. But until this posture is perfected in us in the consummated kingdom, this oscillation must happen every day — indeed, many times each day.[13]

Practicing the Reception of God's Grace

Brother Lawrence is well known for his transformative teaching whereby he exhorts people to "practice the presence of God."[14] The aspect of Lawrence's insight that needs special emphasis here is the encounter with God's grace in his presence. We might therefore rephrase Lawrence's dictum: rather than merely practicing the pres-

---

13. Interestingly, Hafemann makes an unnecessary dichotomy between God's grace as cause and as enablement: "God's grace and calling do not enable obedience. Rather, they bring it about. Obedience to the covenant stipulations is the inextricable expression of the calling and election of God in the lives of his people" (Hafemann, "The Covenantal Relationship," 64–65). The causative grounding of transformation is always to be found in God's redemptive initiative. But it does not follow from this that his grace does not *enable* obedience. The two are compatible together.

14. E.g., Brother Lawrence, *The Practice of the Presence of God*, updated by Ellyn Sanna (Uhrichsville, OH: Barbour, 1998).

ence of God, we must "practice the *reception* of his grace." But we will find that this does not come easy for us as descendants of Eden's rebellion. Even as Christians, saved by grace, we are quick to return to life in our own sufficiency, even as we strive to obey God! But covenantal discipleship rebukes this arrogant independence and replaces it with the posture of reception. And it is in this posture that we will find enablement.

Accordingly, another arrow is needed in our discipleship diagram to capture this dynamic:

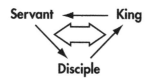

Having been graced by the Servant, we follow the King. But in order to do this consistently, we must return to the Servant often, reflecting on and receiving his gracious enablement for each day, each task, each decision, each need, each temptation. In this way, we will learn to live New Covenant lives, constantly remembering and receiving God's redeeming, enlivening, and enabling grace to us through Christ. As a result, we will naturally and joyfully heed Jesus' summons to kingdom righteousness. In this grace-enabled reality, his "yoke" will be "light."

The Spirit's Role

In and through all of this, the Spirit—the hallmark blessing of the inaugurated New Covenant—will be active (Acts 2:1–4, 16–18, 33; cf. Ezek. 36:26–27; Joel 2:28–29). But how does he enable us? How do we "keep in step" with the Spirit (Gal. 5:25)? I would suggest that we frequently speak about the Spirit's ministry in terms that are so vague as to leave us without a clear idea of how to access his enablement. Worst of all, his ministry is frequently conceived of as independent from Jesus. We like to use Paul's metaphor of being "led" by the Spirit (Rom. 8:14; Gal. 5:18), but what exactly does this mean? Once again, we are encroaching on a topic that demands much more attention than we have time and space here to devote to it.[15] But Jesus' words about the Spirit give us a bit of insight into what is to be the Spirit's role:

> But when he, the Spirit of truth, comes, he will guide you into all the truth. He will
> not speak on his own; he will speak only what he hears, and he will tell you what is

---

15. See esp. Gordon Fee's massive exegetical study, *God's Empowering Presence: The Holy Spirit in the Letters of Paul* (Peabody: Hendrickson, 1994).

yet to come. He will glorify me because it is from me that he will receive what he will make known to you. All that belongs to the Father is mine. That is why I said the Spirit will receive from me what he will make known to you. (John 16:13–15; cf. 14:26)

We often think that Jesus is solely speaking here about the Spirit's role in bringing to the disciples' minds the propositional truths that they are in turn to speak and teach. Clearly, this is the general focus of Jesus' words here. But Jesus also declares truth through his *actions*. So when Jesus says, "the Spirit will receive from me what he will make known to you," this certainly includes the grace communicated through Jesus' compassionate ministry toward disciples and nondisciples alike.

In other words, as we pause and meditate on the life of Jesus—as we fight for the threshold for this encounter—the Spirit will bring the truths of Jesus' actions to bear on our lives. As we *receive* these truths, the Spirit will be active in enlivening our hearts and minds by the grace of Jesus, *enabling* us to respond to Jesus' call to follow him. This, I believe, gets at much of what it means to be led by the Spirit.

We should, therefore, redraw our diagram once more to show the Spirit's role in every aspect of our discipleship:

The question becomes: Where might this grace be found in Jesus' ministry? Obviously, we can find it in the cross, where Jesus took on himself God's just wrath on our behalf, making it possible for us to be forgiven. Granted. But to reduce the grace that comes through Jesus to the cross would be a mistake of the first order. Building on our discussion in chapter 3, what remains for us to consider are some of the gracious elements that come to us throughout Jesus' life and ministry. To ascertain the fullness of this grace, we will need to see how Jesus ministers in the larger context of what God has been doing throughout the history of his interaction with his people.

SUMMARY

In this chapter, we have seen that the all-encompassing demand of righteous fidelity to God was always to be encountered in the repeated remembrance and reception of God's gracious deliverance and provisions. Ideally, the covenant people in the Old

Testament lived in the iterative pattern of remembrance, reception, and response. That is, the covenant provided regular occasions of remembering and receiving Yahweh's grace toward them throughout their yearly, seasonal, and weekly lives. In response to the reception of those blessings, they were to devote themselves afresh to keeping the covenant demands of righteousness. In this way, obedience to the law was constantly grounded in and empowered by God's prior and sustaining grace.

As New Covenant disciples, we too must learn to live covenant lives, returning repeatedly to the Servant for renewing and enabling grace so as to experience the sort of enablement that will enliven our obedience to the King. In and through all of this, the New Covenant gift of the Spirit will be actively making Jesus' grace present to us.

RELEVANT QUESTIONS

1. What are some of the specific ways in which the lack of the "remember, receive, and respond" pattern is evident today in the culture in which you live?
2. Although the church has done a fairly good job in teaching people the necessity to be saved *by* grace, has your church succeeded in teaching you how to live *in* grace? If so, what are some of the ways in which it has successfully done this? If not, what might change if it did?
3. Do you find yourself living this way?

CHAPTER 13

THE SERVANT WHO IS THE REPRESENTATIVE

But John tried to deter him, saying, "I need to be baptized by you, and do you come to me?" Jesus replied, "Let it be so now; it is proper for us to do this to fulfill all righteousness."

Matthew 3:14–15

Jesus answered, "It is written: 'People do not live on bread alone, but on every word that comes from the mouth of God.'"

Matthew 4:4

One of the most successful television programs in recent years has been the talent competition *American Idol*. With its weekly international audience of around thirty million people, its popularity continues unabated. What makes the show so compelling is the opportunity it offers to witness completely unknown people rise from anonymity to the heights of international fame and fortune. As such, the competition provides what could be understood as "representatives" of the public, for whom access to such notoriety seems remote at best.

As the leading singers progress through the successive rounds, they acquire a massive fan base of people who identify with them and support them with their weekly votes. And yet, the show is called *American Idol*, which indicates that the representative role of the competitors is ultimately eclipsed by distance, as the idolized winner achieves the heights of success unattainable to the masses. The illusion of representation, then, ultimately gives way to reverential remoteness.

One might wonder how such a culture of adulation affects the disciple's apprehension of Jesus. After all, Jesus is the ultimate *Superstar*! Given his impeccable behavior, his life and ministry can easily be viewed as the example that must be emulated, even though it is ultimately unattainable. In the process, the grace of Jesus' representational role is lost amid the exaltation of his achievement. But if we are going to find the enablement that we need to follow him faithfully, his life cannot simply be honored and praised. Rather, we will need to find in him our *repre-*

sentative, for it is in that role that his Servant grace is grounded and the enablement of the New Covenant communicated.

In order to answer the "How" question, therefore, we must perceive and receive the covenantal grace that comes through Jesus, the Servant. To do this, we must consider his actions in the context of the covenantal expectations that he is fulfilling. Let's begin at the beginning of his public ministry—his baptism.

THE BAPTISM OF JESUS
John's Prophetic Identity

As people were walking through the Judean wilderness in the late 20s AD, they encountered what must have been a very passionate and animated man, dressed in a cloak of camel's hair and crying out, "Repent!" Although such a figure in our day might be cavalierly dismissed, the Gospels tell us that crowds of people made the trek from Jerusalem and surrounding villages into the wilderness to hear him. Why? In reality, many of the Jews were waiting for something just like this. Remember, the people of Jesus' day were still anticipating the fulfillment of the covenants. They were also aware of the cessation of the prophetic office.[1] For centuries, it had fallen silent. Then suddenly, there in the desert, the prophetic role finds its voice again.

It's difficult for many Christians to understand John the Baptist and his ministry. This is partly because we often treat him as the herald that he is and move on quickly to the one heralded—Jesus! Some of us also tend to link John's baptism ministry with what is familiar to us—namely, *Christian* baptism. But even then it is difficult to understand why Jesus came to be baptized along with the crowds. Is he repenting of his own sin along with the rest of the people thronging to John in the wilderness? Is it simply a symbolic act, expressing his agreement with John's ministry to Israel?

The result is that the significance of Jesus' baptism is frequently missed, and along with it, the grace that comes to us through it. To recover this significance, we will need to reenter the first-century context and encounter both John and Jesus at the Jordan. As we do, we will discover one of the most important of Jesus' Servant roles—that of the *representative* of Israel.

The Covenantal Demand

John appeals to Isaiah 40 to identify what he is up to: "I am the voice of one calling in the wilderness, 'Make straight the way for the Lord'" (John 1:23b). As the "voice" in the wilderness, John understands his role to be that of exhorting the people to

---

1. The author of the second-century BC book known as 1 Maccabees betrays the awareness of the absence of the prophetic voice. When the Maccabees reclaimed the temple after the Antiochene violation, they removed the defiled stones from the temple and stored them "in a convenient place on the temple hill until there should come a prophet to tell what to do with them" (1 Macc. 4.46; cf. also 14.41; 1QS 9.11; *m. 'Abot* 1.1; *b. Yoma* 9b). As a confirmation of this perspective, it is also important to note that there are no new additions to the developing Old Testament canon during this era.

prepare for the Lord's coming. But what is John trying to accomplish by calling people out to the Jordan? Why is preparation needed?

Isaiah's Prophecy

As we noted earlier, Isaiah is referring in chapter 40 to God's deliverance from the Babylonian exile, when Judah's "hard service" will be completed and when she will have received from the Lord "double for all her sins" (Isa. 40:1–2). Then God will provide a deliverance from exile that will even eclipse the original exodus in glory (cf. 43:16–21). For Isaiah, the return from the exile will be a repetition of the pattern of God's deliverance of his people, which he initiated in the original exodus.[2]

We also previously noted that Isaiah (along with the rest of the preexilic prophets) expects the returning exiles to be a righteous people whose hearts will be transformed and wholly devoted to the Lord—they will be "the Holy People" (Isa. 62:12). Unexpectedly, however, these preexilic prophecies find only partial fulfillment. The exiles to Babylon do come home, obviously, and they do generally avoid the idolatry of their forefathers. But it isn't long until they once again fall into various forms of covenant unfaithfulness. This is where Malachi's prophecy comes in.

Malachi's Prophecy

Malachi lives *after* the exile during the time when the nation's unfaithfulness is reappearing. Malachi bemoans this reality, impugning both the priests specifically (Mal. 1:6–14; 2:1–9) and the people generally (2:10–17; 3:5–15). He therefore warns that the cycle of God's purging judgment of his people is about to recur. This will not transpire unannounced, however, for God's prophetic messenger will be sent first to prepare the way: "I will send my messenger, who will prepare the way before me. . . . See, I will send the prophet Elijah to you before that great and dreadful day of the LORD comes" (Mal. 3:1; 4:5). Jesus affirms, in Matthew 11:7–14, that John the Baptist is this first messenger: "And if you are willing to accept it, he is the Elijah who was to come" (11:14; cf. 11:10, which quotes from Mal. 3:1).[3]

A second messenger will then appear:

> "Then suddenly the Lord you are seeking will come to his temple; the messenger of the covenant, whom you desire, will come," says the LORD Almighty. (Mal. 3:1b)

---

2. See Watt's discussion of the "new exodus" motif that Mark develops (Rikki E. Watts, *Isaiah's New Exodus in Mark* [rev. ed.; Grand Rapids: Baker, 2001], 79–82).

3. Based on Mal. 4:5, a Jewish belief developed in the reappearing of Elijah before the coming of the Messiah (cf. Sir. 48:9–10; *1 Enoch* 90:31). To explain how Malachi can refer ostensibly to Elijah's future return without necessarily intending to mean this *literally*, Hengstenberg appeals to messianic passages that depict David reigning again (Jer. 30:9; Ezek. 34:23; 37:24; Hos. 3:5). What must be meant is simply the resurgence of his kingly line (E. W. Heng-

stenberg, *Christology of the Old Testament* [Grand Rapids: Kregel, 1970], 630–32). When John denies that he is Elijah in John 1:21, this must mean that he is aware that he is not *literally* the eighth-century BC prophet. Jesus' reference to him as the Elijah who fulfilled Malachi's prophecy should be taken to imply that John functioned in the same pivotal role in the history of Israel as did the original Elijah (cf. Luke 1:17); so also Pieter A. Verhoef, *The Books of Haggai and Malachi* (NICOT; ed. R. K. Harrison and Robert L. Hubbard Jr.; Grand Rapids: Eerdmans, 1987), 340–41.

When this second messenger comes, he will purify the Levites the way a smelting furnace refines metal (3:2–4). But he will condemn the "evildoers" so completely that neither "root" nor "branch" of them will survive (4:1; cf. 3:5). Those faithful to God, however, will experience climactic deliverance on that day (Mal. 4:2). It is significant that this messenger will make a division between the righteous and the unrighteous *within* the covenant people.[4] Since this is the case, the way preparer's role will be one of summoning the people to repent and to return to the Lord of the covenant before it's too late.

John's Ministry of Preparation

As these two texts find their fulfillment in John's ministry, the twin themes of judgment and blessing prominently emerge. Functioning as the fulfillment of "Elijah," John comes to a nation that is still mired in covenant unfaithfulness and standing under the ominous threat of the second messenger's coming.[5] In John's parlance, this figure is the "more powerful one" coming after him. In the same way that Malachi expects the unrighteous to be destroyed as "stubble" in a furnace, John expects the "one coming after him" to wield the "fire" of judgment to divide the unrighteous from the righteous, removing from the nation its unrepentant "chaff" (cf. Matt. 3:11–12). Therefore, preparation is imperative.

Consequently, John echoes Malachi's warning that those who are not prepared spiritually will be condemned and destroyed, regardless of their Jewish heritage (Matt. 3:7–10). But those who repent will be gathered into the barn like "wheat" (Matt. 3:12)—an obvious metaphor for the kingdom. These will experience the new ministry of the Holy Spirit (Matt. 3:11; cf. Ezek. 36:27; Joel 2:28–29).[6] In view of this impending time of fulfillment, John calls the people to a repentance that will renew their fidelity to the covenant, preparing them to survive the devastating judgment of the one coming after him, and to receive his blessings. Then will the ultimate fulfillment of Isaiah's prophecy of the return from exile transpire.

John's intention, therefore, is to prepare the people for what he believes will be the

---

4. Verhoef, *Malachi*, 332. The use of fire as a metaphor for God's judgment is common. For instance, Moses identifies God as a "consuming fire," who will surely bring upon the nation the curses of the covenant if the people prove faithless (cf. Deut. 4:24–28; cf. also 9:3; 18:16; 32:22; 1 Kings 18:38; Pss. 21:9; 50:3; 78:21; 79:5; 83:14–15; 89:46; Isa. 4:4; 5:24; 10:16–17; 29:6; 30:27; 47:14; 66:15; Jer. 21:14; Ezek. 39:6; Amos 1:4; 2:5; 7:4; Zeph. 1:18; 3:8; Mal. 3:2; 4:1; cf. also *Jub.* 9:15; 36:10; *1 Enoch* 10:6; 54:6; 90:24–27; *Pss. Sol.* 15:6; *4 Ezra* 7:36–38; 13:4; 1QS 2.7–8, 15; 4.13). Note also the use of fire in the burnt offerings of the temple, where sacrificial animals bear the judgment for their repentant beneficiaries (e.g., Lev. 1:9–17; 3:3–16; etc.). For the association of the Spirit and fire, see Joel 2:28–30; 1QS 4:13, 21. On the use of the "axe" in a judgment context, see Isa. 10:15. Note also the cutting down or the pruning of trees as a common judgment image in Isa. 6:13; 10:33–34; 32:19; Ezek. 31:12; Dan. 4:14; cf. Jesus' use of the same image later—e.g., Matt. 7:19; Luke 13:7; cf. also Mark 11:14, 20. The imagery of God's "healing" the nation is especially prevalent in Isaiah (cf. Isa. 29:18; 30:26; 32:4; 35:5–6; cf. also Isa. 50:4–5; Ex. 15:2; Pss. 103:3; 146:8; 147:36).

5. Jesus explicitly identifies John as Malachi's "Elijah" (Matt. 11:14; cf. Mal. 4:5), citing Mal. 3:1 to characterize his ministry (Matt. 11:10; cf. also Mark 9:11–13; Luke 1:17; and the similar descriptions in 2 Kings 1:8 and Mark 1:6). By identifying John as this prophet, who himself is the fulfillment of prophecy, Jesus affirms that John is "more than a prophet" (Matt. 11:9).

6. It is probable that John linked the "fire" with the judgment that the "stronger one" would execute and the Holy Spirit with the purification that God would effect through the "stronger one's" ministry (Nolland, *Matthew*, 147), though "fire" has purifying qualities in some Old Testament contexts (Isa. 1:25; Zech. 13:9; Mal. 3:2–3; cf. Carson, "Matthew," 105). The greater strength of the coming one is likely in reference to the greater efficacy of his baptism (I. Howard Marshall, *The Gospel of Luke: A Commentary on the Greek Text* [NIGNT; Grand Rapids: Eerdmans, 1978], 146).

The winnowing fork or shovel was used to gather up the broken pieces of stalk and loosened grain so as to toss them together into the air on a windy day. The wind would blow the light chaff away, leaving the heavier seed to drop back to the threshing floor. By means of this metaphor, John images the separation between the righteous and the wicked that he expects at the arrival of the one coming after him. The use of the adjective "unquenchable" stresses the finality of this judgment (cf. Isa. 34:10; 66:24; Jer. 7:20).

end-time purging of the nation about to be accomplished by the "more powerful one" after him (cf. Mal. 3:1–4; 4:1–6). This is why the situation is so dire. John is urgently summoning the nation to respond with repentance and righteousness at the last hour, just prior to this great day of the Lord.

John's Baptism

Why does John baptize the people? Throughout the Old Testament, the need for purity before the Lord was taken for granted. As we noted previously, this was especially true for the priests who stood before God in the temple. To accomplish ritual purification, they meticulously washed themselves before performing their mediatorial duties. These washings were effective because the Hebrews understood that the person is a unity of body and soul—what is done to the external body is also true of the internal, repentant spirit.[7]

The prophets eventually draw on this imagery as they look forward to the emergence of the purified remnant. Pride of place here goes to Ezekiel's expectation:

> For I will take you out of the nations; I will gather you from all the countries and bring you back into your own land. *I will sprinkle clean water on you*, and you will be clean; I will cleanse you from all your impurities and from all your idols. (Ezek. 36:24–25; emphasis mine; cf. also Ps. 51:2; Isa. 1:16–18; 4:2–4; Jer. 4:14).

When God brings the exiles home, he will cleanse them with water as if they were priests! The result will be a people transformed from within and indwelt by the Spirit of God—a people who finally will be faithful to God's demand for righteousness:

> I will give you a new heart and put a new spirit in you; I will remove from you your heart of stone and give you a heart of flesh. And I will put my Spirit in you and move you to follow my decrees and be careful to keep my laws. (Ezek. 36:26–27; cf. Joel 2:28–29; Isa. 44:3; cf. also Deut. 30:6; Ezek. 11:17–20; Zech. 13:1; 1QS 4:20)

In preparation for God's great work of judgment and purification, then, John is fulfilling the prophetic expectation of the cleansing of the people.[8] To accomplish this, John summons the nation out into the wilderness—the same place where Yahweh tested the children of Israel in the first exodus and through which they traveled in their return from Babylon. Significantly, John calls Israel out to the *other side* of the Jordan—the east bank, away from Jerusalem, symbolizing a new beginning

---

7. Cf. Hos. 6:1–6; Amos 4:4–6; Zech. 7:1–7. This comes out clearly in David's famous prayer of confession after his adulterous union with Bathsheba. He pleads, "Cleanse me with hyssop, and I will be clean; wash me, and I will be whiter than snow" (Ps. 51:7). For laws pertaining to cleansing by washing in various contexts, see Ex. 19:10; 29:17; 30:17–21; Lev. 1:9, 13; 6:27; 11:25, 39–40; 13:53–59; 14:8, 9, 47; 15:1–33; 17:15–16; 22:6; etc.

8. Notice Ezekiel's similar expectation of God's purging and preparation of the people in the wilderness (Ezek. 20:33–38; cf. also Hos. 2:14–23; 1QS 8:12–16; 9:17–20).

for the nation (John 1:28; 10:40). Those who are cleansed through repentance and baptism then "reenter" the land through the Jordan, reminiscent of the return from exile and the original exodus itself. By this means, John is culling out the purified remnant, prepared for the coming of the "more powerful one after him."

Jesus' Gracious Provision

And so we come to the crucial question: Why does Jesus come to John to be baptized?[9]

An Agreement with John

At the very least, Jesus is signaling his agreement with John that the nation needs purification from its sin. This accord is confirmed by Jesus' parallel baptism ministry through his disciples along the Jordan in the subsequent days (John 3:26; 4:1–2). It is also indicated by the identical summaries that Matthew uses to describe both Jesus' and John's preaching: "Repent, for the kingdom of heaven has come near" (Matt. 3:2; 4:17). Jesus clearly agrees with John on Israel's need of repentance in light of the kingdom's near approach. His participation in John's baptism underscores this.

But does Jesus' coming to John indicate that he too perceives his own need for repentance? John suggests otherwise when he objects to Jesus' baptism: "I need to be baptized by you, and do you come to me?" (Matt. 3:14). It is possible that John's knowledge of Jesus' personal righteousness is behind his hesitation, although more likely John is referring to Jesus' superior baptism.[11] Rather than washing the people merely with water, Jesus will be the one who dispenses the purifying Spirit. Such a one hardly needs John's baptism. So what is Jesus trying to accomplish here?

A similar agenda was practiced at the Qumran settlement on the shores of the Dead Sea. These Jews characterized themselves as those who had separated from the impure nation so as to prepare the way of the Lord in the wilderness, according to the prophecy of Isaiah 40. Here they studied and practiced the law in preparation for the last days when the kingdom of God would come. Removed from what they considered to be impure sacrifices and rituals in the Temple, the Qumranians supplemented their scrupulous adherence to the Torah with a posture of repentance, symbolized by daily baptisms, known as lustrations. They did this to maintain a state of individual and corporate purity. John's message and practice should be seen at least partially against their background.[10]

Identification with the Nation

If Jesus is not being baptized for his own sin, there might be another reason for his coming to John. John's baptism is a corporate event. The *nation* needs repentance

---

9. For a list of the numerous interpretations of this event, see Nolland, *Matthew*, 152.

10. On the similarities and differences between John and the Qumranians, see Ben Witherington III, "John the Baptist" *DJG*, 384; Craig Blomberg, *Jesus and the Gospels* (Nashville: Broadman & Holman, 1997), 216.

11. Carson, "Matthew," 107. For Jewish expectation that the Messiah would be free from sin, cf. *Pss. Sol.* 17.36; 1QSb 5; *T. Jud.* 24.1; cf. also *T. Levi* 18.9.

and cleansing. But if Jesus does not need this for himself, his participation in John's baptism likely implies that he is presenting himself as the righteous one, identifying with the unrighteous.[12] This brings into play the common Jewish notion of "corporate solidarity,"[13] where one member of a group can stand for the rest. In this way, Jesus is taking Israel's need onto himself. This provides the clue to decipher Jesus' words in response to John's hesitation: "Jesus replied, 'Let it be so now; it is proper for us to do this to fulfill all righteousness'" (Matt. 3:15). Whatever we make of this statement, we must interpret it in the context of both Jesus' and John's ministries. The key terms for us to consider here are "to fulfill" (*plerōsai*) and "righteousness" (*dikaiosynē*).

An example of corporate solidarity is provided by the high priest, who bore the names of the twelve tribes of Israel engraved on two onyx stones mounted on his shoulders (Ex. 28:9–12). When he entered the Most Holy Place to make atonement for all of Israel on the Day of Atonement (Lev. 16:3–17), he did so as their *representative*. A representative role is also true of the scapegoat, who bore the sins of the nation away into the wilderness (16:20–22).

Matthew's use of the verb "to fulfill" implies the notion of bringing to fullness what was prefigured in the past. It is the verb that introduces several of Matthew's quotations of the Old Testament, whose messages and historical patterns now are understood to be "filled up" to their end-time fullness.[14] In Jesus' teachings, "righteousness" is simply "God's demand upon man."[15] It refers to behavior involving holiness, integrity, justice, and mercy, each of which is heralded by the prophets.[16] In Matthew, it is the doing of the Sermon of the Mount.[17] In Luke, John calls even tax collectors and soldiers, people who were held in contempt for their abuse and graft, to righteous behavior (Luke 3:10–14).

So what does Jesus mean by the phrase "to fulfill all righteousness"?[18] As we have repeatedly seen, the prophets expected the eventual emergence of a purified remnant—a remnant that John was self-consciously trying to bring about. It is most likely that Jesus is referring to this theme here. By means of his identification with the nation in its dire need, therefore, Jesus is affirming that he is acting as Israel's *representative* in bringing about *in himself* the long-awaited fullness of righteousness.[19] Consequently, Jesus presents *himself* as the purified remnant—the remnant of *one*![20] As such, Jesus stands as the realization of the very goal of John's ministry.

12. Cf. also Cranfield, *Mark*, 52; Hagner, *Matthew 1–13*, 57.

13. See Lunde, "An Introduction," 37–38.

14. Matt. 1:22; 2:15, 17, 23; 4:14; 8:17; 12:17; 13:14, 35; 21:4; 27:9; cf. also 26:54, 56.

15. Benno Przybylski, *Righteousness in Matthew and His World of Thought* (SNTSMS 41; Cambridge: Cambridge Univ. Press, 1980), 94.

16. E.g., Ex. 23:6; Lev. 19:15; Deut. 16:19–20; 24:17; 27:19; Pss. 11:7; 33:5; 103:6; 106:3; 112:5; Prov. 11:1; 16:11; 20:23; Isa. 1:17; 10:1–2; 29:21; 56:1; 61:1; Jer. 9:24; 21:12; Ezek. 22:29; Hos. 12:6–7; Amos 2:7; 5:12, 24; 8:5; Mic. 3:9; 6:8–12; Hab. 1:4; Zech. 7:9–10; Mal. 3:5.

17. Cf. Matthew's use of the word *dikaiosynē* in Matt. 5:6, 10, 20; 6:1, 33. Most importantly, Jesus testifies that John came in "the way of righteousness" (21:32), which must refer to the righteousness of the kingdom of God—namely, the right behavior that results from a right relationship with God (see Nolland, *Matthew*, 154; Przybylski, *Righteousness*).

18. For a discussion of some of the various scholarly options, see Davies and Allison, *Matthew*, 1:321–3.

19. That is not to say that Jesus was accomplishing this in the baptism itself, but rather that he is affirming that he will live the life for which John and the prophets were calling.

20. Cf. also Lane, *Mark*, 54–57.

The Representative Servant King

Earlier, I referred to the identification of Jesus by the voice from heaven at his baptism, which is largely repeated at his transfiguration on the mountain: "And a voice from heaven said, 'This is my Son, whom I love; with him I am well pleased'" (Matt. 3:17; cf. 17:5). As I noted then, this statement draws on two Old Testament themes, implicitly identifying Jesus as David's heir and Isaiah's Servant of the Lord. In the first place, "You are my Son" parallels the psalmist's restatement of the divine promise to David: "I will proclaim the LORD's decree: He said to me, 'You are my son; today I have become your father'" (Ps. 2:7; cf. 2 Sam. 7:14a). God thereby identifies Jesus as his heir who will rule with a "rod of iron," dashing his enemies "to pieces like pottery" (Ps. 2:9–12). If this is all that the heavenly voice had to say, we would expect Jesus' baptism to be his regal anointing, such that his subsequent ministry would involve the forcible bringing of the kingdom of God, eventually landing him on the throne in Jerusalem.

But second, the divine voice refers to Jesus also as the one in whom God is "well pleased." This is likely an allusion to God's promise regarding the Servant of the Lord in Isaiah 42:1: "Here is my servant, whom I uphold, my chosen one in whom I delight; I will put my Spirit on him, and he will bring justice to the nations." You can see how the Spirit's descent on Jesus is tied closely to this image in Isaiah 42. As the fulfillment of Isaiah's Servant of the Lord, Jesus is identified as the one who will reestablish the nation after the exile (49:5–6), extend a blessing to the Gentiles (42:2–4; 49:6), and representatively bear in himself the condemnation that the nation had merited (53:4–12). We will delay a fuller discussion of these texts until the next chapter, but it is sufficient for now to note that the righteous Servant accomplishes the restoration of the nation precisely because of his close *identification* with the sinful servant and through his Spirit-anointed, *representational* role on their behalf.

Once the themes of Davidic King and Servant of the Lord are identified as flowing into the same river, it is easy to see the reason for the turbulence that results. How can it be that Jesus is the great Son of God, the Son of David, who comes to reign victoriously, and at the same time the righteous Servant of the Lord, whose representative suffering will bring about the forgiveness and healing of the nation?[21] These two roles appear to be in such contradiction that no one person could fulfill them both! We Christians often move too quickly to the New Testament resolution without truly feeling the tension—and therefore the wonder—of this confluence. Shockingly, they come together in Jesus, now equipped with the Spirit to accomplish his tasks as Servant and King.[22]

All of this suggests that in his baptism Jesus begins his ministry in a most remarkable way—coming not as the royal, end-time *judge* of Israel that John envisages, but as the Spirit-empowered, end-time *representative* for Israel. John calls on the people to prepare themselves for the righteous judgment of the "more powerful one" who will come after him. As the long-awaited, righteous King, Jesus will

21. Cf. Carson, "Matthew," 109–10; Meyer, *Aims*, 116–29.
22. Cf. Joel Green, *Luke* (NICNT; Grand Rapids: Eerdmans, 1997), 186–187; R. T. France, *Mark* (NIGTC; Grand Rapids: Eerdmans, 2002), 55, 77.

indeed summon the people to a righteousness appropriate to the arrival of the kingdom of God. But as the Servant, he also identifies himself with Israel's failure so that he might also bring about the solution to their need, by providing in himself the fulfillment of the demand of righteousness.

As the Servant anointed by the Spirit, he will also cleanse others along the way as he reestablishes the nation that will be defined by discipleship to him. Thus, it will be through his "fulfillment of all righteousness" that the nation will truly be purified and formed anew, and the end-time blessings will overflow to the nations. The true remnant, true Israel, will both be determined *by him* and brought into being *through him*—the Servant King!

JESUS' WILDERNESS TESTINGS

How, then, do Jesus' wilderness testings contribute to this picture? However we interpret them, they are surely to be seen in close connection with the baptism. Having been anointed in the Jordan by the Spirit as God's Servant King, Jesus is led (Mark = lit., "cast out") by the Spirit into the wilderness to endure a direct attack from Satan. This means that this is a divinely appointed confrontation. It is commonly assumed that the purpose of the temptation narrative is to provide us with the example or model of how to endure temptation. As such, the message is: "Do likewise." While this is an appropriate inference, it misses the mark in terms of its *primary* function in Jesus' ministry.

Once again, let's consider the covenantal demand to which this event in Jesus' life is related, before reflecting on Jesus' gracious provision.

The Covenantal Demand

Our discussion in chapters 3 and 4 uncovered the covenantal pattern that proved to be consistently true throughout the Old Testament—namely, that the covenants are always grounded in God's gracious provisions and commitments, but this always leads to the demand of covenantal faithfulness. In the case of the Mosaic Covenant, we learned that the exodus and Yahweh's commitments to Abraham provide the gracious context in which the law is given to the nation at Sinai.

In the wake of this grace, the law expresses God's covenantal demand of righteousness from the people, involving holiness and trust. Unfortunately, the narrative of the Israelites' travels in the wilderness repeatedly demonstrates the failure of the people to respond to God's gracious provisions with faithfulness. Jesus' wilderness testings connect with this historical and covenantal background.

Jesus' Gracious Provision
History Recapped

Matthew has already tipped his interpretive hand a bit in his remarkable use of Hosea 11:1 in Matthew 2:15: "And so was fulfilled what the Lord had said through the prophet: 'Out of Egypt I called my son.'" In so doing, Matthew appropriates a verse that is not only nonprophetic in its original context, but which is also descriptive of the entire nation of Israel in the original exodus. Notice Hosea's reference to the people of the exodus and their eventual covenantal faithlessness:

> When Israel was a child, I loved him,
>   and out of Egypt I called my son.
> But the more they were called,
>   the more they went away from me.
> They sacrificed to the Baals
>   and they burned incense to images. (Hos 11:1–2)

This is the verse Matthew presents as being fulfilled in Jesus' departure from Egypt with his parents.

How should we explain this fulfillment? Matthew is simply doing what we have seen others do, employing a correspondence-in-history lens to present Jesus as *reenacting* the history of Israel and bringing it to its fullest expression. As God brought Israel out of Egypt in the nation's early years, so is he bringing Jesus, Israel's representative, out of Egypt. In contrast to Israel's covenant failure (see Hos. 11:2–7), however, Jesus will prove faithful. This is where the temptation narrative fits.

The background for Jesus' wilderness temptations, then, is Israel's wilderness wanderings. During those forty years, God tested that generation again and again. Unfortunately, he repeatedly found them wanting. Now Jesus steps into the same kind of situation as Israel's representative. Although he is not out there for forty years, Jesus experiences similar testings in a condensed period at the conclusion of forty days of fasting.

Jesus himself makes this mirroring even stronger by quoting from Deuteronomy 6 and 8 in his responses to Satan's temptations. In the Old Testament context of these passages, Moses is calling Israel's attention to the things they learned (or should have learned) from God during their time in the wilderness. As they stand on the threshold of entering the land of promise, Moses enjoins them to covenant faithfulness, unlike their rebellious and unbelieving forebears. By appropriating these words in his own experience, Jesus is declaring that *he* is the one who will do what Israel in the past failed to do. He is the true *Son* of God who is bringing Israel's failed history to its successful completion!

History Fulfilled

Each of the temptations, therefore, finds resonance in the Old Testament history of Israel. It is because Jesus is reenacting the history of the Hebrews in the wilderness that making bread for himself would be wrong. In order to succeed where the wilderness generation failed, he must not complain about his lack of bread (Ex. 16:1–3, 6–8; cf. Num. 11:4–15), but rather trust in the Lord, "feeding" on his words (Matt. 4:4; cf. Deut. 8:1–3). Carson writes:

Israel demanded its bread but died in the wilderness; Jesus denied himself bread, retained his righteousness, and lived by faithful submission to God's Word.[23]

Rather than repeating the Hebrews' demand that the Lord prove that he is with them (Ex. 17:1–7), Jesus will once again trust in God's provision. Thus, he will not fall for Satan's misuse of the psalmist's declarations of trust (Ps. 91:11–12) to force God's hand (Matt. 4:7; cf. Deut. 6:16). Such would actually have been *unbelief* masked by an appeal to the Scriptures. And rather than resorting to idolatry, as the Hebrews did to ensure safe passage to their inheritance (Matt. 4:9; cf. Ex. 32:1–6), Jesus will worship God alone and wait on him in the path chosen for him (Matt. 4:10; cf. Deut. 6:13–14). By means of his successful weathering of these tests, Jesus demonstrates that he will indeed be the one who supplies Israel's need by living out the righteousness so long awaited by the prophets.

"Jesus did not turn stones into bread. Nor did he force God to send angels. Instead he trusted the Father in heaven — and all his needs were met . . . in time food was given him, and angels appeared. . . . As God once miraculously gave Israel manna in the desert, so now he feeds his Son — his Son who, unlike Adam, did not succumb to temptation and so received the food which the first man ate in paradise before the fall."[24]

Luke broadens the scope of Jesus' representation even further to include the whole of humanity by placing Jesus' genealogy between the baptism and the temptations. Luke's unexpected ordering is implicitly explained through his tracing of Jesus' lineage all the way back to Adam, suggestively identified as the "son of God" (Luke 3:38). Coming close on the heels of Jesus' identical naming at the baptism — "You are my Son" (3:22b) — this suggests Luke's intention to cast Jesus' successful repelling of Satan's insidious attacks as the obedience for which God has been looking ever since Eden.

Understood in this way, the primary message of the temptations is not one of *model*, so as to send the message, "*Do*." Rather, the message pertains to Jesus as *representative*, declaring the good news, "*Done!*"

EMPOWERMENT FOR DISCIPLESHIP

How do Jesus' baptism and temptations enable us to live faithfully as his disciples? The answer lies in applying to this encounter the discipleship dynamic that we learned in the previous chapter. That is, what is it that I should *remember* here? How do I *receive* Jesus' grace that comes to me on the banks of the Jordan and from the arid hills of eastern Israel? Finally, how do I *respond* appropriately?

It is worthwhile *remembering* why Jesus steps into that river and then travels off

---

23. Carson, "Matthew," 113.

24. Davies and Allison, *Matthew*, 1:374. Notice also the parallelism between Jesus' fasting and Moses' fasting for forty days and nights on Mount Sinai when he went up to get the second set of tablets from the Lord (Ex. 34:28; Deut. 9:9–11).

into the wilderness to do battle with Satan. The nation stands under the darkening clouds of impending judgment because of their failure to produce the righteous fruit of repentance. Unexpectedly, Jesus identifies himself with the nation in its failure, bringing to fulfillment the covenant faithfulness that had always eluded them and leading to his provision for all of humanity. Consequently, Isaiah's stark contrast between the lives of the sinful and righteous servants finds fulfilling expression in Jesus' actions in these narratives. The need is clear to John. The time is short before the Lord visits his people in judgment. Surprisingly, Jesus steps into that interval and provides what is needed.

This, then, is what must be *received* daily by faith. Jesus has become the representative covenant partner with God, graciously fulfilling the covenant demand of obedience on our behalf. This is why the New Covenant is a *grant* covenant. As Paul writes:

> Therefore, since we have been justified through faith, we have peace with God through our Lord Jesus Christ, through whom we have gained access by faith into this grace *in which we now stand.* (Rom. 5:1–2; emphasis mine)

For those of us beaten down by the inconsistency of our walk of discipleship, Jesus' provision of covenant faithfulness on our behalf is good news indeed. For others of us who subtly slip into a reliance on our own acts of righteousness in relation to Jesus' commands, this is also good news. For all of us, the partial nature of our repentance from sin literally cries out for the wholehearted repentance that Jesus accomplishes on our behalf, living it out consistently in the crucible of the wilderness testing. In each scenario, the thoughtful reception of Jesus' representative Servant work offers liberation from our repeated failures to live faithfully.

This is what it means to live in the *grant* nature of the New Covenant. It is *God* who has provided this to us in Christ's representative work. It is *Jesus'* righteousness in which we stand. That is why Christians are now baptized into Jesus (Gal. 3:27). For it is in him alone that righteousness and life are found (Col. 3:4a). And since we live in the inaugurated kingdom where we still have the tendency to rely on our own strength and merit, we must return to the reception of this grace each day. When we do, we will experience the Spirit's renewing of our fickle devotion to Jesus, impelling us to follow him.

The answers we have discerned to the "Why" and "What" questions leave us no avenue to avoid Jesus' call to righteousness. Yet, it is in this grace-empowered context that we must hear that summons. Reflecting on and receiving Jesus' representative work, we must each day incline our inconsistent hearts in the direction of the one who supplies the grace and leads us to an empowered walk of obedience. The world lies in the shadow of meaninglessness and despair. The poor languish without hope. The weak and lonely look in vain for aid and compassion. The deceived pursue fulfillment in the wrong places. They are all around us. Jesus, therefore, calls us to rise out of that river with him, to live as the remnant people of the New Covenant, trusting in God's timely provision for our own needs and following our King to bring hope and light into dark places:

> You are the light of the world.... Let your light shine before others, that they may see your good deeds and glorify your Father in heaven. (Matt. 5:14a, 16)

SUMMARY

Jesus therefore comes to John at the Jordan to signal from the outset that he is the one who will fulfill the goal of the Baptist's own ministry—the singling out of the righteous remnant before the time of the great judgment. To do so, Jesus identifies himself with the nation's need in the Jordan and then begins the resolution of Israel's failed history in his representative wilderness testings. As such, Jesus presents himself as the remnant of "one," providing in his own life the fulfillment of the long-awaited covenant righteousness.

What difference does this make for us, as disciples of Jesus? Knowing that Jesus has stepped into our need and has provided what we are incapable of achieving makes all the difference indeed. Knowing that Jesus turned away from sin on our behalf, not just once but throughout his life, has the power to liberate us from our shortcomings as covenant partners of God. Repeatedly remembering and receiving the gracious provision that Jesus accomplishes at the Jordan and in the wilderness offers to us the potential of supplying renewal and divine empowerment for covenant faithfulness.

RELEVANT QUESTIONS

1. How does understanding John's intention in his baptism ministry affect your understanding of God's desires for his people? How does this affect how you view your own life in relation to sin?
2. How has this explanation of Jesus' baptism and wilderness testings impacted you? How might meditation on these aspects of Jesus' ministry affect how you live out your discipleship?
3. What are some of the ways that Christians deny the sufficiency of Jesus' representative life?

CHAPTER 14

THE SERVANT WHO IS THE REDEEMER

But he was pierced for our transgressions,
  he was crushed for our iniquities;
the punishment that brought us peace was on him,
  and by his wounds we are healed.

Isaiah 53:5

After he has suffered,
  he will see the light of life and be satisfied;
by his knowledge my righteous servant will justify many,
  and he will bear their iniquities.

Isaiah 53:11

I grew up listening to the famous radio personality Paul Harvey. My favorite of his program features was "The Rest of the Story." Typically, Harvey would take his audience through an interesting narrative, retelling the story of some significant person, yet without divulging who the person was along the way. When he finally unveiled the person's identity, listeners were treated to a satisfying moment of insight, as their previous knowledge of that person was filled out by the background information supplied by Harvey. I recall my frequent smiles as Harvey concluded the segment in his signature voice, "Now you know, the *rest* of the story."

So is there more to be learned about the background to the story of Jesus' crucifixion? Is there a similar "rest of the story" to the joyous event of Jesus' resurrection? Are there fresh insights that might deepen our experience of the grace that comes through each of these? Obviously, there is always more with Jesus. In chapter 3, we considered Jesus' role in fulfilling the Passover lamb and Isaiah's Servant of the Lord to help us understand the ways in which Jesus provides the atonement anticipated in the New Covenant. Now, however, let's take a closer look at Isaiah's prophecy regarding the Servant to see if there is more to this story so that we might discern more deeply the way in which Jesus brings this redeeming figure to fulfillment.

THE COVENANTAL PROVISION OF THE SERVANT OF THE LORD

Probably the best-known Old Testament prophecy in Christian interpretation is Isaiah 53. With the stunning similarity between the prophet's description of the Servant, the crucifixion narratives, and Christian theology, it appears to be an inescapable conclusion that Jesus is its fulfillment. When Jesus *himself* makes this connection just hours before his flogging, this conclusion is confirmed. I cited this verse earlier, but it bears repeating here:

> It is written: "And he was numbered with the transgressors"; and I tell you that this must be fulfilled in me. Yes, what is written about me is reaching its fulfillment. (Luke 22:37 from Isa. 53:12)

Jesus therefore presents himself to his disciples at the Last Supper as the fulfillment of Isaiah's suffering Servant. So when he repeatedly affirms that his suffering is foretold in the Scriptures,[1] this chapter likely plays a prominent role in his mind.

But what is Isaiah referring to as he delivers his message of redeeming hope? Because of the dominance of the Christian interpretation of Isaiah 53, it is difficult to read this chapter in Isaiah's own context. Ironically, however, if we see *only* the New Testament fulfillment in Jesus, we will actually miss some of the deeper significance that comes from understanding the interpretive pathways down which the New Testament writers progressed—pathways that culminated in Jesus but had temporary destinations elsewhere. Because this is so difficult, I would especially encourage you to follow this argument with your Old Testament open at your side.

Isaiah's Reference regarding the Servant
Isaiah's Exilic Reference

The entire last third of Isaiah's prophecy is patently addressing the nation as it moves toward and through its unavoidable exilic fate. Having shown the palace treasures to the Babylonian emissaries (Isa. 39:1–2), King Hezekiah is told by Isaiah that they will all become the property of the king of Babylon (39:5–7). This sets the framework for the remainder of the book. So, when the next chapter begins with a message of comfort to the people, informing them that their "hard service" has been completed (40:2) and that God will soon bring them through the wilderness (40:3–5), the prophet must be referring to the nation's return from the Babylonian exile. As I noted earlier, the prophet restates the content of Isaiah 40 three chapters later, specifying its application to the judgment of Babylon and the resulting liberation:

---

1. Matt. 26:24, 54; Mark 9:12; 14:21; Luke 18:31; 24:44, 46; also implied in the *necessity* of his death; e.g., Matt. 16:21.

This is what the LORD says—
>   your Redeemer, the Holy One of Israel:
"For your sake I will send to Babylon
>   and bring down as fugitives all the Babylonians,
>   in the ships in which they took pride." (Isa. 43:14; cf. 43:19–21; cf.
>   46:1–47:15; 48:20–21)

Later, God announces that this homecoming will result from the judgment of Babylon through the Lord's conscripted agent—Cyrus, the king of Persia (Isa. 44:21–45:7, 13; 48:14–22). Since the chapters leading up to Isaiah 53 oscillate between the guilt of Israel (48:1–11; 50:1; 51:17–20), the judgment of Babylon (46:1–13; 47:1–15; 51:21–23), and the restoration of Israel,[2] the implication is strong that the exile is still the prophet's focus in chapter 53.

This is made even more secure by the exilic context expressed in the first half of Isaiah 52. Though the city is presently "a captive," the prophet exhorts Jerusalem to awaken and don "garments of splendor." The reason for this is that it is about to "sit enthroned," removing the "chains" from around its neck (52:1–2). What this refers to is explained in the next several verses as the prophet recounts the history of Israel's stages of bondage, explicitly naming Egypt and Assyria as past locations of imprisonment (vv. 3–4). This strongly implies that God's reference to the *present* exile must refer to their Babylonian oppression:

"And now what do I have here?" declares the LORD.
"For my people have been taken away for nothing,
>   and those who rule them mock,"
>   declares the LORD.
"And all day long
>   my name is constantly blasphemed." (Isa. 52:5)

Thus, those who "mock" and "blaspheme" his name (v. 5) must be the Babylonians, who interpret their victory as evidence of their gods' superiority over Yahweh.

When the mood changes in Isaiah 52:6–12, however, the prophetic reference must be transitioning to the return from the Babylonian exile. Just as the military runners precede the army's return to Jerusalem to provide the city with the "good news" from the battlefield, so the prophet envisions heralds who announce the news of the captives' return—an event that evinces Yahweh's reign (v. 7). With their arrival, the Lord will return to Zion, his place of enthronement:

Listen! Your watchmen lift up their voices;
>   together they shout for joy.
When the LORD returns to Zion,

---

2. Isa. 45:13, 17, 25; 46:13; 48:12–21; 49:1–7, 8–26; 50:4–9; 51:1–16.

> they will see it with their own eyes.
> Burst into songs of joy together,
>   you ruins of Jerusalem,
> for the LORD has comforted his people,
>   he has redeemed Jerusalem. (Isa. 52:8–9)

The "redemption" or "salvation" that is seen by all nations, therefore, should be understood within this context as the unexpected return of the exiles to Jerusalem from Babylon (v. 10). Whereas it had appeared that Babylon's gods had triumphed, the sovereign reign of Yahweh will become evident once again when he brings his people home.[3] As they depart from the defiled city, they are not to bring with them anything impure, even as they bear in their arms the temple vessels to Jerusalem (v. 11; cf. 48:20).[4]

Once again, Isaiah caps his argument with a graphic image. How shall he pronounce that resounding "yes" that God's great work demands? He pictures a besieged city breathlessly awaiting the news of the outcome of a decisive conflict. If the news is victory, they are delivered; if the news is defeat, all is lost. Suddenly, on a distant hill a runner is seen. What is the news? As he comes nearer it can be seen that he is waving a victory palm and not so much running as dancing. The Lord has won! Let the singing begin!"[5]

All of this sets the stage for Isaiah 52:13–53:12. In light of the foregoing textual evidence, it must at least be admitted that Isaiah's historical reference is the Babylonian exile and the subsequent return of the Jews to Palestine. This has been his focus beginning in chapter 40 and culminating in 52:1–12. It is also important to recognize that the prophet has repeatedly described *Israel* as his "Servant" throughout this section of the book.[6] So, whoever the Servant is, he is to be *identified* with Israel, yet *distinguished* from those in the nation who are guilty of covenant unfaithfulness (42:19).[7]

Although we will never be able to identify with certainty Isaiah's own referent for the Servant, this contextual evidence suggests strongly that he expects a righteous representative to endure with the rest of the nation the tragedy of Jerusalem's destruction

---

3. Isa. 46:1–13; cf. 44:6–20; 45:15–17, 20–25; 49:7, 24–26.

4. From the post-Easter vantage point, it is easy to reject this interpretation as falling far short of the universal and end-time language that Isaiah uses to describe the effects of this return. Oswalt writes, "Is that the only deliverance God has to offer to the human race, the only redemption the Holy One of Israel has to give the watching world?" Hardly! That deliverance, as wonderful as it will be, is only the barest object lesson for a deliverance, a redemption, that will touch even nature itself (*Isaiah: 40–66*, 372). But it is important to reckon with the prophetic expectations prior to the exile. They saw painted on their broad prophetic canvas the entirety of the redemptive work that God will accomplish through his people. That is, through God's dealings with them, the blessing of Yahweh will extend to all nations (Gen. 12:3; 17:5–6). Thus, Isaiah's expectation is that the redemption of Judah from exile will ultimately result in the extension of this universal blessing (e.g., Isa. 42:10–12; 49:6; 56:6–8).

But, lacking a temporal reference beyond the exile and return, Isaiah clumps God's ultimate purposes together with those that turn out to be foreshadowings—foreshadowings that prior to the exile appeared to be the last act. Because we have the advantage of having seen the consummation of this pattern, we must be careful not to endow that perspective to Isaiah, nor to deny his accurate portrayal of the return from exile as linked closely with God's ultimate redemptive action.

5. John Oswalt, *The Book of Isaiah: Chapters 40–66* (NICOT; ed. R. K. Harrison and Robert L. Hubbard Jr.; Grand Rapids: Eerdmans, 1998), 367.

6. Cf. Isa. 41:8–9; 43:1, 10; 44:1–2, 21; 45:4; 48:20; 49:5–6.

7. For a brief summary of views concerning the identity of the Servant, see Thomas R. Schreiner, *New Testament Theology: Magnifying God in Christ* (Grand Rapids: Baker: 2008), 262–65. Schreiner also provides good reasons why the Servant cannot be coterminus with Israel.

and the agony of the exile to Babylon. Since he is righteous, however, this suffering is not the result of his own sin. Rather, he is caught up in the consequences of Judah's covenant unfaithfulness and suffers along with them as the righteous one. This is why the Servant is described as appalling, disfigured (52:13), and having nothing of beauty to attract others (53:2–3). The righteous Servant is so identified with the nation in the suffering and disgrace of the exile that he shares its shame (53:4b). In other words, he looks like the rest of the nation as they endure the covenantal curse at the hands of Babylon's king; he is oppressed and "taken away" (53:8a).

But because of his righteous life, his undeserved suffering functions as the curse remover for the nation. Isaiah has made it clear throughout his prophecy that the nation goes into exile because of its sin (Isa. 50:1). Thus, the exile is the covenantal curse. Accordingly, when Isaiah describes the Servant as taking up "our pain" and bearing "our suffering" (53:4), he is bearing the nation's curse. As the innocent one (53:9b), he suffers for the rest of the nation, being "pierced for our transgressions" and "crushed for our iniquities" (53:5). He even experiences death on their behalf, being "cut off from the land of the living" (53:8b) and given a grave among the "wicked" and "rich" (53:9a). The result of this righteous "offering for sin" (53:10b) is the "healing" of the nation (53:5d) and the justification of many (53:11b). And though he dies, he also sees his "offspring" and the extension of his days (53:10c), such that "he will divide the spoils with the strong" (53:12a, b).

The Servant as the Remnant in the Exile

It is easy to see why the Christians assigned this passage to Jesus. Though innocent, he suffered and died on behalf of others. Because of this, God vindicated him through the resurrection so that he would see his "offspring" and revel in the "spoils" of victory. Things line up so nicely, it seems almost impossible to see them any other way.[8]

But it is also clear that Isaiah's frame of reference is that of the exile of Judah to Babylon and their return to the land. This aspect, then, leaves us with an interpretive dilemma. On the one hand, we could conclude that Isaiah's expectation—that the atoning, righteous suffering of the Servant would occur in the context of the exile—did not take place until Jesus' crucifixion. That is to say, his perspective was "telescoped" so that it caught in its line of sight the centuries-later suffering of the righteous one on the cross. This is obviously a typically Christian interpretation.[9] And it could very well be the right one. Plenty of times the expectations of the prophets are postponed until a point later than was their expectation.

---

8. Dempster helpfully identifies the royal dimensions of the servant, showing the applicability of the New Testament appropriation of this theme in relation to Jesus. What he does not do, however, is wrestle with the historical contexts of the various Isaianic texts that struggle to fit with an easy one-to-one prophetic relationship with Jesus ("The Servant of the Lord," 128–78).

9. E.g., Oswalt, *Isaiah: Chapters 40–66*, 320–408; more implicitly, J. Alec Motyer, *The Prophecy of Isaiah: An Introduction & Commentary* (Downers Grove, IL: IVP, 1993), 422–44.

On the other hand, it is also possible that Isaiah is referring to someone who actually did experience the devastation of the Babylonian exile, but whose suffering foreshadows that of Jesus. I have become convinced of this latter position, such that Isaiah is understood to be using the singular "servant" to refer *corporately* to the small number of covenantally faithful Israelites at the time of the Babylonian invasion. Taken in this way, Jesus was not the only, nor even an initial, fulfillment of Isaiah 53. Rather, once again we have a case of correspondence in history, where an earlier event foreshadows the greater fulfillment that comes in Jesus. This may seem implausible at first blush, but let's take a closer look.

Is there any evidence that would support a reference to a righteous remnant in the nation during the exile? In reality, yes, there is. The prophet seems to refer to this group in Isaiah 51:1a, identifying them as "you who pursue righteousness and who seek the LORD." The prophet exhorts these people to be comforted by the remembrance of their origin in Abraham and Sarah:

> "Look to the rock from which you were cut
>   and to the quarry from which you were hewn;
> look to Abraham, your father,
>   and to Sarah, who gave you birth.
> When I called him he was only one man,
>   and I blessed him and made him many.
> The LORD will surely comfort Zion
>   and will look with compassion on all her ruins;
> he will make her deserts like Eden,
>   her wastelands like the garden of the LORD.
> Joy and gladness will be found in her,
>   thanksgiving and the sound of singing. (Isa. 51:1b–3)

Though these righteous ones are ensnared in the covenantal judgment merited by the remainder of the nation, there remains hope.[10] This is because of the Abrahamic promise to which Isaiah is alluding here: "When I called him he was only one man, and I blessed him and made him many" (Isa. 51:2b). God will be faithful to these promises. Therefore, their eventual deliverance and restoration to the land is covenantally assured:

> Hear me, you who know what is right,
>   you people who have taken my instruction to heart:
> Do not fear the reproach of mere mortals
>   or be terrified by their insults.
> For the moth will eat them up like a garment;

---

10. The objection might be raised to this interpretation by noting that in Isaiah 53, the Servant suffers *on behalf* of others, not *with* them. Yet, it is likely that Isaiah is referring to those after the exile who benefit from the Servant's exilic suffering. Had the remnant not borne the covenantal curse righteously, there would have been no future for the nation.

the worm will devour them like wool.
But my righteousness will last forever,
     my salvation through all generations. (Isa. 51:7–8)[11]

This righteous remnant, then, looks like the rest of the nation in the exile, being involved in the identical fate as the unrighteous. But their suffering ends up serving as an atoning, curse-bearing offering, resulting in the blessing of God to the nation after the exile. This explains why death and burial can be assigned to the same Servant who eventually sees his "offspring" and the extension of his days, without necessarily ascribing *literal* resurrection to an individual in the context of the exile. Of those who made up the righteous Servant in the time of Nebuchadnezzar's invasions, some did die. Others survived into the exile (e.g., Ezekiel, Daniel, and his companions). Some even lived to see the return (Ezra 3:12). But what evidence is there that Isaiah could be speaking about the remnant corporately in Isaiah 53?

In the first place, Isaiah consistently uses "servant" to refer to "Israel" throughout these chapters (see passages cited above).[12] Second, in the immediately succeeding chapter the metaphor changes from the singular "servant" to the singular "barren woman" (Isa. 54:1, 6–7). But here again the reference is a corporate one to refer to the nation in the exile. Third, in 65:8–16, the prophet utilizes the plural of the same word for servant (*'ebed*) that he employs in 52:13, but now the corporate reference is made clear. Once again, the context is that of the exile and return. But a distinction is made between his "servants ... who seek me" (65:9b, 10c; cf. 51:1a, 7a) and those who are guilty of idolatry and evil (65:11–12). To depict the situation, Isaiah employs the image of a clump of grapes that has been crushed and apparently used up. Yet, it is preserved because there is still "juice" remaining in it:

This is what the LORD says:
"As when juice is still found in a cluster of grapes
     and people say, 'Don't destroy it,
     there is still a blessing in it,'
so will I do in behalf of my servants;
     I will not destroy them all.
I will bring forth descendants from Jacob,
     and from Judah those who will possess my mountains;
my chosen people will inherit them,
     and there will my servants live." (Isa. 65:8–9)

The perspective of this prophecy seems to be *before* the exile. Those who are unfaithful to the covenant in their idolatry and evil ways will be destined "for the

---

11. Cf. the strikingly similar description in Isa. 50:4–9, where most commentators see a reference to the Servant; see also 46:3–4.

12. It is true that Isa. 42:1 can be interpreted as paralleling the clearly messianic passages, Isa. 9:6–7 and 11:1–10a (cf. N. T.

Wright, *Jesus and the Victory of God* [Christian Origins and the Question of God vol. 2; Minneapolis: Fortress, 1996], 602). But since the prophet identifies the servant here as "Israel," it could just as well be interpreted as referring to the remnant.

sword" and the "slaughter" (Isa. 65:11–12). This is likely a reference to the impending judgment of the exile. But for his servants who seek him, there will be a return from exile:

> Therefore this is what the Sovereign LORD says:
> "My servants will eat,
>   but you will go hungry;
> my servants will drink,
>   but you will go thirsty;
> my servants will rejoice,
>   but you will be put to shame.
> My servants will sing
>   out of the joy of their hearts,
> but you will cry out
>   from anguish of heart
>   and wail in brokenness of spirit.
> You will leave your name
>   for my chosen ones to use in their curses;
> the Sovereign LORD will put you to death,
>   but to his servants he will give another name." (Isa. 65:13–15)

If this is accurate, the Servant of Isaiah 53 may very well refer to the remnant group of Israelites to which the servants who seek the Lord in Isaiah 65 belong.

Note the belief in the atoning and restoring effect of the suffering by the righteous martyrs under the second-century BC persecution at the hands of Antiochus Epiphanes IV: "These, then, who have been consecrated for the sake of God, are honored, not only with this honor, but also by the fact that ... the homeland [was] purified — they having become, as it were, *a ransom for the sin of our nation*. And through the blood of those devout ones and their death as an *expiation*, divine Providence preserved Israel that previously had been afflicted" (4 Macc. 17:20–22; emphasis mine).[13]

All of this lends additional weight to the notion that the righteous Servant in Isaiah 52–53 is a corporate reference to the righteous remnant in Israel who are caught up in the destructive judgment of the exile, but whose suffering functions in a curse-bearing way to allow God to show mercy once again to his people in bringing them back to the land. We must bear in mind that the temple's sacrifices will have ceased by the time the exile is in full swing. So it is difficult to identify how atonement might be made for the nation during the exile, apart from the atoning

---

13. Cf. also 4 Macc. 18:3–4; 2 Macc. 7:37–38; possibly also Dan. 11:33–35; 12:3. This sort of theology is also evident among those living in the Dead Sea community known as Qumran, who assume that their own suffering and that of their Teacher of Righteousness would result in the opportunity of salvation for themselves and others (1QpHab 8.1–3; 1QM 1:11–12). Thus, the idea that the end of Israel's oppression would be accomplished by the suffering of the righteous few, even including the notions of vicarious atonement, can be traced from Isaiah on through the time between the testaments. It is significant that in each of these cases, during the exile, the time of Antiochus's persecution, and the time after the Teacher of Righteousness had been deposed from the temple, the atonement for the nation is understood to derive from a sacrifice apart from those offered in the temple. Jesus may have drawn on this developing theology in his definition of his messianic path.

work of the righteous. But God will do this because his own glory and faithfulness to his covenantal commitments are at stake (48:9–11).

The Servant as the Remnant Returning from the Exile

If Isaiah's reference for his suffering Servant is the righteous few during the Babylonian exile (Isa. 49:19–21, 24; 51:14), the expectation that "he will be raised and lifted up and highly exalted" (52:13b) must be interpreted along these same lines. It is again tempting to rush to Jesus here with the language of being "raised." But it is much more likely that the prophet's reference is to the unexpected exaltation of the remnant because of the surprising favor granted to the remnant by Cyrus, God's chosen instrument of redemption who will accomplish God's purpose in allowing Jerusalem to be rebuilt (44:28; cf. also 45:1, 13). Indeed, Cyrus is God's summoned "bird of prey" (46:11) through whom Israel will be exalted: "I will grant salvation to Zion, my splendor to Israel" (46:13b).

Thus, after suffering as "an offering for sin," the Servant will be brought back to the land. He will "see his offspring" and the extension of his days. Just as the descendants of the "barren woman" will experience the need for more space (Isa. 54:1–3), so the Servant of chapter 53 will "see his offspring" in their resettlement of the land. But he will do so after experiencing what is implied to be a resurrection: he will "see the light of life" (53:11a) after the apparent death of the nation in the exile.

This interpretation finds similar expression in the prophecy of Ezekiel. In his famous "valley of dry bones" vision, the exilic prophet depicts the nation in exile as so many disconnected skeletons:

> The hand of the LORD was on me, and he brought me out by the Spirit of the LORD and set me in the middle of a valley; it was full of bones. He led me back and forth among them, and I saw a great many bones on the floor of the valley, bones that were very dry. He asked me, "Son of man, can these bones live?" (Ezek. 37:1–3)

God then directs the prophet to prophesy to the "breath" to give life to the reassembled and enfleshed skeletons: "So I prophesied as he commanded me, and breath entered them; they came to life and stood up on their feet—a vast army" (Ezek. 37:10). Finally, God provides the interpretation of the vision:

> Then he said to me: "Son of man, these bones are the whole house of Israel. They say, 'Our bones are dried up and our hope is gone; we are cut off.' Therefore prophesy and say to them: 'This is what the Sovereign LORD says: My people, I am going to open your graves and bring you up from them; I will bring you back to the land of Israel. Then you, my people, will know that I am the LORD, when I open your graves and bring you up from them.'" (Ezek. 37:11–13)

Once again, the return from exile is likened to a miraculous resurrection from the dead. Though the nation appears to be cut off from the land of the living, strewn about as so many bleached bones in the sun, God will yet respond miraculously to breathe new life into his people, calling them forth from their exilic grave. As you read on, the prophet foresees the return, not only of the southern tribes, but also of those in the north, so that the children of Israel will once again be one united nation (Ezek. 37:15–23). Then the people will be graced with God's empowering presence so as to be faithful to the eternal covenant God will make with them, and the Davidic king will once again reign over them (37:24–28; 36:27). Ezekiel's prophecy certainly resonates with this interpretation of Isaiah 53.[14]

JESUS' GRACIOUS PROVISION AS THE SERVANT OF THE LORD

Since Jesus is "numbered with the transgressors" on the cross, the New Testament proclaims that he indeed brings this historical prophecy to fulfillment. He is the climactic fulfillment of Isaiah's Servant of the Lord. Following Jesus' lead, the gospel writers allude to this portion of Isaiah repeatedly in their descriptions of Jesus' ordeal, without necessarily using identical wording.

- The theme of facial disfigurement and public despising from Isaiah 53:3 (cf. 52:14) is picked up in Jesus' mistreatment and mocking by the soldiers (Matt. 27:28–30).
- The wounding of the Servant (Isa. 53:5) is likely understood to relate to the effects of the flogging and the crucifixion endured by Jesus (Matt. 27:26, 35a; John 19:34; 20:27).
- His silence before his judges (Mark 14:61) may allude to the refusal of the oppressed Servant to open his mouth (Isa. 53:7b, d).
- The reference to the soldiers leading Jesus away to be crucified likely corresponds to the Servant being led away "like a lamb to the slaughter" (Isa. 53:7c).
- His crucifixion between two insurrectionists (Matt. 27:38) echoes the Servant being "numbered with the transgressors" (Isa. 53:12).
- Finally, his burial in Joseph of Arimathea's stone-hewn tomb (Matt. 27:57–60) matches the description of the Servant being assigned a grave "with the rich" (Isa. 53:9b).[15]

The gospels' implicit presentation of Jesus as the Servant of the Lord is secure. How then does Isaiah's "rest of the story" help us understand and appreciate

---

14. This is not to say that Isaiah does not have a literal resurrection anywhere in his purview, for in Isa. 25:6–8 he looks forward to the day when God's end-time blessings (depicted as a lavish feast on Mount Zion) will be experienced by Israel and all of the nations. When this happens, death itself will be undone, literally (cf. also Dan. 12:1b–3).

15. This identification continues throughout the New Testament writings; e.g., 1 Peter 2:22–25 (cf. Isa. 53:4–7, 9); Acts 8:32–33 (= Isa. 53:7–8); Rom. 10:16 (= Isa. 53:1); and many other allusions. See esp. Dempster, "The Servant of the Lord," 165–77.

Jesus' crucifixion and resurrection more fully, so that we can also discern more clearly the grace that comes to us through the true Servant?

Jesus' Crucifixion as the Remnant's Atoning Exile

First, Jesus' role as the crucified Servant of the Lord brings to consummation the exilic suffering of the righteous remnant. In so doing, Jesus once again brings a pattern in Israel's history to its grand fulfillment. In the last chapter, we saw how Jesus does this in his baptism and wilderness testings as the nation's righteous representative. In chapter 3, we noted Jesus' role in bringing the Passover lamb to its fulfillment. Now, as he brings the Servant to its culmination, he himself experiences the reenactment of the exile and the suffering of the righteous remnant within it.[16]

Jesus, therefore, is the *true* suffering Servant who fulfills Isaiah's prophecy in a way that no one else could. With his righteous death, the covenantal curse of the law is removed once and for all by the one man who did not need atonement for his own sins. Those included in the corporate expression of the Servant during the Babylonian exile were undoubtedly "blameless" under the law, even as Paul later describes himself (cf. Phil. 3:6). Such did not entail moral perfection, but rather consistent covenant obedience in response to the ongoing grace provided through the temple sacrifices. But Jesus' fulfillment of the Servant's role eclipses any prior fulfillment, since his suffering fulfills even the sacrificial system *itself* (implied in his fulfillment of the Passover lamb), providing the consummate atoning death (Isa. 53:10).

The remnant Servant in the exile suffered *with* the unfaithful servant, so that their suffering benefited those who would come later ("his offspring"). But Jesus' suffering fulfills this pattern individually, offering to those who trust in him an avoidance of the wrath that would otherwise justly fall on them. Paul would later affirm, "God made him who had no sin to be sin for us, so that in him we might become the righteousness of God" (2 Cor. 5:21; cf. Heb. 5:2–3; 9:7, 12–14). For this reason, Jesus brings Israel's covenantal curse to an end and initiates the New Covenant at the same time. Yet, his fulfillment is both tragic and surprising, cursed as he is not only by Gentiles, but also by his own countrymen.

"This effect in the Servant is the measure of how seriously God takes our rebellion and crookedness. We typically wish to make light of our 'shortcomings,' to explain away our 'mistakes.' But God will have none of it. The refusal of humanity to bow to the Creator's rule, and our insistence on drawing up our own moral codes that pander to our lusts, are not shortcomings or mistakes. They are the stuff of death and corruption, and unless someone can be found to stand in our place, they will see us impaled on the swords of our own making and broken on the racks of our own design. But someone has been found. Someone has taken on himself the results of our rebelliousness, and we have been given the keys of the kingdom."[17]

---

16. See esp. Wright, *Victory of God*, 592–611. The prayer of the Levites during Nehemiah's reforms after the return from exile may provide confirmation that the returnees understood they were still effectively in exile because of their subjugation to Persia (Neh. 9:36–38).

17. Oswalt, *Isaiah: 40–66*, 387.

Jesus' Resurrection as the Remnant's Return

Since Jesus is clearly identified with Isaiah's Servant of the Lord in his passion, it is unavoidable to perceive the continuation of this association in his resurrection. That is to say, if Jesus' crucifixion brings the suffering of the Servant in the exile to its end-time completion, his resurrection must similarly bring the Servant's return from exile to completion. What was *metaphorical* in the prophetic depiction of the return of the nation to the land, however, has now become

The law characterizes a person who is executed under its provisions as being under God's curse: "If anyone guilty of a capital offense is put to death and their body is exposed on a pole, you must not leave the body hanging on the pole overnight. Be sure to bury it that same day, because anyone who is hung on a pole is under God's curse" (Deut. 21:22–23). By the first century, the Jews were applying this text to those who were crucified.

literal in the return of Jesus to physical life. Admittedly, this connection is not explicitly made by the gospel writers. But since it entails the logical progression of Jesus' Servant identity and coheres so well thematically with Isaiah's prophecy and other prophetic images, its appropriateness is difficult to gainsay. Several insights tumble out of this connection as well.

First, God's raising Jesus from the dead reverses the initial conclusion that Jews living at that time must have had as they viewed that beaten and broken Galilean on the cross. Accursed and rejected, he was receiving the just desserts of his fraudulent claims (Deut. 21:22–23). Like the remnant among the rest of the nation in the ignominy of the exile, there is no discernible difference between Jesus and the two insurrectionists crucified with him. Each suffers under the same condemnation. But when Easter morning breaks with the discovery of the empty tomb, this verdict is explosively reversed. Rather than abandoned by God to his accursed end, Jesus' innocence is vindicated in the only way possible, signaling the beginning of the ultimate return of the righteous people of God. As the purged nation walked home under Cyrus's safe passage and the dead nation rose again from the valley of dry bones, so also Jesus' resurrection brings to grand *inauguration* the end-time return of God's people to the Lord.

Second, the Lord's glorious sovereignty is revealed to the world. The Gentiles who observed the defeat and destruction of the Israelite nation undoubtedly concluded the impotence of Yahweh to save his people and the superior strength of their gods. But all of this was undermined with the unprecedented return of the Jews to Palestine. Exiled nations simply did not return to their land in those days of empire building. As a result, kings undoubtedly "shut their mouths" (Isa. 52:15b), their prideful boasting silenced, as they witnessed the glory of Yahweh's deliverance.

In a similar way, as Jesus' last breath expires, many of the Jews standing by garner grim satisfaction at the defeat of Beelzebul's deceptive work in Jesus' ministry. But as the news of Easter morning's miracle becomes public, those who hear are faced with the reversal of everything. For rather than Beelzebul being defeated in Jesus' *crucifixion*, he is undone in Jesus' *resurrection*. Yahweh, with whom Jesus had repeatedly identified himself, is vindicated in this unexpected way, and the Sanhedrin's astonishing service to the prince of darkness (Luke 22:53) is exposed at the same time that it is shattered.

Third, God's mysterious work in his Servant is realized. As I noted above, the Gentile nations' conclusion regarding the reason for Israel's exile was Yahweh's defeat. But when the southern tribes were dramatically released from their captivity, an entirely new interpretation was close at hand. Rather than being deservedly condemned, it was now possible to perceive that the Servant suffered innocently with the nation so as to bear the consequences of the nation's covenantal unfaithfulness. By this means, the way was paved for Judah's return to the land. Consequently the Gentiles' eyes were opened: "For what they were not told, they will see, and what they have not heard, they will understand" (Isa. 52:15c).

The same is true in the wake of Jesus' resurrection. Whereas the initial inference reached by most observers must have included the defeat of Jesus' "god" and the confirmation of his personal guilt, his resurrection offers a different conclusion. Far from meriting his suffering, his role of righteously bearing the guilt of the nation so as to provide forgiveness and renewal for the nation is compellingly proclaimed.

EMPOWERMENT FOR DISCIPLESHIP

How then does the "rest of the story" about Jesus' death and resurrection help us answer the "How" question? What impact does this have on our obedience as disciples of Jesus? What are we to *remember* and *receive* here? Hopefully, the words, "Jesus died on the cross for me," have taken on new meaning. If so, we may be able to appreciate the grace that comes through Jesus at a deeper level. As a result, we are also able to perceive more clearly the demand it brings. Let me explain.

The Disciple's Inclusion in the Return from Exile

First of all, we are able to view our relationship to Jesus' crucifixion within the larger drama of God's interaction with Israel. However one understands Israel's status in the first century, it still had not experienced the *consummation* of the Servant's atoning work. Jesus' death is the climactic fulfillment of that wrath-bearing sacrifice. Those of you who are of Jewish descent, therefore, are able to participate in this climactic fulfillment of your history. Those of us who are Gentiles similarly are included, since this event brings to culmination the covenants, opening the floodgates of God's blessings to the nations.

It is significant, in this regard, that Jesus soon sends out his disciples to proclaim his ministry and message to all nations. As we have seen, this implies that the Abrahamic promise to bless all nations (Gen. 17:2–6, 16) is now being fulfilled. Beginning with the rebellion of Adam's seed traced in Genesis 3–11, the nations had languished in exilic separation from God. As such, they lay under the pall of God's judgment. Paul describes their lot this way:

> Remember that at that time you were separate from Christ, excluded from citizenship in Israel and foreigners to the covenants of the promise, without hope and without God in the world. (Eph. 2:12)

Thankfully, God's call of Abraham had all peoples in its salvific scope from its inception (Gen. 12:3; 17:4–6). This covenantal expectation is now realized in and through Jesus and has extended to all nations. As those who are former members of the nations in exile, we have received these dramatic fulfillments of Israel's heritage as our own. This means that we too are being included in this return from exile. Once again, Isaiah prophesies this in Isaiah 52:15:

> ... so he will sprinkle many nations,
>   and kings will shut their mouths because of him.
>   For what they were not told, they will see,
>   and what they have not heard, they will understand. (Isa. 52:15; cf. also 49:7; 45:20–25; esp. vv. 22–23 and the connections to Phil. 2:10–11)

This likely refers to the cleansing function of sprinkling, reminiscent of the priestly purity requirements (cf. Lev. 14:7; Num. 8:7; 19:18–19). Thus, it will not only be Israel's sin that the Servant will bear, but this atonement will extend to the nations who now understand and come to believe the "message" (Isa. 53:1). Although they initially interpreted Israel's exile to imply the defeat of Israel's God, they eventually see that Yahweh was sovereignly working through this event, effecting the removal of Israel's covenantal curse through the suffering of the righteous few among them.

Now, the work of Jesus the Servant can function as a "light for the Gentiles," so that God's salvation might "reach to the ends of the earth" (Isa. 49:6). We Gentile believers are among those exiles who have been gathered beyond the exiles of Israel (Isa. 56:8), participating in the prophesied inclusion of the Gentiles in the people of God, represented in this passage by two of the ancient enemies of Israel:

> In that day there will be a highway from Egypt to Assyria. The Assyrians will go to Egypt and the Egyptians to Assyria. The Egyptians and Assyrians will worship together. In that day Israel will be the third, along with Egypt and Assyria, a blessing on the earth. The LORD Almighty will bless them, saying, "Blessed be Egypt my people, Assyria my handiwork, and Israel my inheritance." (Isa. 19:23–25)

Consequently, our redemption through Jesus is to be understood as part of this massive, overarching covenantal flow, beginning from Abraham (Gen. 12:3), continuing through Israel (Ex. 19:5–6), mediated through Jesus (Gal. 3:16, 19, 24), and on to the Gentiles (3:25–29). As Paul will write later,

> But now in Christ Jesus you who once were far away have been brought near by
> the blood of Christ. For he himself is our peace, who has made the two one and
> has destroyed the barrier, the dividing wall of hostility.... Consequently, you are
> no longer foreigners and strangers, but fellow citizens with God's people and also
> members of his household. (Eph. 2:13–14, 19)

Far from understanding our relationship to Jesus in individualistic terms, we should
see that our following after Jesus participates in the fulfillment of the sweeping
covenantal flow laid out in Scripture!

Our entire lives must then be determined by this gracious reality. As we live
each day, we must do so *remembering* that our righteous representative has borne
the curse of the covenant on our behalf, so that both Israel and all nations might be
redeemed. As Jews who have come to embrace Jesus as their Messiah or as Gentiles
now incorporated into the people of God, we ought to remember often our exilic
past so that the marvel of our inclusion in the Abrahamic blessings might renew
our wonder and gratitude for Jesus' cross work on our behalf. In the *reception* of
that gracious reality, each day, we are to *respond* in faithfulness to Jesus, who is also
our King.

The Disciple's Participation in the Servant's Mission

In chapters 3 and 12, we observed how the grace of the exodus was the presupposition of the obedience demanded by the law. Repeatedly, the people are exhorted
to remember that God delivered them by bringing them out of Egypt, and then in
light of this grace to respond with faithfulness to the covenant. The return from
the exile is understood as the repetition of this kind of grace, mediated through the
suffering of the righteous minority within the nation. Now Jesus' crucifixion fulfills
this pattern *climactically*. And to this grace we must respond.

If the interpretation of Isaiah's Servant presented in this chapter is essentially
on target, it also carries implications concerning the Christian's participation in the
Servant's mission. As we have seen, Isaiah's original reference is likely a corporate
one, as he anticipates the few covenantally faithful Jews who are ensnared in the
judgment of Judah to serve as the Servant of the Lord. Even though Jesus climactically fulfills the Servant figure in his crucifixion, this does not mean that there is
no longer any application of it to anyone else. Paul, for instance, presents himself
and Barnabas as fulfillments of the Servant's role in providing a light to the Gentiles (Acts 13:47; cf. Isa. 49:6). Thus, Jesus' fulfillment—although exhaustively
fulfilling the Servant's *atoning* function—is found to create the *paradigm* for his
followers' missional lives.

That is to say, the Servant moves from a corporate reference in the exile, narrow-
ing to the singular embodiment in Jesus, but then broadening out again to include

his followers who carry the Servant's ministry forward. This might be depicted in a "bowtie" fashion:

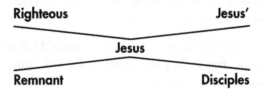

This confirms again the triangular nature of the discipleship dynamic. Having been graced by the Servant, the disciple follows the King, and ends up emulating the Servant.

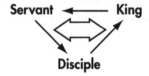

Accordingly, Jesus enjoins his followers repeatedly to pick up their crosses as they follow him (e.g., Matt. 10:38; 16:24; Luke 14:27), anticipating the same treatment from others that he received (Matt. 10:24–25). Peter echoes his master's words as he quotes from and alludes to Isaiah 53 in his instructions to Christian slaves who are being mistreated, even though they are living righteous lives:

> To this you were called, because Christ suffered for you, leaving you *an example, that you should follow in his steps.*
>
> "He committed no sin,
>   and no deceit was found in his mouth."
>
> When they hurled their insults at him, he did not retaliate; when he suffered, he made no threats. Instead, he entrusted himself to him who judges justly. "He himself bore our sins" in his body on the cross, so that we might die to sins and live for righteousness; "by his wounds you have been healed." For "you were like sheep going astray," but now you have returned to the Shepherd and Overseer of your souls. (1 Peter 2:21–25; emphasis mine)

So even though Jesus characterizes discipleship to him as being "light" and "easy," this is not to deny the costly and often painful life to which he calls us (Matt. 26:37–44).

Paul also seems to utilize this imagery to characterize his own suffering in the process of building the church: "Now I rejoice in what I am suffering for you, and I fill up in my flesh what is still lacking in regard to Christ's afflictions, for the sake of his body, which is the church" (Col. 1:24). Far from indicating that he is atoning for sin, Paul is willingly identifying himself with Jesus so as to share in his sufferings (Rom. 8:17; 2 Cor. 1:5; Phil. 3:10). He knows that it will be through this means that the world will come to see the one Servant whose death truly does atone for sin (Rom. 3:25; 2 Cor. 2:14–16; 5:21).[18]

As we argued in chapter 10, this is what is meant by living as "the least" (Matt. 25:40). Whether God calls us to live among a different people group far from our homeland or to live faithfully among our coworkers and neighbors, our self-perception should be determined by this missional reality—the nations of the world are still in exile and their only hope is to perceive the true Servant through those who already have been brought "home" by his grace.

This was Paul's focus as he responded to God's grace to minister the gospel in a "priestly" way among the nations (cf. Rom. 15:14–21). It was his life calling to make Christ known where his name was not named (15:20). In this way, "Those who were not told about him will see, and those who have not heard will understand" (15:21; cf. Isa. 52:15). It is this gracious purpose that has vivified Servant discipleship throughout the history of the church, so that the nations will come to God's mountain and share in the Lord's feast (Isa. 25:6–8). How can we do anything else?

SUMMARY

Jesus' representative role is culminated in his crucifixion and resurrection. As the fulfillment of the righteous remnant within Israel, Jesus brings the pattern of the remnant's suffering to completion. Accordingly, he bears the judgment merited by the covenantally unfaithful nation, opening the door for renewal and restoration. His resurrection, then, is the inaugurated consummation of the nation's return from exile, revealing the mysterious work of God and the expansion of his blessings to the nations. As those who have been redeemed by the servant's atoning work, we have been graciously included in this return from exile from God. It is this grace that must be *received* every day.

Moreover, since Jesus is our representative Servant, our identity is now defined by his life. We must, therefore, *respond* to his grace by living out the role of the Servant ourselves among the nations where we live, faithfully seeking righteousness, yet embracing whatever loss may come for the sake of the mission. In this way, others too may see "what they were not told" and understand "what they have not heard" (Isa. 52:15).

---

18. Barnett similarly perceives Paul's self-perception to run along servant lines. Paul Barnett, *Paul: Missionary of Jesus* (Grand Rapids: Eerdmans, 2008), 118–33.

RELEVANT QUESTIONS

1. How does viewing Jesus as the fulfillment of the righteous remnant deepen your appreciation of the gracious nature of his suffering on the cross?

2. How does understanding his resurrection as the inaugurated consummation of God's people from exile amplify its grace toward you?

3. What specific things in your daily life ought to change as you respond to this grace and participate in the mission of the servant to the nations?

CHAPTER 15

THE SERVANT
WHO IS THE
RESTORER: PART 1

When Jesus reached the spot, he looked up and said to him, "Zacchaeus, come down immediately. I must stay at your house today." So he came down at once and welcomed him gladly.

All the people saw this and began to mutter, "He has gone to be the guest of a sinner."

But Zacchaeus stood up and said to the Lord, "Look, Lord! Here and now I give half of my possessions to the poor, and if I have cheated anybody out of anything, I will pay back four times the amount."

Jesus said to him, "Today salvation has come to this house, because this man, too, is a son of Abraham. For the Son of Man came to seek and to save what was lost."

Luke 19:5–10

To help finance my extended years of schooling, I worked for ten summers as a commercial fisherman in Bristol Bay, Alaska. It was often a miserable and draining experience, though many aspects were also thrilling. One of these was the arrival of the beluga whales. Each summer, a day would come when the whales showed up en masse out in the bay. The telltale whooshes of their forceful exhalations through their blowholes would be heard all over the surface of the water, followed by the glimpse of their stark white backs arcing through the surface of the dark water before they slid once more into the depths. For the uninformed tourist, this was simply a rare opportunity to see nature's stunning beauty on a massive scale. But for the veteran fisherman, this visual display meant so much more. You see, the beluga pods follow the large schools of salmon as they migrate up the coast of the Alaskan Peninsula, harvesting as many fish as possible before they escape beyond their reach up the spawning rivers. Because of this, when the white backs of the belugas show up, the fishermen know the fish have arrived!

In a similar way, when Jesus walked around Galilee during his ministry, he did several things that caught people's notice. He healed many, he cast out demons, he reached across religious and social boundaries to care for the marginalized, and he called apparent nobodies to follow him. To a gospel "tourist," these offered a magnificent display of Jesus' power and grace, confirming that he was the Messiah. But the mere confirmation of his identity was only part of their significance. To the informed, first-century Galilean these visible displays pointed to so much more. Having considered his Servant roles of "representative" and "redeemer," let's consider in these next two chapters Jesus' role of "restorer." By viewing these actions through the lens of the covenantal and prophetic expectations of the Old Testament, we too will perceive the covenantal grace that flows below the surface of these dimensions of Jesus' ministry.

JESUS' CALLING OF THE DISCIPLES

One of the most familiar of Jesus' actions is his calling of the twelve disciples. Since Jesus extends the call of discipleship to the rest of us as well, those first disciples have often served as *models* for us, depicting what we ought and ought not to do in response to Jesus. As a result, the lives of Peter, John, Andrew, Thomas, Matthew, and Judas have become valuable illustrative fodder for countless sermons and theological lessons. And such they should be, for they provide us with encouragements, rebukes, and challenges concerning living our lives as disciples of Jesus in the real world. But if this is all we see here, we are not seeing enough—and surely not the grace that is there. Models are examples that we need to *emulate*. To perceive the grace, we must place this ministry action within the larger context of God's promises to Israel—promises that are nurtured by the prophets.

The Covenantal Hope

From its inception, Israel consisted of the descendants of the twelve sons of Jacob, resulting in twelve tribes within the nation.[1] But as we have already discussed, the nation eventually divided into two separate kingdoms before each one was individually conquered and exiled. The northern kingdom with its ten tribes was finally overrun and dispersed by Assyria in 721 BC, with the defeat of Samaria, its capital city. The southern kingdom, comprising the remaining two tribes, was defeated and exiled by Babylon in 587 BC, after a series of invasions that culminated in the destruction of Jerusalem and its temple. Although the exiles from Judah experienced an organized and sustained "return" to the land, the exiles from Israel never did, giving rise to the expression "the ten lost tribes" of Israel.

Thus, when the prophets look forward to the time of Israel's blessing, central to these conceptions is the expectation of the return of these exiles not only from

---

1. Cf. Gen. 35:22b–26; 49:1–28; Num. 1:1–54; 26:1–65; Josh. 13:8–21:45.

Assyria, but also from wherever they may have landed. God will *reconstitute* Israel in the last days, finally bringing its exile to an end:

> When I have brought them back from the nations and have gathered them from the countries of their enemies, I will be proved holy through them in the sight of many nations. Then they will know that I am the LORD their God, for though I sent them into exile among the nations, I will gather them to their own land, not leaving any behind. (Ezek. 39:27–28; cf. also Ezek. 37:1–28; *Pss. Sol.* 17)[2]

Significantly, Isaiah 11 locates this expectation in the time of the messianic king's coming:

> In that day the Lord will reach out his hand a second time to reclaim the surviving remnant of his people from Assyria, from Lower Egypt, from Upper Egypt, from Cush, from Elam, from Babylonia, from Hamath and from the islands of the Mediterranean.
>
> > He will raise a banner for the nations
> >   and gather the exiles of Israel;
> > he will assemble the scattered people of Judah
> >   from the four quarters of the earth. (Isa. 11:11–12)

Later, he identifies the Servant's ministry as one that will bring Israel back to God:

> And now the LORD says—
>   he who formed me in the womb to be his servant
> to bring Jacob back to him
>   and gather Israel to himself. . . . (Isa. 49:5)

As seems obvious, therefore, this is one of those actions that merges the careers of both the Servant and the King.

It is true that many of the exiles from Judah did return from Babylon, beginning in 538 BC. But even those who returned did not experience the sort of autonomy and climactic blessing that was expected after the exile. The presence of the Roman legions throughout the borders of Israel in the time of Jesus offered daily confirmation this was not the case. And Rome was simply the latest in a series of oppressors who had dominated Palestine, almost without interruption, since the exile began.[3] Moreover, the people were not purified and wholly faithful to the covenant in the way that was expected of the returned-from-exile generation.

---

2. This hope for the return from exile shows up repeatedly in the prophets; e.g., Isa. 43:14–21; 45:13; 51:14; 56:8; Jer. 28:2–6; 29:8–14; 46:27–28; Lam. 4:22; Ezek. 36:24; Hos. 1:10–11; 2:14–23; Mic. 2:12.

3. Following the Assyrian and Babylonian conquests, Palestine was subjugated by Persia (539–333 BC), Alexander the Great (333–323 BC), the Ptolemies in Egypt (323–198 BC), the Seleucids to the north (176 BC–140 BC), and the Romans from 63 BC on. The brief interlude of freedom from 140 to 63 BC witnessed the Jewish Hasmoneans reigning through the high priesthood, which also caused great offense to some Jewish groups.

Consequently, even *after* the return of Judah from Babylon, Zechariah gives voice to a still-future expectation when God will finally provide his people with a permanent peace in the land:

> But I will encamp at my temple
>   to guard it against marauding forces.
> Never again will an oppressor overrun my people,
>   for now I am keeping watch. (Zech. 9:8)

At that time the Lord will finally send forth the Davidic king to bring the messianic peace to the earth (Zech. 9:9–10), resulting in the consummation of the blessing to the Gentiles:

> This is what the LORD Almighty says: "I will save my people from the countries of the east and the west. I will bring them back to live in Jerusalem; they will be my people, and I will be faithful and righteous to them as their God.
> "... And many peoples and powerful nations will come to Jerusalem to seek the LORD Almighty and to entreat him."
> This is what the LORD Almighty says: "In those days ten people from all languages and nations will take firm hold of one Jew by the hem of his robe and say, 'Let us go with you, because we have heard that God is with you.'" (Zech. 8:7–8, 22–23; cf. Gen. 12:2–3; 17:3–6)

In light of this history, it is not surprising that the disciples traveling on the Emmaus road articulate this expectation in relation to Jesus: "but we had hoped that he was the one who was going to redeem Israel" (Luke 24:21a). The verb translated "redeem" (*lytroō*) carries the sense of liberating a slave. By their use of this word, they imply their perception of Israel's present bondage. Though they had set their hopes on Jesus, he had been crucified and their bondage continued. The true end of the exile had not yet happened. For when that takes place, God will also bring to consummation his promise to Abraham to bless all nations through them.

Jesus' Gracious Provision

Seen against this background, we can appreciate the significance of Jesus' selection of *twelve* disciples, for it certainly cannot be coincidental that Jesus chooses the same number as the makeup of the nation. Rather, this purposeful action declares that he is consciously bringing about the beginning of the fulfillment of this prophetic and covenantal hope, restoring the nation that will eventually draw people into it from the ends of the earth. This helps to explain Jesus' concern not only to mentor his disciples, but also to send them out on missionary journeys both to Israel (cf. Matt. 9:35–11:1; Mark 3:13–19; 6:7–11; Luke 9:1–5) and to the nations (Matt. 28:18–20). These twelve are therefore being presented as the restored nation in embryo.

What is more, the nation is being restored by grace. This is because the disciple band is hardly impressive. Representing widely diverse agendas, less than impressive economic standing, and, in some cases, outright questionable character, the disciples' inclusion in this restored nation is explained solely as the result of Jesus' compassionate and inclusive call. It only comes about because of God's gracious summons to unlikely people. Taken in this way, the call of the disciples represents a repetition of the gracious deliverance of the nation from the exile. As such, it functions as a sign of the arrival of the time of God's blessing.

Somewhat surprisingly, however, the writers of the Gospels do not indicate the tribal associations of any of the disciples. Jesus is therefore reconstituting Israel without attempting to recover the former definition of its makeup. Membership in this restored nation, therefore, does not fall along tribal lines. Rather, this is determined solely by the response to Jesus' call for discipleship. Israel is being reconstituted and redefined at the same time. In this way, God's promises to Abraham that he would be both the conduit of blessing to the nations and the father of many nations (Gen. 12:3; 17:4–6) are coming to their fulfillment through Jesus. Since Jesus is the true Son, true Israel is being defined *Christologically*!

JESUS' TABLE FELLOWSHIP

We have already considered Jesus' table fellowship in chapter 8. Yet because of its importance in Jesus' ministry, it merits a second visit here, this time grounding it more fully in its covenantal framework.

The Covenantal Demand and Promise

We learned in our discussion of the "Why" question that within the conditional framework of the Mosaic Covenant, the ongoing experience of its covenantal blessings is dependent on the people's response of faithfulness to God's gracious provisions. This included, of course, their repentance and reception of restoring grace through the temple. Accordingly, their continued enjoyment of abundant life in the land of promise is rooted in covenant faithfulness. This is especially expressed by the prophetic chorus calling for repentance and a return to the covenant to fend off the threat of the exile. Then, after God's gracious redemption of the nation from the exile, the postexilic prophets such as Malachi and John the Baptist once again give voice to the call for righteousness within the covenantal framework. Only those who fear the Lord and respond with righteousness will survive the coming judgment (Mal. 4:2–6; Matt. 3:1–12; Luke 3:7–17).[4]

---

4. It is obvious that the Essenes at Qumran took this agenda seriously, removing themselves completely from the sinful nation and maintaining perpetual ritual purity on the shores of the Dead Sea. Blomberg's assessment (cited earlier) bears repeating here: "One of the main reasons for the Qumranians' withdrawal into the wilderness was to form the truly righteous remnant of God's people and spur his apocalyptic intervention to redress the horrible injustices of the present age, an intervention for which no other segment of Judaism was, in their opinion, properly preparing" (*Contagious Holiness*, 84).

This background helps to explain the Pharisaic concern regarding purity at the table. This is because meals foreshadowed the coming kingdom, when all the people will sit down at the abundant feast that God will one day provide (Isa. 25:6). Since the kingdom will be populated only by the righteous, it is understandable why the religious leaders were concerned to allow only the right kind of person to participate in the symbolically charged context of the table. Although issues of ritual impurity and social class also were in play, the key to the "right kind of person" was determined by moral purity. Thus, the righteous would never knowingly sit down with an unrepentant sinner, such as an adulterer, a murderer, a tax gatherer, or a thief. Since impurity was considered to be *contagious*, to sit with such people would result in personal defilement. It would also imply that the repentance of sinners was of little importance.[5]

"Even more so than in the Old Testament, intertestamental Judaism viewed mealtimes as important occasions for drawing boundaries. Dining created an intimate setting in which one nurtured friendship with the right kind of people, eating the right kind of food.... Fundamental among those principles was the notion that unclean people and objects constantly threatened to corrupt God's holy, elect nation and individuals within it. Like literal physical disease, we may think of ritual impurity as contagious. The idea of a godly person's holiness rubbing off on and transforming an unclean or unholy person scarcely seems to have been countenanced."[6]

In this light, the Pharisees' agenda made sense. They tried by teaching and example to move the nation to faithfulness by maintaining in their homes and social gatherings the sort of purity that was expected of the priests, as they awaited the arrival of the kingdom. Disrespecting these boundaries, however, would only further delay the kingdom's arrival. Jesus' table fellowship with sinners, therefore, serves to challenge these boundaries and to offer a picture of the kingdom that is radically different.

Jesus' Gracious Provision

Placed in this religious context, Jesus' purposeful transgression of these boundaries proclaims his gracious provision of that to which the table pointed. He obviously knows the offense of his actions. But by sitting down with such individuals as the tax collectors and sinners, Jesus is demonstrating God's pursuing grace toward those who could not purify themselves: "It is not the healthy who need a doctor, but the sick" (Matt. 9:12–13).

Jesus is, therefore, presenting a living parable to confront people with God's gracious invitation to sinners to be reconciled with God and to receive a share in the blessings of the kingdom. Those sitting with Jesus did not merit their place at the table. And that is just the point. Jesus' action signals the ongoing, gracious return of the exiles in the present and points ahead to the final "banquet" in the king-

5. McKnight, "Who Is Jesus?" 64. Cf. Luke 15:1–2; 8:1–3; 10:38–42; 19:7.

6. Blomberg, *Contagious Holiness*, 93. It is for this reason that Jesus' table fellowship would have been incomprehensible to the Qumranians, who "were consumed by the desire to remain pure by the avoidance of everything impure. No thought was given to the possibility that holiness might rub off on and cleanse that which was unclean" (ibid., 85).

dom's consummation, at which these returnees will feast: "Many will come from the

east and the west, and will take their places at the feast with Abraham, Isaac and Jacob in the kingdom of heaven" (Matt. 8:11; Luke 13:29).

But not only does Jesus extend grace to the unlikely; he also undoubtedly looks for repentance in response. Zacchaeus is a classic example of this dynamic, even though Luke does not explicitly mention a meal. Jesus' gracious pursuit of the notorious tax collector, even to enter into his defiling home and likely sit at his table, melts

"In Judaism … table-fellowship means fellowship before God, for the eating of a piece of broken bread by everyone who shares in the meal brings out the fact that they all have a share in the blessing which the master of the house had spoken over the unbroken bread. Thus Jesus' meals with the publicans and sinners … are an expression of the mission and message of Jesus … eschatological meals, anticipatory celebrations of the feast in the end-time…. The inclusion of sinners in the community of salvation, achieved in table-fellowship, is the most meaningful expression of the message of the redeeming love of God."[7]

his idolatrous heart and moves it to profound repentance and just repayment (Luke 19:8). Once again, prior grace leads to the response of righteousness.[8]

EMPOWERMENT FOR DISCIPLESHIP

In the previous two chapters, we considered Jesus' Servant roles of representing and then redeeming those who cannot save themselves. Accordingly, the grant nature of the New Covenant is established and confirmed. But the covenantal purposes of God are not simply to redeem and forgive his people. He is also interested in transforming them to reflect his image. Jesus' call of his disciples and his table fellowship express this goal.

We have seen that God enters into covenantal relationships with people in the context of his prior grace. Similarly, when the prophets look forward to the consummation of God's relationship with humanity, they once again emphasize the necessity of the divine initiative if the purified and righteous remnant is ever to come about. Jesus' call of the unlikely to be his disciples and his pursuit of the sinful at the table repeat this pattern, affirming in the process that God is working through *him* to redeem, cleanse, and transform Israel.

As such, Jesus is fulfilling the Servant King's role of "restorer." Israel could *not* achieve what God demanded. Her long and tragic history, littered with the debris of her unfaithfulness, attests to this. Jesus' gracious calling of the diverse disciple band and his open invitation to sinners to join him at the table depict this. Let's then consider how these ministry actions of Jesus help us answer the "How" question, again applying to them the "remember, receive, and respond" paradigm we have been suggesting.

---

7. Joachim Jeremias, *New Testament Theology: The Proclamation of Jesus* (New York: Charles Scribner's Sons, 1971), 115–16.

8. See Blomberg, *Contagious Holiness*, 167.

Graciously Called so as to Call Others

Meditating on the gracious significance of Jesus' call of the twelve disciples has the potential of reminding us of our own gracious inclusion in the true people of God. Like the disciples, our inclusion is not based on our impressive résumés or impeccable pedigrees. As the redemption of the Jews from exile declares the covenantal pattern of God's gracious initiative toward his people, so also does our inclusion repeat it. This is true whether we are Jewish or Gentile: we all have been graciously included in this reconstitution of the people of God. As Paul writes:

> He came and preached peace to you who were far away and peace to those who were near. For through him we both have access to the Father by one Spirit. Consequently, you are no longer foreigners and strangers, but fellow citizens with God's people and also members of his household. (Eph. 2:17–19)

Pausing regularly to remember and receive again the grace of our inclusion in the fulfillment of the Abrahamic promises will open the window of a stale discipleship to a fresh and invigorating breeze of covenantal grace—grace that will enable us to participate in the multiethnic call to others.

As we have seen, Jesus mediates to us the command to love our neighbors as we love ourselves. Reflecting frequently on the implied breakdown of ethnic barriers in Jesus' discipleship summons will move us to respond with reconciling pursuit of others around us, regardless of their ethnicity or social class. Genuinely receiving this gracious reality will transform us into a passionate nullifier of divisions, both within and without the church.

In fact, whenever I spend time with this theology, I find myself looking with new eyes at the diversity of people that I pass on the sidewalk. Seeing the faces of various ethnic groups moves me to reflect on my own gracious inclusion in the people of God and fills me with a desire to *revel* in the multiracial nature of the body of Christ. Taking delight in pursuing genuine relationships of love and respect across racial boundaries among disciples is an *inevitable* result of the reception of this grace. To the extent that we are not moved in these directions, we are fighting against what God is proclaiming through Jesus' call of the disciples—through his call of us.

Accordingly, the reception of this grace ought to fuel our passion for evangelism and missions. Since Israel in exile images the reality pertaining to the rest of the nations, and since we are among those who have now been brought near (Eph. 2:13), our grace-empowered response should be to become passionate about the ongoing mission to the world. Sharing our faith with those around us, involving ourselves in ministries of justice and mercy, and stewarding our resources to further these ministries both close to home and around the world should all flow out of our fresh experience of this grace. But again, the key is for us to remember and receive it *often,* so that the Spirit enlivens our response of obedience by making the things of Jesus present in our lives.

Graciously Invited so as to Invite Others

The same is true of Jesus' table fellowship with sinners. Reflecting afresh on Jesus' gracious invitation to join him at the kingdom table liberates us from the despair of personal failure and the clamor of legalism. We don't belong at the table with Jesus. Yet each day, Jesus waves us in to the banquet of kingdom blessings that one day will be brought to their fullest expression.

Obviously, this theology fits nicely into our celebration of the Lord's Supper. But it certainly should go beyond that to a *daily* experience. Regularly allowing Jesus to grace us at the table reminds us of the grant nature of the New Covenant and of Jesus' gracious pursuit that continually prepares us for its consummation in the kingdom to come. As was true of Zacchaeus, receiving anew Jesus' gracious invitation to sit with him at the table will soften our hearts and send us into each day filled with gratitude and humility, empowered to invite others to Jesus' table who are also just as unworthy.

SUMMARY

Learning to reflect on and receive the grace embodied in Jesus' calling of his disciples and his invitation to sinners to sit at table with him has the potential of renewing our awareness of our identity and the nature of our participation in the blessings of the kingdom.

Recognizing daily that we have been graciously included in the end-time ingathering of God's people continually reminds us of who we are and what our role is in the world in which we live. We have been privileged to participate in the ongoing fulfillment of God's bringing of the nations back from their exiles, not because of the impressive nature of our personal credentials, but solely because of the gracious initiative of the God who calls.

This, then, should remind us always of the role we have in the world — that of responding in the empowerment of this grace to pursue others who yet need to come, regardless of their ethnicity, social standing, or moral purity. Having been graced, we are invited to participate in the gracing of others. Similarly also, receiving the grace of Jesus' table fellowship every day reminds us of our gracious inclusion in the kingdom blessings and impels us from that table to invite others who similarly cannot purify themselves so as to merit a place at the feast.

In both cases, Jesus provides the covenantal grace that empowers covenantal faithfulness.

RELEVANT QUESTIONS

1. How does meditating on your gracious inclusion in the restored people of God affect your life today as a disciple of Jesus? In what ways is your self-perception changed and how does this affect your awareness of your role in the world?

2. In what ways might you respond with a similar gracious outreach to others around you, regardless of ethnicity, moral, or economic status? Are there specific people who are brought to mind as you reflect on this?

3. How might you approach each day differently if you were to begin it by sitting with Jesus at his gracious table?

4. What needs to change for these responses to happen in your life? From what priorities and perspectives might Jesus' grace be moving you to repent?

CHAPTER 16

THE SERVANT
WHO IS THE
RESTORER: PART 2

When evening came, many who were demon-possessed were brought to him, and
he drove out the spirits with a word and healed all the sick. This was to fulfill what
was spoken through the prophet Isaiah: "He took up our infirmities and bore our
diseases."

Matthew 8:16–17

The man from whom the demons had gone out begged to go with him, but Jesus
sent him away, saying, "Return home and tell how much God has done for you."
So the man went away and told all over town how much Jesus had done for him.

Luke 8:38–39

It is worth remembering that one of the major roles of Isaiah's Servant of the Lord
is that of bringing Israel and the nations back to God (Isa. 49:5–6), restoring the
relationship that had been broken. In the previous chapter, we began our consideration of this "restorer" role of Jesus, focusing on the call of his disciples and his
gracious table fellowship. In both cases, God's gracious initiative is primary, communicating to Israel and us that it will be through Jesus that the restoration will
come. In this chapter, we will continue our focus on this theme, moving on to Jesus'
healing and exorcism ministries. To do so, we will again view these actions through
the lens of the Old Testament.

JESUS' HEALING MINISTRY

There is a real sense in which the significance of Jesus' miracles is misunderstood
and even somewhat misapplied by many Christians. The importance of these powerful actions, so it is maintained, is to prove his identity. Utilized in this way, Jesus'
miracles provide people with the best apologetic for his identity as the Son of God.
Although this is certainly *part* of their function (cf. John 10:37–38; 20:30–31),
this approach mutes what is likely their most important aspect—namely, to dem-

251

onstrate the fulfillment of the gracious blessings of the kingdom as it breaks into the present age. As we have already discussed, the Jews anticipated the transformation of the world when the kingdom arrived, including both the spiritual and physical realms. Jesus' healing miracles flow from this stream. But to perceive this, we need to see them once again in the context of Scripture's covenantal framework.

The Covenantal Demand and Promise
The Covenantal Imagery of Judgment

It is significant that several Old Testament prophets use physical ailments to portray spiritual realities. The images of "blindness" and "deafness" are especially used as ciphers for *spiritual* dullness and hardness. This imagery is grounded in the warnings Moses gives to the Israelites regarding the curses that will come on Israel for covenant unfaithfulness:

> The LORD will afflict you with madness, blindness and confusion of mind. At midday you will grope about like a blind person in the dark. (Deut. 28:28–29a)

As a result of the individualization of this curse, those who suffered under one or more of these maladies were often considered under God's covenantal curse. At least in some segments of first-century Judaism, a maimed Jew was not considered a full Israelite and was kept at bay from several aspects of social and religious life. Those who were blind, lame, leprous, deaf, or dumb were marginalized and even ostracized (e.g., Mark 5:24–34), with no hope for restoration.

But the prophets utilize this imagery *metaphorically* to depict covenant unfaithfulness. Accordingly, after Judah has forsaken the covenant, Ezekiel is told that he lives "among a rebellious people. They have eyes to see but do not see and ears to hear but do not hear, for they are a rebellious people" (Ezek. 12:2). Similarly, Isaiah is commissioned to prophesy to a people who hear but will not understand, and who see but will not perceive (Isa. 6:9). As a result, the effect of Isaiah's ministry will largely be one of judgment, exacerbating the problems of spiritual blindness and deafness:

> Make the heart of this people calloused;
>   make their ears dull
>   and close their eyes.
> Otherwise they might see with their eyes,
>   hear with their ears,
>   understand with their hearts,
> and turn and be healed. (Isa. 6:10)

The same imagery resurfaces later in Isaiah's description of the rebellious "servant of the LORD"—a description of unfaithful Israel that we have considered previously:

"Hear, you deaf;
    look, you blind, and see!
Who is blind but my servant,
    and deaf like the messenger I send?
Who is blind like the one in covenant with me,
    blind like the servant of the LORD?
You have seen many things, but have paid no attention;
    your ears are open, but you hear nothing. (Isa. 42:18–20; cf. also 59:9–10;
        Jer. 5:21–23; 6:10; 17:23; 44:5; Zech. 7:9–14)

This imagery comes to a climax of sorts when King Zedekiah witnesses the execution of each of his sons by his Babylonian conquerors. Then Zedekiah's own eyes are put out with a sword and he is led as a blind man in chains to Babylon (2 Kings 25:1–7). As the last Davidic king before the exile, Zedekiah serves as a poignant representative of Israel's covenant infidelity.

The Covenantal Imagery of Restoration

Understood in this context, it is significant that Isaiah describes the eventual deliverance of the people as the recovery of various physical abilities:

Strengthen the feeble hands,
    steady the knees that give way;
say to those with fearful hearts,
    "Be strong, do not fear;
your God will come,
    he will come with vengeance;
with divine retribution
    he will come to save you."
Then will the eyes of the blind be opened
    and the ears of the deaf unstopped.
Then will the lame leap like a deer,
    and the mute tongue shout for joy." (Isa. 35:3–6)

Isaiah goes on to locate this deliverance in the time of the people's return from exile, when they will no longer be impure or foolish:

And a highway will be there;
    it will be called the Way of Holiness;
    it will be for those who walk on that Way.
The unclean will not journey on it;
    wicked fools will not go about on it....
But only the redeemed will walk there,
    and those the LORD has rescued will return.

> They will enter Zion with singing;
>> everlasting joy will crown their heads.
> Gladness and joy will overtake them,
>> and sorrow and sighing will flee away. (Isa. 35:8–10; cf. also 43:5–8)

Indeed, when the exile is over and the righteous king reigns, the previously impaired people will be restored to wholeness:

> See, a king will reign in righteousness
>> and rulers will rule with justice.
> Each one will be like a shelter from the wind
>> and a refuge from the storm,
> like streams of water in the desert
>> and the shadow of a great rock in a thirsty land.
> Then the eyes of those who see will no longer be closed,
>> and the ears of those who hear will listen.
> The fearful heart will know and understand,
>> and the stammering tongue will be fluent and clear.
> No longer will the fool be called noble
>> nor the scoundrel be highly respected. (Isa. 32:1–5)

It is obvious that Isaiah is using the recovery of physical abilities to represent the people's gracious recovery of *spiritual* health and faithfulness. In Isaiah's expectation, those returning from exile and living under the reign of the righteous king will finally be righteous themselves, mirroring the righteous Servant of the Lord, whose senses are attuned to God:

> The Sovereign LORD has given me an instructed tongue,
>> to know the word that sustains the weary.
> He wakens me morning by morning,
>> wakens my ear to listen like one being taught.
> The Sovereign LORD has opened my ears;
>> I have not been rebellious,
>> I have not turned away. (Isa. 50:4–5)

All of this prepares for what comes in Jesus' ministry of healing.

Jesus' Gracious Provision

With Isaiah's use of this imagery in mind, we should note that Jesus quotes from his prophecy to characterize his healings and ministry to the poor as evidence for his identity as the kingdom-bringer (Matt. 11:4–5; from Isa. 35:4–6; 61:1). This Old Testament framework, therefore, situates Jesus' miracles of healing in the context of Israel returning to their covenant God. Isaiah looked forward to the day when God would bring his people back to the land and heal them of their rebellious hearts. He looked forward to a time when the nation would be whole in every sense of the word—seeing, hearing, and declaring his truth. Though the return from exile brought partial fulfillment, the postexilic persistence of the nation's unfaithfulness implied the need of another, more glorious fulfillment in the future.

Jesus lays claim to this expectation by means of his healing ministry, offering to the one healed and to those who witnessed the miracle the invitation to respond to him in faith so as to be healed spiritually as well. This means that those whom Jesus healed image the wholeness and fidelity of God's people under his reign. This is not to deny the importance of the physical nature of the healing. God's kingdom salvation is holistic! Nor is it to minimize the social dimensions—those healed by Jesus were being restored to full membership in the community. But the spiritual aspect of the healings cannot be overlooked. By performing these prophetic signs of the kingdom in a literal, physical way, Jesus is declaring what he is bringing. The time of the purified and righteous people of God's kingdom has arrived![1]

Therefore, Jesus calls on those who observe his healings to repent. Although a portion of the nation had returned to the land, the prophetic expectation of the spiritual transformation of the people had not been fully realized. Jesus' miracles declare the onset of that returned-from-exile reality, pointing beyond themselves to the inbreaking of the kingdom, characterized by physical *and* spiritual wholeness! The Servant of the Lord is among them! Matthew confirms this by identifying Jesus' healing and exorcism ministry as fulfilling the work of Isaiah's Servant:

> When evening came, many who were demon-possessed were brought to him, and he drove out the spirits with a word and healed all the sick. This was to fulfill what was spoken through the prophet Isaiah:
>
> > "He took up our infirmities
> > and bore our diseases." (Matt 8:16–17; cf. also 12:15–21)

Jesus' going to the sick and unclean, therefore, most likely pictured the sick, deaf, blind, and leprous nature of Israel as a whole. The irony of the situation is thus exposed. Those who were previously presumed to be under the curse because of their defiling ailments and handicaps are purified by Jesus' healing touch and permitted to rejoin the community. But the community itself is still impure. Thus, Jesus calls for repentance from those who witness his healings:

> Then Jesus began to denounce the towns in which most of his miracles had been performed, because they did not repent. "Woe to you, Chorazin! Woe to you, Bethsaida! If the miracles that were performed in you had been performed in Tyre and Sidon, they would have repented long ago in sackcloth and ashes.... If the miracles

---

1. Jesus' healing ministry is also linked with his messianic identity. This is suggested by the repetition of the query on the part of the crowds, "Could this be the Son of David," in the context of his healing power (e.g., Matt. 9:27; 12:23; 20:30–31; 21:14–15).

that were performed in you had been performed in Sodom, it would have remained to this day. But I tell you that it will be more bearable for Sodom on the day of judgment than for you." (Matt. 11:20–24)

This point is powerfully made in the wake of Jesus' healing of the man born blind in John 9. Having intentionally violated the Sabbath traditions by making mud and healing on the Sabbath, Jesus is condemned by the Pharisees as a "sinner" (9:24b). Though they hear the healed man's rationale for viewing Jesus as a prophet (vv. 17b, 30–33), they refuse to "listen" and throw the man out (v. 34). Later, Jesus again encounters the man and invites him to respond both to the gift of physical sight and his hearing of Jesus' voice (v. 37) by believing in him as the Son of Man. In this way, the man's healing is completed, bringing this miracle of the recovery of physical "sight" to its holistic goal (v. 38). The Pharisees, however, continue to deny their blindness (v. 40) and are condemned (v. 41).

> "The crippled, the lepers, the blind, the poor, the hungry, the mourners, the sinners, the ostracized, the unimportant, unpowerful, and unpromising, were all types imaging the real ... situation of Israel vis-à-vis God. They were types of Israel-to-be-saved. The eschatological reversal of their situation — the poor made rich, the mourners comforted, the lepers cleansed — imaged the eschatological restoration of Israel."[2]

Understood within the framework of Old Testament expectation, the healed man functions as a harbinger of the nation's final condition in the consummated kingdom — healed and whole, both physically and spiritually. Thus, Jesus' call for repentance and faith in the wake of this gracious display of the kingdom blessings is the spiritual counterpart to the physical reality. The fulfillment of the divine promise to heal his covenant people comes through Jesus.

JESUS' EXORCISM MINISTRY

"But if it is by the Spirit of God that I drive out demons, then the kingdom of God has come upon you" (Matt. 12:28). Having just healed a blind and mute man by casting out an impairing demon, Jesus leaps to this audacious inference — the kingdom has arrived in his ministry! Though he demonstrates the veracity of this claim in multiple ways, this is Jesus' clearest affirmation of the kingdom's presence preserved for us in the Gospels. Once again, let's explore the background of this aspect of Jesus' ministry so as to discern any greater significance in these actions.[3]

---

2. Meyer, *Aims of Jesus*, 171.

3. Exorcisms are prominent in Jesus' ministry. After his initial battle with Satan in the wilderness and the calling of the disciples, Mark recounts as the first event in his Galilean ministry the exorcism of the demon from a man in a Capernaum synagogue (Mark 1:21–28; cf. also 5:1–20; 7:24–30; 9:14–29). Luke gives a similar picture (Luke 4:31–37; 8:26–39; 9:37–43; 11:14–26). This emphasis is not as prominent in Matthew, though it is significant. Matthew's emphasis on Jesus' teaching ministry qualifies the exorcism ministry a bit (cf. Matt. 8:28–34; 15:21–28; 17:14–20). Jesus' reputation as an exorcist is also confirmed in the Jewish Talmud (*b. Sanh.* 43a) and in an ancient, non-Christian papyrus (*Papyri graecae magicae* [ed. K. Preisendanz; Leipzig: Teubner, 1928], 4:3019–20).

The Promise of Divine Deliverance

Prior Foreshadowings

The prior foreshadowings of this aspect of Jesus' ministry are more difficult to identify than in relation to other ministry actions insofar as the Old Testament lacks a
robust development of the defeat of Satan in the last days. Much more prominent
is the theme of the defeat of the gods of other nations. We saw this especially in
our consideration of the implications for Babylon's gods in the Servant's return
from exile. But the overall tenor of the prophetic rhetoric is that the gods of other
nations are but dead objects of wood and stone,[4] and not that they are empowered
by Satan.[5]

A more fruitful backdrop to Jesus' exorcisms lies in the Eden narrative, where
the serpent certainly depicts Satan and his corrupting influence in the world (Gen.
3:1–7). Because of Eve and Adam's capitulation to his wiles, the entire biblical
theme of judgment, atonement, and redemption ensues. Thankfully, the eventual
demise of Satan is depicted even here in this context. God announces to him the
enmity that will exist between him and the offspring of the woman. Though this
message depicts a struggle, God promises the eventual crushing of Satan's head by
the woman's son: "And I will put enmity between you and the woman, and between
your offspring and hers; he will crush your head, and you will strike his heel"
(Gen. 3:15). The implication is that the authority that was ceded to the serpent will
one day be recovered, resulting in his undoing.

Satan's influence pops up occasionally from that point forward (1 Chron. 21:1;
Zech. 3:1–3), especially in the Job narrative (Job 1:6–12; 2:1–7). But for the
most part he disappears from view in the biblical literature. Still, in light of Eden's
portrayal, when the prophets depict the righteous, Spirit-empowered righteousness
of the New Covenant people, the inference is easy to make that Satan's influence
will then be gone.

When we consult the intertestamental literature, however, a dramatically different picture emerges. Likely under Persian influence, what is latent in the Old
Testament blossoms into full flower. Satan's influence in the world is depicted in
graphic detail, mediated through his meddling and deceiving angels:

> The third was named Gader'el; this one is he who showed the children of the people
> all the blows of death, who misled Eve, who showed the children of the people how
> to make the instruments of death (such as) the shield, the breastplate, and the sword
> for warfare. (*1 Enoch* 69:6)

---

4. E.g., Isa. 40:19–20; 41:22–24; 44:9–20; 46:1, 6–7; Jer. 50:2.
There is the interesting struggle between the angel sent to Daniel
and the prince of the Persian kingdom (Dan. 10:12–14). Since it is
an angel and he is given free access to Daniel through the mediation
of Michael (v. 13), the struggle must be undertaken in the spiritual
realm. This surely foreshadows the struggle that characterizes Jesus'
exorcisms.

5. Though this is the case, there are at least hints in the Old
Testament that demons lie behind idols (Deut. 32:17; Ps. 106:37).

But when the messianic age arrives, Satan and his powers will be undone. When the great day of judgment comes, God will send forth his angels and they will root out all the fallen angels and imprison them forever:

> Then the valley shall be filled with their elect and beloved ones (fallen angels); and the epoch of their lives, the era of their glory, and the age of their leading (others) astray *shall come to an end and shall not henceforth be reckoned.* (*1 Enoch* 55:4; emphasis mine; cf. also 10:4–6; 21:10; 54:6; *T. Sim.* 6:6; *T. Levi* 18:12; etc.)

New Testament Confirmation

This perspective is shared in general by the New Testament writers. Paul describes this world as being under the dominion of Satan (2 Cor. 4:4; Col. 1:13), resulting in temptations and oppositions.[6] Peter echoes this assumption, depicting Satan as a prowling "lion," looking for hapless victims (1 Peter 5:8). Paul further develops this warfare, portraying Jesus' resurrection and ascension as the event that strips Satan of his power, subordinating him and his underlings to his dominion (Eph. 1:20–21; Col. 2:15; cf. Rom. 16:20).

Similarly, John affirms that Jesus' mission is to destroy Satan's works (1 John 3:8; cf. also Heb. 2:14) and finally condemn him at the final judgment (Rev. 20:10). Given this conceptual context, it is not difficult to see why the Jews took for granted that the kingdom's arrival would also be the occasion at which Satan would be judged and condemned.

Jesus' Gracious Provision

It is obvious that Jesus presents himself as the one through whom this battle will be won. At the judgment, the Son of Man will consign the "goats" to the "eternal fire prepared for the devil and his angels" (Matt. 25:41). Similarly, the Son of Man will send forth his angels at the end of the age to cull out of his kingdom and judge all those who "cause sin" and "do evil" (13:40–43). Since Jesus identifies the weed-planting "enemy" as "the devil" (v. 39), Satan's judgment is here strongly implied.

Putting this expectation together with his claim to have inaugurated the kingdom, Jesus views his exorcisms as the inauguration of the end-time judgment. In this way, the exorcisms themselves reveal the presence of the reign of God and point ahead to the ultimate demise of Satan. This is what informs Jesus' kingdom logic in Matthew 12. Far from working in league with Satan, which would only ensure the fall of his kingdom (v. 26), Jesus takes the battle to Satan's doorstep. Accordingly, his exorcism of the impairing demon from the blind mute is evidence

---

6. See 1 Cor. 7:5; 2 Cor. 2:11; 11:14–15; 1 Thess. 2:18; 2 Thess. 2:9; 1 Tim. 5:15; 2 Tim. 2:26; cf. also James 4:7.

of his attack on Satan's dominion, setting free a man who could not have escaped on his own. In Jesus, the authority bequeathed to Satan by Adam is being reclaimed by Jesus.

This is yet another of his ministry actions where Jesus' identity as the Servant fuses with his messianic identity (cf. Matt. 15:22). As such, he also provides confirming evidence that he is indeed the Son of David (v. 23). Although Jesus numbers himself generally with other Jewish exorcists of that era who also were performing exorcisms by the power of God (12:27), he sets himself apart by his claim that his exorcisms are accomplished "by the Spirit of God." Twelftree comments that no other Jew seems to have made this claim in that era.[8]

Given the association of the outpouring of the Spirit on the Messiah in the time of the kingdom (Isa. 11:2; but cf. 42:1), Jesus' claim here implies that he is being empowered by the end-time Spirit associated with the coming of the kingdom. Coupled with the emphatic "I" (egō) — "But if I drive out demons by the Spirit of God" — Jesus appears to be making an implicit messianic claim. Accordingly, Jesus is emphasizing his own authority and identity:

> In other words, on the strength of this saying we can conclude that Jesus did not think the kingdom of God was arriving where the Spirit was but where the Spirit was empowering him to perform exorcisms.[9]

His messianic identity is, therefore, once again coupled with his role as healing Servant within this context (Matt. 12:15–21).

Twelftree appeals to Isaiah 24:22 as evidence of a two-stage judgment of the fallen angels: "They [the host of heaven] will be gathered together like prisoners in a pit; they will be shut up in a prison, and after many days they will be punished." A similar perspective seems to be expressed in 1 Enoch 10:4–6. His conclusion, then, is that Jesus viewed his exorcisms as the first stage of this two-stage judgment.[7] Confirmation of this may come in the query of the spirits influencing the Gerasene demoniac: "And they begged Jesus repeatedly not to order them to go into the *Abyss*" (Luke 8:31; emphasis mine).

The crowd's subsequent question, "Could this be the Son of David" (Matt. 12:23), suggests the Jewish expectation that the Messiah would perform miracles to demonstrate who he was. It may also imply the Jewish tradition that Solomon had learned how to exorcise demons, possibly because David himself lent a healing presence to Saul when the latter was tormented by the evil spirit (1 Sam. 16:1–23). Referring to Solomon, Josephus writes: "God also enabled him to learn that skill which expels demons, which is a science useful and sanative to men. He composed such incantations also by which distempers are alleviated. And he left behind him the manner of using exorcisms, by which they drive away demons, so that they never return, and this method of cure is of great force unto this day."[10]

7. Graham H. Twelftree, *Jesus the Miracle Worker: A Historical and Theological Study* (Downers Grove, IL: IVP, 1999), 270; idem, *Jesus the Exorcist: A Contribution to the Study of the Historical Jesus* (Peabody, MA: Hendrickson, 1993), 223–24.

8. Twelftree, *Miracle Worker*, 269. Twelftree also contends that there is no "certainly pre-Christian literature" that depicts "a mes-

sianic figure doing battle with Satan through the relatively ordinary healing of exorcism." He then concludes that Jesus was the first who made the connection "between exorcism and eschatology" (*Jesus the Exorcist*, 227; also 127, 173, 182–89).

9. Ibid., 269.

10. Josephus, *Ant.*, 8.2.5 §§45–49.

EMPOWERMENT FOR DISCIPLESHIP

How do these two aspects of Jesus' ministry empower discipleship?

Healed to Heal Others

In the first place, we should recognize that Jesus' healings declare this to be the beginning of the time when God is healing and transforming his people. Whether we ponder the testimonies to this reality in the gospel records or listen to the many people in the present day whose healings confirm the ongoing presence of Jesus' kingdom power, we have been privileged to live in the age of Jesus' inaugurated fulfillment of the climactic restoration of God's people.

Credible reports of healings abound throughout the world, as people pray in faith for Jesus' healing touch. Missionaries frequently describe God's healing power dissipating the darkness that pervades people groups. In my interaction with college students, I have heard numerous stories, testifying to experiences of healing that are inexplicable outside of the supernatural realm. It has happened in my own family. It has also been demonstrated in the lives of some of my close friends. One of them was marvelously healed of numerous internal injuries and ailments that had inflicted such pain and impairment that his very survival was frequently in question.[11] This is the gracious reality in which discipleship is to be lived.

Since Jesus' healing ministry is bound up with God's covenantal faithfulness to restore the nation, it first of all offers to us an ongoing invitation to participate in God's gracious provision for his recalcitrant and exiled people. As those who have similarly been called out of exile from God, Jesus' healings commend to us hope and grace concerning the continuing expressions of both physical and spiritual malaise that persist in testifying to the kingdom's incomplete fulfillment in our own lives. We ought, therefore, to hear Jesus' offer to touch our eyes as well, to bring healing to our physical and spiritual ears, tongues, and legs, so that we too might participate in this progressive fulfillment of the return from exile.

This may result in both physical and spiritual healing, or only in one of these. The two do not always happen at the same time. The physical healing of the blind man in John 9 is only completed when the man comes to faith after his interrogation by the Pharisees (9:38). Therefore, if physical healing is granted, the spiritual dimension hovers in the air, beckoning us to a deeper healing as well. If the physical healing is withheld for divinely known reasons, the spiritual healing always remains on offer. And though we may have experienced this spiritual renewal before, the inaugurated nature of Jesus' kingdom necessitates the ongoing reception of this grace.

---

11. I am referring in this regard to the experience of William Beeson. What is especially significant about Willie's case is that he has extensive medical evidence of the miraculous changes that took place in his body, apparently suddenly. Willie's story is available in his book, *The Impossible Miracle: A True Account of a Modern Day Miracle* (Mustang, OK: Tate, 2008).

As Israel was diseased and impaired spiritually, so also are we, even as people of the inaugurated New Covenant. As we sit before Jesus with the impurity of our minds, the frailty of our love, the self-centeredness of our focus, or simply the brokenness of our lives, that places us in the posture of reception. We must allow Jesus to touch us afresh every day so that his healing grace and power flow again into our lives, opening our eyes in order to see his glory, unstopping our ears in order to hear his truth again, strengthening our legs in order to leap for joy in his salvation, and loosening our tongues in order to proclaim his praises anew.

Then, in the enablement of these renewals, Jesus beckons us to participate in this ministry in the lives of those around us. That is, we must respond to this restorative grace by living out who we now have become — redeemed people living under the reign of our righteous King. For like the Servant of the Lord, our eyes now are able to see his glory, our ears are receiving instruction from the Lord, and our legs are being strengthened to do his will (Isa. 35:3 – 5; 50:4 – 5). Thus, even as the purified exiles are exhorted not to be defiled as they leave Babylon on their return journey home (Isa. 52:11), we too ought to be renewed in our devotion to the righteous life of the Servant.

Second, we must take seriously the implications of the continuing presence of the kingdom's power to pray for healing in the lives of others. Jesus' redemptive ministry is holistic. Therefore, we too must be a people known for the mediation of Jesus' healing power. Jesus conferred this authority to his disciples as they went out on their missionary journeys (Matt. 10:8a; cf. John 14:12 – 14) — an authority that continues to be exercised in the early church after Jesus' departure (e.g., Acts 3:1 – 10; 5:15 – 16; 14:8 – 10; 20:9 – 10; likely suggested by 14:3). It will not do to consign all of this evidence to the apostolic age, especially since it appears in the general instructions in James (James 5:14 – 16). This, coupled with the immense evidence of contemporary healings today, exhorts us to be praying in Jesus' name for the healing of people. May it not be true of us what was said of those living in Nazareth:

> He could not do any miracles there, except lay his hands on a few sick people and heal them. He was amazed at their lack of faith. (Mark 6:5 – 6a)

At the same time, this must be held in tension with the reality of the inaugurated nature of the kingdom. Jesus did not heal everyone. Nor will everyone who has faith be healed in our day. God's redemptive purposes are not yet consummated. Consequently, when physical healing is granted, we must respond with worship and renewed devotion. When it is sovereignly withheld, we must still respond with submission and renewed devotion, taking comfort in his ever-present grace in the midst of ongoing suffering (2 Cor. 12:9). Either way, Jesus' healing grace is perpetually available to empower us to emulate the Servant's life, bringing the healing of compassion into the lives of those whom God brings into our paths.

Delivered to Deliver Others

Jesus' exorcism power similarly communicates delivering grace and the summons to respond. For apart from Jesus' authoritative rebuke of Satan's power and dismissal of his minions, there is no hope that Eden's tragedy will ever be reversed. At times the evil that is present in this inaugurated stage of the kingdom threatens to undermine the moorings of our hope. Evil abounds on every side. Satan's power seems unchecked. That is why the power of Jesus' exorcisms is so important. By taking the battle directly to the evil one, Jesus gives us a glimpse of Satan's inevitable demise. Evil will not have the final say. Jesus' exorcisms assure us of this. Though it often does not seem so, the day of reckoning is drawing nearer. The present defeat of Satan in Jesus' exorcisms serves notice to the world who indeed will reign supremely in the end. Learning to meditate on this *aggressive* grace and living in its hopeful implications is a vital part of the life of the empowerment of discipleship.

Since God has indeed transferred us from the "dominion of darkness and brought us into the kingdom of the Son he loves" (Col. 1:13), since he has "disarmed the powers and authorities" (2:15), and since he now sits enthroned "far above all rule and authority, power and dominion, and every name that can be invoked" (Eph. 1:21), we should respond to this gracious deliverance with the careful severing of all ties with the demonic in our own lives. Having been delivered from Satan's dominion, we can experience the progressive confirmation of this reality in the increased surrender of our lives to the reign of Jesus. Emboldened and empowered by Jesus' binding of the strong man (Matt. 12:29), our discipleship can increasingly display the reality of this victory in the purity and consistency of our covenant faithfulness.

Finally, we should move forward into the fray. Carrying the authority that Jesus has now restored to us in his name (e.g., Matt. 10:8b; Acts 5:16; 16:16–18), we should be encouraged to an active participation in the spiritual war waging all around us in the lives of people.[12] In fact, Jesus' statement, "Whoever is not with me is against me, and whoever does not gather with me scatters" (Luke 11:23), almost certainly implies a call for his followers to become involved in the ministry of exorcism.[13] We are a delivered people. May we live in such a way that this same deliverance can flow through us to others.

SUMMARY

Seen against the foil of Old Testament anticipations, Jesus' healing and exorcism ministries declare once again the necessity of the divine initiative if God's people

---

12. For helpful discussions of spiritual warfare and the authority of Christians to wage it, see, e.g., Clinton Arnold, *Three Crucial Questions about Spiritual Warfare* (Grand Rapids: Baker, 1997); Timothy M. Warner, *Spiritual Warfare: Victory over the Powers of This Dark World* (Wheaton: Crossway, 1991); Charles H. Kraft, *I Give You Authority: Practicing the Authority Jesus Gave Us* (Grand

Rapids: Chosen, 1997).

13. Graham H. Twelftree, *In the Name of Jesus: Exorcism among Early Christians* (Grand Rapids: Baker, 2007), 96. Twelftree concludes this in light of the preceding and succeeding verses, all of which have to do with spiritual warfare.

are to be delivered and transformed. On the one hand, Jesus' healings announce the onset of the people's climactic return from exile, when they truly will see, hear, and declare his praises. These actions affirm that the time of Israel's end-time transformation is at hand and summon people to repent. On the other hand, Jesus' exorcism ministry functions as the inauguration of the end-time judgment of Satan and his dominion.

As such, these encounters presage not only Satan's eventual demise, but also Jesus' eventual, absolute reign. They serve, therefore, to demonstrate God's aggressive grace on our behalf, defeating an enemy that is far beyond our abilities to fight. In both of these ministry actions, then, Jesus demonstrates the kingdom's potency, providing a glimpse into the end of the age when these inaugurated fulfillments will be consummated—in Satan's final condemnation and judgment and in the ultimate transformation of the people into the image of Jesus.

Remembering and receiving these expressions of Jesus' grace should move us to respond with covenantal faithfulness in the living out of lives of sight, hearing, and proclamation, unencumbered by the impairing power of Satan. In this way, we will be empowered to follow him in mediating those same dimensions of grace to those around us.

RELEVANT QUESTIONS

1. What are the areas in your own life that amount to covenant unfaithfulness? In what ways are you spiritually blind, deaf, mute, lame, or leprous? What would it look like for you to inject yourself into the narrative of Jesus' ministry and experience him touching you in your impurity, even as a disciple already saved by grace?

2. How might you respond to this healing and cleansing touch? What opportunities exist for you to respond to Jesus' pursuing grace by reaching out into the community where people languish in their own darkness? Who might be the marginalized around you that you could "touch," allowing the grace of Jesus to begin having access to their lives? How might you broaden your vision even more broadly to participate in relief efforts and compassion ministries around the world?

3. In what ways are you allowing Satan to have a foothold in your life? How might you respond to Jesus' exorcisms, both in your personal life and in your ministry?

4. What needs to change for these responses to happen in your life? From what priorities and perspectives is Jesus' kingdom grace moving you to repent?

CHAPTER 17

THE SERVANT WHO IS THE REIGNING KING

I am poured out like water,
    and all my bones are out of joint.
My heart has turned to wax;
    it has melted within me.
My mouth is dried up like a potsherd,
    and my tongue sticks to the roof of my mouth;
    you lay me in the dust of death. . . .
All the ends of the earth will remember
    and turn to the Lord,
and all the families of the nations
    will bow down before him. . . .
They will proclaim his righteousness,
    declaring to a people yet unborn:
    He has done it!

Psalm 22:14–15, 27, 31

Then Jesus came to them and said, "All authority in heaven and on earth has been given to me."

Matthew 28:18

We've covered a lot of ground in our pursuit of the answers to our three main questions. Along the way, we've learned much about the nature of the covenants that God makes with his people and how life is to be lived within them. We've also learned a great deal about Jesus and the ways in which he brings to fulfillment the covenantal themes of grace and demand.

Although I admit the paradigm I have drawn is a bit too neat, it is helpful to subsume these two themes under Jesus' roles as Servant and King. As the fulfillment of the Servant of the Lord, Jesus supplies the consummation of God's grace in the establishment of the New Covenant and its blessings. As the fulfillment of the promises regarding the Messiah, Jesus is the King who mediates the fulfilled law to his New Covenant disciples and summons them to follow him. This distinction, though helpful, breaks down at several points, since Jesus also provides grace as the King. This is inevitable since he fulfills both roles.[1] Nowhere is this overlap clearer than in his crucifixion.

We already considered this event through the lens of the Servant of the Lord in chapter 14. As we bring to completion our pursuit of answers to the "How" question, it is appropriate that we revisit these final events in Jesus' earthly life, this time discerning Jesus' experience of the cross and resurrection as the fulfillment of his role as King.

THE DAVIDIC KING'S OPPRESSION

"My God, my God, why have you forsaken me?" (Matt. 27:46; cf. Ps. 22:1). I recall wrestling with this question from Jesus in my adolescent years. Was Jesus doubting his relationship with God at the bitter end? Was he finally crushed by fear and despair? Was his unshakable trust in God finally crumbling? How could this be reconciled with his earlier claims to be "one" with the Father and his open-eyed anticipation of his cross ordeal? Thankfully, the text permits us once again to discover more of what Jesus was encouraging us to see and thereby the covenantal grace that is seeping through.

The King's Oppression

It is possible that the historical reality behind Psalm 22 pertains to the betrayal and intrigue associated with Absalom's conspiracy against David (2 Sam. 15–18), though certainty is never possible. Whatever the actual situation facing the king, he is wrestling with the dissonance between his ongoing intimate relationship with Yahweh ("My God, my God") and God's inaction, in spite of his promise never to remove his lovingkindness from him or from those in his line (2 Sam. 7:15).

On the combination, "My God, my God, why have you forsaken me?" Goldingay comments: "The expression encapsulates the personal relationship of suppliant and God. That is here belied by the Deity's inaction. . . . "My God" and "abandon" do not fit easily in the same sentence. The fact that the term *'el* by nature points to the awesome and mighty nature of God underlines the point. If the mighty and awesome creator God is with us, that solves problems. So why is this not so?"[2]

David's agonizing lament, therefore, finds covenantal linkage with the tortuous confusion expressed by the poet in Psalm 89, likely composed in the wake of Nebuchadnezzar's overthrow of Jerusalem and the subsequent exile of King Jehoiachin to Babylon (2 Kings 24:12). In this psalm, the speaker repeatedly appeals to the solemn covenant oath that God made with David:

> I have made a covenant with my chosen one,
>   I have sworn to David my servant,

---

1. This is most clearly seen in John's vision of the heavenly throne room in Rev. 5. There, the "Lion of the tribe of Judah, the Root of David" is depicted as the "Lamb, looking as if it had been slain" (5:5–6). See Thielman, "The Atonement," 124–25.

2. John Goldingay, *Psalms*; vol.1: *Psalms 1–41* (Baker Commentary on the Old Testament; Grand Rapids: Baker, 2006), 325.

"I will establish your line forever
    and make your throne firm through all generations.". . .
I have found David my servant. . . .
I will maintain my love to him forever,
    and my covenant with him will never fail.
I will establish his line forever,
    his throne as long as the heavens endure.
If his sons forsake my law . . .
I will punish their sin with the rod,
    their iniquity with flogging;
but I will not take my love from him,
    nor will I ever betray my faithfulness.
I will not violate my covenant
    or alter what my lips have uttered.
Once for all, I have sworn by my holiness —
    and I will not lie to David —
that his line will continue forever
    and his throne endure before me like the sun. (Ps. 89:3 – 4, 20 – 36)

This then sets up the contrast with the king's present experience of apparent abandonment by God:

But you have rejected, you have spurned,
    you have been very angry with your anointed one.
You have renounced the covenant with your servant
    and have defiled his crown in the dust. . . .
How long, LORD? Will you hide yourself forever?
    How long will your wrath burn like fire? . . .
Lord, where is your former great love,
    which in your faithfulness you swore to David?
Remember, Lord, how your servant has been mocked,
    how I bear in my heart the taunts of all the nations,
the taunts with which your enemies, LORD, have mocked,
    with which they have mocked every step of your anointed one. (Ps.
        89:38 – 51)

Two reliable facts — the covenantal promise of Yahweh and the reality of David's fallen throne — are contradictory in the highest sense. So the poet struggles to make sense of it all.

Jesus' citation of Psalm 22:1 evokes the pattern of this covenantal tension and invites those witnessing his crucifixion to locate their confusion within that framework. In so doing, he also invites them to find its resolution within that same framework.

Jesus' Fulfillment of This Pattern

Much to the dismay of the religious leaders, Pilate affixes to Jesus' cross the charge that captures the biting irony of the event: "THIS IS JESUS, THE KING OF THE JEWS" (Matt. 27:36b; Luke 23:1–3; John 18:33–37). Then, with his provocative cry, the crucified Jesus gives voice to his sorrow, joining his lament with David as he writes Psalm 22. This combination channels our perception of Jesus' suffering through the lens of this psalm and David's own experience, inviting us to ponder the notion of a suffering king.

As we move through the gospel narratives, numerous parallels and allusions to this psalm emerge. The most obvious of these comes from the mouths of the religious leaders, seeking to capitalize on the contradiction created by Pilate's placard above a crucified man. Sarcastically, they quote from Psalm 22, mocking Jesus for his acceptance of the messianic title "Son of God":

"The acts of casting the crown into the dust, spurning the covenant, and destroying the fortifications (Ps. 89:39–40) would usually be associated with the activities of Israel's enemies. Here, however, God is the perpetrator of the hostile acts. How can these deeds be reconciled with his 'love,' 'faithfulness,' and 'covenant' celebrated in the hymn and oracle (vv. 1–37)? The destruction of Israel's fortification system (v. 40) and the cries and scorn of the enemies' victory leave God's people with little hope. God has abandoned his people; more than that, he has rejected the covenant of love, i.e., the covenant with David."[3]

> "He saved others," they said, "but he can't save himself! He's the king of Israel! Let him come down now from the cross, and we will believe in him. He trusts in God. Let God rescue him now if he wants him, for he said, 'I am the Son of God.'" (Matt. 27:42–43; cf. Ps. 22:6–8, 17; Luke 23:35)

Likewise, Jesus' expression of thirst (John 19:28) matches the psalmist's torment (Ps. 22:15). Both Jesus and the psalmist experience wounding to their hands and feet by their enemies (Ps. 22:16; John 20:25, 27). Although nothing in the Gospels explicitly picks up the description of Jesus' bones being visible for all to see, Jesus' garments are divided among the soldiers (Matt. 27:35; John 19:24), cohering with the Roman practice of crucifying their victims in the nude and the psalmist's desperation (Ps. 22:17–18). What was true of David, then, finds

"What these mockers scornfully ridicule, what they regard as impossible, what they look upon as the wild claim of a charlatan is paradoxically the truth. The words with which they so confidently taunt Jesus, 'Son of God,' 'king of Israel,' are fully true.... The key piece of information unknown to the mockers is that Jesus undergoes in his humiliation and crucifixion nothing other than the intended will of God. Their notion of the Son of God, the messianic king of Israel, as a triumphant, self-assertive, and powerful figure was mistaken — or at least partially so since he will ultimately appear as such in his future parousia. They cannot guess that they are speaking the truth about Jesus. In their blind opposition to the truth, they but accomplish the will of God."[4]

3. Willem A. VanGemeren, *Psalms* (EBC rev. ed; ed. Tremper Longman III and David E. Garland; Grand Rapids: Zondervan, 2008), 5:678–79.

4. Hagner, *Matthew 14–28*, 840.

tragic repetition in the oppression of Jesus. Although he is the king whose heart beats in unison with Yahweh's, his own people betray and turn against him. And Yahweh remains silent. Once again, the enduring validity of the Davidic promises hangs in the balance.

THE DAVIDIC KING'S VINDICATION

The King's Vindication

Significantly, in both Psalm 22 and 89, the concluding word is one of faith. The final verse in Psalm 89, however, was not part of the original composition. Rather, it is the repetition of the refrain that concludes each of the books of the psalms (cf. also Pss. 41:13; 72:19; 106:48; 150:1–6). Coming as it does at the end of this lament, however, it offers to the reader the invitation to respond to the tension created by the second half of the psalm by a reaffirmation of the unconditional promises of God to David (89:3–37), foreshadowing also the victorious acclamations of psalms yet to come (e.g., Pss. 93–99).

The expectation of vindication is voiced more explicitly in Psalm 22, as David repeats his cry for deliverance (vv. 19–21) in full confidence that God will yet be true to his word. And the result will be praise and worship to God throughout the generations of Israel:

> For he has not despised or scorned
>   the suffering of the afflicted one;
> he has not hidden his face from him
>   but has listened to his cry for help. (Ps. 22:24)

In response to this anticipated intervention, David renews his commitment to reign justly and righteously so that the poor will be given food and the righteous will praise God (Ps. 22:26). He goes on to affirm that the ripples of his rescue will not stop at Israel's borders. They will reach to the ends of the earth, resulting in worship from all nations being given to the Lord (vv. 27–28). Indeed, no one will be exempt — all will praise God and acknowledge his faithfulness (vv. 29–31). They will sing the Lord's praises because "He has done it!" (v. 31c). Almost assuredly, David is linking his own deliverance to the preservation of his kingly line (cf. 2 Sam. 7:13, 16) and the extension of its dominion to the ends of the earth (e.g., Ps. 2:8).[5]

---

5. This also helps us understand David's expectation in Ps. 16. In this psalm, David expresses his confidence in God's protection. God is his "refuge" (v. 1) and the one in whom he finds all good things (v. 2). Because of God's gracious provision in his life (v. 6), David experiences assurance that God will indeed deliver him in what sounds like a resurrection (vv. 9–11). Although David's meaning is hotly debated, it seems best to conclude that he is expressing here his expectation of God's deliverance from whatever threat he presently is experiencing. But David also perceives the connection between his own rescue and the preservation of his line, implied in vv. 5–6 and in his reference to his "portion" and "inheritance." Peter confidently ascribes David's words in this psalm only to Jesus in Acts 2:25–28. It is likely that this conclusion is to be explained by Peter's awareness of David's corporate reference in the context of the Davidic Covenant (v. 30) and the climactic nature of Jesus' fulfillment of this pattern in the Davidic line.

Jesus' Fulfillment of This Pattern

It is easy to see that Jesus' resurrection connects with David's expectation of deliverance and restoration. As the great fulfillment of the Davidic line (Matt. 22:45), Jesus' resurrection both resolves the temporary tension caused by God's inaction during the crucifixion and brings to culmination the universal scope of the blessings anticipated by David. Though Jesus is oppressed for a time, God's promises to David once again prove trustworthy. His resurrection confirms that Jesus truly is David's greater son, who will reign on David's throne forever (Luke 1:32–33). And with his vindicating resurrection, Yahweh's reign over his people is once again established (Isa. 52:7).

This brings us to our final text. It is significant that Jesus prefaces his Great Commission with these words: "All authority in heaven and on earth has been given to me" (Matt. 28:18). Jesus is here alluding to Daniel 7:14, where the Son of Man receives universal kingly authority from the Ancient of Days:

> He was given authority, glory and sovereign power; all nations and peoples of every language worshiped him. His dominion is an everlasting dominion that will not pass away, and his kingdom is one that will never be destroyed. (Dan. 7:14)

Since I discussed this text in chapter 10, I will be brief here. I noted there that the remarkable manner in which this king's sovereignty over all nations is to be accomplished—at least in this age—is through the proclamation of the gospel through his disciples. If we bring the vision of Psalm 22 together with this expectation, we can achieve further clarity. For included in the disciples' proclamation of the good news of Jesus is his deliverance from the bonds of death, which brings to consummated expression the deliverance David himself experienced. Thus, the blessings that David anticipated are here linked to the compassionate, kingdom mission of Jesus' disciples—disciples who have seen firsthand the vindication of David's greater son and who carry on his Servant role of pursuing grace and mercy:

> The poor will eat and be satisfied;
>> those who seek the LORD will praise him—
>> may your hearts live forever!
> All the ends of the earth
>> will remember and turn to the LORD,
> and all the families of the nations
>> will bow down before him,
> for dominion belongs to the LORD
>> and he rules over the nations.
> All the rich of the earth will feast and worship;
>> all who go down to the dust will kneel before him—
>> those who cannot keep themselves alive.

> Posterity will serve him;
>> future generations will be told about the Lord.
> They will proclaim his righteousness,
>> declaring to a people yet unborn:
> He has done it! (Ps. 22:26–31)

EMPOWERMENT FOR DISCIPLESHIP
God's Gracious Fulfillment of the Davidic Promises

As we have seen, Jesus' resurrection brings to covenantal consummation David's expectation of vindication (Ps. 22:24) and universal reign (22:25–31). Consequently, we should perceive in this event the fulfillment of God's gracious covenantal promises that he made to David (2 Sam. 7:11b–16). Even though there were times when God appeared to have forsaken his line (e.g., Pss. 22 and 89), even in the experience of his greatest heir, he has in the end proven faithful. He has defeated the enemy of the people of God (Eph. 1:19b–21; Col. 2:15; Heb. 1:14–15; 1 John 3:8) and now sits enthroned at the right hand of the Almighty (Acts 2:31–35; 7:56; Eph. 2:6; Col. 3:1; Heb. 1:3, 13; cf. Ps. 110:1). David's throne has indeed been established forever!

"[The church's] witness to God's victory in the future is based on a victory already achieved in history. It proclaims not merely hope, but a hope based on events in history and its own experience. Indeed, the church is an eschatological community not only because it witnesses to God's future victory but because its mission is to display the life of the eschatological Kingdom in the present evil age. The very existence of the church is designed to be a witness to the world of the triumph of God's Kingdom accomplished in Jesus."[6]

Meditating on this gracious reality has the potential of lifting the face of those disciples who languish in the apparently unending hegemony of evil in this world. In Daniel 7, when the Son of Man receives his dominion, so also do the saints of the Most High (Dan. 7:18, 27) who are being persecuted on the earth (vv. 21, 25). Remembering God's faithfulness to David and assenting to the reality of Jesus' enthronement, far above all rule and authority that stands against us (Eph. 1:19–23), should enable us to press on, bearing the cost of discipleship and knowing that one day we will share in his vindication!

The Christian's Inclusion in the Vindicated King's Reign

Jesus' reign has begun and his disciples have already entered into that reign. God's redeemed people finally have the righteous King for whom they have awaited for centuries. We are the privileged ones to live in the new era of this fulfillment. The

---

6. Ladd, *The Presence of the Future*, 337–38.

grace that this represents summons us to surrender afresh each day to this gracious Servant King, making his reign visible to those around us—a dominion that will one day be visible to all (Eph. 1:9–10; Phil. 2:10–11). If we do so even today, taking up his ministry of grace, mercy, and justice, the "poor will eat and be satisfied" (Ps. 22:26a) and "all the families of the nations will bow down before him" (22:27b). Buoyed by the grace of God's deliverance of our King, we must respond to his absolute summons to covenantal fidelity, even as we lift our praises as the people who were "unborn" at the time of Jesus' vindication, but who now live in the hope generated by his resurrection. Truly, "He has done it!" (22:31).

SUMMARY

As in the case of the Servant of the Lord's experience, Jesus' crucifixion and resurrection bring to fulfillment the pattern of the oppressed and vindicated Davidic king. Though Good Friday might lead one to deduce Yahweh's abandonment of Jesus, Easter morning declares the truth of Jesus' innocence and divine approval. Consequently, the Davidic Covenant has come to climactic fulfillment as Jesus steps permanently into his reigning authority. Since we are those whose righteous King has been vindicated and enthroned, may we daily receive his gracious reign so that we might in turn be empowered to participate in the extension of his gracious dominion over all nations of the earth.

RELEVANT QUESTIONS

1. In what ways does understanding Jesus' suffering and resurrection as the fulfillment of the Davidic promises change your relationship to him as King?
2. What difference does living under the gracious reign of the vindicated Son of David make in your everyday life?
3. What specific things in your daily life ought to change as you respond to this grace and participate in the extension of Jesus' reign to the nations?

THE ANSWERS TO
THE "HOW" QUESTION

In answering the "Why" and "What" questions, we learned that the nature of the New Covenant implies that the demand of righteousness from its people is not at all diminished in comparison to the Mosaic Covenant era. Even though Jesus is the representative covenant member who fulfills this demand in his own life and offers its righteous benefits to us by faith, the expectation of righteousness from us, the people of the New Covenant, is absolute. Since we have received final atonement for our sin, since we have experienced the internalization of the law, since we have a righteous king reigning over us, and since we have been graced with the internal witness and enablement of the Spirit, our righteousness ought to shine forth like the sun and draw the nations to Yahweh. The urgency of the "How" question becomes obvious at this point in the discussion.

IMPLICATIONS FROM
THE INAUGURATED KINGDOM

We began our discussion of this question by examining Jesus' teachings regarding the kingdom of God. We discovered that the kingdom he brought was only *inaugurated*—it was not consummated. I suggested this implies that some of the New Covenant benefits associated with this kingdom have similarly only been inaugurated, leaving us with only partially transformed hearts and spirits that are incompletely surrendered to the Spirit.

The prophets did not foresee this inaugurated stage of the kingdom, which accounts for Jesus' ascription of the word "mystery" to it. This, then, helps us understand the dissonance between the absolute descriptions of the righteous, purified people of the New Covenant era and our own inconsistent fidelity to God. How are we to live in this reality? I suggested that the answer lies in learning what it means to live in covenant with God.

When we looked at how life in the covenants was lived in the Old Testament era, we discovered that the law's commands were always encountered in the repeated pattern of *remembering* God's gracious deliverance and provisions. But the people did not merely remember God's faithfulness, the law also provided for yearly, seasonal, and weekly times of renewed *reception* of those provisions. Only in this grace-empowered state would the people be able to *respond* faithfully to the all-encompassing demand of God on their lives.

As we reflected on how to apply these insights to the "How" question, I suggested that the inaugurated nature of our transformation necessitates an ongoing and persistent reception of grace so as to be enabled to live faithfully to the New Covenant demands. Every day, disciples of Jesus must return to the Servant for the grace that empowers conformity to the King's demand to live out the life of the Servant. In all of this, the New Covenant gift of the Spirit will be actively taking what is from Jesus and making it present to us, including not only his teachings and demands, but also his grace.

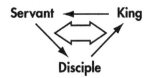

This is the discipleship dynamic that empowers profound obedience, without devolving into a binding form of legalism, for it is profoundly grounded in the grace of a grant covenant.

IMPLICATIONS FROM JESUS' SERVANT WORK

Learning to remember and receive the multifaceted grace that comes through Jesus in his different roles is, therefore, the means to living faithfully in this New Covenant era. For instance, learning to remember Jesus' consummate representative work on our behalf and pausing long enough so that the Spirit brings this gracious truth alive in our hearts again will enable us to live in Jesus' completed righteousness instead of our own frail attempts. This in turn will enliven our own efforts to respond to Jesus' provision with lives of repentance and righteousness.

Pausing often to receive the grace of Jesus' redeeming work in his crucifixion and resurrection, by which he absorbed the covenantal curse on our behalf and then experienced God's vindication, will constrain our hearts in turn to pursue those around us who are still in exile from God. They too need to see the Servant so that they will understand God's grace that comes to them through Jesus. Repeatedly being moved by this profound grace will increasingly enable us to emulate his life among the nations, willingly accepting the risks associated with the cross.

Similarly, frequently receiving Jesus' restoring grace will enable our own obedience to his command to love others as ourselves. Reckoning with our unworthiness to be included in the restored people of God, our inability to cleanse ourselves so as to merit a spot at the kingdom table, or our powerlessness to heal ourselves of our covenant unfaithfulness will open us up to the reception of Jesus' pursuing grace. In these ways, we will be empowered to follow him in mediating those same dimensions of grace to those around us, regardless of their ethnicity or social class. Likewise, learning to meditate on the aggressive grace of Jesus' exorcism ministry and receiving its hopeful implications have the potential of lifting our heads as his disciples in the present day, of winning our allegiance to his kingly reign, and of enabling our active participation in his power encounter ministry.

Finally, as we live in the gracious reality of the vindication and enthronement of our gracious King, our hearts will be inclined to surrender afresh to participate in the ministry of extending his kingdom to all nations and all peoples — but always with the empowering song in our hearts, "He has done it!"

If we were to summarize this theology, we might think of it this way:

Grace foils legalism.
But grace fuels righteousness.

Those who live in grace simply cannot continue living under the illusion that it is by means of their righteous actions that they are acceptable before God. By its very nature, grace nullifies pride and autonomy, rectifying the posture bequeathed to us by Adam and Eve. This means that rediscovering how to live in grace involves the recovery of what it means to be *human*! In the process, the role of grace is restored as the means by which we are transformed to reflect the righteous character of God.

This is covenantal discipleship.

PART THREE

REFLECTING ON RELEVANCE

CHAPTER 18

FOLLOWING THE SERVANT KING TODAY

For this reason, since the day we heard about you, we have not stopped praying for you. We continually ask God to fill you with the knowledge of his will through all the wisdom and understanding that the Spirit gives, so that you may live a life worthy of the Lord and please him in every way: bearing fruit in every good work, growing in the knowledge of God, being strengthened with all power according to his glorious might so that you may have great endurance and patience, and giving joyful thanks to the Father, who has qualified you to share in the inheritance of his people in the kingdom of light.

Colossians 1:9–12

What, after all, is the purpose of discipleship, if not to foster transformation into the image of the great Rabbi himself—Jesus? Apart from transformation, there will be no mission. Apart from mission, there will be no worship from every corner of the globe. For this reason, it is important that we conclude this exercise in biblical theology with a few further reflections on the relevance of what we have learned. This is precisely what the framers of this series on biblical theology have sought to achieve. For if the theology that we distill from the biblical text does not impact our daily lives, we have not completed our task. This is why this series is called "Biblical Theology for Life"—offering books that communicate the empowering *life* of God, shaping the *life* of people in covenant with him. This study has sought to facilitate this outcome, culminating in this definition of covenantal discipleship:

> Covenantal discipleship is learning to receive and respond to God's grace and demand, which are mediated through Jesus, the Servant King, so as to reflect God's character in relation to him, to others, and to the world, in order that all may come to experience this same grace and respond to this same demand.

Bearing this conception of discipleship in mind, let's consider some of the ways in which the answers we have found are relevant to contemporary life. Admittedly, my horizon is significantly limited to what I know in my own apprehension of American culture. I hope these thoughts will spur your thinking to build bridges and make applications to the setting in which you live as a disciple of Jesus.

THE RELEVANCE OF THE ANSWERS TO THE "WHY" QUESTION

Reclaiming the Contours of Discipleship

In their enlightening study of the religious and spiritual lives of American teenagers, Christian Smith and Melinda Denton have delineated the fuzzy contours of a popularly held version of Christianity among contemporary youth. Dubbed "Moralistic Therapeutic Deism," its adherents perceive God to be at their beck and call, even though he is not particularly involved in their lives. That is, apart from those occasions when he intervenes to address a specific problem or need, he recedes from view. As a result, though the moralism of this belief system assumes all "good" (= "nice") people go to heaven, its God does not demand much of anything from his people, especially if those demands would compromise Christianity's narcissistic goal—that of fostering a sense of well-being, happiness, and peace.[1] Smith and Denton's conclusion is deeply troubling:

> It is not so much that U.S. Christianity is being secularized. Rather more subtly, Christianity is either degenerating into a pathetic version of itself or, more significantly, Christianity is actively being colonized and displaced by a quite different religious faith.[2]

When the authors of the study inquire regarding the sources of this variant form of Christianity, they indicate it is actually deriving from the adults who have parented and mentored these young people in the faith. In other words, the extent to which Moralistic Therapeutic Deism (MTD) is affecting the church is likely more far-reaching than merely among its youth.[3]

Since it is likely that variations of this theological worldview have seeped into many churches at a variety of levels, it is worthwhile to use it as a foil against which the relevance of covenantal discipleship might be discerned. Let's take each main element of MTD in turn, and compare it with what our study has uncovered.

Moralism by its very nature denies the necessity of divine grace to bring about salvation. Even in the insipid expression of needing to be "nice" to enter heaven, MTD is a form of legalism that mocks the absolute demand of an all-holy God. Our analysis of the biblical covenants has demonstrated that throughout history

---

1. Christian Smith, with Melinda Lundquist Denton, *Soul Searching: The Religious and Spiritual Lives of American Teenagers* (Oxford: Oxford Univ. Press, 2005), 162–65.

2. Ibid., 171.

3. Ibid., 166.

God has always been the initiator of the divine-human relationship by means of his pursuing, providing, and promising grace. This persistence makes the necessarily gracious nature of God's salvation clearly discernible. Consequently, there has never been an era when *any* kind of legalism has been the basis of acceptance before God.

"This God is not demanding. He actually can't be, because his job is to solve our problems and make people feel good. In short, God is something like a combination Divine Butler and Cosmic Therapist: he is always on call, takes care of any problems that arise, professionally helps his people to feel better about themselves, and does not become too personally involved in the process."[4]

This truth finds resounding confirmation in the New Covenant, which is grounded first in Jesus' representative covenant righteousness, whereby God's absolute demand is met in his perfect obedience, and second in his role as representative curse-bearer, bringing to fulfillment all prior expressions of atonement. Thus, New Covenant disciples stand in Jesus' righteousness alone *by faith*. The stunning absence among many professing Christians today of a keen awareness of their utter dependence on divine grace must be addressed by a return to the good news about Jesus.

We have also learned that covenantal grace never diminishes God's high call to righteousness. This is especially true of the New Covenant, whose prophetic expressions depict a set-apart, Spirit-filled people who consistently follow and obey their righteous messianic King. Consequently, to characterize Jesus' demand of righteousness as simply that of being "nice" falls far short of his preservation of the Old Testament command to reflect the character of God (Lev. 19:2; Matt. 5:48).

Even in circles where more traditional understandings of Christianity are held, the problem of a truncated call to righteousness is rampant. Often, this is the result of a sanctified concern not to fall into legalism, lest grace be diminished in the process. The result is often a lethargic, lukewarm, and compromising lifestyle that is difficult to distinguish from other "nice," law-abiding people in the neighborhood. Active righteousness — not just the avoidance of bad language, drunkenness, and adultery, but the kind that pursues personal uprightness in all areas of life and extends itself to the unlikely, the underprivileged, the marginalized, and the oppressed — is all too often absent from the lives of professing Christians.

This is why learning the proper relationship between God's grace and his demand is so important. From the beginning, God's longing has not changed. He has always desired a people of his own, living in his gracious care and responding to that grace with surrendered hearts, all for the purpose that they will display his character throughout his creation. As we have seen, this was his stated desire even before the fall. His Edenic intention is that humanity will respond to his grace by ruling over the earth, stewarding it within the ambit of his attributes.

---

4. Ibid., 165.

This desire remains unchanged throughout the successive covenants that follow, culminating in the New Covenant. Now, through Jesus' fulfillment of the Old Testament expressions of covenantal grace, God has laid claim to an even greater righteousness in the lives of his people than ever before. The deeper grace of Jesus does not translate into reduced obedience to him! On the contrary, the deeper the grace, the higher are God's expectations of righteousness from those who are privileged to receive that grace. Jesus himself affirms, "For I tell you that unless your righteousness surpasses that of the Pharisees and the teachers of the law, you will certainly not enter the kingdom of heaven" (Matt. 5:20). As I have argued, this statement reflects Jesus' expectation of righteousness from those privileged to experience the transforming and enabling blessings of the kingdom. Those of us who have been so privileged must not delude ourselves into thinking that Jesus doesn't really mean what he says. As we have seen, biblical faith inevitably expresses itself in obedience. Where the latter is lacking, the former is most likely illusory.

Our survey has also made it clear that God is not some kind of benevolent "Divine Butler," whose raison d'être is to cater to the narcissistic desires of the true "masters" of the universe—us! Rather, God's provisions of grace and sustenance to his covenant partners are for the purpose of enabling them to respond to his demands. God graciously pursues people not simply to effect their redemption, but also to empower their transformation. Moreover, God has called his people into *his* drama of history, to participate in *his* purposes in the world. To characterize God as a "therapist" implies that our comfort in *our* stories is the main focus of God's concern and denies Jesus' discipleship call to pick up our crosses in the fulfillment of his commands.

Finally, rather than a deistic God who winds things up and periodically checks in with his creatures, God presents himself in the Bible as our King. Consequently, his reign is constant and his demands are all-encompassing. There is no hint of a distant, disinterested God in Scripture. Jesus' call to discipleship is a call to enter into this *kingdom*. No aspect of life is lived outside of his kingly reign.

Revising Our Evangelistic Methods

Our consideration of the "Why" question has also suggested that we need to think carefully about how we present the gospel to others. In their revealing study on the perceptions of Christians in American society today, David Kinnaman and Gabe Lyons note the effect of an easy believism on the frequently shallow nature of people's commitments to Christ:

> How deep is the faith you convey to outsiders? What type of depth are we asking our friends and neighbors to have? A get-saved approach ignores the fact that most people in America have made an emotional connection to Jesus before; now they need much more than a one-dimensional understanding of him.

More of the same lightweight exposure to Christianity, where a decision for Christ is portrayed as simple and costless, will fail to produce lasting faith in young people.[5]

Overemphasizing salvation by grace through faith gives people only half of the covenantal story. Rather, we need to think long and hard regarding how we might communicate the gospel, always safeguarding God's free grace but also being honest about the nature of entering into covenant with him. Presenting Jesus not only as the Servant who redeems and forgives, but also as the King who demands loyalty and devotion, is an important task facing the church today. Unless we do a better job at the front end of people's Christian experience, we are likely to draw them into an inadequate version of discipleship that may never be corrected. We must help people not only to fall in love with the Savior, but also to fall at the feet of the King.

> "Intentionally or not, we promote the idea to outsiders that being a Christ follower is primarily about the mere choice to convert. We do not portray it as an all-out, into-the-kingdom enlistment that dramatically influences all aspects of life."[6]

Developing an Informed Discipleship

This naturally leads to a more robust conception of how to move people into a deeper understanding of discipleship. In light of the sobering frequency of people leaving the church after initially being drawn in through some evangelistic effort, our attention must increasingly be given to facilitating spiritual formation and growth in understanding. Unfortunately, what is often missing in this regard is the focus on *articulacy*.

Smith and Denton affirm that *in*articulacy in relation to faith commitments actually *undermines* the reality of those commitments for those who hold them. They conclude:

> ... religious faith, practice, and commitment can be no more than vaguely real when people cannot talk much about them. Articulacy fosters reality. A major challenge for religious educators of youth [and I would add "adults" as well], therefore, seems to us to be fostering articulation, helping teens to *practice talking about* their faith, providing practice at using vocabularies, grammars, stories, and key messages of faith.[7]

But how this is done must be carefully examined. Too often, the church has sought to remedy the problem of inarticulacy through the memorization of individual verses and isolated stories.[8] But these are usually disconnected from the over-

5. David Kinnaman and Gabe Lyons, *Unchristian: What a New Generation Really Thinks about Christianity ... and Why It Matters* (Grand Rapids: Baker, 2007), 76. This is especially important since most people in the U.S. have already experienced and rejected an emotional commitment to Christ. Their prior "skin deep" exposure to Christianity has resulted in a large number of jaded, "*de*churched individuals*" (74).

6. Ibid., 79.

7. Smith and Denton, *Soul Searching*, 267–68; emphasis theirs. They note that it appeared most young people they interviewed had not ever been asked by an adult to articulate their faith and to explain why it mattered (133).

8. See the insightful article by David R. Nienhuis, "The Problem of Evangelical Biblical Illiteracy," accessed online at Modern Reformation: www.modernreformation.org/default.php?page=articledisplay&var1=ArtRead&var2=1110&var3=main.

all biblical narrative—as if their meaning and significance could be discerned in pristine isolation from their literary and historical contexts.[9]

If Christians, both young and old, are to understand the answer to the "Why" question, we must do a much better job of creating an ethos of knowing and articulating the longitudinal contours of the biblical narrative and the nature of the relationship that God desires to have with his people. What is needed is a concerted effort to trace the big story of the Bible, including such things as the covenantal flow and the expectation of the kingdom of God. Unfortunately, this kind of teaching and preaching is curiously absent from many Christian fellowships. On one occasion after teaching a basic lesson on the kingdom to an adult Sunday school class, an elderly man approached me and said, "I've been sitting in these pews for over forty years and I've never heard anything like that." I frequently hear of the same experience from my college students who have grown up in the church. This state of affairs must change.

Learning to conceive of discipleship in the context of "covenant" requires that Christians acquire a good knowledge of what covenant entails generally, as well as its specific provisions in its New Covenant expression. Too often, the essence of the New Covenant is presented as the fulfillment of the sacrificial system and the end of the law. But as we have seen, Christians need to think clearly about what it means that the law is internalized in the hearts and minds of God's people. They need to reflect on the role of the Holy Spirit in fashioning believers into people obedient to God in everything. They need to consider the implications of the arrival of the righteous Davidic King, who reigns over them and leads them into righteousness. They need to think about their missional role of displaying God's character in the world so that the nations might be drawn to their light.

"We want to create a community ethos of habitual, orderly, communal ingestion of the revelatory text. We do so in the hope that the Spirit of God will transform readers into hearers who know what it is to abide before the mirror of the Word long enough to become enscripturated doers; that is, people of faith who are adept at interpreting their individual stories and those of their culture through the grand story of God as it is made known in the Bible."[10]

Until we teach people what the New Covenant is about, the church will be characterized by varieties of discipleship that fall woefully short of the biblical vision.

Even though Jesus has provided the fulfillment of the grace of the covenants, his command to respond to that grace with absolute righteousness is crystal clear! Jesus called his disciples "salt" and "light." Let us begin to think deeply, both individually and corporately, about how we might actually begin living that way in the world. Within the framework of the New Covenant, this is *not* optional!

9. A great example of this is the frequent citation of Jer. 29:11, as if it were a promise directly applicable to the modern Christian in every circumstance. Its reference to God's intention to redeem the exiles languishing in Babylon in the sixth century BC is almost never even considered, nor how this promise might be mediated through Jesus to the modern disciple.

10. Nienhuis, "The Problem of Evangelical Biblical Illiteracy."

THE RELEVANCE OF THE ANSWERS TO THE "WHAT" QUESTION

As with one voice, the prophets describe the people of the New Covenant/Kingdom era as being characterized by profound righteousness. Having experienced the transforming blessings of this covenant, their own righteousness will emanate forth in such a way as to fulfill their role as priests to the nations. Isaiah's lofty portrayal is typical of this expectation:

> Arise, shine, for your light has come,
>   and the glory of the LORD rises upon you.
> See, darkness covers the earth
>   and thick darkness is over the peoples,
> but the LORD rises upon you
>   and his glory appears over you.
> Nations will come to your light,
>   and kings to the brightness of your dawn. (Isa. 60:1–3; cf. Zech. 8:23; etc.)

Since the fulfillments of the covenantal hopes have come in Jesus, those who claim to have experienced this reality ought to resemble these prophetic expectations.

Sadly, such is all too often not the case. Rather, non-Christians typically perceive hypocrisy, compromise, and superficiality. As proof, Kinnaman and Lyons cite a 2007 study that offers insight into the private lives of many professing Christians:

> When asked to identify their activities over the last thirty days, born-again Christians were just as likely to bet or gamble, to visit a pornographic website, to take something that did not belong to them, to consult a medium or psychic, to physically fight or abuse someone, to have consumed enough alcohol to be considered legally drunk, to have used an illegal, non-prescription drug, to have said something to someone that was not true, to have gotten back at someone for something he or she did, and to have said mean things behind another person's back.
>   No difference.[11]

I suppose this should not be surprising if the essence of Christianity is simply to provide its followers "therapeutic benefits" (as in MTD), or simply to save people from an eternity in hell and not to bring about their transformation. The call to a biblical definition of lived-out righteousness is therefore unheard by many today:

> This is not a religion of repentance from sin, of keeping the Sabbath, of living as a servant of a sovereign divine, of steadfastly saying one's prayers, of faithfully observing high holy days, of building character through suffering, of basking in God's love and grace, of spending oneself in gratitude and love for the cause of social justice, etcetera. Rather, what appears to be the actual dominant religion among

---

11. Kinnaman and Lyons, *Unchristian*, 47.

U.S. teenagers is centrally about feeling good, happy, secure, at peace. It is about attaining subjective well-being, being able to resolve problems, and getting along amiably with other people.[12]

Given this state of affairs, the relevance of the answer to the "What" question is obvious.

Rediscovering Who Jesus Is

Likely because we Christians do not often think through the relationship between the Mosaic law and the New Covenant, we do not always feel the weight of Jesus' role as the Prophet who articulates for us the end-time nature of God's demand. That is, we do not wrestle with the ways in which Jesus "fulfills" the law by mediating its final expression.

But the reality is that he is indeed the Prophet whose mandate outstrips that of Moses himself—who stands before us as the only one who has supreme authority to articulate God's claim on our lives. What's more, he is also the King who embodies the heart of God and thus commands us to follow him down the pathways that he forges before us. Somehow, the message of God's grace in Christ has opened up the possibility of making obedience to Jesus' prophetic and kingly summons *optional*. But if we hold our answers to the "Why" question together with a fresh appreciation of Jesus' true identity, we will return to the posture of submission in which covenantal discipleship is possible. Robed in supreme authority, Jesus stands before us, summoning us to follow him absolutely. We must learn to reject the delusion that our concern to avoid legalism permits us to pick and choose which of his commands we actually obey.

Rediscovering the Reality of His Commands

Our answers to the "What" question have introduced us to the difficult topic of how the law is mediated to us through Jesus. In a time when meaty sermons and challenging Sunday school lessons are on the wane, the need has never been greater for leaders in the church and individual thinking Christians to wrestle with these issues in biblical theology. Various pastors have expressed to me their fear of going too deep for their congregations. Consequently, they "put the cookies on the lowest shelf" and concentrate on evangelistic sermons and lessons filled with application. These trends must change.

While effectively communicating into our cultural contexts must always remain essential to our task, pastors, teachers, and lay leaders must begin again to challenge the church to think scripturally regarding these matters. Otherwise, individual Christians will be left to define the nature of their relationship with God on their own; such thinking will result in permutations that fail to reflect the biblical

---

12. Smith and Denton, *Soul Searching*, 163–64.

reality. My hunch is that when people are given something solid into which they can sink their teeth, they will discover how truly hungry they have been. They will also perceive more acutely the sharp edges of Jesus' discipleship summons.

One of the most important things that this study has affirmed is that, while the law as a covenantal era has ended, this does not mean that its demands have been rescinded. Rather, they have been fulfilled in Jesus' *teaching*, placing the same demand on us. Even in the case of those laws that have been made obsolete by the nature of their fulfillment, their call to righteousness is preserved by Jesus. Accordingly, the suspension of the food laws, the sacrifices, and the requirement of circumcision implies an age when the righteous *goals* of those institutions and laws have arrived. The same pattern applies to Jesus' ending of Moses' more relaxed provisions for divorce.[13] The bar has been *raised* from the Mosaic era, not lowered!

As we have come to understand Jesus' discernment of the heart of the law, we have discovered that the Old Testament command to love God in an all-consuming way and our neighbors as ourselves is *still* God's demand on us as his people. There has been no change in this whatsoever. Accordingly, any of our traditional practices or behaviors that hinder acts of mercy, compassion, and truthfulness are to be jettisoned as simply wrong. We must realize that getting involved personally and sacrificially in the needs of those around us and around the world is *unavoidable*, even if that means surrendering the need to protect and defend our own rights. Rather than conceiving of discipleship as some kind of pathway to prosperity, it is the means by which God's gracious provisions might flow through us to others.

Whether that be helping out at a homeless shelter to feed and care for the needy, investing a week in a camp for underprivileged or abused or handicapped children, graciously giving of our financial resources to kingdom causes, housing women caught in crisis pregnancies, adopting children out of hopeless circumstances, championing the rights of the oppressed and the trafficked, volunteering at AIDS care facilities, or supporting the feeding and care of children in far-off lands through various agencies of mercy, we must realize that this is our *nonnegotiable* calling. All of these and many others are indicative of what it means to live under Jesus' reign. There will be no faithfulness to Jesus apart from them.[14]

---

13. Yet, the statistics concerning divorce rates continue to suggest that American Christians are not faring too well in this arena. In a 2008 study, the Barna Group found that 26 percent of those adults identifying themselves as "evangelicals" had experienced a divorce. But when grouped with "non-evangelical born-again Christians," the resulting statistical average of 32 percent was virtually identical to the rate within the population as a whole (based on data accessed online at www.barna.org/family-kids-articles/42-new-marriage-and-divorce-statistics-released). Whichever way one looks at these figures, it is clear that the righteous patterns demanded by Jesus, which would almost assuredly result in much lower rates of divorce, are wanting, even among apparently committed Christians.

14. Thankfully, calls for Christian involvement in such matters as social justice, racial reconciliation, and environmental care are increasingly being heralded. E.g., Mae Elise Cannon, *Social Justice Handbook: Small Steps for a Better World* (Downers Grove, IL: IVP, 2009); Emmanuel Katongole and Chris Rice, *Reconciling All Things: A Christian Vision for Justice, Peace and Healing* (Downers Grove, IL: IVP, 2008); Miroslav Volf, *Free of Charge: Giving and Forgiving in a Culture Stripped of Grace* (Grand Rapids: Zondervan, 2005); Steven Bouma-Prediger, *For the Beauty of the Earth: A Christian Vision for Creation Care* (Grand Rapids: Baker, 2001); Stanley Hauerwas and Jean Vanier, *Living Gently in a Violent World: The Prophetic Witness of Weakness* (Downers Grove, IL: IVP, 2008).

This is because the full-orbed ministry of the kingdom, which Jesus' disciples were to carry out in their missionary journeys, includes not just the *proclamation* of the gospel of the kingdom. It also entails the *demonstration* of the presence and nature of that kingdom. Consequently, ministries of healing, mercy, and even spiritual warfare are integral to the fulfillment of the mission.

But this will take a much greater investment of both time and resources by a much higher percentage of the Christian population than is presently the case.[15] Only in this way will the proclamation of the gospel and Jesus' provision of atoning grace through the cross be couched in the kind of ministry that he himself conducted, allowing people to see the nature of the true King who reigns. In this way, we will participate in the completion of the Abrahamic promise to bless all nations through his offspring. This is *what* Jesus commands us to do!

> Is not this the kind of fasting I have chosen:
> to loose the chains of injustice
>   and untie the cords of the yoke,
> to set the oppressed free
>   and break every yoke?
> Is it not to share your food with the hungry
>   and to provide the poor wanderer with shelter —
> when you see the naked, to clothe them,
>   and not to turn away from your own flesh and blood?
> Then your light will break forth like the dawn,
>   and your healing will quickly appear;
> then your righteousness will go before you,
>   and the glory of the LORD will be your rear guard.
>   (Isa. 58:6 – 8)

THE RELEVANCE OF THE ANSWERS TO THE "HOW" QUESTION

Learning to Live in Grace

Since we Christians live in the age in which the kingdom of God has only been inaugurated, our obedience to these kingdom demands will never be complete. In fact, apart from learning the answers to the "How" question, we will only experience frustration, compromise, and bondage, wedged as we are between Jesus' absolute demand of kingdom righteousness and our own partial transformation. We must, therefore, learn to view our present experience through the lens of the *inaugurated* kingdom and discern our desperate need of daily grace. In this way, we will acquire the covenantal perspective that makes sense out of our journey, helping us to avoid the cynicism, lethargy, and subtle hypocrisy so common in our day.

One of the things that astounds me at the same time that it saddens me is the frequent testimony that I receive from students and adults alike that they have never

---

15. Although Christians give to the church and nonprofit organizations at a rate unparalleled by any other group, it is still striking that only about 9 percent of "evangelicals" give at a rate of 10 percent or greater. Data accessed online at www.barna.org/congregations-articles/41-new-study-shows-trends-in-tithing-and-donating.

really understood the notion of *enabling* grace, even though they have spent years in solid, biblically grounded churches. You will recall the word association exercise that I conduct with my students in relation to the notion of "disciple" or "discipleship" — not one has yet responded by offering "grace" or "enablement" in response. Somehow, the two just don't go together. Similarly, among the interviews included in Smith and Denton's study, the role of grace in the living out of the Christian life is hauntingly absent.

This situation is quite telling. Unless we do a better job of teaching Christians where to find the resources for discipleship, we will only succeed in frustrating them at best and deluding them at worst. This is because the main obstacle that blocks the path of genuine discipleship is often not so much *why* we should obey Jesus or even *what* it is that he commands us to do. Rather, the crux of the matter turns on the *means* by which this obedience is to come about. Given this reality, the resources offered by the answers to the "How" question become essential.

" ... the church is called to be for the world what Jesus was for Israel: not just a moral lecturer, nor even a moral example, but the people who, in obedience to God's strange vocation, learn to suffer and pray at the place where the world is in pain, so that the world may be healed."[16]

These resources are to be found, of course, in the framework of biblical theology. Specifically, we must learn again how to live in covenant with God, now in its New Covenant expression. Given the iterative weakness of our surrender to Jesus' authority and the frequent frailty of our resolve to follow him, our lives of discipleship must regularly be punctuated by intentional pauses at the feet of the Servant, not only *remembering* his grace, but thoughtfully *receiving* it. In this way, the Spirit will bring the grace of Jesus to bear on our hearts, softening them, inclining them toward God, and enabling them to *respond* to the virtuous demands of our King.

Learning to Respond to Grace

What, indeed, will nudge us to extend a helping hand to the beggars we pass daily at the intersections of our habitual itineraries? What will induce us to enter into significant relationships with people whose lifestyles and morality stand at significant variance to our own, so that opportunities to communicate God's love might arise? Will not the contemplation of Jesus' death and resurrection against the backdrop of Israel's exile and return remind us of our own former state in exile from God, so that we might look through Jesus' eyes at those who yet languish in that darkness? Will not the repeated experience of Jesus' healing power, cleansing away our recurring blindness and leprosy, galvanize our concern for those who yet have not experienced his gracious touch? Will not our hearts be renewed in compassion as we hear Jesus invite us again to his gracious table, inclining our hearts in the process to pull out a chair for another whom Jesus is also waving in?

16. N. T. Wright, "The Truth of the Gospel and Christian Living," in *The Meaning of Jesus: Two Visions* (ed. Marcus J. Borg and N. T. Wright; New York: HarperSanFrancisco, 1999), 224.

What will move us to reach across racial boundaries to combat the various kinds of ethnic divisions that continue to plague us, even within the church? Will it not be through the sincere remembrance and renewed reception of Jesus' gracious summons to join the messianic community of true Israel in which racial identity is no longer a defining issue? Will not these daily encounters with the Servant empower us to turn in similarly gracious and inclusive ways toward others whose ethnic, moral, or economic backgrounds render them "unlikely" candidates as well? As Katongole and Rice write:

> There are two movements in this story, and the order is important. The first movement is about God and what God has done in Christ. The second is about the transformation this first movement has enacted in the world and in the lives of people.... Because a Christian vision of reconciliation is rooted in the story of God's people, we can grasp the vision only as we learn to inhabit the story. The story shapes us in the habits of God's peculiar people; the more we get it down inside us, the easier it is to resist the temptations of this world's prevailing visions.[17]

I recall watching the national news one evening when a lengthy report was aired on the racial reconciliation that was transpiring in a stunningly effective way in the Rock of Our Salvation Church in Chicago. I watched spellbound as then senior pastor Raleigh Washington and several other church members witnessed to the transforming grace of Jesus that made such reconciliation possible. Not only did this story confirm the basic thesis presented in this book, but it also indicated the massive appeal that gracious discipleship has in this increasingly graceless world.

What will bring renovation to our inner lives, from which our lust, anger, and coveting seep? What will open our eyes to Satan's wiles to entrap us so that our lives yield his unseemly crop? Will not resting in Jesus' willingness to step into the waters of repentance on our behalf deliver us from our own paltry attempts at purity and thrill us with the realization that we stand blameless and without reproach in him? Will not Jesus' successful repelling of Satan's enticements on our behalf and his aggressive attack on his strongholds liberate us to live in his victory over darkness? Will not the sheer costliness and unexpectedness of this grace wean us away from our drooling after the very things Jesus came to destroy?

In the process, we will learn to live our lives in the framework of the Bible's narrative, allowing its promises, expectations, and fulfillments to govern our existence. Along the way, we will learn not only to be saved *by* grace, but also how to live *in* grace. We will learn not only to live *in* grace, but also to respond *to* grace. Only then will true and increasingly consistent discipleship be realized in us, leading to the mediation of God's great covenant blessings to others around us — so that they too will follow the great Servant King.

---

17. Katongole and Rice, *Reconciling All Things*, 43, 46.

SCRIPTURE INDEX

OTHER ANCIENT LITERATURE INDEX

SUBJECT INDEX

The Mission of God's People

A Biblical Theology of the Church's Mission

Christopher J. H. Wright;
Jonathan Lunde, General Editor

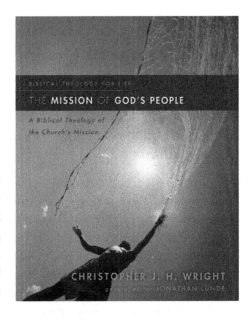

Chris Wright's pioneering 2006 book, *The Mission of God*, revealed that the typical Christian understanding of "missions" encompasses only a small part of God's overarching mission for the world. God is relentlessly reclaiming the entire world for himself. In *The Mission of God's People*, Wright shows how God's big-picture plan directs the purpose of God's people, the church.

Wright emphasizes what the Old Testament teaches Christians about being the people of God. He addresses questions of both ecclesiology and missiology with topics like "called to care for creation," "called to bless the nations," "sending and being sent," and "rejecting false gods."

> *"What do theology and mission have to do with each other? This book powerfully answers the question."*
> — John Goldingay, Professor, Fuller Theological Seminary

As part of the Biblical Theology for Life Series, this book provides pastors, teachers and lay learners with first-rate biblical study while at the same time addressing the practical concerns of contemporary ministry. *The Mission of God's People* promises to enliven and refocus the study, teaching, and ministry of those truly committed to joining God's work in the world.

Available in stores and online!

Three Views on the New Testament Use of the Old Testament

Stanley N. Gundry, Series Editor;
Kenneth Berding and Jonathan Lunde,
General Editors

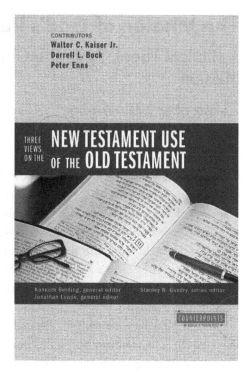

To read the New Testament is to meet the Old Testament at every turn. But exactly how do Old Testament texts relate to their New Testament references and allusions? Moreover, what fruitful interpretive methods do New Testament texts demonstrate? Leading biblical scholars Walter Kaiser, Darrel Bock, and Peter Enns each present their answers to questions surrounding the use of the Old Testament in the New Testament.

Contributors address elements such as divine and human authorial intent, the context of Old Testament references, and theological grounds for an interpretive method. Each author applies his framework to specific texts so that readers can see how their methods work out in practice. Each contributor also receives a thorough critique from the other two authors.

A one-stop reference for setting the scene and presenting approaches to the topic that respect the biblical text, *Three Views on the New Testament Use of Old Testament* gives readers the tools they need to develop their own views on this important subject.

Available in stores and online!

We want to hear from you. Please send your comments about this book to us in care of zreview@zondervan.com. Thank you.

ZONDERVAN.com/
AUTHORTRACKER
follow your favorite authors